vernment, Labor, and Inflation
age Stabilization in the United States
niel Quinn Mills

his timely work analyzes how government,
bor unions, and management in the
nited States have dealt with the problem
controlling inflation. Daniel Quinn Mills
xplores formal wage controls in light
f the rich body of historical experience
om the world wars to the recent Phases I
hrough IV. Economic issues are analyzed
om the broad perspective of politics
nd industrial relations.

Mills is uniquely qualified to write a
omprehensive study of wage stabilization
or he not only served as chairman of the
tabilization committee of the construction
ndustry but was also on the Cost of
iving Council. The book is written in a
style that makes it accessible to all who
are interested, and is thoroughly docu-
nented from primary and secondary
sources. *Government, Labor, and Inflation*
will stand as a valuable reference for
officials who formulate public policies
and for representatives of management
and labor.

Arguing that experience has provided
us with important lessons, Mills demonstrates that controls can be only one
element of a general economic program.
The formation of successful incomes policy
with its attendant effects on politics and
industrial relations, must be based on
the combined contributions of public
agencies and private labor and management groups. Mills surveys the complexities

the various interest groups
icy change and stresses
f understanding the motiva-
arket behavior.
emphasis is on the design,
arrangements, and institu-
cessary for flexible wage
licies. The discussion
ese policies are dependent
hat changing income and
hips have on the increase
s and prices. Mills brings
ions to his discussion of the
tween the industrial
n and incomes policy. He
pact of wage controls
argaining and discusses
oute settlements during
tion. In a final chapter,
points to future directions
in inflationary periods.
NN MILLS is an economist
or of industrial relations
hool of Management,
Institute of Technology.
r of *Industrial Relations and
onstruction.*

D1445200

(Continued on back flap)

Daniel Quinn Mills

Government, Labor, and Inflation

Wage Stabilization in the United States

The University of Chicago Press

Chicago and London

The University of Chicago Press
Chicago 60637
The University of Chicago Press, Ltd.
London

Library of Congress Cataloging in Publication Data

Mills, Daniel Quinn.
  Government, labor, and inflation.

  Includes bibliographical references and index.
  1. Wage—price policy—United States.   2. Labor
policy—United States.   I. Title.
HC110.W24M55   331.2'1'01   75-9685
ISBN 0-226-52951-7

DANIEL QUINN MILLS is an economist
who is professor of industrial relations at the
Sloan School of Management, Massachusetts
Institute of Technology. He is the author of
*Industrial Relations and Manpower in Con-
struction.*

Contents

v

Preface

This volume was written during three years in which I taught at the Sloan School of Management at MIT, and served the government in various capacities on the Construction Industry Stabilization Committee and the Cost of Living Council. The book was undertaken for two purposes: to contribute to current public understanding of stabilization policy and to provide a source book for future reference by officials and observers of stabilization efforts. Furthermore, I had a personal reason for writing this book, in that the effort helped structure my own thinking and contributions to the development of the stabilization program in recent years.

The historical material in the book is based as much as possible on primary sources, although there is also much reliance on the analytic literature regarding the programs of World War II and the Korean period. Personal observations provided the framework for the material concerning the 1971–72 stabilization program. As an official of the CISC beginning in 1971 and of the COLC in 1973–74, I have had an almost unparalleled opportunity to study at firsthand the operation of the most recent stabilization program. The complete story of the CISC is not included in this volume, however, but will be told elsewhere.

Many persons have helped me in the preparation of this study. My debt to John Dunlop is enormous. I also appreciate the support of my colleagues at the Sloan School, especially Charles A. Myers, Abraham Siegel, and Douglass V. Brown. Ms. Gail Coleman was responsible for part of chapter 2 of this book. Mrs. Joyce Yearwood and Ms. Patte Macpherson assisted in the preparation of the manuscript. All errors and omissions are, of course, my responsibility alone.

Part I

Experience with
Stabilization Policy
in the United States

The beginning of wisdom is to recognize that there are honest issues to be resolved, and that the critical questions are who shall decide those issues, by what standards and by what procedures.

Paul Freund, letter to the New York Times *June 25, 1971*

1. Wage Stabilization Policy and the Modern Economy

The Renewed Importance of Stabilization Policy

Until recently, formal wage and price controls were an unusual aspect of national economic policy in the United States. In fact, until 1971 formal controls had been put into practice only during times of war. There were many reasons for the reluctance of the government to impose direct controls and for private interests to oppose them. Leading economists argued for reliance on the role of the decentralized activities of buyers and sellers in the marketplace to establish the prices and volume of commodities and services. Intervention by public authorities to set prices and output by decree was believed to be not only a largely futile exercise but also one with important undesirable secondary effects. The change in attitude toward economic policy which accompanied the depression of the 1930s stressed a more activist public policy with respect to aggregate employment and production but relied upon management of the government budget and the national money supply to achieve its ends. Then, during World War II and the Korean War, formal wage and price controls were exercised. Following the two wartime periods of formal controls, there was a wide acceptance of a view that the anticipated disadvantages of direct controls had been confirmed by experience. Three major disadvantages were identified. First, controls required a large and expensive bureaucracy to administer; second, they appeared to many to be inherently inequitable; and, third, controls seemed through error and delay to result in unnecessary inefficiency in production. It was thought that these disadvantages might be tolerable for short periods in an emergency but certainly in no other context.

Because of the general acceptance for many years after the end of the Korean War of the view just described, it must be surprising that in 1971 the Nixon administration embarked on the first use of formal wage and price controls in a largely peacetime economy; and that this effort was accompanied by encouragement from the public, many economists, and representatives of both political parties. The change in opinion which caused controls to be welcomed in 1971 had not suddenly come. During the 1960s there had been a continual drift in the direction of resort to controls in this country and abroad. In Western Europe repeated use of incomes policies had been made through the 1960s and the preceding decade, and the American decision was influenced by European efforts.

The process by which the negative attitude toward controls of the first half of the century became an advocacy of controls in the 1960s and 1970s, though of great interest, is not our primary concern here. Rather, our purpose is to study what has been learned about the application of formal controls as an element of economic policy. For example, what has our experience (including that of 1971–72) taught us about the possible uses of controls? What can be accomplished, and what cannot be done? How are controls best formulated and administered? How does the economic environment affect a stabilization program? What is the impact of a stabilization program on other public objectives, particularly in the industrial relations area? And, can the unfavorable aspects of the impact of controls on collective bargaining be minimized?

There is a rich deposit of historical experience to reward the analyst of stabilization policy. There have been substantial differences among various periods in the administration of stabilization programs and even more important differences in the economic and political environments in which the programs operated. These differences facilitate a comparison of stabilization efforts. Also interesting is the tendency of certain basic issues of content and procedure in a stabilization program to arise in each period, although often with distinctive trappings reflecting changing economic and political circumstances.

Yet the emphasis in this volume is not historical but analytic. Considerable attention is devoted to the relationship of wage stabilization policy to aspects of the behavior of labor markets, especially the economic and institutional factors affecting wage determination in the United States. The interaction of stabilization policies and market forces is of great importance, for wage stabilization programs are more than a set of regulations regarding compensation. They are, rather, an attempt by the government to control the behavior of labor markets in order to achieve wage restraint but without too greatly distorting the efficiency of the markets in recruiting, training, allocating, and motivating workers. John Hicks many years ago warned of the importance of these matters. "The same forces which determine wages in a free market are still present under regulation," he said, "they only work rather differently."[1] A major object of this study is to determine how forces which affect wages tend to operate during a stabilization program, as well as to determine the methods by which stabilization policy can be accommodated to labor market forces.

Definition of Wage Stabilization Policy

Wage stabilization policy is one of a group of policies of the United States directed toward economic and industrial relations behavior. Stabilization policy is normally a short-term effort, which is conducted within the context of the continuing development of economic and industrial relations policy generally. In the economic sphere, stabilization policy must be distinguished from the fiscal and monetary policy of government, and from federal policies with respect to the distribution of income (including tax and transfer policies). In the industrial relations sphere, stabilization policy must be distinguished from the practice of collective bargaining in the United States with its reliance upon the use of the strike or lockout as a determinant of disputes. Stabilization policy must be accommodated to both economic and industrial relations; that is, stabilization programs require some limitations on the expansiveness of fiscal and monetary policy and some understanding with respect to limitations on the use of the strike or lockout.

We have distinguished stabilization policies from economic and industrial relations policy. But how can stabilization policy be described? Wage stabilization is not the sort of unilaterally determined and executed governmental economic policy that fiscal or monetary policy is. Rather, it is substantially more akin to public policy with respect to industrial relations, in which a legal framework has been constructed and applied by the government to regulate the relationships of private organizations and individuals. The structure of industrial relations policy was developed with substantial inputs from labor and management and depends to a very large degree for its operation on their cooperation or acquiescence. This pattern of development is very much unlike that of fiscal and monetary policy but is quite analogous to wage stabilization policy. Too often in the public discussion of national wage policy, there emerges a conception of a stabilization program as a set of governmental regulations established to govern the rate of increase of compensation. In this conception, stabilization policy is a unilateral act of the government in pursuit of its economic policy objectives, and the stabilization program involves only the drafting of regulations and perhaps their enforcement by the executive branch or the courts.

In fact, stabilization policy has two major aspects, only one of which is recognized by those who hold the view just described. One aspect of wage and price stabilization policy is an arrangement between the government and private groups as to how each will contribute to a national economic policy. A second aspect is the administration of the stabilization program itself. In this country, the first aspect has historically involved an arrangement between management, organized labor, and the president and Congress. There are also matters of major importance involved in the day-to-day administration of a stabilization program. An agreement among groups in society that a stabilization program is necessary does not automatically insure that machinery can be established that will effectively administer the program. A general agreement as to the form, content, and objectives of an incomes policy can be usefully converted into reality only if certain requirements of comprehensiveness and fairness in administration can be supplied. The essence of the administrative problem of wage stabilization is the interrelationship of wage rates among groups of workers, firms, industries, and areas. The administrative machinery must prevent workers and employers in individual situations from taking advantage of the stabilization period to pursue their own objectives at the expense of others. Neither the competitive forces of the product market nor the politics of labor organizations will permit individuals in positions of leadership to support actively (not simply in word but in deed) a general program which operates to their own organization's serious detriment relative to other groups. The problem is not primarily the enforcement of stabilization policies, though that is one aspect. More important is the question of the quality of the design of the detailed machinery and procedures of stabilization authorities in adjusting the general goals of policy to the interrelationships of wages, prices, product markets, and labor costs in the individual operations of the economy. Further, stabilization authorities must seek to prevent individual organizations from using stabilization procedures and rules to further noneconomic objectives against other organizations or individuals. These aspects of the administration of stabilization policy are of extraordinary complexity. If they are performed poorly, the result will be the erosion of the effectiveness of the stabilization program.

The Modern Economic Problem

Sources of Inflation

It is common for various periods in our country's history to be characterized as having a particular economic problem. In the 1930s the problem was depression and associated massive unemployment. The decade of the 1940s was dominated by the problems of wartime mobilization and peacetime reconversion. Since the fundamental economic problems of earlier periods can be so easily characterized, it is not surprising that a characterization should also be sought for our current economy. The one most often offered is that during the post–Korean War period, with the brief exception of 1966–69, the basic problem in our economy has been the persistence, simultaneously, of price and wage inflation and a somewhat slack economy.

What are the sources of inflation? Unfortunately, there is a well-known controversy among economists over the causes of inflation. One group tends to give greater emphasis to the role of the effective quantity (volume times velocity) of money in determining the rate of inflation; the other group emphasizes the combined effect of spending decisions by consumers, business, and government (especially the balance between federal receipts and expenditures) measured against the output capacity of the economy.[2]

However, the explicit points of theoretical dispute between the two groups are far fewer and far less significant for an understanding of the inflationary problem than might be thought.[3]

The basic issue dividing the groups relates primarily to the relative role and form of fiscal versus monetary policy in the control of inflation. The monetarists remain suspicious of the traditional tendency of the state to manipulate the currency to further political objectives, domestic or foreign, and thereby debase the value of the money supply (with a resultant impact on prices and wages which may be referred to as inflation). The other school is less suspicious of the activities of government and tends to support an activist and discretionary authority to adjust fiscal and monetary policy to pursue national goals.

Both groups tend to view inflation as a problem primarily of the aggregate variables in economic life, including the total supply of money, the balance or imbalance of the entire federal budget (by whatever measure is preferred of the budgetary situation—cash, administrative, or other), the aggregate volume of employment and unemployment, and so on. There is little concern expressed by either side in this debate for the role in inflation of particular sectors and the interactions among prices, wages, and product and labor markets.

Whatever the general cause of inflation, it manifests itself as rising prices in particular product markets. Often, general inflationary movements have their origin in particular markets where demand has increased, costs have risen, or production has declined. The distribution of rising prices is rarely uniform in the economy; some sectors are affected more strongly than others. Furthermore, in our economy some sectors are much more likely than others to respond to demand or cost pressures through price and wage increases rather than through other means (for example, through increased production, or delays in delivery, or a form of rationing). The effect of changed economic circumstances is to generate price and wage increases in these sectors. The more uneven the expansion among sectors (and thereby the more uneven its impact on occupations, firms, geographic areas), and the more prolonged its continuation, the greater will be the differences which develop in the adjustments in wages, prices, and financial holdings or obligations of firms and individuals. Distortions will thus be introduced into the overall structure of wages, prices, and finances. These distortions are the seeds of future adjustments in money wages and prices; they are the essence of that element of the problem of inflation which outlives the period of initial price pressures.

But inflation is not the only aspect of the peculiar economic problem of these times. As one prominent American economist has said, "the really intractable problem in our modern economy is that inflation occurs simultaneously with the existence of underutilized resources.... An inflation which did indeed start with the over-heated economy of the late 1960's ... persisted for ... years after the over-heating disappeared, and persisted through a period of substantial unemployment."[4] This emphasis on the apparent anomaly of inflation and substantial unemployment existing simultaneously is characteristic of much economic analysis in recent years. Schultze apparently believes, as do others, that when aggregate unemployment is rising or high, wage and price increases should be caused to moderate. In consequence, most efforts by economists to analyze the behavior of the post-Korean economy have involved the effort to identify the form and magnitude of the relationships between the aggregate rate of wage (or price) change and the unemployment rate.[5] These explanations (referred to as studies of the Phillips curve, after the author of a seminal article)[6] have popularized the concept of a trade-off by which a lower rate of inflation results from a higher unemployment rate. Various investigations have explored the effect of the quantitative characteristics of the trade-off changes in the composition of the labor force, of changes in industrial structure, profit levels, output per manhour, and so on. The common ground of these studies is the view that aggregate unemployment and aggregate inflation are causally linked and that achieving both wage and price stability and low unemployment by breaking this link constitutes the major problem of modern economic policy, one substantially different from the economic problems of the past.

Yet, in a careful analysis, the supposedly intractable problem of the trade-off between unemployment and inflation is more apparent than real. Not that these two problems might not exist simultaneously; in fact, they often do. Inflation and unemployment are both major economic and social problems and both result in some cases from largely similar causes, but the causal connection between the two factors is far less direct than is assumed by many economists.[7] Unemployment is one of many factors which affect some wage-price interactions, and is affected by them in turn. Unemployment rates respond to increasing economic activity, as do wages and prices, with the aggregate unemployment rate tending to decline (the degree of decline depending on the elasticity of the labor force, among other things) and wages and prices tending to rise. The impact of the rate of unemployment on particular wages and prices differs among labor markets. In some labor markets much unemployment exercises a substantial pressure to keep wages from rising. This is especially true in less structured, weakly organized labor markets and in those involving considerable product market competition. In other labor markets, wage and price behavior is substantially insensitive to unemployment levels. This is especially true of strongly structured, strongly organized markets which are associated with little product market competition. In the aggregate, the impact of unemployment on wage levels depends on the distribution of unemployment among various labor markets. Further, the influence of other factors, including rising consumer prices and wage interrelationships, can eliminate the net impact generally of rising unemployment rates on wage inflation. In consequence, the aggregate rate of unemployment is generally only one of a group of factors affecting the rate of inflation in wages and prices and, in the short run at least, is not likely to be a dominating influence unless substantially higher rates of unemployment than those reached since the depression of the 1930s were to occur.[8]

If there is no straightforward causal connection between the aggregate rate of unemployment and the aggregate rate of wage (or price) inflation, then the coexistence of substantial unemployment and rising wages and prices is not so mysterious as it has seemed. And economic analysis, rather than being directed first at illuminating the supposed connection between the two, and then at seeking some policy to break the connection, might be better directed at the long-term management of the economy so as to avoid the doubly undesirable circumstance of too high unemployment and too much inflation. We need not lose hope that it is possible for careful economic policy to result in moderate inflation and low unemployment.

Some potential inflationary situations are more difficult than others, however. In circumstances which appear to be very threatening to price stability, government in the United States has sometimes sought through direct price and wage controls to limit inflation. Since American economic society is characterized by the considerable influence of business firms, producers' associations, and labor unions, wage and price controls involve the government directly in the behavior of the various institutions of the economy. The result is the complex political, social, and economic process which is the topic of this book. But in order to understand this process, we must first explore the impact of an inflationary surge on the behavior of economic organizations.

The Problem of Competing Groups

A period of inflation introduces into an economy a variety of unsettling forces, especially a considerable uncertainty as to the future of wage and price relationships. These uncertainties affect the behavior of many organized groups in our society, including management and labor in the collective bargaining process. In a democratic society, struggles over the distribution of the national income and over relative pay status take place not only through the political process but within the private economic sphere as well. In our society, with a largely free system of collective bargaining, private economic power in part determines the outcome of such struggles. It is not possible to find in American history a period when there were no disputes over relative status and pay; and such disputes remain a feature of our economy. Yet in recent years the bitterness of the struggles, the variety of groups involved, and the forums in which they are waged have been enlarged. Much of economic stabilization policy depends on the impact which changing income and wage relationships have on the rate of increase in money wages and prices. In consequence, this topic is one which will concern us at length throughout this study. In later chapters, however, we will be primarily concerned with the interdependencies of particular wage rates. In this introductory section an initial survey is made of the more general process of competition among groups and of its effect on economic stability.

How earnings and status are to be distributed among individuals and groups occasions as much dispute and activity of various sorts as does concern over actual living standards. This is, of course, an obvious point. Yet the evidence of statistics in recent years has seemed to be such as to obscure the significance in the economy of the struggle over relative position. For example, the share of national income in the United States going to various claimants (including workers, corporations, and so on) has remained generally stable over many years; so also, though to a lesser degree, has the distribution of income among elements of the population.[9] This stability might be thought to suggest a lessening of disputes over income distribution and status. Yet, as Livernash has pointed out, even constancy of the income shares (between labor and business) is not inconsistent with union efforts to push up money wages to prevent a redistribution of income by government policies.[10] In addition, the problem of allocating proprietors' income (also associated with changes in the form of business organizations) creates great difficulties for measuring any changes which might have occurred in gross factor shares.[11] In any case, the analysis of gross income shares, relevant though it may be to certain generalized economic concerns, is not particularly significant for understanding the day-to-day problems of the economy, for these occur among smaller groups. Often disputes between groups of workers are involved, rather than between employers and workers, and the evidence of these disputes does not appear in aggregative data.

To those who have attempted to probe beyond the somewhat artificial stability of aggregate shares and of the income distribution, what appears to have occurred in the inflationary period of the late 1960s, in particular, is a major struggle over relative positions carried on by various groups. Price inflation threatened to reduce the real income of various groups, stimulating efforts to protect living standards. But, at the outset of the boom in the early 1960s, the ready availability of capital funds for investment, the willingness of Congress to enact spending programs, the increasing tightness of the labor market, and the profitability of businesses all suggested that efforts not only to retain relative position in the distribution of income but also to improve position might be successful.[12] Further, the inflation itself and the obvious efforts of various groups placed each organization or interest group in a position of concern as to the path of future adjustments which others might make, so that substantial anticipation of future increases became an unsettling force.

There are a great many ways in which elements of society may attempt to preserve or enhance their relative position in the distribution of society's resources. Unions are confined primarily to bargaining for wage increases as a mechanism to affect the distribution, but in some cases other means are attempted. For example, some unions seek to promote (often in cooperation with management) the use of the product they produce. Others may lobby for public funds to support the product market, either by direct purchases by various governmental units, or by incentive or subsidies to private consumers.[13] Unions, acting in concert, generally lobby for federal economic policies or legislation such as increases in the minimum wage which tend to support their individual wage claims in collective bargaining. But unions are not the only organizations which act in this manner. Agricultural interests (especially farmers, to whom the prices of farm products and personal income are very closely related) have long sought, with relative success, to protect farm incomes through national legislation. More recently, educational institutions have sought to protect levels of employment, salary levels, and amenities in clerical support and physical facilities through efforts to obtain public and private money to support education directly (as well as for university-conducted research and development).[14] Medical societies of various sorts initially welcomed or opposed Medicare as their political and ideological postures required. But by the 1970s federal assistance for medical treatment, with the significant support it provides for incomes in health industry, was widely, though not uncritically, accepted in the industry. Homebuilders, after weathering several years of a depressed housing market in the late 1960s, obtained from the Congress subsidy programs which contributed markedly to the revival and boom of housing in the early 1970s.[15] The health insurance industry, facing substantially rising costs for medical care, has obtained special legislative assistance in a variety of forms, including a special exemption from certain aspects of controls in the Economic Stabilization Act of 1971. Finally, even groups which had traditionally fared poorly in competition with others over economic status became more active in the late 1960s. For example, public expenditures on income-maintenance programs of various types rose rapidly, primarily as a result of a substantial increase in the number of persons receiving public assistance (or welfare).[16] Increases in the amount of aid available to the individual family or recipient were much more limited.[17]

These examples are adequate to suggest that the economic environment of the late 1960s was highly unstable and quite threatening to various groups of workers and businessmen. From the viewpoint of any particular firm or union, there was a limited degree of responses available in the attempt to protect or enhance their economic position. Some groups, operating alone or in concert with others, possessed substantial power or influence at the collective bargaining table, others in the product market, others in state legislatures or the Congress, and others in the executive branches of various levels of government. But in a decentralized, often competitive, economic system each group remained responsible for its own success or failure in achieving its economic objectives.[18] The turmoil which ensued was largely the result of an unreasonably expansive federal economic policy which generated both uncertainties and opportunities in the private economy. Private groups reacted to threatened changes in their economic position in a variety of ways, many of which had unfortunate consequences for price and wage stability.[19] It is important to understand that what many observers assume to be an automatic process by which aggregate economic expansion is transferred into rising prices and wages is, in fact, not automatic at all but is subject to various mechanisms and influences which yield changes in the relative position of economic groups. In this process some groups gain, some lose, and the process itself generates pressures for the adaptation of traditional pricing and pay procedures to respond to threatened changes.

We have noted above that the problem of groups competing for relative economic position in the society is a general one, involving not only labor and management but agricultural interests, public employees, small business-men, proprietors, professional persons, and so on.[20] But what of the special problems of management and labor, the groups that are the principle concerns of our study? It is normally recognized by employers and unions that a prolonged competition for relative position may be self-defeating. That is, the impact of continual readjustments may have a cumulative effect on the price of a product, or on the price level generally, which is undesirable. Yet, in a decentralized economy there is ordinarily no mechanism by which the competition can be halted. Organizations (whether firms or unions) which attempted to halt the competition unilaterally could reasonably anticipate to achieve no more than a worsening of their own position.

There is no escape in our society from the attempt to resolve these matters in some way. Normally, the issue is left to the action of employers and individual workers or to collective bargaining. The procedure is decentralized but flexible. When unexpected events occur and the government so conducts economic policy that substantial uncertainties and instabilities are introduced into the system, our customary procedures may not work well. When government further complicates the issue by rapid adjustments in the relative position of certain groups (for example, in the 1960s, public employees and those receiving public assistance), the actions may be meritorious, but pressures may develop in the private sector which are substantially threatening to wage and price stability.

Thus, what is often required for wage restraint—and, thereby, for anti-inflation policy—is a moratorium on the struggle for relative economic place. In some circumstances an agreement to suspend the struggle can be reached. Such an arrangement may take one of several forms, as evidenced in the past. There may be a general agreement to suspend competition for pay temporarily (as in World War II); or an agreement to suspend the competition in a certain sector for a temporary period (as evidenced by the periods of wage stabilization in a single industry); or an order by government to suspend competition (though this can be only partly effective without acceptance by private groups). A stabilization policy must by its very nature involve a moratorium on the struggle for relative economic position. How this may be achieved is the subject of later chapters.

The Role of Stabilization Policy in Controlling Inflation

When the government is concerned with a rising price level but is unwilling or unable to manage fiscal and monetary policy consistently in such a way as to eliminate the cycle of economic expansion and contraction, one is not surprised that it should turn to direct controls as a possible solution to its problems. The temptation to respond to inflation by outlawing price and wage increases is always present. But can inflation actually be restrained in such a simple fashion? Whatever might be said of some sectors of the economy, it remains true that in many product and labor markets the forces of supply and demand continue to exercise an important influence. How, then, would competitive markets respond to controls? With hoarding, with black markets? And yet, is there any way to prevent wage inflation without resort to a stabilization program?

Two periods of wartime controls (World War II and Korea) and the experience of 1971–72 have left a residue of opinion regarding controls, but a residue of a remarkably inconsistent nature. There are those who look favorably on the experience of wartime stabilization and argue for direct controls in a largely peacetime economy as well. Perhaps the most persuasive advocate of this position is John Kenneth Galbraith of Harvard. "At full employment," he argues, "there is no mechanism for holding prices and wages stable. This stabilization ... is a function of the state ... and [therefore] a system of wage and price restraint is inevitable in the industrial system." As to the likelihood of success for controls in limiting inflation, Galbraith simply notes that "during both conflicts the wage-price spiral was successfully contained by controls."[21] Galbraith's position has received support from several other economists. Robert Lekachman told a Congressional committee, "I judge that the best feasible incomes policy commences with a freeze of wages, prices ... and ... dividends ... [After the freeze] remaining under control will be prices, wages and dividends in industries dominated by large corporations engaged in bargaining with national trade unions."[22] Similarly, and not unexpectedly, the officials placed in charge of the stabilization program in 1971–72 were strong in their convictions that it could be successful in restraining inflation.[23]

Other groups of observers have drawn very different conclusions from the experience of past stabilization programs. For some the net result of controls is judged to be nil; for others controls are themselves a positive agent for inflation. To the first group controls are incapable of withstanding market pressures[24] and at best generate inefficiencies, additional costs, and unwarranted interference into the affairs of the private economy.[25] The arguments of the second group hold that controls are themselves agents of inflation in several ways. First, controls are said to strengthen monopolies and thereby undesirable pricing behavior. "When," asked Milton Friedman, "was the last time—or, for that matter, the first time—that a Government regulatory body weakened or offset monopoly rather than strengthened it ... the simple fact is that Government control of prices and wages will, if it lasts, strengthen monopoly."[26] Second, controls are said to foster inflation itself in the following ways: by distorting pressures for wage and price increases into noncontrolled or weakly controlled sectors (e.g., food); by being "more effective in putting a floor under rises in the slower sectors than in putting a ceiling on prices in the fast-rising sectors"; and, by "encouraging economic irresponsibility" in fiscal and monetary policies.[27]

There are thus two extreme views, each voiced by prominent spokesmen and respected academic observers: one, that controls are effective in limiting inflationary pressures; another, that controls are at best ineffective or at worst a contributing factor to inflation. Yet neither view is balanced; nor can either view provide guidance as to what contribution a controls program can make to the overall objective of economic stabilization.[28] In fact, what we have to learn from previous periods of controls is not a once-and-for-all judgment as to their efficiency but, rather, more limited lessons: for example, that controls are only one element of a general stabilization program; that they are a scarce resource, one which erodes rapidly and can be of use only for a few short years without major overhauls; that they are cumbersome and expensive in terms of economic efficiency, equity, and economic freedom. But they are not to be eschewed totally, for they have at times served very important purposes.

The basic issue may be phrased in this way: given the best available mix of fiscal and monetary policy, what role can direct controls play in stemming an inflation; by what means and in what circumstances are the best results likely to be obtained? A tentative judgment might be offered that controls can be useful in retarding the rate of increase of wages and prices when there is a favorable economic environment, a favorable political environment, a professional administration of the controls program, and when such other weapons of stabilization policy are available as the circumstances demand. The particular characteristics which make economic or political conditions favorable and which characterize professional administration of a program are explored in later chapters of this book. Where these conditions are not met, a stabilization program may either fail or even have undesirable results, so that the different views of stabilization programs cited above may be understood to reflect in large part different judgments as to the environment and administration of the program.[29] Furthermore, there are a variety of different types of wage stabilization programs, characterized by the criteria for wage and fringe benefit increases, the breadth of coverage, and so on. That set of controls which is optimal for stopping an inflationary bulge may not be best for permanently altering the inflationary structure of the economy.[30] Thus, the objectives of the stabilization program may also condition its characteristics and the judgments of observers as to its success or failure.

During both the Second World War and the Korean War a considerable amount of attention was devoted to the limited contribution which wage stabilization could make in an overall stabilization program. For example, President Roosevelt on April 27, 1942, listed a seven-point program which was the framework of anti-inflationary policy during World War II. In addition to wage controls, the program included heavy personal and corporate taxation, price ceilings, sale of war bonds, commodity rationing, and discouragement of credit and installment buying. During the Korean period, on December 15, 1950, at its sixth meeting, the tripartite (labor, management, and public) Wage Stabilization Board unanimously adopted a statement on the place of wage policy in the prevention of inflation. The resolution was developed against the background of the World War II experience and the peculiar circumstances of the Korean War immediately after the Chinese intervention, and it remains a thoughtful and instructive document. The solution to the inflation control problem, in the WSB's view, involved three elements: first, expansion of production; second, minimizing of aggregate consumer demand; and third, control of specific areas of the economy. A list of measures to achieve each of the three elements was offered. Suggested measures to minimize consumer demand included higher taxes, less nonmilitary government spending, and limited credit expansion. Suggested measures to control specific areas of the economy included consumer credit controls, real estate credit controls, rent controls, price controls, controls over speculative commodity markets, limitations on business investments, direct allocation of scarce materials and goods, and, last, stabilization of compensation. Regarding the latter, the WSB argued, "the stabilization of wages ... will not by itself attack inflation at its sources, but will merely conceal and defer its effects, while permitting a pressure of hidden spending power to build up."

That wage and price controls can serve only as an element of an anti-inflation policy is no less true in the 1970s than it was two decades ago when the WSB issued its statement. The role of fiscal and monetary policy, of production policy and of credit and other direct controls, remains important. But we will not, in this work, explore at length the full range of anti-inflationary policies. Rather, we are concerned with the peculiar characteristics of wage stabilization policies: their development, design, and administration. It will be necessary from time to time to discuss the economic policy environment in which they operate, but that will not be our primary focus. This study is not, therefore, an economic analysis of inflation and the role of stabilization policy, though these topics are integral to our broader concerns. There are two reasons for this emphasis. First, there are already numerous technical monographs which treat the economic theory of inflation in an exhaustive fashion. Many of these have provided inputs to this study. But those aspects of stabilization policy which involve political compromises, dispute settlement, collective bargaining, and wage interrelationships are badly neglected in these studies. Second, too many narrowly economic analyses of anti-inflationary policy simply assume the effectiveness of an incomes policy in limiting wage and price increases or are at pains to assert effectiveness post hoc.[31] Stabilization policy sometimes receives treatment akin to asserting that price and wage increases can simply be outlawed. Such studies are not based on a careful evaluation of what a stabilization policy is (either in abstract or in a particular case), how it operates, and what it can or cannot do in various circumstances.[32] It is these issues which this book explores. A stabilization program is not a simple tool of economic policy. Rather, it has profound industrial relations and political aspects.[33] An understanding of stabilization policy which reveals its wider implications, problems, and limitations may suggest to some that it would be effective in a certain context, to others that it would not be effective. The purpose of this study is to provide the information on which judgments about the content and effectiveness of wage stabilization policy can be made.

2. Experience with
Wage Stabilization
Programs
before the 1970s

The United States has a rich history of various types of wage stabilization programs which have occurred in a variety of economic and political circumstances. This chapter provides a description of the programs from World War I through the mid-1960s. The following chapter describes the most recent program, that of 1971–72. The sequence of events in stabilization policy, the economic and institutional environment of the policy, the criteria for wage increases, and the administrative arrangements employed are given emphasis. A critical analysis of stabilization policy, which draws on the historical experience described here, is presented in later chapters. The organization of this chapter and the next is largely chronological but not exclusively so. Within each period of stabilization policy there is also some categorization by topic. This combination of formats was necessary to prevent the description of changes in policy from becoming so complex, confusing, and time-consuming as to obscure more important themes in each of the programs.

Some readers might wonder at the relative distribution of material in these chapters. The most detailed treatment is accorded to the period 1971–72 for three reasons. First, other sources are the least satisfactory and accessible to the reader for this period. Second, the 1971–72 period represents in many ways a departure from the practice of past periods and so merits special study. For example, the period is distinguished by being the first attempt to restrain inflation by direct controls on a comprehensive basis in other than a wartime emergency. Third, this period is the most recent, and its experience is probably the most prominent in the minds of readers. The emphasis given pay controls in 1971–72 does not mean, however, that those controls are the ones which most merit study. On the contrary, the most impressive and professionally competent application of controls remains the experience of World War II. It is certainly appropriate to measure succeeding periods of control by the standards of 1942–45. For this reason, the National War Labor Board of World War II is accorded a fairly comprehensive summary.

Also included are sections on the National War Labor Board of World War I, the Wage Stabilization Board of the Korean War period, and the guideposts of the Kennedy-Johnson administration. Although the National War Labor Board of World War I was exclusively a disputes-settling mechanism (without stabilization responsibilities), its development, organization, and administrative procedures initiated a tradition in the manner by which wage stabilization boards have been operated in the United States. The Korean machinery is important in its application of controls in a twilight zone between total war and a peacetime economy. In many respects the Korean program explored aspects of stabilization policy which would be of substantial importance in the 1970s as well. The guideposts period (1962–66), interesting in itself, was also significant in providing the immediate background to the 1971–72 controls program. But the guideposts were a very small-scale operation by the standards of the other periods and receive, accordingly, little discussion below. Also, a section is included on the development in Western Europe of so-called "incomes policies"—analogous in some ways to American stabilization policy—in the period since World War II. The use of incomes policies abroad and the experience obtained have significantly affected American attitudes toward employment of stabilization policy in a peacetime economy.

The National War Labor Board of World War I: Formation and Organization

The Economic and Institutional Environment

American participation in World War I was brief by the standards of other major military conflicts in which we have been involved. Yet, during the eighteen months the United States was at war, the government faced major labor problems in two areas—work stoppages, which imperiled needed production, and rising wages and prices. The government's response to these problems, particularly the former, established a procedure sometimes imitated in later periods.

With the advent in 1914 of war in Europe, the cost of living began to rise rapidly in the United States. From June 1915 until June 1917 prices increased 26 percent; and by December 1919 prices were almost double the August 1915 levels.[1] In many industries and localities, however, there were no wage increases in the 1915–17 period. Not until 1919–20 did wages on average catch up with rising prices.[2] Thus workers on the whole experienced a falling standard of living throughout the war period.

Establishment of the National War Labor Board

The number of work stoppages increased as the war approached, and a national labor policy seemed essential to provide the stability required for efficient war production. The Council of National Defense assumed leadership at the request of various defense agencies and in September 1917 invited the National Industrial Conference Board, a group of seventeen national employers' associations, to submit a proposal for the creation of a federal board to settle labor disputes.[3] On December 13, the council called an interdepartmental conference of representatives from the Navy Department, the War Department, the Labor Department, the American Federation of Labor, the Shipping Board, the Aircraft Board, and the council itself. This conference suggested establishment of "machinery which will provide the immediate and equitable adjustment of disputes in accordance with the principles to be agreed upon between labor and capital and without stoppage of work."[4]

On January 4, 1918, President Wilson directed the secretary of labor to organize the recommended machinery. The secretary appointed a seven-member council, including a public chairman, two representatives each of employers and wage earners, a representative of women, and an economist. This council recommended appointment of a tripartite twelve-member conference to negotiate collective bargaining agreements during the war, "having in view the establishment of principles and policies which will enable the prosecution of production without stoppage of work."[5]

In accordance with the council's memorandum, the secretary created the War Labor Conference Board (WLCB) on January 28, 1918. The National Industrial Conference Board and the American Federation of Labor were each called upon to appoint five members as representatives of employers and wage earners, and each group chose a public chairman to preside on alternate days. On March 29 the WLCB issued a unanimous report, recommending the establishment of the National War Labor Board to adjust labor disputes for the period of the war. The report suggested that the board's membership should be in the same number and established in the same way as its own membership, and proposed certain powers and functions for the board. In addition, the WLCB proposed principles to govern the proposed board's decisions on employer-employee relations. The most important principles included the prevention of strikes and lockouts, the recognition of the right of workers to organize and bargain collectively, the ability of the employer to continue existing conditions (to continue to have a nonunion shop, for example), and various principles of wage adjustment. The secretary of labor then appointed the members of the conference board to be members of the NWLB. On April 8, 1918, one year after the United States entered the war, the president made a formal proclamation, approving the appointment of the board and making public its principles.

Thus the board was established by government with the support of management and labor, who together determined its functions and its policies. It was created by the president, rather than by Congress, which made no appropriation and conferred no authority upon the board.

Organization of the Board

The original members of the board were the twelve members of the WLCB, including William Howard Taft and Frank P. Walsh as joint chairmen, and five members each from managment and labor. The president also appointed ten umpires, from whom a final arbitrator was to be appointed if the board was unable to reach a unanimous decision in an individual case. In addition, there was a staff of about 250 when the board was in full operation, headed by the secretary of the board. The staff was organized into six departments, four of which handled the administrative functioning of the board. The department of examination held preliminary hearings and assembled all testimony and data for the board, often making further hearings before the board unnecessary. Another department had the duty of overseeing the carrying out of an award of the board. To further expedite cases, the board formed sections composed of one member each from labor, management, and the public (the chairmen made up the section on public utilities cases). If the section reached agreement, the decision was submitted to the board and usually approved. If the section did not agree, the full board took the case.

The Operation of the Board

It should be emphasized that the board was officially a dispute-settling body, not a wage stabilization board. The approach of the board, as expressed in its Resolution of July 31, 1918, was to decide each case on its own merits and to reserve making rules "until its judgments have been sufficiently numerous and their operation sufficiently clear to make generalization safe."[6] However, there was no provision for enforcement of the decisions of the board. In joint submission cases the parties could sue for breach of the private contract by which the dispute was submitted to the board. Otherwise, enforcement depended on the pressure of public opinion, the support of other governmental agencies, and the obligation accepted by employers and employees in having their representatives sit on the board. Further, the president had the authority to seize a facility involved in a dispute. But there was no directly comparable authority to compel the workers to return to work—only the potential withdrawal of draft-exempt status or the refusal to provide placement in war industries by the U.S. Employment Service.[7]

Criteria Applied by the NWLB

Board Actions in Dispute Cases. The attempt to prevent strikes and lockouts was one of the major functions of the NWLB and other disputes-settlement boards. Although labor and management generally agreed that there should be no strikes, major strikes did occur. Frequently, work stoppages occurred in industries where there was no mechanism for settling disputes. In addition, some encouragement was given to strikes by the board's policy of giving first consideration to disputes in which a strike was threatened. However, fear of strikes at a time when uninterrupted production was essential induced the government and many employers to remove causes of unrest by adjusting wages and improving sanitary and housing conditions.[8] It should be noted that strikes were not legally prohibited during the war, and no attempts were made to prevent strikes by court injunction.[9] In general, the frequency of strikes slowed after the NWLB was set up, although the board could not compel parties to submit to its jurisdiction.

In three cases where a party refused to comply with the board's award, President Wilson did take action. First, in the Western Union case, work stoppages spread across the country as a result of the dismissal of men for union affiliation. The company refused to comply with a board recommendation to reinstate the strikers, even at the president's request. When the employees threatened to strike again, the government seized the company.[10] Second, in a similar case, the Smith and Wesson Company refused to obey a board decision, and the government took over the company.[11] A third significant case involved the Bridgeport, Connecticut, munitions companies. Employees were dissatisfied with a board decision involving the classification of trades and minimum wage rates, and struck. The president wrote the employees, requesting that they return to work on the threat of being barred from employment in any war industries in the community or from placement by the U.S. Employment Service elsewhere in the country, and on the threat of removal of their draft exemptions. When the employees voted to return to work, the president wrote the employers, who were refusing to let them return, insisting that the strikers be reinstated.[12]

Right to Organize and the Preservation of Existing Conditions. One of the most important principles agreed to by the NWLB was the right of workers to organize and to bargain collectively with their employers. Employers were forbidden to discharge workers for union activities, but workers were also forbidden to use coercion to induce other workers to join the union or to compel employers to bargain with the union.[13] However, in a company where there was an open shop (that is, union and nonunion workers), and bargaining was with company employees only, "the continuance of such conditions" was not to "be deemed a grievance."[14] Thus the employers were not necessarily required to recognize unions with whom they did not meet before the war, but in some instances employers were required to recognize committees established by their employees.

In order to encourage worker morale, the NWLB promoted collective bargaining by establishing shop committees. Among the most far-reaching orders to this effect were issued in the Bethlehem and Bridgeport cases, in which local boards of three members from each side were created to resolve disputes not covered by the NWLB. The boards were presided over by a chairman appointed by the secretary of war.[15] Often, however, difficulties with shop committees arose because of employer hostility to any form of collective bargaining and because of union objections to a committee composed of both union and nonunion men.[16]

Recognition of the right of workers to bargain collectively and to organize into trade unions was the biggest concession made by management to labor in conjunction with the NWLB program. In turn, the unions relinquished their demands for the closed shop generally and for union recognition in companies where such conditions did not exist before the war. The issue of collective bargaining rights, nonetheless, caused most of the disruption of production (through strikes) during the war.

Wage Criteria. The governing principle employed by the board for determining wages and working conditions was the comparison with prevailing standards in the area. In addition, the right to a living wage which would "insure the subsistence of the worker and his family in health and reasonable comfort" was recognized.

In making wage comparisons, the board considered area practice, the needed skill and responsibility, the nature of the work; it also required equal pay for equal work (a principle explicitly established for the employment of women).[17] The result of the use of comparative criteria for wages was a marked tendency toward standardization of wage rates among firms. Further standardization occurred because of increased mobility and high competition for labor, resulting from tight wartime labor markets. Most employers, however, resisted wage standardization, asserting that it always involved a leveling of rates upward. In addition, employers wished to be able to reward their most efficient and most skilled workers individually, a practice which sometimes was alien to collective bargaining and in some situations served to disguise discrimination against union members.[18]

As noted above, the board explicitly recognized the right to earn a "living" wage. The board never formulated a standard for the living wage but preferred to decide each case on its own merits. A cost of living section was established by the board to study the question of what would constitute a minimum subsistence level and a minimum comfort level.[19] Cost-of-living increases were applied by the board as a matter of course, though never explicitly recognized as a controlling principle.[20] Moreover, it was recognized that wage decisions could not be expected to be of indeterminate duration, so that six months was generally set as the duration of an award. Finally, the board rejected the ability of the employer to pay as a criterion in granting wage increases.

The Wage Stabilization Program of World War II and Reconversion

During World War II the government faced three different labor problems that had to be adjusted for war production to proceed smoothly. The first problem was to settle labor disputes with minimum interference with production; the second was to limit wage increases as part of a program to stabilize wages and prices in the economy; and the third was to utilize efficiently the nation's manpower for both the armed forces and production. As the war progressed, these issues became more difficult in some ways. For example, in the first stages of the direct American involvement in the war (after December 7, 1941) settlement of disputes over economic issues was a limited problem because employers were often able to grant higher wages and charge higher prices. However, with the application of wage and price controls in mid-1942 dispute settlement became more difficult. At the same time, the wage structure best suited for inflation control was not necessarily best for the allocation of manpower to defense needs. The World War II stabilization program was developed and modified over time in an effort to satisfy to the greatest degree possible these three objectives of public policy—uninterrupted production, wage and price stability, and maximum war-related output.

The National Defense Mediation Board

By the winter of 1940–41 the situation in the European war had become so unfavorable to the Allied powers that major armaments production efforts in the United States were necessary. American labor and management recognized that emergency measures would be necessary to curtail the strikes that were accompanying the revival of business activity with increasing frequency and that appeared to be threatening the nation's safety.[21] Following informal discussions with management and labor, the president established the National Defense Mediation Board by Executive Order 8716 on March 19, 1941. The board was given authority to hear disputes cases which were certified to it by the secretary of labor after the parties (often assisted by the Federal Conciliation Service) failed to settle the dispute. With a view toward avoiding work stoppages, the board was empowered to provide mediation, or, at the request of both parties, arbitration; to help establish methods to resolve disputes which would arise in the future; and to investigate the issues of a dispute referred to it, make findings of fact, and publish recommendations.[22] The board was required to refer cases concerning union representation to the National Labor Relations Board and, in practice, also referred questions of unfair labor practices to the NLRB.[23]

The National Defense Mediation Board was composed of three public, four management, and four labor representatives (two chosen from the AFL and two from the CIO). In the ten-month period of its life, from March 19,

1941, to January 12, 1942, the board received 118 cases—a small enough caseload to make decentralization to regional or industry subordinate boards unnecessary.[24] In all cases the board first attempted to mediate the dispute. However, if the parties did not reach agreement, the board was empowered to issue a recommendation which public opinion or governmental authority might persuade the parties to accept. Although recommendations were not binding, recalcitrant parties faced the possibility of a public request by the president for compliance, cancellation of government contracts, or seizure of property by government. It should be noted, however, that in thirteen of the twenty-six cases in which the board issued recommendations a public refusal was made by at least one party to abide by the recommendation.[25]

A dispute in the coal industry ended the effectiveness of the board. In the *Captive Mines* case, the primary issue in dispute was the union's demand for a closed shop. On September 15, 1941, John L. Lewis called out forty thousand miners in the coal mines of the steel industry, beginning a series of strikes. Lewis agreed to submit the case to the NDMB for a final recommendation but refused to commit himself to accepting it in advance. The board issued a decision against the union and the CIO members left the board in protest. The miners struck again. Finally, arbitration by a specially empaneled board which was acceptable to and included Lewis resulted in a decision in favor of the union. This experience, however, left the NDMB effectively crippled for the remainder of its existence.[26]

The National War Labor Board

Formation. Shortly after the resolution of the *Captive Mines* case, Japan attacked the United States military installations at Pearl Harbor, and the combatant role of the United States in the war began. With the National Defense Mediation Board virtually inoperative, some government action was necessary for dispute settlements, especially because the requirements of war production were now accelerating. A bill restraining aspects of collective bargaining had already passed the House of Representatives, and a more stringent bill, prohibiting strikes, had been proposed in the Senate.

At the suggestion of both the AFL and the CIO, President Roosevelt convened a labor-management conference on December 17, 1941, emphasizing the importance of industrial peace and asking for recommendations for a disputes-settlement machinery. Twelve representatives from labor and management met. The conference agreed that (1) there would be no strikes or lockouts, (2) disputes except those involving union security would be settled amicably, and (3) tripartite machinery would be set up to resolve disputes. However, there was strong disagreement between management and labor as to the appropriate method for resolution of disputes on union security. Senator Thomas, associate moderator of the conference, proposed a three-point resolution, incorporating the first and third points of agreement. For the controversial second clause, Senator Thomas proposed the phrase, "All disputes shall be settled by peaceful means." However, management wished to add a fourth point, specifically forbidding board action on union security. Both the three- and four-point resolutions were presented to Roosevelt, who announced that: "Government must act in general, the three points agreed upon cover of necessity all disputes that may arise between labor and management." Roosevelt thereby attempted to create agreement where there was none. In response, the management representatives issued a statement accepting the president's direction but suggesting that, in determining its procedure, the board should decline to accept cases dealing with the closed shop issue.[27]

As a result of the labor-management "agreement," the president established the National War Labor Board by Executive Order 9017 on January 12, 1942 (simultaneously disbanding the National Defense Mediation Board). The NWLB was given original jurisdiction over disputes cases after consultation with the secretary of labor; the president did not detail the board's structure, policies, or procedures but provided for settlement of disputes through mediation, voluntary arbitration, or arbitration under its own rules. The responsibility to develop criteria for disputes settlement was left to the new tripartite board, which chose to act on a case-by-case basis, establishing general rules through decisions in particular cases.

During the period from January to October 1942 in which the board was limited to a dispute-settling function, its case load was fairly small. On October 2, 1942, however, President Roosevelt issued Executive Order 9250, providing for a wage stabilization function of the board. Thereafter, the board was deluged by voluntary applications for wage adjustments and by disputes cases. Several approaches to decentralization were suggested. On the national level, the staff increased its role in analysis and screening of cases. Regional directors were appointed to process voluntary cases and make decisions on certain issues which were reviewable by the board. Tripartite committees, initially appointed in a consulting role to the regional directors, eventually became regional boards with authority to make decisions on both disputes and wage adjustment cases. The War Labor Board also established seventeen industry-specific agencies to hear cases. The size of the industry or the geographic region covered by an agency varied, as did its jurisdiction regarding types of cases.[28]

The National War Labor Board was made up of four members each from the public, management, and labor. The public members were prominent citizens chosen by the president who were not closely identified with either management or labor or the administration itself;[29] labor's representatives were chosen equally by the AFL and the CIO; industry's representatives were recommended by businessmen from the National Association of Manufacturers and the Chamber of Commerce. Delegation of board activities to agencies other than the board itself was eventually extended to such a degree that 84 percent of all cases were referred to regional boards and industry commissions, the NWLB retaining only those cases which were industry-wide or involved significant issues of policy.[30]

Operations of the Board. For the first few months of its existence, the board was preoccupied with union security issues and was reluctant to establish principles regarding wage increases. However, on April 27, 1942, the president issued a seven-point program to combat inflation and directed the board to stabilize wages. The labor representatives continued to insist that the board place emphasis on collective bargaining, treating each case individually rather than forming in advance generally applicable principles. The public members agreed. Realizing the importance of providing guidance for voluntary wage adjustments, however, the board on July 16, 1942, issued a decision in the *Little Steel* cases regarding permissible wage adjustments. Increases were permitted for the steelworkers based on the difference between the wage increases which they had already been granted and the increase in the cost-of-living over a base period. The formula provided that firms would be permitted to increase wages to a level not to exceed 15 percent above the average straight-time hourly earnings in January 1941. The 15 percent figure equaled the rise in consumer prices from January 1941 to May 1942. In a later case (*Remington Rand Company*, July 27, 1942), the board described the purpose of the *Little Steel* formula: "What the formula will do is place a terminal on the race between prices and wages and prevent the beginning of another upward spiral of general wage increases with their inflationary effects." The *Little Steel* formula, developed in the context of a dispute case in 1941, was to become the standard for general wage increases throughout the war.

On April 8, 1943, following a 5 percent rise in the cost-of-living over a six-month period and considerable agitation for relaxation of the *Little Steel* formula, the president issued Executive Order 9328, the "hold-the-line" order, allowing wage increases only to correct substandards of living and to compensate for the rise in the cost-of-living in accordance with the *Little Steel* formula. The order initially appeared to remove much of the NWLB's discretion in administering stabilization. At the board's request, the director of economic stabilization issued a clarifying directive, restoring authority to approve minimum noninflationary adjustments to aid in the effective prosecution of the war or to correct gross inequities. This policy was later elaborated in the wage-rate "bracket" system. Following the "hold-the-line" order, there were no other major policy directives for the duration of the war, although additional limited modifications of the program were made.[31]

In the spring of 1943 the number of strikes and lockouts began increasing rapidly, including a particularly important series of work stoppages in coal. In response, Congress passed the War Labor Disputes Act over a presidential veto. The act, however, did little more than reaffirm the board's existing authority, adding to it the power of subpoena. On August 16, 1943, the president issued Executive Order 9370 to insure compliance with board awards. The order authorized the director of economic stabilization to withhold any benefits or contracts entered into with employers who did not comply with board orders, and similarly to withhold certain benefits from noncomplying unions. In addition, the War Manpower Commission was authorized to modify draft deferments or employment privileges of individuals, if necessary to enforce the stabilization program.[32]

The voluntary no-strike, no-lockout pledge on which the War Labor Board was founded expired with the end of the war in August 1945. The operations of the board were terminated on December 13, 1945, and delegated in part to a successor agency, the National Wage Stabilization Board.

Criteria for Wage Adjustments. The administrative criteria used by the NWLB are analyzed in detail in later chapters. Here it is sufficient to summarize the wage stabilization policy of the NWLB following the "hold-the-line" order in the spring of 1943. This policy consisted primarily of four elements. First, proposals for general wage increases were measured against the *Little Steel* formula. Second, brackets of sound and tested wage rates were developed by area and occupation and were used in evaluating claims for changes in interplant wage relationships. Third, increases were permitted to raise wage rates up to specific levels in order to correct substandards of living. Fourth, wage increases proposed primarily to direct the flow of manpower were approved in a few instances.[33]

Standards for Nonwage Issues in Dispute Cases. In order to maintain wartime production the National War Labor Board was required to consider many disputes which involved issues other than wages. The most controversial issue presented to the board was union security. The unions argued for a closed shop to compensate for the loss of the strike weapon. The employers insisted that the law required only that a union representing a majority of the employees be recognized as exclusive bargaining agent—that is, the unions should not be allowed to take advantage of the war to improve their position. After six months of debate and experimentation in a number of cases, a workable solution was reached by the board, though still with industry members dissenting. In *Norma Hoffman Bearings Corp.* (no. 120, August 24, 1942),[34] the board worked out the language of what was to be the standard maintenance-of-membership clause, requiring all employees who were union members fifteen days after an order of the board, and all new members, to maintain their membership in good standing as a condition of employment.

No employee was required to become a member of the union. Maintenance-of-membership was generally ordered unless the union was irresponsible, which in practice meant that it had violated the no-strike pledge. The board also usually ordered checkoff of union dues and initiation fees when requested by the union. To reduce work stoppages, the board promoted the establishment of grievance machinery for the settlement of disputes over the administration of collective bargaining agreements, including provision for final settlement by arbitration. Such machinery was especially important in handling disciplinary and discharge cases.[35]

Compliance. Over 95 percent of the 17,650 dispute cases before the War Labor Board were settled without further threat of disruption. Many of the remaining cases involved misunderstanding rather than defiance of the board. Where further clarification and persuasion were not successful in inducing compliance, the defiant party was called to "show cause" at a public hearing as to why the board order was not being obeyed. In 1943, the War Labor Disputes Act gave the board the power to subpoena parties for the hearings. It also affirmed the power of the president to seize a plant where compliance could not be obtained and provided that there would be no change in wages or conditions of employment at the seized plant without approval of the board and the president.

In forty cases it was necessary for the president to seize a plant. In situations (nineteen in number) where the employer had failed to comply with a board order, the government put the order into effect. Where the union had failed to comply with a board order and a strike was in process (twenty-one instances), the strike usually stopped when the government took over the plant. Thus, in most cases seizure was successful. However, in two cases seizure was only partly successful at best, and in two other situations seizure appeared useless.

The National Wage Stabilization Board

After V-J Day, August 14, 1945, President Truman issued a series of executive orders limiting the powers of the National War Labor Board and announced that it would be dismantled after a forthcoming labor-management conference. Under pressure to relax controls, the president announced in Executive Order 9599, dated August 18, that voluntary wage increases could be made without the approval of the board in cases where there would be no request for a subsequent price rise. In addition, he reinstituted Executive Order 9250, relaxing the circumstances under which a wage increase could be granted in those cases for which board approval was still required. Disputes were to continue to be handled by the board. The construction industry was expected to experience sharp increases in wages, for the manpower supply was especially tight and there was a great demand for civilian housing. Therefore the construction industry was subjected to a continuation of the authority of the Wage Adjustment Board. On October 16, 1945, the National War Labor Board announced that it would terminate no later than January 1, 1946, in accordance with the president's message of August 16. At the same time, the board announced that it would later announce a program to continue administration of the Stabilization Act.

Prior to abolishing the NWLB, the administration made a last effort to preserve stabilization policy. The war had ended unexpectedly in August 1945, and soon thereafter labor had withdrawn its no-strike pledge. The entire stabilization program was thereby imperiled, for without a no-strike pledge the wage criteria were no longer enforceable. Further, with the end of the war it was obvious to the American people that the claims for wage increases and readjustments which had built up during stabilization must somehow be accommodated. Therefore, the president called for a national labor-management conference on August 16, 1945, "to work out by agreement means to minimize the interruption of production by labor disputes in the reconversion period." The conference convened on November 5, 1945, with delegates representing the AFL, the CIO, the Chamber of Commerce, the National Association of Manufacturers, the United Mine Workers, and the Railway Brotherhoods (the last two then nonaffiliates of either the AFL or the CIO). Public delegates attended and chaired conference sessions, but did not vote.

President Truman addressed the conference on November 5 at its first session. He directed his remarks primarily at the rising spectre of numerous industrial disputes. "The American people ... never expected anything like the amount of strife which has been threatened," the president commented. Significantly, he suggested, "If [collective] bargaining produces no results, then there must be a willingness to use some impartial machinery for reaching decisions ... that is the way to keep production going."[36]

At the first meeting of the executive committee of the conference on November 7, Philip Murray, president of the CIO, suggested a resolution which provided that the framework for collective bargaining should be the president's recent wage-price message. Murray emphasized the need for a resolution of the issue of wages if problems of collective bargaining and industrial strife were to be solved. On November 16, the management side replied, suggesting the conference "not consider national wage policies" but confine its attention to improving the machinery of collective bargaining. John L. Lewis of the United Mine Workers in essence supported the employers, suggesting a positive resolution of the issue by declaring for a program of higher productivity and higher wages (the program followed in the late 1940s and early 1950s by the mine workers in encouraging mechanization of the mines in return for economic benefits). A bipartite subcommittee, on which the CIO refused to serve, declared the conference not to be a wage conference. So ended the administration's attempt, with the support of important elements of organized labor, to find grounds for agreement between management and labor which could permit the extension of the no-strike pledge and wage stabilization machinery into the reconversion period.

The failure of the labor-management conference to agree to an extension of the no-strike, no-lockout pledge forced the administration to pursue a less desirable policy. On November 6, the president had requested that the NWLB set up a tripartite division to carry out the remaining functions of the board until its termination. The personnel of the new division were later transferred to a new agency which functioned until the Stabilization Act expired. On December 31, 1945, Executive Order 9572 dissolved the National War Labor Board and established the National Wage Stabilization Board, a six-member, tripartite body. The new agency operated as an independent, quasi-judicial body within the Department of Labor.[37]

Just before its dissolution, on December 29, 1945, the National War Labor Board announced the regulations which its successor agency was to administer. A new cost-of-living formula allowed increases of up to 33 percent over the January 1941 average straight-time hourly earnings in those cases which required board approval. Moreover, the bracket concept, which restricted correction of interplant inequities, was abandoned.[38]

Because of the failure of the labor-management conference to renew the no-strike, no-lockout pledge, there was no mechanism for resolving disputes. The National Wage Stabilization Board had control only over certain voluntary wage adjustment cases, particularly those in which a price increase was requested under a continuing program of price controls. Serious problems arose in some industries when the wage offers which management made under the constraints of price stabilization failed to meet the demands of the unions. A type of three-way bargaining developed in which the unions bargained with management and the government over a wage increase, while management bargained with the government over a price increase. The stabilization program virtually collapsed in the context of a complex dispute involving the basic steel industry in early 1946, but it was not until February 24, 1947, that the NWSB was officially dissolved by executive order of the president.

The Record of Stabilization, 1941–46

Prices and wages were restrained on average, but not frozen, during the World War II period. From January 1941 through July 1945, the Consumer Price Index rose about 33.3 percent. On average, basic wage rates during that period increased only about 24 percent. In the period of maximum restraint by the NWLB, from October 1942 to April 1945, basic wages increased about 8 percent, as compared to 15 percent from January 1941 to October 1942. Due to the War Labor Board's policy of restraining wages but not gross earnings, however, gross weekly earnings rose 70.5 percent between 1941 and 1945, an increase in real weekly spendable earnings of 24 percent for a family of four. Thus only about one-third of the increase in weekly earnings was due to a change in the basic wage rate. Other factors included longer hours at premium pay; shifts to higher paying industries or regions or to more skilled occupations; liberal administration of merit increases, adjustments in piece-rates, and increased output by piece-rate workers. These other factors were largely reversible (earnings would potentially decline as the need for high production fell) upon return to a more normal economy and exerted their greatest effect on earnings in the early months of the war when the economy was moving into full production. Rationing, however, diverted much of the gain into savings. Following the war, a wage-price spiral occurred, which was just ending as the Korean War began.

The Wage Stabilization Board During the Korean War

Formation of the Board

In June 1950 the Korean War broke out. An immediate inflation began, in part because people expected it, although there were few actual scarcities.[39] As a result of strong consumer demand and high profits, several labor agreements were voluntarily reopened and wage increases provided. In many cases new wage negotiations resulted in cost-of-living escalator clauses and improvement factors, patterned after the General Motors–United Automobile Workers agreements of 1948 and 1950 (the latter a five-year agreement). In general, however, industrial relations were relatively peaceful.[40] Meanwhile, the actual production levels which would be necessary to fight the war were uncertain. The defense budget was only 7 percent of total production at the end of 1950 and would rise to only 18 percent by the end of 1951 (well below the proportions in World War II).[41]

On July 19, 1950, President Truman requested emergency legislation to aid military production and to control inflation. The Defense Production Act of September 1, 1950, provided the president with the authorization he had requested to establish priorities and allocate scarce war materials, to control consumer and commodity speculation, and to offer production loan guarantees and other financial incentives to business. In addition the act provided the president with power to control prices and wages, which he had not requested. Title IV of the act called for voluntary action by business, agriculture, labor, and consumers; but also authorized selective or general price ceilings accompanied by simultaneous wage stabilization. Only very general standards for the administration of controls were provided. Furthermore, the act provided that no ceiling could be set for agricultural products below parity levels.[42]

President Truman issued Executive Order 10161 on September 9, 1950, to implement the new act. Under the order, the president established an Economic Stabilization Agency and provided that, subordinate to the economic stabilization administrator, would be a director of price stabilization and a Wage Stabilization Board.[43] Considerable controversy occurred over whether to establish a tripartite wage board or a wage stabilization agency similar to the Office of Price Stabilization, which would not be tripartite. The proposed agency was to be limited to wage stabilization functions, with no dispute-settlement responsibilities. The duration and extent of the war effort was uncertain. If dispute-settlement machinery became necessary, one viewpoint held that a tripartite board would be necessary. But it was agreed that wage stabilization alone did not require tripartitism.[44] Meanwhile Stuart Symington, chairman of the National Security Resources Board, sought the creation of the United Labor Policy Committee, composed of representatives of the AFL, the CIO, and independent unions, to formulate a program for labor's participation in the NSRB. This committee then pressed for labor participation in the new wartime agencies.[45] Furthermore, the National Advisory Committee on Mobilization Policy, an agency established by Symington to represent industry, agriculture, labor, and the public, expressed no objections to the creation of a tripartite wage stabilization board.

Ultimately, a decision was made by the administration to form a nine-member wage stabilization agency, with three members each from labor, industry, and the public, all to be named by the president. The Wage Stabilization Board, established under Executive Order 10161, was to make recommendations to the administrator of the ESA and to perform those wage stabilization functions which he had assigned. Title V of the Defense Production Act had authorized the president to call a labor-management conference as a preliminary to setting up dispute-settlement machinery. Such a conference was never called.

Even after the extent of the potential war effort began to be understood, direct controls were not attempted for over two months. On December 18, 1950, the WSB issued a unanimous resolution expressing the view that direct controls have only a partial role in curbing inflation. The members of the board were convinced that voluntary controls were unrealistic. In consequence, the board made no response to an administration request for a voluntary wage stabilization program. But the board did discuss partial controls. Later the Council of Economic Advisers urged the economic stabilization administrator to intercede in the basic steel negotiations, but no action was taken. Price controls were placed on the automobile industry, however, and the Defense Production Act called for accompanying wage controls. The WSB encountered strong opposition to wage controls by both the union and the automobile companies. The industry argued that wages were already stabilized by the existing five-year collective bargaining agreements, signed in 1949. The board, faced with the decision to either breach the long-term contracts or adopt policies allowing the agreements to continue to operate, recommended only that workers should not be paid more than the amount provided in the existing collective bargaining contracts. A decision to impose general wage and price controls was announced, and a freeze became effective January 25, 1951.[46] Meanwhile the labor members of the WSB were becoming increasingly dissatisfied with their role in the defense structure generally, and especially with the board's lack of authority to settle disputes. An occasion for the expression of their dissatisfaction came with the adoption by the WSB of General Wage Regulation 6 on February 15, 1951. Regulation 6 allowed voluntary wage increases of up to 10 percent more than the straight-time wages on January 15, 1950. The board would consider granting increases in other cases where January 15, 1950, was not a normal base period or in rare and unusual cases where it was necessary to ease a manpower shortage. In a dissent to the adoption of General Wage Regulation 6 by the WSB, the labor members stated:

> [We] have repeatedly urged that the Board move promptly to establish machinery for handling labor disputes. These urgent requests have been completely ignored.... This is a fundamental issue. No wage stabilization board can hope to set a wage policy and then remain aloof from the controversies which might develop over its application or interpretation.[47]

Upon instructions from the United Labor Policy Committee, the labor representatives withdrew from the board on the night the other board members voted to adopt regulation 6. On February 28 labor representatives withdrew from all levels of the defense program.[48]

The president continued negotiations with the labor representatives through the next three months and assumed some of the powers of the inoperative Wage Stabilization Board. He had signed regulation 6 with misgivings and, to increase flexibility in granting wage increases, issued General Wage Regulations 8, 9, and 10, dealing with escalator clauses, rates for new plants, and tandem relationships among plants.

Establishment of a Reconstituted WSB

Desiring an operating Wage Stabilization Board, President Truman established a 17-member National Advisory Board, headed by Chief Mobilizer Charles E. Wilson. Labor agreed to work with the NAB on April 5 and returned to the defense program under a reconstituted WSB as recommended by the advisory board. The WSB was reestablished and redefined under Executive Order 10233, issued April 21, 1951, with George W. Taylor as chairman. The board was to be an eighteen-member body with a limited dispute-settling function in addition to its wage stabilization responsibilities. It was authorized to hear a dispute case where the parties jointly agreed to submit the dispute to the board, either for a recommendation or for a binding decision. The parties alone were to decide whether to submit the dispute to the board and which issues should be submitted. Upon referral by the president, the board could also hear cases that were a substantial threat to the national defense. The WSB was then to investigate the dispute and make a recommendation to the president.

The Final Reorganization of the WSB

The Defense Production Act was amended in 1952 to provide for a substantially different Wage Stabilization Board.[49] The old board was prohibited from issuing any orders except as to pending cases until July 30, 1952, when the new board would start functioning. The WSB remained an eighteen-member tripartite agency, now chaired by Archibald Cox; its members were subject to Senate confirmation, however, for terms expiring May 1, 1953. The authority of the board was limited to making recommendations regarding general policies and regulations to the economic stabilization administrator on issues of wage stabilization—that is, setting the limits of permissible increases. The board was to have jurisdiction only over labor disputes involving interpretation of its stabilization policy and recommendations.

In the *Bituminous Coal* case, the WSB made an attempt to maintain the wage stabilization program. John L. Lewis had negotiated an increase of $1.90 a day for the United Mine Workers. The board was prepared to approve an increase of only $1.50. In consequence, the mine workers struck on October 10, 1952, shortly before the presidential election. Coal stockpiles were adequate for several weeks, but public pressure to end the strike was great. Moreover, both the UMW and Harry Moses, of the northern coal operators, were content with the negotiated agreement, and neither was willing to negotiate a new agreement within the board's guidelines. After a prolonged stalemate, David L. Cole, director of the Federal Mediation and Conciliation Service, arranged a secret conference between Lewis, Moses, and Roger L. Putnam, director of economic stabilization. Lewis and Moses argued that the board had misapplied its criteria, and Putnam, primarily interested in ending the strike, promised to consider their appeal.[50] After a formal conference in the White House, President Truman ordered approval of the full negotiated increase on December 3, 1952. The president suggested that his decision was the result of a belief that the case was unique (therefore involving no precedent for other industries) and that the approval of the entire agreement was in the interest of industrial peace, particularly during the transition to the Eisenhower administration.

Functioning of the WSB

The tripartite national board consisted of eighteen members, representing industry, labor, and the public. The chairman and vice-chairman were chosen from among the public members. The staff of the board was headed by the office of the executive director. Under the executive director were the Review and Appeals Committee, the National Enforcement Committee, the Office of Disputes, and the Committee on Health and Welfare Plans. The Review and Appeals Committee processed most of the cases over which the national board had original jurisdiction, in addition to appeals from the decisions of the regional boards. It was obligated to stay within the board's policies and could not issue decisions, only recommendations. A unanimous recommendation was rarely questioned by the board, however.[51]

Fourteen regional boards, patterned closely after the national board, were set up late in the summer of 1951. Each board had twelve members, representing labor, industry, and government. Industry members were nominated by chambers of commerce, boards of trade, and other business organizations, and were then reviewed by the industry members of the national board. Nominations for the labor representatives were made by state federations of labor and industrial unions councils. Public members were reviewed by both sides.[52] Associated with each regional board was a regional enforcement commission, which heard cases of violations of stabilization regulations referred to it by the regional general counsel's staff. The regional boards had no dispute-settling powers and concentrated on stabilization issues, under the supervision of the national board. The guidance of the national board was often inadequate, however. Under a General Wage Procedural Regulation of September 20, 1951, regional board decisions were to be reviewed by the national board (or the Review and Appeals Committee) only when the decision was contrary to established policies or presented an important, novel case. In practice, however, it has been charged that only passing reference was made to these criteria at best, and the cases were heard de novo on their merits. In consequence, it is argued, the Review and Appeals Committee reversed 43 percent of the appeals from the regional boards with little explanation for the reversals in the minutes of the committee.[53]

Industry boards were established for the construction industry and the automobile industry. The Construction Industry Stabilization Commission was a twelve-member tripartite commission established at the request of the Building and Construction Trades Department (AFL) and nine national contractors' associations under GWR 12, May 31, 1951. The CISC functioned as an autonomous agency as long as it stayed reasonably within the policies of the WSB. Furthermore, approval of the board on cases where the CISC exceeded agreed upon wage formulas was usually obtained.[54] As in World War II, the Detroit regional board was given authority to handle all stabilization cases involving the automobile industry.[55]

Only the national board had authority to resolve disputes cases, and it was authorized to act only after all collective bargaining and mediation procedures had failed and only upon referral by the president or by both parties voluntarily. The board then made recommendations to the president or made recommendations or a binding decision to the parties, depending upon whether the parties had agreed to accept a board decision. The board had disputes authority during the period July 20, 1951, through May 7, 1952, only. During that time it reviewed thirty-four disputes cases, twelve upon referral by the president and twenty-two from voluntary submissions by the parties to the disputes.[56]

The Record of Wage Stabilization

The record of wage stabilization during the Korean War was mixed. The rate of increase in adjusted hourly earnings in manufacturing during the Korean conflict was perhaps below that of World War II.[57] But the economic environment in 1950–53 was significantly less expansive than during the Second World War, and therefore the achievement of the stabilization program in the Korean period was not so marked when measured against the probable rate of wage inflation in the absence of controls. During the Korean War, certain major employers appeared to have been concerned primarily with avoiding industrial strife rather than with preventing the granting of large wage increases and fringes (as evidenced by the level of negotiated settlements in major industries during the Korean period). The Wage Stabilization Board frequently attempted to establish wage ceilings at the levels created by major collective bargaining agreements, partly in order to maintain industrial peace and particularly when faced with an employer's willingness to pay the negotiated rates. Price increases were generally allowed by price stabilization authorities to offset the wage increases. In fact, the argument has often been made that the WSB had little if any discernible effect in controlling wages.[58] In 1950, straight-time earnings in most industries were moving at about the same rate as the cost-of-living. By January 1953, money wages had so outdistanced the cost-of-living that real hourly earnings had increased 6.9 percent over January 1950 in the durable goods industry, 3.8 percent in nondurable goods, and at least 5.4 percent in fifteen of twenty-two industries studied.[59]

Incomes Policies Abroad, 1946-72

During the post-World War II period many countries of Western Europe pursued policies designed to control the rate of increase of wages and prices. There were substantial differences among nations in the content of these policies, and in some cases substantial evolution occurred over time in the policy followed by a single nation. Nevertheless, a generic term came to be applied to the various efforts—"incomes policies." The development of incomes policies abroad is important to a study of stabilization policy in the United States for two major reasons. First, the efforts abroad to control prices and wages suggested a type of policy to American government officials and academics. In the United States a demand for an "incomes policy" developed, the impetus being American economic problems and European economic policies. This largely uncritical borrowing of a policy was encouraged by a tendency to view Western European and American economic problems as very much alike. The concern in Western Europe for reconciling low unemployment with a greater measure of price stability provided a striking parallel to American problems. Further, the fact that incomes policy was directed at the control of wages and therefore at the activities of trade unions, also struck a responsive chord in the United States. Thus, despite substantial differences between the Western European nations and the United States (and among the Western European nations as a group) in economic, political, and institutional characteristics, the existence of incomes policies in Europe established a presumption for their employment in the United States.

Second, in the interdependent international economy of the 1960s, the reliance of Western European governments on incomes policies as a tool to control inflation led those same governments to expect that a serious attempt to control domestic inflation in the United States would necessarily entail resort to incomes policies of some nature. Thus, in the recurrent crises over the United States balance of payments deficits in the 1960s and early 1970s, European creditors of the United States demanded an American incomes policy as evidence of an intention to control inflation.

A number of conclusions have been drawn by American observers from the varied experience of European countries with incomes policies. Unfortunately, analysis of European experience has been, with a few exceptions, no less controversial than most evaluations of stabilization policy in the United States. For example, the following five propositions about incomes policies may be found in most American discussions of European wage-price policy. In each case, however, there are substantial inaccuracies in the propositions, so that they are of limited usefulness as a guide to American policy. The first proposition is that an incomes policy is a necessary and useful tool of wage-price policy. However, generally little or nothing is offered by observers as to the particular form and content of policy other than the goal of reducing wage and price increases to some target rate. But even the most cursory review of European experience demonstrates a variety of policies that have experienced failure as well as success in different instances. The second view, in apparent contradiction to the first, is that incomes policies abroad have been on the whole unsuccessful. The Nixon administration, until August 15, 1971, was adept at citing European experience as evidence of the uselessness of incomes policies to control inflation. But this judgment, like the first proposition just cited, is a distortion of a more complex record. What might be offered in place of these two inconsistent assertions (of success on the one hand and failure on the other) is the view that we know little from European experience about the causes and cures of inflation as a general problem.

A third proposition is that the trade unions have a major causal role in inflation, so that incomes policies have been promoted primarily as a method of controlling the unions. The unions are often faulted not only as a major contributor to inflation but also as unwilling for political purposes to support incomes policies except in some circumstances involving a labor or socialist government.[60] Yet to generalize from the behavior of unions in Europe, whatever it may be, to the very different context of the United States is particularly hazardous. Fourth, the role played by problems regarding the income distribution in the development and management of incomes policies has been stressed by students of the European experience. In Europe, according to a common interpretation, attempts to develop an incomes policy among management, labor, and government often provoke difficult disputes over the distribution of income.[61] Yet such disputes are more commonly a major political problem in Europe than in the United States and would be almost as likely even in the absence of incomes policies.[62] Further, in Europe appeals for a different distribution of income may serve rather as a popular public response[63] by labor to more basic but more complex elements of dissatisfaction with incomes policy.[64] In consequence, the assertion that stabilization policy in Europe (and by extension in the United States) must involve difficult problems of income distribution is not proven.

Fifth, some observers have chosen to rely on European experience to suggest that a wage control program is only effective to the degree that no exceptions are allowed from the target established for wage increases. It is argued, for example, that the "productivity" criterion for increases in the British policy of the late 1960s provided a loophole through which large wage increases were approved, effectively damaging the controls program. But a more balanced appraisal suggests that the value of the single norm for wage increases as a policy instrument is not established by European experience. Turner pointed out that in Great Britain the provision of exceptions for productivity resulted in its use as a "safety valve to permit pressures which might otherwise have led to industrial conflict to escape."[65] Further, Ulman and Flanagan noted that percentage norms were abandoned in several countries in the late 1960s because of a tendency to become not maximum increases but minimum, and the authors suggested in consequence that "perhaps the way out is to explore . . . a no-norm policy."[66]

These five commonly expressed lessons of European incomes policy are largely incorrect. However, there are several conclusions for American policy which might fairly be drawn from a review of the European experience. First, incomes policies are no panacea. In some circumstances, however, a restriction of the rate of wage and price increases seems to have occurred in part as a result of an incomes policy.[67] But, they do not necessarily result in an improvement of the long-term price and wage behavior of an economy.[68] Where there has been failure, the reasons are often not hard to identify. Second, an important aspect of incomes policy which has been too little studied is the use of the policy as a temporary substitute for, or even a device to obtain, fundamental reforms in the operation of the economy or certain of its sectors. In Britain, incomes policy encouraged the improvement of productivity in British industry. The importance of achieving structural adjustments in the economy as a condition of wage-price stability is reinforced by the evidence from Europe that incomes policies (like stabilization policies in the United States) inevitably erode with the passage of time and cannot be relied upon to provide long-term stability. Third, the initiation of an incomes policy does inevitably raise other issues in its context. The economic policies of the government with respect to growth, prices, and the distribution of income become, to a degree, issues in the form of the incomes policy. Whether or not these issues become destructive to a desired wage policy depends largely on how they are handled by the government and private groups. Fourth, industrial disputes and work stoppages always contain the potential of seriously damaging an incomes policy. European experience provides considerable recent evidence of this, including the French general strike of 1968, the Swedish public employees strike of 1970, and the British coal strike of 1972. Thus, there is no evidence from Western European experience that industrial relations considerations can be successfully eschewed in an incomes policy in favor of exclusive reliance on economic objectives and criteria.

Finally, a study of European experience suggests strongly by comparison the importance of the peculiar institutions, economy, and historical experience of the United States. There are basic differences between American and Western European labor market institutions which cause wage determination to occur in a very different framework and with different characteristics. In Western Europe unions tend to be much weaker at the plant or local level than in the United States, and unions are often unable to exert a significant measure of influence over the behavior of workers at the local level.[69] Wage rates are often negotiated at the national or industry-wide level in Europe and are actually minimum rates to which local adjustments may be applied. In consequence, national negotiations regarding wage rates become political matters in a sense not often the case in the United States, and wage adjustments are made in response less to labor market and product market factors than to other considerations. Also, because of the structure of Western European unionism, earnings more accurately reflect market conditions and may diverge very markedly from negotiated rates. This is especially true in Sweden, where compensation practices rely heavily on piece rates. In Denmark, national wage negotiations have established a highly egalitarian structure of wage rates which has been substantially modified at the local level to reflect skill and other differentials. In Great Britain, incomes policies have even in some instances had the support of unions, which can "control the setting of wage rates but not the actual movement of earnings."[70] In the Netherlands, wages paid above legal rates have been referred to as "black wages."[71] The result of the European pattern of bargaining has been a continued problem of so-called "wage drift," by which earnings (and wages actually paid at the job site) rise above the nationally negotiated levels. From the perspective of economic stabilization, wage drift has often been the primary problem in Europe.[72]

In the United States, on the other hand, labor unions tend to be quite strong (by European standards) at the local or plant level. There is little competition among organizations at the plant level, union discipline of the work force is good (so that wildcat strikes, for example, are infrequent), and negotiated wage rates are most often those paid (so that there is little problem of wage-drift). In consequence, the participation of American unions in a wage stabilization program has historically provided much greater substance to the enforcement and success of the policy at the workplace than is possible in Europe. The American tradition in wage-price stabilization machinery, including the tripartite character of wage stabilization boards, has reflected the peculiar strength of the American labor movement at the workplace. Thus, the American tradition of stabilization policy is very special and unusual in several respects, and should not be confused with what is loosely referred to as "incomes policies" abroad.[73] European experience with incomes policies, while interesting and in some ways instructive, is of far less importance with respect to the American situation than is historical experience with stabilization in the United States itself.

Wage-Price Guideposts in the United States, 1962–68

In 1962, during the second year of the Kennedy administration, the

President's Council of Economic Advisers announced wage-price guideposts for the American economy. The guideposts were carefully described by a student of the period as a "specific and systematic governmental, rather than tripartite, statement of standards for non-inflationary price and wage behavior which would, however, rely chiefly on acceptance by those influenced by the policy for its effectiveness."[74] The guideposts had a rather checkered career from 1962 to 1969, when the newly elected Republican administration formally abandoned them. However, the experience with the guideposts greatly affected American thinking about economic policy, occasioning bitter disputes among observers as to the best methods of influencing wage and price behavior in the economy. Further, the lessons of the guidepost years, though differently interpreted by various individuals, exerted a profound influence on the structure and administration of the far more extensive program of wage-price controls established in 1971.

Early in 1962, the CEA announced the wage-price guideposts in its annual economic report. The wage standards called for increases in wages and fringe benefits in each industry to be equal to the trend rate of increase in output per man-hour in the economy as a whole. Four exceptions were provided. Increases might exceed the productivity guideline where there were labor shortages or substandard wages. Increases should fall below the productivity guideline where there was considerable unemployment in an industry or in cases involving exceptionally high levels of wages and fringe benefits. The council noted that, if compensation rose at the same rate as output per man-hour, labor costs per unit of output would be unchanged, so that there would be no pressure on prices from labor cost increases. Prices, therefore, should not change where compensation increases were equal to the productivity change in the particular sector, industry, or firm involved; prices should fall where compensation rose less rapidly than productivity; and prices should rise where compensation rose more rapidly than productivity. In 1963, the annual report of the council reaffirmed the guidelines. In 1964, President Johnson supported the guideposts in the president's own economic report, a step President Kennedy had not taken.[75] Further, the 1964 report of the CEA established the guidelines figure at 3.2 percent per year. The year 1964 was perhaps the heyday of the guideposts, in which they experienced an unusual degree of overt presidential support. In 1965, the guidelines were reaffirmed but began to be undermined by expansion of the economy and tightening labor markets; in addition disputes between the government and several industries (including, especially, steel and aluminum) developed over price increases. Wage settlements in a number of instances also exceeded the guidelines. In January 1966 the council reaffirmed the 3.2 percent guideline. Early in 1966, wage increases were negotiated in construction, metropolitan transit, longshoring, and other industries well above the guidelines. In the summer of 1966, President Johnson helped to mediate an agreement between the International Association of Machinists and five airlines which the union had struck on July 8. The resulting agreement was estimated to cost 4.3 percent, but President Johnson, announcing the agreement over national television on July 30, described the increase as noninflationary since it conformed to the *industry's* rate of productivity improvement.[76] Unfortunately, the IAM membership failed to ratify the agreement, and the strike resumed. On August 19, the union accepted an increase of about 5 percent, ending the strike. In 1967–68 the guidelines were essentially abandoned.

Guideposts policy had been characterized by three fundamental elements. First, a single percentage figure for wage increases was used almost to the complete exclusion of other considerations. The original statement of the guideposts had provided for certain exceptions to the productivity rule (as noted above). In the succeeding years, however, the council's interpretation of the policy did not evolve toward a more flexible program but rather hardened into an insistence on a 3.2 percent as the proper rate of increase for compensation in all situations. For example, during 1966, Budget Bureau director Charles L. Schultze, testifying to Congress on a pay raise for federal employees, rejected a liberalizing interpretation of the council's exception for low-wage workers. "It isn't really catch-up," Schultze testified, "it has to do with employees who are grossly underpaid. It is a need basis, not a comparability exception."[77] Furthermore, in its January 1966 economic report, the council continued to rely on the 3.2 percent standard despite increasing evidence that many wage adjustments could not be contained within that figure and despite the opportunity to raise the percentage (since measured productivity in the most recent five-year period, the term of measurement originally selected, had increased). A result, in part, of the council's immobility, was the bargaining debacle described above which occurred in the summer of 1966.

Second, the guideposts constituted a wage-price policy developed and administered exclusively by the executive branch of the federal government. There was no congressional action with respect to the guideposts, though once they were existent they became a topic of testimony in many congressional hearings. Nor were private industry and labor sources involved in the development or administration of the guideposts. Rather, they constituted, as one participant has commented, "an exercise in Presidential staff initiative."[78] The Council of Economic Advisers not only formulated the guideposts but served as the operational body in their administration, reflecting a desire by the council to be involved in the defense of economic policy.[79] President Kennedy tolerated this ambition of the council, and President Johnson actively supported it (at least through 1966). Federal actions under the guidelines policy were very much of an individual character, unrelated to any perceptible general policy. This type of involvement was, in part, a result of the small size of the council, its many duties, and its lack of procedure for handling review of wage and price decisions. For example, one member of the council has stated that, during the guideposts period, individual newspaper or television reporters who contacted the council to get a government response to a proposed wage or price increase were "the most frequent source of information for major price increases."[80]

Third, the guideposts were directed at large firms and labor organizations, reflecting the council's concern with the application of discretionary market power by these organizations.[81] Concentration on large firms and unions had the virtue of minimizing the staff required to administer the guideposts and was also an inevitable result of an information system for price and wage increases which relied primarily on newspaper reporters.

Analysis of the effectiveness of the guideposts has rested on measuring the extent of voluntary compliance. Statistical models of the economy during the guidepost period give different estimates of the effectiveness of the guideposts. Sheahan, relying strongly on Perry, concluded that "price and wage behavior was more restrained than it had been in the preceding decade."[82] Eckstein and Brinner support this view.[83] Others do not. Black and Kelejian suggest that a stable composition of aggregate demand was responsible for moderate wage-price behavior in 1962–1966.[84] And Gordon noted simply that the econometric models he tested did not suggest an independent role for the guideposts.[85] As to the effectiveness of the guideposts in changing the behavior of negotiators in collective bargaining disputes, John Dunlop commented:

> I know of no person actually involved in wage setting on the side of industry, labor organizations, or as a government or private mediator or arbitrator who thinks that the guideposts have had on balance a constrictive behavior.... The guideposts probably have had no independent restraining influence on wage changes in private industry.[86]

There has been much criticism of the guideposts in the United States. For simplicity and brevity in exposition, the more meritorious objections may be summarized into four major types. First, the guideposts represented only the position of the federal administration with respect to wage-price policy, not a consensus among private groups or even a policy sanctioned by Congress. In consequence, the social and political (in a broad sense) basis of the guideposts was too narrow to support an effective stabilization policy. Second, the guideposts were unreasonably inflexible and, furthermore, were formulated in such a manner that they were essentially irrelevant to private decision-making. In practice, both wage and price decisions in the private economy are the result of the evaluation of many factors. The guideposts tended increasingly to stress the appropriateness of only a single percentage target as a wage criterion; the wage criterion, less productivity gains, was the only one used for price increases. Further, the standard for wage adjustments was the trend rate of increase in output per man-hour nationally, a concept which has had no direct significance in individual wage adjustments (whether determined by collective bargaining or by an employer's unilateral decisions). In a sense, the guideposts sought to remove most discretion from wage adjustments by specifying a single percentage figure. Both the complexity of many situations (after all, not all compensation can or should rise by the same rate) and the independence of private decision-makers resisted so inflexible a policy. Third, the Council of Economic Advisers was largely incapable, by virtue of its small size and limited expertise, of administering a comprehensive wage-price policy. Many wage and price adjustments that were made during the guideposts period were unknown to the council and slowly eroded the standards established. Wage-price policy which is intended to affect the behavior of firms and unions requires a fairly elaborate administrative structure, necessitated by the volume of wage-price decisions in our economy and by the complexity of their interrelationships. The council had no capacity to administer the wage-price policy on any but a hit-or-miss basis. In consequence, when economic expansion in 1965–66 began to cause wage and price increases to accelerate, the guideposts did not restrain the acceleration but rather collapsed. Fourth, the guideposts policy was totally without a disputes-settlement machinery. When collective bargaining threatened to result in increases above the guideposts, the government was forced to rely on either public opinion or presidential intervention to settle the dispute according to the criterion. Unfortunately, public opinion is rarely successful in settling strikes, though its support is often sought by both sides, and presidential intervention is a limited and not necessarily successful initiative. The absence of a disputes machinery in the guideposts period was so glaring that some observers questioned the existence of a wage-price policy at all, implying that all that really existed was a general exhortation by the government to private parties and a group of government press releases condemning certain firms and unions for failing to abide by the suggestions offered by the government.[87]

The guideposts were abandoned in the late 1960s, but the debate among their supporters and detractors did not cease. The experience was inconclusive generally, though both sides held their own positions with substantial certainty. Probably, it is accurate to add that the supporters of the guidelines did derive several additional lessons from their experience and the arguments of critics, although these items clearly were not fundamental to their approach. First, it would be useful to obtain some support from labor and management for the policy. For example, in 1968, the economic advisers of Vice President Humphrey wrote, "a successful new approach must involve the participation of labor and management in the formulation of the principles. The principles must somehow be 'ratified'."[88] Second, enhanced capacity to settle disputes within the guidelines would be helpful. Thus, Gardner Ackley in 1971, suggested that in behalf of incomes policy it was necessary to "do something" about the mediation service, presumably to increase its capacity to act as an anti-inflationary tool.[89] Third, the guideposts had been formulated too narrowly; and cost-of-living increases should be added to productivity as a fundamental element in deriving the standard for percentage increases in wages, and material costs as well as wages should be factors for establishing price standards.[90] Fourth, wage-price policy required greater coercive powers over management and labor than the guideposts policy had possessed. Finally, a greater degree of due process in the administration of wage-price policy would be consistent with national ideals without undermining the policy, and therfore a more elaborate administrative mechanism than the council was appropriate.

3. Pay Controls:
1971-73

Establishing a Stabilization Program

The Economic Situation Prior to Controls

The period of the late 1960s was the climax of the longest business expansion in American history. After an uncertain beginning in 1962–63, real output rose steadily and unemployment rates fell throughout the period. In part, the expansion was associated with the Vietnam War buildup, but the expansionary fiscal policy which largely generated the boom was not solely a result of military spending.[1] Perhaps the critical decision in economic policy during these years was the decision in 1968 by the Johnson administration to run the largest federal budget deficit of the entire decade, at a time when the economy was already strongly expansive. The result was a further impetus to the economy which set the stage for the inflationary pressures of the succeeding several years.

By 1971 the problem of inflation and an overheated economy which Richard Nixon had received upon taking office in 1969 had been transformed into the twin problems of rising prices and rising unemployment. The public, as evidenced by opinion polls, came increasingly to favor government controls over prices. In mid-1971 some 60 percent of those polled favored direct controls.[2] Responding to the increasing public pressure, the Democratic-controlled Congress had enacted in 1970, against President Nixon's wishes, an Economic Stabilization Act, providing the president with authority to invoke direct controls at his discretion. Nixon first employed his authority under the act to establish on March 29, 1971, a tripartite board to administer a wage stabilization program in the construction industry. From April 1971 until August of that year the administration maintained a position against employing controls generally or in any industry other than construction.[3] The demands for federal action from congressmen, the press, and the public grew steadily more intense during this period.

The Freeze on Wages and Prices

Confronted in August 1971 with a crisis in the international balance of payments, the president and his advisers studied a series of alternative policies assembled by the President's Council of Economic Advisers. There was apparently little discussion with business or labor interests regarding the monetary crisis or the actions being considered by the administration. The matter was treated as government policy, not as a national issue involving private parties as well. Only after a course of action was determined were elements of the private sector informed of the consideration of a change in public policy. It appears that the leaders of the labor movement, and most business organizations, found out about the freeze and the development of a stabilization program from the news media.

The decisions reached in August were such a substantial departure from the previous economic policy of the Nixon administration that they were referred to as a "New Economic Policy." Briefly, the NEP included suspension of convertibility of the dollar into gold for the first time since 1934, imposition of a temporary 10 percent surcharge on imports, establishment of a freeze on wages and prices in the economy generally, and a package of fiscal actions designed to expand the economy (including, for example, repeal of the 7 percent excise tax on automobiles, and a tax credit to business). Congress eventually modified aspects of the program in various ways, but without affecting its general framework.[4]

As part of the NEP, the president invoked the Economic Stabilization Act of 1970 to impose an immediate ninety-day freeze on wages, prices, rents, and salaries, and created a cabinet-level committee, the Cost of Living Council (CLC), to administer the freeze and to advise on further stabilization policies. The CLC developed the principal policies of the freeze period and delegated their administration to the Office of Emergency Preparedness. The CLC was chaired by the secretary of the treasury and had a small professional staff headed by an executive director. During the stabilization period which followed the freeze, the council served as the central coordinating body for the various controls agencies and as the highest policy-making body short of the president himself. In this sense, the Cost of Living Council replaced the economic stabilization agencies of previous periods of controls. Initially, the council did not recognize the important coordination functions, especially between wage- and price-control agencies, which it would have to perform. Only over a period of many months did the council's staff come to fulfill these duties. Unfortunately, the council's composition, involving five cabinet members and four directors of White House staff agencies (including the Office of Management and Budget, and the Council of Economic Advisers) was not well suited for detailed administrative responsibilities.

By mid-September administration of the freeze was generally in good order, and discussions as to what sort of stabilization mechanism should follow the freeze began in earnest. The issues to be decided were much the same as those which had been debated at the advent of earlier periods of stabilization. The issues included whether there should be a mandatory set of controls imposed by the government, how comprehensive the program should be, how controls should be administered, who should set the standards for wage-price behavior and in what manner, and what standards should be set. There emerged various loose groupings of officials within the administration, each with a different view of the appropriate resolutions of these issues. In the weeks of discussion which accompanied the development of the stabilization program, each group sought to influence presidential decisions as much as possible, and the outcome was generally a matter of the president's choosing among or blending together the positions presented to him.

Two aspects of these internal disputes require further comment. First, each group had its close associates in business, labor, the Congress, and the public generally. The information which private parties received regarding the administration's thinking (prior to public announcements) was generally conveyed by those in the administration closest to them. Similarly, the input of private parties to the policy discussions was largely made by an informal process and through that group which included their confidants. This process of communication had unfortunate results. In some cases leaders of private organizations were confidentially informed that the government intended to take a certain important step, only to be told a few days later that the information had been completely false. In some situations private officials and organizations were placed in compromising positions with their own constituents and associates by these mistaken governmental initiatives, with unfortunate consequences for the future of the stabilization program.[5] Second, the disputes within the administration over stabilization policies were so intense and so varied that it became possible for those involved in them to delude themselves into thinking that the critical issue was to achieve the desired resolution of the internal dispute, not to obtain public support and the cooperation of management and labor for the program. Yet both management and labor pressed their views upon whatever elements of the administration would listen.

In the end, the administration made its decision as to the form of the second stage of controls (the so-called "Phase Two") and announced them on October 7, 1972. There had been no formal labor-management conference of the type which preceded the First and Second World War programs. In fact, management and labor were so little aware of the administration's intentions, prior to the October 7 message, that a crisis immediately ensued. Was the tripartite pay board to be "autonomous," as Mr. Meany insisted, in return for his participation, or subject to the dictates of the Cost of Living Council? A round of discussions took place between Mr. Meany and administration representatives which culminated in an initialed assurance from the president that the pay board would be substantially an independent body.

The president announced on October 7, 1971, that controls would be continued after the expiration of the freeze. A tripartite Pay Board was to be established to administer wage controls, and an all-public Price Commission to administer price controls. The Cost of Living Council would retain responsibility for establishing the broad policies of the stabilization effort, including any major exceptions to the coverage of controls. To the Pay Board and Price Commission were delegated the responsibility for developing standards or criteria for wage and price adjustments, as well as administration of the standards. There ensued in the Pay Board, at its first meetings, a debate as to what would constitute appropriate wage standards. On November 8, 1971, the Pay Board by a vote of 10 to 5 (public and employer members voting against labor members) adopted a resolution entitled "Policies Governing Pay Adjustments." This resolution established a "general pay standard" of 5.5 percent for annual increases on or after November 14, 1971, in appropriate employee units. The labor members had submitted a proposal for a 6 percent general pay standard with a fairly liberal procedure for allowing additional adjustments as required to achieve for a group of workers "an equitable position with their counterparts in the economy." With the Pay Board's adoption of the November 8 resolution, the first step in establishing the structure of wage controls was taken.

The Form of the Post-Freeze Stabilization Program

The Objectives of Phase II

Rarely in American history has an administration been so explicit about its goals for economic policy as the Nixon administration in 1969–72. This unusual clarity of purpose extended to the controls program as well. At the outset of the post-freeze program, the Cost of Living Council proposed that the general goal of the stabilization effort should be to reduce the rate of price inflation by the end of 1972 to a range of 2 to 3 percent (about half the pre-freeze rate). This objective was repeated throughout the first half of 1972, and both the Price Commission and the Pay Board established a general framework of policies which they believed to be consistent with the stated goal. As described by the President's Council of Economic Advisers, the policies of the Pay Board and the Price Commission implied the following arithmetic:

> If compensation per hour of work rises by 5½ percent per annum, and if output per hour of work rises by 3 percent per annum, labor costs per unit of output will rise by approximately 2½ percent per annum. If prices rise in the same proportion as labor costs, which are the largest element in total costs for the economy as a whole, then prices will also rise by 2½ percent, a rate within the range of the goal set by the Cost of Living Council.[6]

The reader will recognize the similarity of this approach to that of the

Kennedy administration's "guidelines," to which it in fact owed a substantial intellectual debt. Economists who had been prominent in the development of the "guidelines" had been quite vocal in suggesting the appropriate arithmetic for 1971–72. In part through the influence of Dr. Kermit Gordon of the Brookings Institution, a public member of the Pay Board, they were largely successful in pressing a view of stabilization policy as primarily the technical determination and legal enforcement of a single percentage figure for all wage increases which would achieve the desired average restraint on price increases.

Basic Characteristics of the Stabilization Program

The administrative framework of the stabilization program which was revealed to the public by the president on October 7, 1971, involved several new agencies of government. The cabinet-level Cost of Living Council was continued in existence with responsibility for overall supervision and management of the program. In place of the Office of Emergency Preparedness, the administrative agency employed under the freeze, a tripartite Pay Board and a Price Commission were established. The Pay Board created an Executive Compensation Subcommittee. The Construction Industry Stabilization Committee, existent since March 29, 1971, was continued with a special relationship to the Pay Board. A Rent Advisory Board was established for the Price Commission. And three committees—on interest and dividends, the health services industry, and state and local government cooperation—were established to advise the Cost of Living Council.

The wage stabilization program was distinguished from programs of previous periods in three fundamental ways. First, the Pay Board chose to operate primarily as a regulation-drafting agency, rather than as a case-handling body. The board, in its first public announcement (November 8, 1971), established a general pay standard of 5.5 percent for annual increases over the preceding period. It then proceeded over a period of several months to draft a set of regulations designed to implement the general pay standard in two ways: (1) to describe the method of calculation of any proposed increase for measurement against the standard, and (2) to define exceptions to the general pay standard and to limit the additional pay increases approvable under the various exceptions. In its first order, adopted November 13, 1971, the Pay Board delegated to the secretary of the treasury (and hence to the Internal Revenue Service) authority to "interpret, implement, administer, monitor and enforce the stabilization of wages and salaries pursuant to the criteria, standards and implementation procedures established by the Board."[7] For its own functions, other than drafting regulations, the board proposed to hear requests for pay adjustments involving large units (those of five thousand or more workers), which required advance approval before being placed into effect, and to hear requests from units of any size for increases above the 7 percent maximum established to cover most exceptions permitted.[8] But for most interpretations and applications of the wage stabilization policy, reliance was placed on the Internal Revenue Service. This administrative procedure, adopted to minimize the bureaucracy needed to administer controls, also had the effect of placing considerable responsibility for the stabilization program in an agency with no experience or expertise in either personnel administration or collective bargaining.

Second, to a much larger degree than in the past, the wage stabilization program of 1971–72 was intended to be self-administering by employers and workers subject to its provisions. There were two primary ways in which self-administration was advanced. On one hand, the Cost of Living Council established a classification of firms and employee units involving three tiers. In Tier I were placed employee units of five thousand or more, and these units were required to notify the Pay Board of proposed wage increases and to receive approval of the board before implementing any increase. Tier II units, involving one to five thousand workers, were required to report pay changes decided upon after November 14, 1971, to the Pay Board but not to receive advance approval prior to implementing an increase, unless required to do so by other regulations as described below. Tier III units, involving less than a thousand workers, were not required to report, unless as a result of other than the size regulations, but were subject to the regulations and to spot checks for compliance.[9] (A similar three-tier structure based on annual sales by firms was established for the purpose of price control administration.) Additionally, increases permitted by the general pay standard (5.5 percent) were self-executing by Tier II and Tier III units, as were a number of specified exceptions to the general standard that permitted larger increases. Employers and unions were expected to seek advance approval of any increase *above* that permitted by the various regulations, but theirs was the responsibility of deciding what should or should not require advance approval. The Internal Revenue Service and, in some situations, the Pay Board itself, were available to employers, workers, or unions, as the case might be, to advise as to the interpretation of the regulations.

Third, no mechanism for disputes settlement in collective bargaining negotiations was established by the program (with the exception of the machinery which had been established in March 1971 in construction, which was continued). The unions had not given a no-strike pledge, and important elements of the business community had actively opposed a disputes-responsibility for the Pay Board. Further, the public members of the Pay Board were without any strong desire to participate in disputes-settlement. The Pay Board did not, in consequence, have any means by which to offer assistance (or to decide) disputes between employers and unions in which economic terms were an issue. Pay Board regulations and procedures became operative, in a sense, only after a collective bargaining agreement was reached.

Congress Prescribes Policies for Wage Stabilization

The Pay Board began its operations in the context of congressional debate over extension of the Economic Stabilization Act of 1970. Under the 1970 act the president's authority to impose wage and price controls was scheduled to expire on April 30, 1972. It was necessary, therefore, for the administration to seek extensions of the authorization to administer controls. But in the course of the congressional consideration of the extension, a large number of amendments specifically pertaining to the operation of the program were proposed for inclusion in the act. Several of these inclusions were motivated directly by Pay Board policies adopted in the fall of 1971. Ultimately, Congress rewrote the 1970 act so extensively that the one-page 1970 act authorizing controls became a twelve-page detailed blueprint of the program. On December 22, 1971, the president signed into law the Economic Stabilization Act as amended.

Several policies adopted by the stabilization authorities were substantially modified by the Congress in the new act. A first instance involved the question of retroactivity of wage increases held up by the freeze. The Pay Board and the Cost of Living Council had chosen to interpret the freeze stringently. Producers were not allowed to raise prices during the ninety-day freeze, nor employees to receive pay increases, including those provided to take effect during the freeze by the terms of collective bargaining agreements negotiated prior to the freeze. "Consistency," the government argued, "provided the rationale for disallowing previously negotiated wage increases which were scheduled to become effective during the freeze, in that the bulk of the employees in the Nation are not covered by negotiated contracts and would therefore be ineligible for wage increases during the freeze."[10] However, both the House of Representatives and the Senate were of the view that in certain circumstances wage increases due during the freeze should be paid.[11] Since the 1971 Amendments to the ESA were enacted after the expiration of the freeze (November 14, 1971), increases allowed as of the date originally provided for, required, in most cases, retroactive payment by the employer. The Senate offered to the congressional conference committee on new legislation a provision requiring payment of wage increases due during the freeze if the increases were not "unreasonably inconsistent" with stabilization policies.[12] The House offered a different formulation: that increases should be paid where "prices have been advanced, productivity increased, taxes have been raised, appropriations have been made, or funds have otherwise been raised or provided for in order to cover such increases."[13] The conference committee included *both* provisions in the act and noted in its report, "the conferees agree to both the Senate and House provisions with respect to retroactive pay. The conferees intended to require retroactive and deferred pay under either the House provisions or the Senate provisions, whichever provision would authorize such payments. The conferees also intended that the provisions relating to employment contracts also apply to wage increases which were scheduled to be paid as a result of an agreement or an established practice but which were not allowed to go into effect because of the 90-day freeze."[14]

Following enactment of the legislation, the Pay Board rewrote its regulations to provide for the approval of retroactivity for deferred increases in conformity with the congressional directive. Eventually, most employees received increases due during the freeze retroactively, though, in some cases, as long as eight to ten months after the expiration of the freeze. The motivation for the Pay Board's preoccupation with the issue of retroactivity during the freeze is unclear, since retroactivity had very little bearing on the future course or effectiveness of the stabilization program. Apparently the public and business members of the board, in an attempt to make the freeze absolute by eliminating virtually any pay increases to employees during the ninety days, fought and won a very bitter dispute within the board with the labor members. Congress then legislated into law much of the unions' position on retroactivity. Even after the congressional action, the board continued to devote much attention to the issue of payment for work during the freeze period. Simultaneously, the board permitted all increases previously scheduled to take effect during the freeze to take effect at the end of the freeze (November 15, 1972), reserving only for specific policies and procedures the question of retroactivity (if any) during the freeze. Thus, adjustments of great concern to the stabilization of wages (that is, the establishment of new levels of pay) were allowed by the board to proceed unencumbered, while it devoted great efforts to a matter totally inconsequential with respect to the future course of stabilization policy (the question of retroactivity during the freeze period).

A second instance involved a similar misfortune at the hands of Congress which overtook the public and industry members of the Pay Board with respect to the treatment of certain fringe benefits under stabilization criteria. The Pay Board had adopted a general pay standard, over the objections of the labor members, of 5.5 percent. In the board's initial interpretations of the general pay standard, all increases in compensation, both in the base wage rate (or salary) and in such fringe benefits as health, welfare, and pension programs, were subject to the standard. In the view of both the unions and the insurance industry, the Pay Board's interpretation was unreasonably strict. These groups lobbied in Congress, therefore, for amendments to the ESA which would provide more liberal treatment for fringe benefits. The Congress responded by excluding from the general pay standard contributions by employers to any "pension, profit sharing, or annuity and savings plan ...; any group insurance plan, or any disability and health plan," unless the president determined the contributions to be "unreasonably inconsistent" with the standards for wage increases permitted by another provision in the act. This action of Congress was, in some respects, irresponsible, for a stabilization program cannot operate successfully without careful standards for fringe benefit increases. In consequence, the Pay Board was compelled to establish a group of separate standards for these "excludable" fringe benefits which served to bring these fringes back under controls. (The detailed regulations adopted are described below.) Considerable complexity and confusion were introduced into the compensation criteria of the stabilization program by the act's special provisions for these fringe benefits and the Pay Board's subsequent adoption of special regulations. There can be little doubt, in retrospect, that the board would have better served its purpose by providing, initially, more flexibility for the treatment of fringe benefits, with the likelihood, in consequence, of avoiding congressional action in the matter.

Wage Stabilization Policies Following the 1971 Amendments to the Economic Stabilization Act

The full set of regulations which ultimately emerged from the Pay Board were a complicated and sophisticated creation, requiring some fifty pages of the Code of Federal Regulations in their first full codification in June 1972. There is no way in these few pages to recount in a comprehensive fashion the provisions of the regulations. All that can be done is to give the reader a brief but careful exposure to the structure of regulations and to identify their major characteristics. Three separate elements of the regulations are described below: regulations regarding permissible increases decided upon after the establishment of the stabilization program; regulations applicable to existing pay practices or deferred increases; and special provisions made for certain sectors of the economy. (Although the following pages present highly technical material, there is really no substitute for a careful study of their contents if one wishes to understand the stabilization program thoroughly. Some generalizations are attempted in introductory paragraphs below, but these cannot reflect fairly the full complexity of the regulations or their implications for the practice of collective bargaining or for personnel administration.)

Standards Applying to New Increases

The standards applying to new collective bargaining agreements or pay decisions by employers were of two types: the general pay standard and exceptions. All units of employees were entitled to the general pay standard plus some additional increase for "excludable" or "qualified" fringe benefits. Exceptions providing for approval of additional increases were numerous, but in all but one instance no more than a 7 percent increase in a twelve-month period was to be permitted in the appropriate employee unit. A further provision allowed the board itself to apply various additional criteria to permit an increase of any size justified. It was the intention of the board to permit no more than 7 percent as a self-administered increase (with one exception, as will be seen below).

The general pay standard was established as 5.5 percent increase for a twelve-month period. The board was prepared to allow up to this level of increase in pay without regard to circumstances that might suggest the advisability of a lesser increase (for example, unusually high wage rates in an occupation or industry).[15] The appropriate measure of the increase in an employee unit was to be the average overall increase, so that exceeding the 5.5 percent standard for certain groups of workers within the unit was not prohibited if the average increase was within the standard.[16] The board also described how the increase should be calculated. At first, the "sum of the percentage" method, by which pay increments at various times during a twelve-month period are measured as a percentage of the base-year wage and fringe package and are summed to get the total increase, was suggested.[17] In later regulations a simpler procedure by which the entire adjustment provided to take effect during the twelve-month period (without regard to sequencing of increments, if any) was divided by the "base compensation rate."

The "base compensation rate" was a complicated measure. It was not the base or straight-time wage rate. Rather, the concept involved the addition of straight-time hourly earnings (excluding incentive plans) and employer costs for such items as shift differentials, overtime premiums, vacation, holiday and sick leave, bonuses, severance pay, pension plans, health and welfare plans (but excluding payments required by law, for example, Social Security contributions), divided by the number of man-hours worked during the base period. This concept, the reader will recognize, is close to a measure of total average hourly compensation (measured by hours worked, not hours paid for).[18] The concept was defined for the period preceding the "control" year.

Adjustments made in the control (or succeeding) year in the base compensation rate were more complicated to calculate. Excluded from these adjustments were payments for (1) qualified benefit plans (including pension, annuities, health and welfare), (2) bonafide promotions with the unit, (3) longevity increases, (4) automatic in-grade step increases, (5) employer contributions to certain federal or state plans (including Social Security, and so on), (6) increases required under the minimum wage law

(Fair Labor Standards Act), (7) increases required by federal agency wage determinations (e.g., the Walsh-Healy Act), and (8) pay increases to persons earning less than $2.75 per hour (initially, $1.90 per hour).

The general pay standard of 5.5 percent applied only to the ratio of adjustments in the control year compensation rate, as just described, to the previous base compensation rate. Other standards applied to all adjustments specifically excluded from the above computation. Most important was the exclusion of increases in employer payments for health and welfare, pensions, and annuity plans. One standard (there were several) applying to increases in these payments provided that an increase in contributions necessary to continue existing benefit levels was exempted from all controls. Another provided that increases in benefit contributions of up to .7 percent of the base compensation rate were automatically approvable. This circumstance caused the executive director of the Pay Board to insist that the board's standard for permissible increases in total compensation was 6.2 percent, not 5.5 percent.[19]

The Pay Board developed a list of circumstances in which exceptions would be made to the general pay standard. Some of these exceptions were mandated by Congress, others were determined by the board unilaterally.[20] In general, Congress had provided for two sorts of exceptions. First, the exception of employer contributions to pension, health and welfare, and annuity plans from the general pay standard. Second, authorization was provided to the Pay Board and the Price Commission to make "such general exceptions" as necessary "to foster orderly economic growth and to prevent gross inequities, hardships, serious market disruptions, domestic shortages of raw materials, localized shortages of labor and windfall profits."[21] With respect to "excludable" or "qualified" fringe benefits, the board established a standard with two separate elements, the applicable element being the one yielding the larger increase. First, increases in qualified fringes were permitted up to .7 percent of the base compensation rate (as mentioned above), plus a proportional increase if the unit was entitled to a "catch-up" adjustment above 5.5 percent (excluding "qualified" benefits). Second, if the total contributions made by employers to the qualified fringes in the base period was less than 10 percent of the base compensation rate, an increase of up to the 10 percent level was permitted, so long as the increase did not exceed 5 percent of the base compensation rate. Thus, in the extreme case of an employer with no qualified benefits, it was permissible to increase wages and fringes, except qualified benefits, by 5.5 percent of the base compensation rate, qualified fringes by 5 percent of the base compensation rate—or 10.5 percent in total (with "catch-up" in addition, if appropriate).[22]

Exceptions to the general pay standard (excluding "qualified" benefits) were also permitted for the following reasons.

1. Tandem relationships. Where pay increases for an employee unit had

for at least a five-year period been equal and directly related to increases for another unit, an increase of not more than 7 percent (including the 5.5 percent general standard but excluding the qualified benefit standards) could be approved toward maintaining the tandem relationship.

2. Essential employees. Where increases above those otherwise permissible were needed to attract and retain essential employees, and there had been vacancies for at least three months despite "intensive" recruiting, and there was a reasonable expectation that the increase would be effective, an increase not to exceed 7 percent in total (all other permissible increases included) could be made.

3. Catch-up increases. Where for three years previously increases in a unit did not average 7 percent per year (calculated according to Pay Board procedures), there could be an increase not to exceed 7 percent in total (all other permissible increases included).[23]

4. Intraunit inequities. Where an employer could demonstrate that increases above the 5.5 percent standard were "necessary in order to correct wage and salary inequities in an appropriate employee unit," and other standards as to the nature of the claimed inequities were met, then an increase not to exceed 7 percent in total could be made. The board defined intraunit inequities as deriving exclusively from the introduction of new or changed technology, and a significant requirement provided that not less than 10 percent of the jobs and not less than 25 percent of the employee unit must be affected by a "comprehensive change in production methods and techniques" to qualify for this exception.[24]

The reader will have noticed that for each of the exceptions noted (tandems, essential employees, catch-up and intraunit inequities) a maximum (or "cap") of 7 percent for the "permissible annual wage and salary increase" was established. Thus, though in certain situations an employee unit might appear to fall in more than one category of exception, the exceptions provide additive increases only up to a maximum of 7 percent (or 1.5 points above the general pay standard). The 7 percent was *exclusive*, of course, of increases under the qualified benefit standards.

5. Cost-of-living allowance calculation. Where a pay practice or collective bargaining agreement provided for stepped increments dependent on changes in the cost-of-living ("pursuant to and justified by a generally established escalator formula"), then increases provided by the escalator would be weighted by the length of time during the twelve-month control year during which they were in effect. Thus, cost-of-living increases were treated separately from all other types of increases. For example, if a contract provided for a $0.25 increase January 1, and $0.25 July 1, on a $10 base compensation rate, the percentage increase as calculated by the Pay Board would be 5 percent (not 3.75 percent). However, if the agreement also had an escalator, which yielded $0.05 on April 1, and $0.05 on October 1, the

additional percentage increase would not be calculated as 1 percent (yielding a total of 6 percent for the year), but as 0.5 percent (yielding 5.5 percent for the year). Increases permitted under the cost-of-living exception, calculated as just described, were not to exceed in total the general pay standard (5.5 percent). The result of this provision was to favor stepped increments which were the result of a cost-of-living escalator above any other method of providing wage increases. There was, in fact, no limit on the increase in the money wage rate resulting from a bonafide cost-of-living allowance. In consequence, by July 1973, unions in some areas were experimenting with cost-of-living escalator clauses in ways apparently designed to take advantage of the possibility of raising the final rate of pay by deferring increases.[25]

6. Merit increases. Pay increases in the control year granted pursuant to a qualified (as defined by the Pay Board) merit plan provided for in an agreement or pay practice adopted prior to November 14, 1971, and continued thereafter, did, the board ruled, "constitute an exception to the general wage and salary standard." Thus, increases granted to employees within a range established for a job classification, and based on an evaluation of the individual's performance, were exempted from controls.[26] The merit plan exception was to expire for control years beginning on or after November 14, 1972.

7. Productivity and incentive plans. The Economic Stabilization Act amendments of 1971 provided that the president should not use his authority under the act to "preclude the payment of any increase in wages ... paid in conjunction with existing or newly established employee incentive programs which are designed to reflect directly increases in employee productivity."[27] On February 23, 1972, the Pay Board adopted a policy to implement this statutory requirement. Compensation to employees made pursuant to an existing or newly established productivity incentive program, as defined by the regulations, was exempted from the general pay standards. Productivity incentive programs were defined as formal systems whereby wage and salary payments to an employee or group of employees increase as the measured productivity of the employee or group increases.

8. Additional criteria. The Pay Board's November 8, 1971, policy statement had said, following the setting forth of the general pay standard, that in reviewing both new and existing contracts and pay practices, "The Pay Board shall consider ongoing collective bargaining and pay practices and the equitable position of the employees involved." This provision of the board's statement was coupled with the list of criteria included in the ESA amendments in 1971 to become Section 101.11(d) of the board's regulations (later Section 201.30), entitled "Additional Criteria." Under this section the board itself (since authority to act under Section 201.11[d] was not delegated to the IRS) could approve whatever size increase, if it was found acceptable.

Approvals for increases well above 7 percent in the coal, aerospace, and longshore cases, for example, were made by the board under the provisions of this section.

The application of this "catch-all" (as it was described by the board) section of the regulations was unusual and requires some additional comment. Probably it was both necessary and appropriate that the board provide itself flexibility to approve increases exceeding 5.5 percent or 7.0 percent as required in certain circumstances. In major decisions under this section the board continually cited its reasons for approving a specific rate of increase by reference to the criteria of Section 201.11(d). But the board never attempted to instruct the public in the meaning and application of these criteria. Nor were board case decisions citing Section 201.11(d) intended to establish precedents or interpretations for the guidance of employers and workers. This lack of clarification (one might even say candor) regarding these criteria by the board was particularly unfortunate because the particular criteria—including inequities, traditional practices, and the like—reflected those matters most often involved in collective bargaining negotiations and had been, in fact, the essential criteria of earlier programs of wage stabilization. The failure of the board to provide guidance for industry and labor leadership in the application of these criteria represented in a very pronounced fashion the unwillingness or inability of the board to respond to the needs of collective bargaining. The other criteria provided by the board constituted primarily arithmetic formulas providing for an increase, not to exceed some set amount, for one or another purpose. But regarding the relationships of wage adjustment, which could not be reduced to mere arithmetic formulas, the board provided virtually no leadership to labor and management.

The board's procedures under Section 201.11(d) created other problems as well. There was displayed a surprising lack of concern for equitable treatment in a legal sense—surprising from a board with an otherwise careful concern for the niceties of due process.[28] Yet, Section 201.11(d) was applied by the board with a remoteness, a lack of public explanation of its purposes and provisions, which verged on secrecy. It was not merely a matter of the board exercising its legitimate discretionary role in the interpretation of the criteria in specific instances (for example, in the application of the other exceptions described above). Rather, the criteria of Section 201.11(d) were so broad in scope, so important to collective bargaining, so significant, potentially, to the size of increases that could be approved (in coal, longshore, and railway cases, for example, increases of 12 percent or more were approved), that some indication of the board's interpretation of those criteria was important. The board's failure to amplify these criteria for the general public, combined with its application of the standards to certain cases involving large unions and/or industries, engendered the belief that considerations or approvals of contracts under Section 201.11(d) was available only to particularly influential unions and employers.

Standards Applying to Deferred Increases

The 1971 amendments to the ESA prohibited the president from limiting the level of any wage or salary increase scheduled to take effect after the freeze by the terms of an already existing agreement or pay practice, "unless the President determines that the increase provided in such contracts is unreasonably inconsistent with the standards for wage and salary increases." Thus, Congress appeared to mandate that in 1971–72, as in previous periods of stabilization, contracts existing prior to the stabilization program would be allowed to take effect fully, including wage and fringe benefit increases scheduled to take effect during the period of stabilization. The Pay Board provided in its regulations that "employment contracts and pay practices previously set forth which existed prior to November 14, 1971, will be allowed to operate according to their terms."[29] However, any specific contract or practice could be challenged by a "party at interest"[30] or by two or more members of the board itself. The criterion for board approval of a challenged increase was that it not be "unreasonably inconsistent" with the criteria established by the board. No attempt was made to define more clearly the term "unreasonably inconsistent," although the board implied a definition by two actions. First, in its November 8, 1971, policy statement the board applied the same criteria to deferred increases which were later included in Section 201.11(d). Second, the board required that all deferred increases of greater than 7 percent in an appropriate twelve-month period which affected more than one thousand employees must be prenotified to the board. Four months later the board required a ninety-day notice of an increase of greater than 7 percent affecting more than one thousand workers and prohibited payment of the increase until ninety days after notification. Where the board failed to take contrary action, the increase was permitted to take effect as scheduled (subject only to the prenotification provision). Increases affecting less than one thousand workers could take effect without notification unless there was a challenge and a board order halting some or all of the increase.

The board took no action on cases involving deferred increases until the spring of 1972, despite earlier challenges.[31] On April 5, 1972, the board issued a list of seventy-two deferred increases which had been challenged. On June 7, 1972, the board announced its first action in rejecting proposed deferred increases, limiting proposed increases to 7 percent.[32] Meanwhile, the Construction Industry Stabilization Committee found increases due under some nine hundred collective bargaining agreements existing prior to

March 29, 1971, unreasonably inconsistent with stabilization criteria and obtained modification of the agreements.

Special Provisions for Certain Groups of Workers

The Pay Board sought to minimize the establishment of special commissions and regulations for separate sectors of the economy. To a very substantial degree this was accomplished, especially as compared to the experience of World War II. Apparently the board was of the view that separate commissions and regulations needlessly complicated the administration of the stabilization program, confused the understanding of the applicability of regulations, and enlarged the bureaucracy necessary to administer the program. In consequence, the general pay standard and exceptions were made applicable to virtually all sectors of the economy with but two exceptions. One sector to which specific standards were applied was construction. The union segment of this industry was made subject to a separate set of standards that were equivalent in toto to those of the Pay Board and were administered by the Construction Industry Stabilization Committee (a tripartite body). The nonunion segment of construction was made the subject of a special set of regulations administered by the Pay Board itself. Other exemptions from the stabilization regulations included those exempted from the stabilization program entirely by the Cost of Living Council (in some cases, following congressional directives). These exceptions involved federal employees, employee units of less than sixty persons (except those in construction and health services), and employees with substandard wages.

The 1971 amendments to the Economic Stabilization Act had provided that the president's authority to establish controls "shall be implemented in such a manner that wage increases to any individual whose earnings are substandard or who is a member of the working poor shall not be limited in any manner, until such time as his earnings are no longer substandard or he is no longer a member of the working poor." This provision of the law precipitated a struggle between the Pay Board and the Cost of Living Council as to the definition of "substandard" and "working poor." In early January 1972, the Cost of Living Council recommended to the Pay Board that earnings of $1.90 per hour or less be exempted from the stabilization program.[33] The then tripartite Pay Board responded with a resolution that the $1.90 figure was too low but proposed no alternative figure (though proposals within the board for $3.50 and $2.20 were rejected). On January 29, the Cost of Living Council rejected the Pay Board's recommendation and established the maximum for an exemption under the substandard and working poor provision at $1.90 per hour. Several congressmen and the unions immediately objected that the figure was far too low.[34] Subsequently, several unions and the AFL-CIO itself filed suit in federal court asking that the council's action be overruled, citing an interpretation of the intent of Congress in enacting the substandards provision in the Economic Stabilization Act.[35] On July 14, 1972, the Federal District Court of the District of Columbia ruled against the government but did not establish a figure. Subsequently, the Cost of Living Council raised the substandards exemption to $2.75 per hour. The unions then continued to sue, seeking a higher figure.[36]

In large part the dispute over the substandards definition was influenced by the simultaneous consideration in Congress of a minimum wage bill. The existing federal minimum wage was $1.60 per hour. Labor and liberal congressional leadership wanted an increase to more than $2.00 per hour. The administration opposed so large an increase, and felt, probably with considerable justification, that the definition for stabilization purposes of substandards would affect its position on the minimum wage issue. But the problems of the stabilization program with minimum wage laws were not limited to the federal statute. On June 12, 1972, the Cost of Living Council suspended an order of the District of Columbia Minimum Wage and Industrial Safety Board increasing the minimum pay of hotel and restaurant workers in the District from $1.60 to $2.25 per hour. Subsequently, the Pay Board prepared guidelines to cover state minimum wage law increases exceeding the $1.90 figure. The impact of the substandards ruling by the council was important in some instances. For example, Local 141 of the Laundry and Dry Cleaning Workers in Pittsburgh had negotiated an increase of 40 cents, raising the average hourly rate from $1.94 to $2.34 per hour in the first year of the agreement. The IRS, applying Pay Board standards, insisted on an increase of no more than 13 cents (to a rate of $2.07). The union objected that the effect of the regulations was to lock "service workers into permanent poverty."[37] The redefinition of substandards to $2.75 per hour mooted these issues, of course, and allowed the increases to take effect.

Finally, the Pay Board established a special set of regulations covering the compensation of executives, and other variable compensation. These regulations were directed at a highly specialized area of compensation practices, involving such matters as incentives, bonuses, stock options, perquisites, and so on. Since these provisions of the stabilization program defy brief presentation or summarization and are tangential to our major concerns, we shall not describe them further, with one exception. Executive compensation received from the Pay Board some of its most flexible regulatory language, strikingly absent from the general pay controls (with the partial exception of Section 201.11[d]). For example, regarding the valuation of items of executive compensation that were job perquisites, the board directed that the amount of a perquisite be "the reasonable cost of providing the item to be determined from all the facts and circumstances involved."

Actions of the Pay Board

In the next few pages are described the first major cases handled by the Pay Board, the increasing dissatisfaction of the union representatives with the board, their resignation, and the reconstruction of the board. For the first time, the government of the United States accepted indefinitely a virtually all-public wage control board. Finally, the later actions of the board and some aspects of enforcement of board decisions are described.

Initial Cases

On November 13, 1971, just prior to the expiration of the freeze and the imposition of Phrase II regulations, the national bituminous coal agreement was settled between the United Mine Workers and the coal operators. The agreement called for an increase of some 16.8 percent (as estimated by the Pay Board) in wages and fringes during the first year of its three-year term. The Pay Board considered the agreement under the provisions applying to deferred increases (those provided by agreements negotiated prior to November 14, 1972). Within a week of the settlement, the board voted to approve the agreement, without modification, by a 10 to 3 majority, the labor and business representatives (five each) voting to approve, three public members voting no and two public members abstaining. The employer members issued a statement citing "the equitable position of the employees involved, the complexities of their work, the imperative need of the industry to expand and attract new employees . . . and the ongoing collective bargaining relationships which have traditionally been applied to the coal industry."[38] The public members objected strongly in a dissenting statement and proposed limiting the increase to 12.5 percent in the first year. "This maximum increase was determined by taking into account the general pay standard of 5.5 percent . . . ; a factor of 4.1 percent to make up the deficiency in the health and welfare fund . . . ; and a further adjustment to reflect inter-industry wage relations."[39] Upon approval of the agreement by the board, many miners who had remained away from their jobs returned to work.

A round of negotiations in the railway industry was coming to an end as the Pay Board became operational. On November 16, 1971, the carriers and the Brotherhood of Railway Signalmen agreed on a forty-two-month contract covering the period January 1, 1970, to June 30, 1973. The agreement called for a 46 percent increase over the period and closely paralled agreements negotiated by other railway unions. In part, the settlement had been mandated by congressional action, and in part the increases conformed to the recommendations (issued April 14, 1971) of a presidential emergency board established under the provisions of the Railway Labor Act. Recognizing the circumstances surrounding the agreement, the Pay Board, on

December 9, 1972, approved those provisions of the agreement to take effect after November 14, 1971.[40] The board approved the agreement, with the public members objecting.[41] On January 26, 1972, the board approved a similar (but not identical) agreement (retroactive to January 1, 1970, also) involving the United Transportation Union which had been reached on August 2, 1971, but never ratified by the workers because of the freeze.[42] The board voted 8 to 5 to approve, with four public members and one business member objecting (chairman Boldt abstained).

Finally, in March 1972, the Pay Board took up the longshoremen's agreements from the West and East Coasts. The West Coast agreement had expired in July 1971. A hundred-day strike followed, but was ended on October 9, 1971, by a Taft-Hartley Act injunction prohibiting a resumption of the strike for eighty days. On October 1, 1971, a strike had commenced on the East Coast, though certain ports remained open due to legal action. In late November the administration obtained another injunction to halt the East Coast strike for eighty days. In January 1972, the West Coast strike resumed after the injunction expired, and the administration sought legislation in Congress calling for compulsory arbitration to end the dispute. Meanwhile, the East Coast dispute was settled without a resumption of the strike. Finally, on February 8, 1972, the West Coast strike was settled. Nevertheless, Congress passed a bill calling for compulsory arbitration of the dispute should there be no settlement between the parties. On March 14 the Pay Board held a hearing on the West Coast contract, calling for an increase of 25.9 percent over two years. The wage increase was argued by the parties to reflect in an important way substantial productivity improvements realized on the West Coast docks in the previous decade. The board's staff argued that the West Coast situation might meet "the test of uniqueness" because of the productivity arrangements agreed to in previous contracts, and therefore should be an exception to the general pay standard in some substantial way.[43] On March 16, 1972, the board voted 8 to 5, labor members objecting, to reduce the first year of the agreement from 20.9 percent to 14.9 percent (the entire reduction being in wages, with 4.9 percent excludable fringe benefit increases approved). The board cited as the reason for its approval of an increase above 7 percent "the unique facts ... in the record, including those relating to prior Mechanization and Modernization Plan payments, involving ongoing collective bargaining and pay practices, the equitable position of the employees involved, arrangement between the parties specifically designed to foster economic growth, and other factors."[44] The union members issued a statement saying, in part, "the Pay Board is being used by the Nixon Administration in concert with some of the nation's largest employers to set the stage for permanent legislation robbing employees in all transportation industries of their right to free collective bargaining"[45]—a reference to the administration's proposed legislation for dispute-settlement procedures in transportation industries. On March 22, 1972, the three AFL-CIO members of the Pay Board resigned.

The Unions Resign from the Pay Board

The West Coast longshore case provided the occasion for the resignation of four of the five union representatives from the Pay Board. But the causes of union disaffection with the board went much deeper than the rejection of the longshore agreement. What were the reasons which caused the unions to leave the board and how did the longshore case become the occasion? There were four general sources of union dissatisfaction. Most important, the AFL-CIO from the outset of the stabilization program had conditioned its participation on two factors: that there be effective price control as well as wage control, and that the wage control machinery be a tripartite board chaired by public members and largely independent (in Mr. Meany's terms, "autonomous") from the administration. These were traditional positions for organized labor with respect to stabilization programs and constituted their preferred public posture. By March 1972, the unions were no longer satisfied with the administration's good faith on either of these points. There was considerable unhappiness within organized labor over the apparent confusion and lack of effectiveness in the price control program, particularly with respect to food prices. And the Cost of Living Council continued to establish policy with respect to important aspects of the wage stabilization program without the agreement of the Pay Board (as, for example, in the matter of the determination of the application of the substandards exemption).

Other sources of labor dissatisfaction were the role of the public members of the board, the internal procedures of the board, and the general political situation in which the unions found themselves. The unions objected to both the individuals chosen as public members of the board and these individuals' concept of their function. The president had assured the unions, they stated as early as November 1971, that "the public members would be citizens of high repute, knowledgeability and neutrality. That commitment has not been kept." Rather, "the public members, so called, . . . are handmaidens of the Administration."[46] The internal procedures of the board had reinforced the unions' view that it was not a fair forum. Board discussions were carried out largely by emissaries moving among separate caucuses of the public, employer, and union members. In some instances a Pay Board meeting was convened in the morning, immediately adjourned to caucuses, with the union members left to await a decision, if one was reached, of the public and employer members; then the board was reconvened, often without prior scheduling (and in some cases as much as eight to ten hours after the initial adjournment), and a vote taken. Nor was it uncommon (e.g., in the aerospace case) for a public member to go to the unions' caucus room and begin his suggested resolution of a case (or of a dispute over a regulation) by asserting that the public and employer members had already decided on a position.[47] In part, the situation within the board arose from its practice of permitting at its meetings the presence of "advisors" or "alternates" to the board members. At some times as many as forty to fifty persons might be in the room, and often the public members could not even identify all those present. There was, therefore, no opportunity, even had one been desired, for the board to develop any internal cohesion as a group.

Finally, there was a political element in the unions' decision to leave the board. The AFL-CIO had supported the Democratic candidate, Hubert Humphrey, in the 1968 presidential election which Mr. Nixon won. Throughout Mr. Nixon's administration the AFL-CIO had been strongly in opposition to many of his domestic policies. When the New Economic Policy (including the wage-price freeze) was announced in August 1971, the AFL-CIO issued a statement entitled "The New Nixon Game Plan: Unequitable, Unjust, Unfair, Unworkable."[48] In the spring of 1972 the presidential election was only eight months away, and the unions wished to be free to express actively their opposition to the president. They could not do so, they thought, while remaining on the Pay Board, for in so doing they implied a continuing measure of support. The Pay Board's rejection of the longshore agreements provided a convenient occasion for their resignation.[49]

The West Coast longshore case itself was not simply incidental to the unions' departure, however. The settlement had followed a prolonged strike. The unions had convinced themselves that the agreement merited approval because it reflected increased productivity. The unions even insisted they had prior assurances from Dr. Weber that the agreement would be approved.[50] But the agreement was not approved. Mr. Meany described the board's procedure and decision as "an insult to the labor members." According to Meany, the decision to cut the increase was made privately by the public and employer members, then communicated to the labor members as a fait accompli. Had the procedure been different, Meany suggested, the labor members would have remained on the board.[51]

On March 22, 1972, the AFL-CIO Executive Council issued a statement entitled "The Nixon Economic Program: No Fairness, No Equity, No Justice," and announced the resignation of the AFL-CIO's three members of the board. Only the Teamsters remained on the board. President Fitzsimmons announced that, despite disagreements with the board on numerous occasions, "I still hold to the principle that we must work within the system." But, "in my opinion, both the public and management members of the Pay Board are more concerned with their public image than they are with the proper recognition of the problems of American workers."[52]

President Nixon responded to the resignation of four labor members by reconstituting the Pay Board as an all-public body of seven members and appointing Mr. Fitzsimmons and Mr. Siciliano (an employer member of the board) as public members in addition to the five existing ones. The four other business representatives on the board resigned.

Actions of the All-Public Pay Board and Its Termination

The reconstituted Pay Board resumed its activities with dispatch, following the resignation of the union members. This was much unlike the Korean period, when the resignation of the union representatives had precipitated a crisis in which little was accomplished until a new chairman was found for the WSB and the unions were persuaded to return to the board. In 1972 there was evidently little or no attempt by the administration or the public members of the Pay Board to induce the unions to return. Rather, the board continued to codify its regulations, and its Cases and Appeals Panel continued to handle such appeals for exceptions under its regulations as reached the board itself.

On June 7, 1972, the Pay Board took its first action to reduce a deferred increase. The board ordered that "increases in the vicinity of 11 percent for 4,000 members of the Amalgamated Meatcutters and Butchermen's Union employed by three major food chains in Philadelphia which had gone into effect on March 1, 1972, ... be reduced to 7 percent."[53] The board gave no detailed explanation of the reasons for its actions. In ensuing weeks the board reduced several other increments provided by agreements negotiated prior to November 14, 1971.[54] On June 8, 1972, the board, for the first time, reduced a new agreement to 5.5 percent. Several retail clerks locals in Philadelphia had negotiated an agreement with the Philadelphia Food Store Employers Labor Council calling for an increase of 19 percent on January 9, 1972. The board reduced the increase permitted to 5.5 percent on wages and 1.17 percent in qualified fringe benefits. (These increases had not been placed into effect prior to the board's action.) Simultaneously, numerous new contracts and deferred increases of comparable size were allowed to take effect without objection by the board, which cited various reasons for its actions, including procedural failures by parties challenging deferred increases.

The Pay Board continued to operate through the fall of 1972, recodifying its regulations, and issuing reports on the progress of the wage stabilization program at periodic intervals. Unexpectedly, on January 11, 1973, the president announced the termination of both the Pay Board and the Price Commission and the initiation of a so-called Phase III of the economic stabilization program. Existing wage and price regulations were made advisory to firms and unions, and the administrative functions of the two agencies were incorporated into an expanded Cost of Living Council, except in three sectors of the economy (construction, food processing and retailing, and health services). The Pay Board ceased to receive new cases as of January 11 but continued to operate until February 28 in order to finish its existing case load. Some Phase II cases remained even after February 28, 1973, however, and were disposed of by the staff of the now nonexistent Pay Board.

Why was the board abolished so suddenly in January 1973? In some respects this termination was surprising, for there was no general public clamor for the board's elimination. Rather, the press and many economic commentators were calling for a continuation of the board's activities and further expansion of the price controls program.[55] Nor was there any crisis, such as a work stoppage in a major industry, which precipitated the board's demise. Why, then, were the operations of the Pay Board ended? The administration gave two major reasons. On the one hand, it said, both the existing pay and price controls were creating unfortunate anomalies in product and labor markets. These distortions in the economy were said to be increasing and were threatening the efficiency of the economic system. In order to reduce the unfavorable impact of the controls on the economy, said the administration, relaxation of controls was required. On the other hand, the administration said, the Phase II regulations had not been designed for, and would not be effective in, the altered economic climate which was emerging in 1973. The regulations had been intended to control a cost-push inflation and would not be expected to be adequate to constrain the economic boom, fueled by demand pressures and rapid economic growth, which was emerging.[56] Thus was dismissed the entire experience of World War II and the Korean period in restraining, by price and wage controls, inflationary pressures in an expanding economy. Viewed against the rhetoric of 1972, it seems ironic that at the end of World War II President Truman relaxed controls, arguing, in essence, that the end of a demand-pull inflation obviated the need for them. "With the ending of war production," the president said, "there is no longer any threat of an inflationary bidding up of wage rates by competition in a short labor market."[57]

These were the reasons advanced by the administration to explain the sudden termination of the Pay Board and the Price Commission. But a more basic factor was also at work. Neither the Pay Board nor the Price Commission had developed a constituency. In other words, neither agency was acceptable to those elements of the private sector whose behavior it regulated. Therefore, when the administration privately sounded out both business and labor as to the acceptability of a plan to eliminate both agencies, neither group strongly objected. Business leaders preferred the elimination of the Price Commission to retention of the Pay Board;[58] and union leadership preferred elimination of the Pay Board to retention of the Price Commission. In the latter case, in fact, the unions insisted upon abolition of the Pay Board as a condition of cooperation with the administration on domestic economic policy.[59] The result was that the Phase II program, facing an uncertain future in a changing economic climate, and without business or labor support, was defenseless against an effort to bring about its end.

The Record of the Stabilization Program

It is always hazardous to attempt to evaluate an economic stabilization program while it is in progress or soon after its termination. Yet, certain aspects of the record are already clear. First, the wage-price freeze itself was, to all accounts, substantially effective. The freeze was simple, conceptually, and voluntary compliance was almost complete. The rise of prices and wages all but ceased during the ninety days of the freeze, and the "bulge" of increases which occurred at the end of the freeze was not unreasonably large.[60] Whether the freeze made a lasting contribution to the stabilization program generally is less certain. The proponents of the freeze insist that it contributed to breaking an inflationary psychology in the country and thereby helped create conditions conducive to a stabilization program.[61] That the 1971 freeze had any such effect is, however, difficult to substantiate. While wage and price increases generally did moderate in the aftermath of the freeze, this trend had started well before August 15, 1971. Further, several important collective bargaining agreements reached during or after the freeze, including, e.g., the longshore agreements, reflected little if any moderation induced by the freeze.

The record of Phase II is more difficult to assess. But even here, we may make some preliminary judgments. There were four objectives to which the president's New Economic Policy, announced August 15, 1971 and in which controls were a part, was directed. First, the policy was precipitated by an international monetary crisis. The convertibility of the dollar into gold was suspended, and domestic actions were taken to strengthen the national economy. A currency agreement in December 1971 essentially devaluated the dollar by some 12 percent on average and provided greater flexibility in the foreign exchange markets. For the first year following the NEP, the nation's balance of payments problem was improved. Second, the actions of August 1971 were taken in part to permit a substantial fiscal stimulus to the American economy, and a substantial economic recovery occurred. Third, the package of measures, including suspending convertibility, freezing prices and wages, and providing a fiscal stimulus, were all directed to a large degree at domestic unemployment. In this area the administration also had some success. By the end of 1972, the nation's unemployment rate was edging down to 5.0 percent from the 6.1 percent rate of August 1971. Fourth, the freeze and subsequent stabilization program were directed at a greater degree of wage-price stability than had been achieved in the period since

1966. With respect to increases in prices, the Cost of Living Council had announced a goal of price increases at an annual average rate of 2.5 to 3.0 percent by November 1972. This goal was almost obtained. The Consumer Price Index, for example, rose during the final months of 1972 at an annual rate of roughly 2.9 percent, though a renewed acceleration, based on food price increases, was to occur in the first months of 1973.[62] Also, it is to the credit of the stabilization authorities in 1972 that the wage control program was associated with a lessened frequency of work stoppages in the economy rather than the opposite. In 1972, the proportion of man-days lost due to strikes declined to its lowest level in a decade.

The wage stabilization program itself is the most difficult to evaluate. We have noted previously that there was little consensus within the administration as to the function of the Pay Board apparatus. Virtually the only goal made public was that the board would attempt to keep wage increases in the range of 5.5 percent for 1972, a rate thought to be consistent with a 2.5 to 3.0 percent increase in prices. The Pay Board failed to limit new collective bargaining agreements to this rate of increase in 1972. Rather, first-year increases approved by the Pay Board in 1972 in new collective bargaining agreements that covered more than one thousand employees averaged about 7.0 percent.[63] Increases in the nonunion sector were several percentage points lower, on average, so that the first-year average increase in all adjustments annually was 5.6 percent.[64] Increases in unionized employee units were below preceding years' rates and were more evenly distributed among industries (the increasing stability of construction was especially marked).[65] Finally, increases in average hourly earnings in 1972 were somewhat below those in 1971.

That there was some moderation of wage adjustments in 1972 cannot be doubted—what is subject to dispute is the role of the wage stabilization program in achieving this moderation and the longer-term consequences of the program. The economy was sluggish in the 1969–72 period, and with the completion of the round of wage negotiations in 1971 many of the maladjustments in the wage structure introduced in the 1968–71 period had been removed. These factors suggested a lower rate of increase in 1972 and would have resulted independently of a stabilization program. While no general answer is possible to the issue of the program's effect, the following three items are offered as a tentative judgment on the impact of the 1971–72 wage stabilization program. First, the Pay Board undoubtedly reduced some increases below what they would otherwise have been (e.g., the longshore agreements). Second, the effect of the general pay standard of 5.5 percent was undoubtedly to raise some increases above what they would otherwise have been. For example, the BLS reported that in 1971 the average annual increase in wages in nonunion manufacturing establishments with one thousand or more workers was approximately 5.7 percent (in union establishments approximately 8 percent).[66] Since adjustments in 1972 were expected to be below those in 1971, the general standard had been set at a rate higher than the normal course of the nonunion sector of manufacturing in 1972 was expected to provide. Since the general standard inevitably became a minimum in many situations, there were cases in which increases established in conformity with the general pay standard were higher than otherwise would have been likely. By mid-summer 1972, this effect was apparent, and the Pay Board began to consider changing the general pay standard.[67] Third, the Construction Industry Stabilization Committee served to reduce negotiated increases in construction below what otherwise would have occurred.[68]

Despite the evidence of a slowing of wage increases, the Pay Board was terminated suddenly, after only sixteen months of operations. There was little evidence of a substantial long-term impact of the stabilization effort on the fundamental factors influencing wage inflation in the American economy. What suggestions can be offered as to how the 1971–72 program might have been improved?

First, the willingness of the board to operate in a nontripartite manner was a substantial and largely unrecognized limitation on its effectiveness. Second, the regulations of the board and the stabilization program generally and inappropriately contained important distinctions depending upon the size of the firm or employee unit involved (though the Pay Board and the Cost of Living Council differed to some degree on the degree of application of the size criterion, both contributed to placing unreasonable reliance on it). Third, the board place substantial *over*reliance on self-administration. Fourth, the board coupled with its reliance on self-administration a set of regulations so complex in their terminology as to be almost undecipherable by unions and employers, so that a chaotic and generally unfortunate situation was created in industrial relations generally. Fifth, the board's delegation to the Internal Revenue Service of the function of interpreting its regulations was inappropriate and unsuccessful. The general result was a situation of widespread confusion, disregard of stabilization regulations, and the rapid dissipation of the willingness of elements of society (particularly unionized workers) to cooperation with a stabilization program. Sixth, the effectiveness of the stabilization program in 1971–72 was limited (and threatened prospectively in 1972–73, had it been continued) by its failure to recognize the importance of an effective arrangement for dispute settlement. These disadvantages, which flowed from the structure and operation of the program, were such as to weaken the program in 1971–72 and to affect unfavorably the country's capacity to apply controls in future circumstances. Only the relatively slack economy of 1971–72 and the relatively permissive wage policy of the Pay Board (as compared to what an uncontrolled economy would have generated in that period) allowed the defects of the stabilization program to pass largely unnoticed by the general public in 1972. Yet these limitations of the program, each of which is explored in detail in later chapters, were instrumental in the administration's decision to abolish the Pay Board in January 1973.

Part II   The Foundations of
                               Stabilization Policy

That which is called government, or rather that which we ought to conceive government to be, is no more than some common center in which all parts of society unite.

Thomas Paine, The Rights of Man

4. Establishing a Stabilization Policy

Private-Public Cooperation in a Stabilization Program

Wage policy as an arrangement among the government and private-interest groups is explored in detail in this chapter. We shall consider four major groups of issues. First, why is an arrangement among private groups and the government necessary? What is the role of private groups? Which organizations are to be included in the development of stabilization policy and which excluded? Why must private organizations be involved at all?

Second, if management and labor are to be involved in the development of stabilization policy, by what method or mechanism is this to be done? What are the procedures for their involvement?

Third, what are the traditional concerns of management and labor in the development of stabilization policy? What are the elements that divide the two sides? On what basis have accommodations been reached in the past? And, if management and labor are deeply interested in a stabilization policy, why need the government be involved at all? Why cannot collective bargaining achieve the desired stabilization of wages?

Fourth, a particular form of cooperation among management, labor and government has been the tripartite administration of a wage stabilization program. What have been the lessons of tripartitism in the past? What are the arguments against tripartite administration? What factors favor it? Is tripartitism an appropriate arrangement for a stabilization board today?

The Role of Private Organizations in Establishing a Stabilization Policy

In the United States it has been customary for the leaders of private economic interests to be consulted about the design and development of economic stabilization programs. When the programs have taken the form of formal wage and price controls, the involvement of private groups has been both overt and extensive. In large part this has been in order to secure the cooperation of the private organizations in assuring the success of the program. The form of cooperation by unions and companies with a controls program is discussed at length below. The considerations favoring a role for private groups in developing stabilization policy are not, however, limited to expediency. Rather, public policies with respect to wages and incomes are of critical concern to the interests of private groups—so much so that it is appropriate in a democratic society that they have a role in the development of those policies.

Foremost among the several aspects of a stabilization policy which cause it to be of special interest to the representatives of organized labor and business is its potential impact upon the distribution of money and real income among groups in our society. It has been noted often enough by researchers that incomes policies in Western European nations have brought the question of the distribution of income to the political forefront.[1] In Western Europe periods of wage control have generally been associated with demands for substantial adjustments in the wage structure in the direction of wage equalization. Because government authorities cannot normally achieve equalization, they face a particularly intractable problem in achieving a consensus on the goals and procedures of a wage policy.

In the United States the government is fortunate to confront, to a far lesser degree, demands for a readjustment of the income distribution in the context of a stabilization policy. In part this situation is a result of the lesser strength of socialist ideology in this country. Yet concern for income distribution arises in two important ways in the United States whenever a wage policy is under discussion: in the context of low-wage earners and of internal rivalries among skilled trades and professionals. The representatives of both these groups are extremely anxious that a government stabilization policy not disadvantage their constituents relative to others in the work force and are thereby very deeply concerned with the development of the stabilization policy. During World War II, for example, the wage and price stabilization program, developed in consultation with union and employer representatives, resulted in a relative advantage in the distribution of income to wage earners vis-à-vis profits, to agriculture vis-à-vis other industries, and to low-wage earners vis-à-vis other workers.[2] A stabilization program designed in a different fashion might have resulted in a very different effect on the distribution of income.

Further, wage stabilization programs often occur in the context of other changes in the economic system which are expected to have an impact on the income distribution. The representatives of various groups are understandably concerned that the stabilization policies not have an adverse effect on expected changes in the income distribution favorable to themselves. A period of stabilization has normally been associated with an expanding economy generally, involving real growth, higher employment, and rising government purchases. The net effect of these influences on the distribution of income is to reduce inequality.[3] Union officials in this situation will be anxious to see that not all the redistributive effects of economic expansion are lost as a result of policies ostensibly directed at wage and price stabilization. Employers, conversely, may be concerned that unions not achieve through wage stabilization a degree of income redistribution which they are unable to secure at the bargaining table.

The Cooperation of Private Parties

There are many ways in which either management or labor can move to bring about the demise of a stabilization program. There is, first of all, the workplace itself. Stabilization cannot survive many serious challenges by determined unions employing the strike weapon. Nor can it survive persuasive disregard of its standards by employers. Similarly, either side can often successfully challenge a stabilization program in Congress, effectively gutting the program on what may seem to congressmen and senators to be highly technical, inoffensive issues. In addition, litigation by either side can, potentially at least, so delay and place in question key elements of the stabilization program that it is rendered suspect and largely ineffectual for long periods. Thus, although it is useful for the authorities to win a few visible legal victories to establish the serious intent of the program, excessive litigation can be destructive. Finally, the operations of wage control machinery are predicated to a great degree on the voluntary compliance of local unions and employers with the required regulations, procedures, and decisions. General disregard of the stabilization machinery will leave it operating in a limbo in which it is unaware of what is occurring in the economy and the economy is largely unaware of it.

In consequence, there is a need for cooperation by private organizations with the government in order to make a wage stabilization program effective. What does the requisite "cooperation" entail? At the outset it should be emphasized that cooperation need not involve overt and active support of the program. Historically, few stabilization boards have had overt support from either management or labor, though they may have had, for brief periods, the support of one or the other. This situation is readily understandable and may be expected to continue in the future. Unions are less than enthusiastic regarding wage control boards for reasons too obvious to require elaboration. Business normally opposes controls as an unwarranted interference with the freedom of the private economy. Rather than to have direct wage controls, business would normally prefer legislation to restrict the capacity of unions to negotiate wage increases. Business, like labor, is, therefore, normally a lukewarm supporter of controls at best. Further, the involvement of wage boards in noneconomic aspects of collective bargaining disputes has often caused management to oppose a controls program strongly. Even when the private opinions of business and labor leaders may not be hostile to a stabilization agency, the antagonisms which their constituencies harbor against the stabilization effort may force them into positions of public opposition. For these reasons, the public opposition of both management and labor to the activities of the stabilization agencies is normally a cross which its public representatives and the administration must bear.

If "cooperation" does not mean overt support, then what does it mean? There are two elements of cooperation: what the private parties should do, and what they must *not* do. Because the negative aspects of the required cooperation are the more significant of the two, we begin our discussions with them.

The effective functioning of a wage stabilization body requires that the private parties, industry and labor, do not actively seek to undermine it. If the leaders of management or labor were to seek actively to destroy the program, they would undoubtedly succeed. In fact, the issue would be settled when one side first undertook the program's destruction, even though it might take many months to accomplish overtly. It has not been uncommon, for example, for a program to have been destroyed de facto long before the government made such an admission to the public. However, it may be that elements of either side are in active opposition, or that their voices are those most often carried to the public by the press, without the program being made ineffective—for public opposition alone is normally not conclusive. Isolated areas of deep discontent of both the business and labor sides must be anticipated and can often be contained. But a stabilization program will not survive a general willingness by either industry or labor to seek its end.

In contrast to these negative aspects of cooperation are those of a more positive nature. Positive cooperation by labor and industry can be of great assistance to the stabilization program, and its total absence might cripple the program. First, positive cooperation entails the willingness of the representatives of both sides to give advice to their constituents, advice predicated on a willingness to comply with stabilization objectives. Especially important in this regard are the representatives of labor and management who are on a stabilization board, for they perform a very important service of informal communication with their own groups; failure to perform this function in good faith can be most debilitating. Second, it is very important that both sides accept decisions of the controls machinery. If either side suggests to its constituents directly involved in a decision of the board that the decision should not be accepted but resisted by whatever means are available, the problems of the stabilization agency become very great. Third, it is very important that both sides be willing to seek the resolution of disputes within the context of the stabilization program—not by appeal to other forums (especially political ones). A stabilization machinery which is bypassed for discussions with higher authorities by those whose behavior is its concern, soon loses its value to any group, the administration included. There will, of course, be individual situations in which an appeal to higher authorities is attempted, and these must be handled carefully by the stabilization board.

But when the procedure of seeking another forum becomes general, not simply the action of a "maverick" on either industry's or labor's side, then a stabilization program is endangered.

The reader will observe that these requirements of cooperation with a stabilization program by private parties are quite limited. And they are *all* that is required. But these requirements, limited though they are, do place a great responsibility on public officials of the stabilization agency to establish the arrangements on which cooperation can be based. In this process several factors are significant, including the trust of the public representatives by officials of industry and labor, and the personalities involved on all sides. Therefore, the failure of individual persons in government to inspire the degree of trust and confidence necessary to obtain cooperation (as defined here) can undermine and render ineffectual a stabilization program and yet not be apparent to outside observers.

The Appropriateness of Government Cooperation with Private Parties

Some may wonder whether the involvement of private parties in a government wage stabilization machinery is appropriate in our society, regardless of the reasons advanced above. The development and administration of federal policy through consultation with affected groups may seem to have an unpalatable flavor of government acting as representative, not of the people, but of special-interest groups. Further, some might argue, private groups are not broad enough in constituency, whatever their claims as to whom they represent, to justify their involvement in any special way (other than as citizens, like all other citizens) with governmental policy.

There are various forms in which these objections have been raised. Some oppose economic controls of any kind, and introduce an argument about the involvement of private-interest groups only as a rhetorical device. Others believe an all-governmental stabilization program is most likely to meet their own objective for the program and so oppose the participation of private parties in the development and administration of the program. This particular objection arises often in the context of the decision whether to establish a tripartite or an all-public wage stabilization board. Finally, there are those who are concerned with the relationship of government and private groups because of dangers they perceive which are of a broader nature than stabilization.[4] It is to this concern that we now direct our attention.

The area of this discussion is necessarily one of political and social preferences and, therefore, is not subject to resolution by arguments of a technical or scientific nature. Yet it is possible to reach some conclusions with respect to the relationship of government and private groups in stabilization policy which may be generally accepted. First, for the reasons cited above, the cooperation of private groups is necessary to the success of a stabilization program—this is a direct result of the democratic characteristics of our government favored by those who might argue for the exclusion of private parties from stabilization efforts. The dilemma in their posture is now apparent. To insist that the government in defense of a pluralistic democratic society cannot undertake joint activities with private power centers, is simply to deny to government the possibility of effective action, although much responsibility for wage and price stability continues to reside with government. Some might reply that the dilemma is not so certain as stated here, for other types of policies might equally well achieve wage stabilization. Particularly, it might be said, there are a number of institutional impediments to economic stability which if removed might make controls unnecessary, thus eliminating any necessity for government to cooperate with private parties to achieve stabilization. Yet, as the next chapter will show, there are aspects of wage determination rooted in the most basic characteristics of labor and product markets, which in some circumstances result in economic behavior requiring controls. To take an extreme example, it is difficult to believe that during World War II any proposed structural changes in the labor market could have obviated a need for direct wage controls. Whether controls are necessary in less difficult times is discussed elsewhere in this work.

Second, the arguments against private involvement in stabilization programs neglect important aspects of the role of government in a democracy. Government's role is not exclusively that of a regulator but also of a leader, an advocate, and a device for achievement of public purposes pursued by private groups. With respect to wage stabilization, government's role as a regulator is inherently very limited. This is not to say that public authorities may not issue and publish a set of regulations covering compensation in private industry. However, the capacity of government to enforce the letter and spirit of the regulation without the cooperation of private parties is very much restricted.[5] The private economy is simply too complicated for regulations to work against widespread indifference or antagonism. However, it is likely that most Americans would agree that although a comprehensive regulatory effort by government with respect to compensation is inappropriate interference in the operation of a free society, it may nevertheless be necessary in periods of national stress or peril. Under such circumstances it is appropriate, they might agree, for government to exercise its role as leader in a cooperative effort to establish an economic stabilization program. The administration of the program may then also involve government's function as a regulator, in cooperation with private groups.

The Development of a Cooperative Stabilization Policy

In the United States, private industry, organized labor, and government have traditionally explored the establishment of a cooperative stabilization policy through two sorts of mechanisms: the congressional legislative process and discussions with or under the auspices of the executive branch. In Congress, the "discussion" of stabilization policy is often a very diffuse process. Normally, the various parties (including labor, management, and the administration) present their positions in congressional hearings. Later, elaboration and modification of these positions may be made by the congressional supporters of the various groups in the context of legislative debate.

Legislation and Economic Stabilization

It is uncommon for Congress to legislate with respect to wage stabilization policy alone. Rather, congressional action normally entails some comprehensive package of wage and price stabilization authority and may include standards for implementation by the executive branch of government. In addition, congressional action is normally of a broad character, leaving the detailed regulations and procedures of controls to the executive branch of government—though Congress has intervened in the detailed administration of a program when it is disturbed by the program's content, direction, or results.[6]

It is interesting that, in the United States, Congress has several times provided the administration with enabling legislation for economic stabilization programs in advance of the administration's request. In 1970, for example, the Democratic-controlled Congress passed an Economic Stabilization Act over the objections of President Nixon, who avowed his intent never to invoke the provisions of the act. Because Congress is an extraordinarily complex body which represents many constituencies, it is hazardous to assign a simple explanation for its propensity to enact stabilization legislation against the wishes of a president. It is likely, however, that the following consideration is a major factor. Congress is a first and primary recipient of the complaints of those dissatisfied with the economy. During a prolonged and rising inflation, the pressures on Congress for action to control rising prices become pronounced. The enactment of stabilization authority for the president is both an indication that Congress is concerned about inflation and a method of shifting the initiative for further action to the executive branch. The president, on the other hand, although subject to the pressures of public opinion with respect to rising prices (as is Congress), is normally reluctant to embark upon a stabilization policy. American chief executives are always well aware of the disadvantages of direct economic controls, including the necessary additional bureaucracy and expenditures, the problems of equity in administration, and the likelihood of failure of the program. In consequence, the president is generally anxious to appear to resort to controls only at the insistence of the electorate—an insistence well expressed by congressional action to authorize the use of controls. Also, the need for cooperation by industry and labor in the administration of controls is such that the president may wish to act only upon the demands of the public, in order to better insure the cooperation of private organizations.

Congress, as we have seen, rarely spells out the details of a stabilization program. Rather, an economic stabilization act normally authorizes the president to invoke wage and price controls when, in his opinion, the economic situation requires them. The act customarily provides a general framework for stabilization policy, including, for example, what aspects of the economy may be made subject to direct controls. The Economic Stabilization Act of 1970, for instance, apparently excluded profits from direct controls, requiring the stabilization program which was established in 1971 to attempt to restrain profits primarily through a profit-related policy with respect to the control of prices.

Procedures for Discussion with the Executive Branch

The most extensively used method for discussions among government, industry, and labor regarding a stabilization policy is informal discussion involving the executive branch of government. Initially, the administration may seek the views of leaders of the business community and organized labor. Often, it is necessary to deal separately in the first instance with different elements of each group. In American experience neither business nor organized labor is monolithic in character, so that rarely can one individual or organization speak for all business or all unions. Both the largest firms and the smallest businesses often insist on a separate voice. In consequence, an administration customarily consults the larger employers individually or through industry associations or ad-hoc groups and attempts to deal with representatives of small businessmen as best it can, considering the amorphous character of the group. Alternatively, consultations with labor require separate discussions with whatever formal or informal associations of national labor organizations exist. During much of the World War II and Korean periods the AFL and the CIO separately represented important elements of American organized labor, though for much of both periods the two federations cooperated through a labor policy committee. The United Mine Workers, the major independent, was often included in stabilization discussions as well. During 1971–72, discussions preliminary to the stabilization program necessarily included both the merged AFL-CIO and the major independents, the Teamsters and the United Automobile Workers. It should be obvious that the greater the degree of internal unity in the business and labor communities, the greater the potential ease of these discussions, though not necessarily the achievement of agreement in them. Unfortunately, the existence of disunity on either side may tempt an administration to take policy initiatives with the cooperation of elements of one side only—a sometimes successful and sometimes disastrous course.

It is unusual for the preliminary discussions regarding a stabilization policy to involve the president himself. Rather, top officials of an administration, both cabinet members and White House aides, represent the administration in these discussions. It is common, however, for the president to become involved at either or both of two points. First, the president may be asked to meet with business and labor representatives, separately or together, to press upon them the urgency for action. Such meetings are most often in the form of exhortations and rarely involve detailed discussion or the request for a commitment from the private parties. These meetings are very important, nonetheless, in establishing an atmosphere in which discussions may proceed. Second, toward the conclusion of discussions between the government and the private parties, it may be necessary for the president to confirm for either side the content of an arrangement as to how the stabilization program will work. Confirmation by the president is most likely to be required when an administration is internally divided and the private parties are, therefore, unwilling to accept assurances from anyone except the president. Assurances given by the president which are later violated by the government may have profound consequences, so that these meetings require great care in establishing an explicit understanding as to the commitments asked and made.

A particular problem arises with respect to the partisan character of each administration. In the United States the labor movement has ordinarily been relatively closer to Democratic administrations, and the business community to Republican administrations. Consequently, it might be expected that in developing a stabilization policy each administration would find its relationship to its special constituent a simpler one than that which involves the other. Yet the difficulties encountered have not always been those that have been anticipated. For example, in 1950 President Truman appointed Mr. Charles E. Wilson, president of General Electric Corporation, as director of the Office of Defense Mobilization. In 1951 the unions withdrew from the Wage Stabilization Board in part because of dissatisfaction with their relationship with the Democratic administration, reflected to a degree by Mr. Wilson's important role in the economic stabilization program. But the relationship between an administration and the various private groups can also be better than expected. It can be added here that the possibility of nonpartisan support for a stabilization program arises in part out of the complex character of American administrations, in which a wide spectrum of political ideologies is represented, so that even an administration's opponents may find some special advocates for its views within the administration.

At the onset of each of the World Wars and prior to the reconversion period after World War II, informal discussions among government, industry, and labor were followed by a formal, joint labor-management conference held in Washington, to which the representatives of organized labor and management were invited. The conferences at the start of each war were initially concerned primarily with problems of avoiding work stoppages, not with stabilization policy per se. The conference in 1945 was explicitly concerned with stabilization policy and failed to reach agreement on the continuation of general controls into the reconversion period.[7] No conferences were called during the Korean period or in 1971.[8]

The formal mechanism of the labor-management conference is an interesting element in the development of a stabilization policy. Among its advantages are that it brings into the public eye the participants in and the substance of otherwise informal discussions; it lends an element of urgency and yet of due process to the entire procedure of developing a policy; it prevents stabilization procedures and regulations from appearing with a disconcerting suddenness; and it removes some of the regulatory flavor of action in favor of a more cooperative appearance. The conference has significant disadvantages in that it provides dissidents in either group (labor or management) with a forum from which to attack the proposed actions, and it may, therefore, have an undesired result.

Should the labor-management conference be revived? Should it have been employed, for example, in 1971? If the intent of the administration were a serious and substantial policy of stabilization, one which would require cooperation of private parties, and if the conference could have been expected to have a result favorable to such a program, then a conference would have been a useful device in developing and achieving acceptance of a stabilization policy. Put somewhat differently, one might say that where a stabilization policy is expected to be under considerable stress by virtue of economic conditions, and to be an important part of economic policy generally, then the conference can be very useful as a formal method of establishing a commitment by private parties to a national objective. A conference can, of course, include a much larger representation from labor and management, and in a far more public posture, than can informal discussions. It also has the great value of bringing management and labor together to work out the program, rather than through separate discussions with government officials.

Elements of a Stabilization Arrangement

How explicit an arrangement among industry, labor and government is necessary to inaugurate a stabilization program? The more detail required and the larger the number of issues involved, the less likely is an agreement. What then is necessary in terms of an arrangement, and what is proper for the government to undertake by way of an agreement?

Generally, it is not necessary for the arrangement to be very detailed with respect to what the various groups undertake to do. However, each party must receive an understanding of what the others expect in embarking on a program of controls. More significant than the details of the stabilization program itself, are the intentions of the parties with respect to the economic and institutional environment in which controls will operate (for example, the related issues of aggregate spending and employment, collective bargaining, profits, and so on). This is not to imply that the various groups will seek or give guarantees that there will be no movement in environmental areas. No responsible leaders on any side would expect this. Rather, each group would desire assurances that the stabilization program is sought by others for its own sake, not as a device to achieve progress in other areas. And, in general, the private parties require an understanding of the general direction the government will pursue in the period of stabilization.

A more explicit arrangement may be required when there is deep mistrust among the parties. With a Democratic administration, business may seek more explicit guarantees for matters within its concern than otherwise; the unions, conversely, may require more specific guarantees from a Republican administration. For example, in the fall of 1971 the AFL-CIO insisted on receiving from President Nixon a guarantee of the "autonomy" of the tripartite Pay Board from interference by the Cost of Living Council (an all-administration body) as a condition of labor's participation on the board. Mr. Nixon initialed such a message, which became a public document. This degree of explicitness among the parties is, however, unusual.

The casual observer might expect that there are many factors which would commonly be important elements in the discussion of a stabilization policy among business, government, and labor. A list might include prices (especially those of products most significant in the consumer's budget), the level of employment, unemployment, profits, taxation policy, income transfers, the minimum wage, the level of interest rates, foreign trade policy, the role of collective bargaining, the strike, and others. Each of these matters is a significant aspect of the economic and institutional environment, and it would not seem unreasonable to expect business or labor to seek assurances or concessions from the government with regard to these areas in return for cooperation in a stabilization policy. Further, whatever political matters (presidential appointments, proposed legislation) might be timely during discussions might be expected to become part of any arrangement. However, since government has rarely sought to impose substantial institutional changes (restructuring of industry or of collective bargaining) under the guise of stabilization, there has been much less wide-ranging bargaining regarding a stabilization program than might have been expected. In fact, the list of issues which have been critical to a stabilization program has been surprisingly short, and it has changed very little over several decades. This permanence suggests that fundamental aspects of the relationship among government, labor, and industry are involved, so that the issues deserve careful study.

The Concerns of the Unions

The unions have normally stressed three major areas in private discussions and public debate regarding wage stabilization programs. The first of these is the control of consumer prices; second, control of profits (and the broader issue of equality of sacrifice); and third, the provision of some method of dispute settlement where a no-strike pledge is sought.

Consumer Prices. In all periods of stabilization the unions have expressed considerable concern for the expected behavior of consumer prices and the direction of government policy toward consumer prices. Yet, what is common to the union position over the years is merely a concern for the matter, not any particular position toward it. Perhaps this is surprising. One might have expected the unions to insist on controls on consumer prices stringent enough to allow real wages to rise (that is, a stabilization policy which would permit money wages to rise faster, to some degree, than the cost of living). After all, when money wages rise more slowly than prices, then the real standard of living of workers is likely to fall. Yet, an examination of the historical record reveals that the unions have taken very different positions at various times with respect to the relationship of wages and prices. The primary factors affecting their position have been the economic and political environment in which controls were proposed.

In World War II there was a general expectation among industry, labor, and government leadership that real wages would be required to fall during the conflict.[9] Although the unions accepted this situation as inevitable, involving the sacrifice necessary to win the war, they were nonetheless anxious to minimize the reduction in real wages which would actually occur. In the Korean period, there was no such willingness on the part of union leadership or members to accept a decline of real wages. Thus, when the public members of the WSB suggested a formula which would have the effect of constraining real wages too tightly, the unions left the board. A further variation on the theme occurred in 1971. The standards for wage

increases under discussion never seriously involved a threat to real wages. Quite the contrary, for during the inflation of the mid- and late-1960s prices had risen so rapidly that real wages appeared to decline. The Nixon administration's economic policy contemplated for 1971–72 an average rate of wage increase several percentage points above that of consumer prices, and, in the result, during 1972 real wages rose on average in the economy for the first time in several years. Administration spokesmen were not reticent in pointing to this situation, apparently in the belief that organized labor could not in good faith oppose a stabilization program which generated rising real wage levels.[10] Yet, the influence of other economic circumstances, the divisiveness of other issues and personalities, and the press of political considerations in an election year caused the unions to reject the wage stabilization program and to be unceasing in their condemnation of the machinery of controls.

Profits. The unions have been concerned historically with the attitude of public policy toward profits during a period of wage stabilization. Normally, the unions' position is that profits must not be allowed to rise without bound while wages are controlled. When formal profit controls or excess profit taxes have not been available to the administration, the unions have sought to have controls on product prices used as a surrogate.

The motivations for the unions' concern with profits may seem too obvious to require elaboration. Yet, there are subtleties which become apparent with careful analysis. As in the case of consumer prices, the unions' attitude toward the control of profits is less motivated by an ideological position than by the practicalities of the relationship between union leaders and their members. Profits are commonly watched by workers as indications of a company's ability to pay higher wages; and though profits may not be a good measure of capacity to pay without higher prices, the traditions of unionism give profits an important role in negotiations. A context in which profits are rising rapidly but wages are controlled places union leaders in a very difficult position vis-à-vis their constituents. Cooperation with a stabilization program requires that the union leadership encourage its local affiliates and members to abide by wage stabilization regulations and discourage evasion or challenge. In a situation in which profits are uncontrolled, the capacity of union leadership to perform such a function will be seriously, perhaps completely, undermined.

Because the interest of unions in profits proceeds from a highly practical basis, any number of formulations will serve to adjust their concerns, depending on the peculiar circumstances of the time. There is, thus, no simple formula which can be depended on to satisfy the unions regardless of circumstances. The unions, like other groups in our society, recognize that profits may be low at the outset of a period of stabilization. When profits have been depressed in the years prior to a stabilization program, it may be necessary to allow substantial increases in profits to occur. This was the situation in 1971, when wage and price controls were applied. The unions recognized that wages and prices had expanded rapidly in the years immediately preceding 1971 but that profits had not. Union leadership was potentially agreeable, therefore, to a stabilization program which would, by one device or another, allow a substantial recovery in profits, while wages were under tighter controls.[11]

Union leadership customarily offers for inclusion in a stabilization program the further principle of "equality of sacrifice." By this is apparently meant that if workers are to be restrained in achieving expected or hoped-for economic gains, other elements of society should also be restrained. The judgment as to what arrangements constitute "equality of sacrifice" is, of course, largely subjective, but the implication of the principle is clear. In order to persuade local union leadership and the membership generally to forego hoped for wage increases, it is important that national union leadership be able to point to restrictions not only on corporate profits but also on the earnings of highly paid individuals. If the rich are believed to benefit unduly, despite the stabilization program, the problem of limiting the aspirations of union membership may be insoluble.

A Procedure for Dispute Settlement. The procedures which are to be followed by labor and management in settling disputes are an important element of any stabilization program. In wartime, maintaining production by minimizing work stoppages is a goal in itself and may be pursued independently, to some degree, of a wage stabilization effort. Even in periods when continuity of production is not an all-important goal in itself, a stabilization program requires some means of dispute settlement, or striking unions may compel (or assist) employers to violate wage stabilization regulations. It is usual, therefore, for government to propose to the leadership of organized labor that a no-strike pledge or some partial substitute be given to accompany a stabilization program.

When unions are requested to eschew the strike weapon in some fashion, it is understandable that they would seek some other method of resolving disputes. The unions normally insist that the mechanism for dispute settlement to be established in place of the strike shall cover all issues, economic or noneconomic, on which the parties might be at variance. Thus, the unions seek to have a large number of issues relating to the status of the union, bargaining structure, and other matters, all seemingly extraneous to monetary concerns, become an element of the disputes machinery of the stabilization program. In support of this position the unions point out that in the give-and-take of collective bargaining it is customary to trade off economic against noneconomic items, so that distinction between the two, while unambiguous in concept, may be very impractical. American employers normally have resisted strongly the suggestion that noneconomic items should be subject to any board of recommendation or arbitration. This attitude brings them into direct conflict with the unions, as will be described in detail shortly.

Several remarks should be made in conclusion to this discussion of the unions' concerns with the general framework of stabilization policy. It is apparent from the above analysis that, in the United States, these areas of union concern are not ideologically motivated (though they may each have ideological expressions) but rather relate directly to the capacity of union leadership to provide the cooperation with a wage stabilization program which is sought by the government. It should not be assumed that the union leadership can necessarily prescribe a form of resolution of these matters which will enhance its own position, so that cooperation becomes possible, and yet satisfy other groups in society. Rather, there is a substantial role for discussion among government, business, and labor as to how adjustment of these matters can be made. To fail to allay these concerns of the unions in some effective manner is not to be "tough" with the unions, as elements of government, business, and the press so often suggest, but rather to make the cooperation of union leadership impossible, even if it was willing to attempt to participate in the controls program. Union leaders must be attentive to the general thrust of their constituents' views or they will be ineffective in the stabilization effort and probably be out of their jobs as well. Unfortunately, federal authorities often fail to understand that union leaders represent their members and have limited discretionary authority. For federal officials to fail to reach an understanding with union leadership on the issues discussed above, and then to blame union leadership for failing to cooperate in a stabilization program, is totally disingenuous. Responsible public officials must recognize that the representatives of the workers, like those of business, require a certain environment if they are to be able to cooperate with public policy without serious damage to their own position.[12]

The Concerns of Business

Employers are in a very different posture with respect to discussions regarding the environment of wage controls than organized labor. Since employers are in many ways potentially the beneficiaries of a wage stabilization program, they are not likely to attach major conditions to their support of the program. Rather, employers' primary interests are directed at the price- and profit-control aspects of the general stabilization effort. The reader might ask why business should have any significant influence on the establishment of a wage stabilization program, since corporations stand to benefit from the program so directly.

Employers commonly have two major reservations about a wage control program, both of which, like labor's reservations, must be accommodated in some manner if business leadership is to be able to deliver the cooperation of the business community as a whole with the stabilization program. First, employers are anxious that, when both price and wage controls are to be established, the policies pursued in the two areas should be compatible. Employers are, therefore, anxious to receive governmental assurance in advance that inconsistencies between price and wage criteria will be minimized.

Second, employers in the United States (quite unlike those abroad) have been very strongly concerned with the implications of a wage stabilization program for noneconomic aspects of their relations to labor unions. This concern has been most directly induced by the activities of public authorities in disputes settlement. During World War I, for example, the government supported a major expansion of collective bargaining in return for cooperation by the unions in maintaining wartime production. After the war American employers embarked on a campaign of several years' duration to reduce labor's wartime gains. Later, the Second World War began in the midst of a round of disputes in the newly organized industrial union sector over union security arrangements in collective bargaining agreements.[13] Employers insisted, without success, that noneconomic issues should not be the concern of the National Defense Mediation Board or of its successor, the National War Labor Board. Employers left the World War II period determined to resist any government machinery, even if connected with wage stabilization, that allowed the government to side with labor on noneconomic items in collective bargaining.

Third, in order to avoid government involvement in noneconomic issues, business has normally opposed a disputes function for a stabilization board. The consequences of such oppositon have been significant. When the Korean emergency developed, employers effectively opposed the Wage Stabilization Board's exercise of a disputes-settlement function except in a few cases directly involving the war effort. The employers' action during Korea prevented government involvement in noneconomic items in disputes but at some cost to the effectiveness of the wage stabilization effort. In 1971, business again opposed the establishment of a disputes mechanism. The Pay Board was therefore established without a no-strike pledge from the unions and without any mechanism to settle disputes.

Is a Nongovernmental Stabilization Program Possible?

If, as is argued above, private business and organized labor must be involved in the establishment and administration of a wage stabilization program, then why does the private sector not conduct a wage-price control program without government involvement? This was, after all, the British and Swedish procedure in World War II. Why not a private stabilization machinery in this country?

There are several reasons why government has necessarily been involved with the private parties in each wage stabilization program in the United States. Perhaps the most fundamental reason is that the pursuit of private gain by individuals and groups in the United States has been too deeply engrained for the private parties to effectively restrain one another. American society has supported, with limitations which are minor compared to some of those abroad, the right of private groups to exploit positions of economic power or scarcity. In consequence, in the private sector there is not the cohesion of management and labor, or sense of social responsibility, necessary to the adoption and enforcement of a stabilization program. The two groups have not trusted one another enough to accept the assurances of good faith necessary to such an endeavor. In the United States, therefore, a "voluntary" stabilization program can only be one in which the private parties cooperate with the government, not a nongovernmental effort.

Furthermore, in the United States collective bargaining and product market pricing remain too decentralized to permit effective central control by private parties. In part because of the American support for private gain described above, neither business nor labor has been able to exercise the degree of internal discipline necessary to an exclusively private stabilization effort. Both labor federations and employer associations lack effective control over their affiliates in the economic sphere. The problem is not that all affiliates would ignore a privately established stabilization machinery but that a significant number would be likely to do so—enough to undermine thoroughly a private program.

Tripartitism in the Administration of a Stabilization Program

Wage control in the United States has generally been performed by a tripartite board of management, labor, and the government. In part, this has been because labor insisted upon a role in the administration of wage controls as part of the general stabilization arrangement. But there has long been a controversy regarding the appropriateness of tripartite wage boards. Opponents of tripartitism have argued that involvement of business and labor representatives in the decision-making process of a government agency is inappropriate. During World War II, George Taylor, an advocate of tripartitism, occasionally answered the critics of the NWLB, pointing out that the board had neither been an ineffectual debating society nor a dictatorial regulator.[14] But not all were convinced, so that at the advent of the Korean War a bitter battle was waged within the administration as to the advisability and/or functions of a tripartite board.[15] The performance of the tripartite WSB during the Korean period did little to convert the critics of tripartitism, and a similar dispute over tripartitism occurred within the Nixon administration in 1971. The Pay Board was established as tripartite, but soon, due to the labor members' withdrawal, was converted to an all-public board.

The position of the proponents of an all-public wage stabilization agency was well summarized by the authors of the report on the WSB; since the arguments on either side change little with passing decades, it is useful to quote their description here:

> Proponents of an all-public board argue that there are general public values distinct from, conflicting with, and offsetting values of responsible participation of collective bargaining parties. They would rather see public representatives make and promulgate wage policy, taking technical advice from interested parties but precluding the latter from voting authority. To some extent this view may represent a belief that private party representatives cannot, in the nature of their allegiances, take responsibility for necessary restraint and regulation but will promote joint interests against the general public and carry public members as mediators along with them. On disputed issues, it represents the contrary complaint that the public members of a tripartite board will take a "pro-labor" or "pro-industry" position rather than voting the "center" or otherwise on the merits of the case.[16]

The case for a tripartite wage board includes the following arguments. First, that since a wage control program cannot be effectively pursued over a prolonged period without the cooperation of management and labor, and since their cooperation (especially labor's) includes the demand to participate in the administration of wage controls, there are no viable alternatives to tripartitism. Second, tripartite boards are better informed and tend to develop more practical and effective policies by virtue of the interchange among the three parties. Third, tripartite boards may obtain a degree of general compliance with the stabilization program that a purely governmental body cannot obtain.

The Roles of the Public and Partisan Members of a Board

The essential character of tripartite boards is determined by the interaction of public, labor, and business representatives. Each group of members has certain functions, and the success of the board depends, in large part, on how each group perceives and performs its own role. In the case of each group there are certain attitudes and activities which, if assumed, are profoundly destructive of the functioning of the board. What are the roles of the representatives on the board, and to what errors are they prone?[17]

Public Members. The public members of a wage stabilization board must be able to perform five basic functions. First, public members must represent the stabilization program to Congress and the public generally. They must be able to explain the rationale of the board's policies and its actions in individual cases. Often it is asserted in the press that the essence of this function is to mobilize congressional and public support for the program. It is not. Rather, the essential matter is to defend the board from the attempts of the public and of private-interest groups, acting through Congress, to so amend the stabilization program that it is seriously hampered.

Second, public members have a special responsibility within a tripartite board in the establishment of policy. It is necessary, therefore, that they be persons with a grasp of the economic and institutional factors involved in wage determination. As we will see in later chapters, the complexities of establishing wage policies are very great, and public members without experience in wage-setting and administration are prone to the commission of many serious errors, the result of which may be to undermine the stabilization program. Third, in a tripartite setting, public members must, to a degree, be mediators between management and labor representatives. A solution to a difficult problem of wage policy or to a difficult case which represents a degree of consensus between management and labor may command a greater acceptance at the workplace than any unilateral decision by public members, no matter how wise. Thus, the success of the stabilization program is facilitated by a mediation function. Fourth, public members must generally exercise the deciding ballot on questions of policy and the decisions in particular cases, since management and labor will often be at odds.

In their capacity as decision-makers, public members require good judgment and a large enough degree of independence from either business or labor so that the motives of their actions will not be suspect on grounds of self-interest. Fifth, and last, public members must be prepared to receive considerable criticism and even personal abuse from outside the board for their decisions. In many instances they are required to shoulder alone the burden of responsibility for a compromise worked out in the board but which neither management nor labor representatives are prepared to defend before their own constituents.

Since criticism by the press, by politicians, and by private parties can be extremely strident and bitter, public members must possess a degree of personal courage to do their job well. There is perhaps no better method of introducing a public member to the consequences of his actions at the workplace than to have to explain the board's policies and decisions to aggrieved local unions or employers. But this, as we have said, takes courage.[18]

There are certain hazards which the public members of a board must be careful to avoid. The most important are associated with a tendency to adopt too completely the position of either partisan side of the board (that is, either labor or management). With respect to management, there is a tendency for public members to support uncritically management's position on economic issues. This is a result of the greater sympathy of the management side of a board for the stabilization objectives of the public members. Yet, in several respects, management objectives have often not been in common with public objectives with respect to wage stabilization. First, the management of particular companies and their representatives on the board may be far less anxious to restrain wage increases than public members expect. During World War II, because of the very tight labor market and the high volume of demand, this was especially true. "The general assumption during the early days of the stabilization program," reported a former executive director of the NWLB, "was that employers would be only too happy to keep their wage costs down; and, at least for a time, no one fully realized the extent to which some employers would go in order to secure or retain desperately needed manpower."[19] In the Korean period, and even more so during 1971-72, looser labor and product markets made this employer attitude less common. Second, employers often have a very high preference for certain aspects of short-term as opposed to long-term wage restraint. The reason is that restraint of expected wage increases may occur after prices have been raised in anticipation, so that a "windfall" profit is gained by the employer. For public members of a stabilization board to support this employer preference, without other reasons of a substantial nature, contributes little or nothing to the stabilization program itself (since prices are already advanced) and threatens to undermine the credibility of the program with workers. Third, the most subtle of these dangers is that the public members may fail to recognize when employers are proposing a course of action which is intended only to use the stabilization machinery to strengthen their own bargaining position with unions. Thus, the employer representatives might propose that stabilization authorities establish a guideline for wage increases, which the employers may then exceed in collective bargaining in return for union concessions of various kinds, or under the threat of a strike. Having settled for a figure above the guidelines, the employers may then publicly charge the stabilization authorities with failure to enforce the guidelines and demand that the negotiated increase be reduced. Such an employer policy is not only potentially destructive of honest collective bargaining but of the stabilization program as well. There are a variety of subtle, but effective, devices which public members of a board may employ to minimize the use by business of this tactic, but it cannot be fully eliminated.[20]

Public members of a board can also be too amenable to the position of the union members on major issues of policy. For example, business representatives have for years accused the public members of stabilization boards of favoring, to an unreasonable degree, union positions on nonwage items. Without examining the merits of employer objections, we may cite as examples the companies' complaints regarding union security demands, check-off provisions, certain fringe benefits (now recognized to be economic items in a sense not true during the Second World War, for example), and aspects of bargaining structure. It is not hard to conclude that the NWLB was perhaps too considerate of noneconomic demands by unions in disputes cases, since management has, in response, successfully limited the disputes function of subsequent boards.

Finally, an unintended advantage of the role of public members on a tripartite stabilization board has been the training of numerous persons who later served private industry and the government as mediators and/or arbitrators. William E. Simkin, a former director of the Federal Mediation and Conciliation Service, has pointed out that of the small group of mediators (outside the FMCS) used by the government (in the 1960s) in very difficult industrial disputes or in the ongoing industrial relations of certain industries, all received their introduction to industrial relations through the NWLB or WSB.[21]

Partisan Members. From the viewpoint of public policy toward stabilization, partisan members potentially may make several contributions to the operation of a stabilization board. First, and of very great significance, they may supply special knowledge and expertise in the problems of an area, industry, or occupation with which the board is concerned.[22] Second, they may assist the board to understand unstated aspects of a case which are internal to union or management organizations (this may be especially important in resolving a disputes case).[23] Third, they may suggest avenues of compromise in the settlement of policy or case controversies within the board. Fourth, they are often able to inform the public members as to what aspects of a policy or case decision have broad significance and therefore must be considered or qualified carefully. Fifth, in many instances they may serve as a liaison between the board and companies and unions affected by board actions. This avenue of communication may be very important to the board in ascertaining the true facts of a situation and the issues involved. In some cases, union and employer members may directly be the representatives of the workers or management involved in a matter before the board. Sixth, partisan members may take part, by voting, in the decisions of the board. Seventh, partisan members are especially valuable in suggesting to a board the occurrence of new developments in the economy or in industrial relations which require some response by the board or which raise problems of a long-run policy nature. This list, although not complete, is impressive.[24] It is not too much to say that, in the absence of partisan members, public members of a stabilization board tend to be isolated and ill-informed.

Not all partisan members of a board exercise the same degree of influence in the performance of these functions. A board is, after all, a group of individuals and is subject to the interpersonal aspects of group dynamics. Several factors contribute to the influence, or lack of it, which an individual labor or industry member of a board may exert. First, the importance of the company or union which he represents and the degree of his leadership role within it are very important. While a mere spokesman for a large organization may have little weight, the organization's president may carry a great deal, particularly with respect to matters affecting his organization. Second, the ability of a partisan representative to judge an issue on wider elements than those narrowly related to his own organization's interest is particularly important in establishing influence with the public members or the members from the other partisan groups. Third, a willingness to make and carry out hard decisions, especially decisions opposed to a man's short-term interests, creates a substantial degree of influence and respect. Fourth, and finally, the personality, imagination, and knowledge of an individual can be important in determining his degree of influence.

There are certain problems in the operation of a tripartite board specific to management and labor representatives. With respect to management, three problem areas may be identified. First, the selection of management representatives for a board is complicated by the lack of unity in American management. There are rivalries among the various employer associations (including, among the major groups, the Chamber of Commerce, the National Association of Manufacturers, and the National Industrial Conference Board), and between big business and small business, and among employers in various industries. Furthermore, the selection of employer representatives is made complicated by the need to choose among the professional staff of employer organizations or the chief executives (or staff representatives) of individual firms. Association staff executives are more likely to have a greater breadth of knowledge and comprehension of industry generally than corporation executives but are less likely to have the high respect which business affords chief executives of firms. In consequence, employer representatives on a board are normally chosen, after consultation with various business groups, to reflect divisions within the business community based on geography, industry, size, and other factors. Second, because the self-interest of employers generally lies with the success of wage stabilization efforts, employer association members of the board often have a less difficult role than their union counterparts. But, employer representatives often have very little capacity to affect the behavior of individual firms or local employer associations, except through a mild form of persuasion. In consequence, where union leadership is called upon to participate in the enforcement of the board's awards and to assist in ending strikes, employer representatives whose constituents are, in most cases, the beneficiary of these actions, are often unable to be of assistance in the effort. The union representatives often respond to this situation by charging, justly in many instances, that they are required to bear an unreasonably large burden of responsibility for the stabilization program's success. Third, employer representatives have in many cases, because of internal considerations in the board, had to bear public responsibility for the approval of wage increases or even noneconomic adjustments which employers generally objected to. And it is often an inadequate response to criticism that some concessions must be made to obtain others.

The position of union leaders serving on a wage stabilization board is necessarily a bit anomalous and subject to misinterpretation by those outside the board. Union members may feel that the leadership has betrayed them by its participation and, despite denials by their leaders, may be convinced that under-the-table deals are being made in the confines of the board. Conversely, persons not sympathetic to the unions often believe that the very presence of organized labor on a stabilization board indicates that the special interests of powerful groups are being given undue consideration, or that the unions, by their presence on the board, are in a position to sabotage its operations. Because of these conflicting views, and because neither is close to the truth, it is useful to explain the role of the unions on a board.

There are several reasons why union representatives may agree to serve on a wage stabilization board. First, a request to serve on a board established by the president, acting within his powers delegated by the Constitution or Congress, tends to require union leadership to honor the request as public-spirited citizens. Second, it is incumbent upon union leaders to participate in a board's deliberations to the extent necessary to protect the members of their various organizations. Representation of union members in various forums before public and business leadership is an essential element of the duties of union officials. Third, a stabilization board cannot function well in the absence of labor members. For them to fail to participate would invite the president to take another initiative, the specific nature and result of which could not be predicted. In consequence, participation on a tripartite board, with the always reserved right to resign, often appears preferable. Fourth, a basic position of the unions in discussions regarding the context and content of a wage stabilization program normally is that collective bargaining be protected from interference to the greatest degree possible. Participation on a stabilization board permits union leadership to exercise influence for this purpose.

The Functioning of Tripartite Boards

A great deal could be written regarding the many aspects of the internal operations of tripartite boards. In order to set some limits to the length of our inquiry, however, we will explore here only four of the major aspects of the operation of tripartite boards. First, what are the implications of voting by partisan members of a board on its policies and on cases which come before it? Is the public interest distorted? Are public members unduly influenced by their partisan colleagues? Second, how has the prerogative of partisan members to withdraw from a board been used? Conversely, what keeps a board together? Third, is there too much bargaining which occurs within a tripartite board, as opposed to evenhanded application of the law? Is bargaining within a board inappropriate? Fourth, would a more quasi-judicial approach to the board's activities better serve the public interest?

Voting strength on tripartite boards has, in the past, always been divided equally between public, employer, and labor representatives. There is no necessary reason for this, and it has sometimes been proposed that public members should have a majority vote. Historically, there has been no need for such an arrangement (at least until recently), because public members generally cast the deciding votes by siding with either management or labor, who were in opposition to each other. The few instances in which public members were outvoted by a combination of employer and labor members were of no importance.[25] Unfortunately, in 1971–72, the Pay Board's public members were outvoted in a series of important cases by a combination of labor and employer representatives, raising in a serious fashion for the first time the question as to whether public members alone ought to have a deciding vote. Yet, to a great degree, this issue is quite artificial. For in a well-functioning board there is an important distinction between formal, recorded votes and the actual decision-making process. Decisions are made through a procedure of discussion intended to develop a consensus, perhaps involving as well one or more straw votes, allowing board members to express their true viewpoints. This is very important, because business and labor representatives are often the best judges of the true best interests of the public, and some device is necessary to permit them to express these views off-the-record. Their constituents, however, have not chosen them to represent the public interest but for more narrow interests, and they cannot publicly repudiate that duty. Thus, the formal vote, often taken after a decision is made, reflects the formal, narrow, public positions of each group. Early in the experience of the NWLB, industry and labor members sought to vote formally their own best judgments rather than their organizations' formal and public positions. Pressure on those representatives who sought to follow this course soon brought it to an end.[26] It is, perhaps, unfortunate that in public affairs such subterfuges as straw votes, taken separately from formal votes, must be employed, but given the nature of human beings and human institutions, it is inevitable. The right of industry and labor representatives to withdraw from a tripartite board is fundamental to their willingness to participate and thereby is critical to the preservation of an important degree of voluntarism in a stabilization program. Nor have management and labor failed to exercise this right when they so desired. Since the establishment of the NDMB at the outset of rearmament before World War II, various union groups have withdrawn from tripartite boards on two occasions, and employers have withdrawn on two occasions also. Unions have threatened withdrawals seriously on two other occasions; employers on two, also.

Two generalizations may be offered about these instances. The first is that, in many of the instances of withdrawal or threatened withdrawal, the basic issues which union or employer representatives were protesting were aspects of general economic policy, not matters internal to the wage boards. A second generalization about the actual withdrawals is that whatever their causes, they initiated crises in the stabilization program which required its abandonment or substantial modification. This result is the logical expression of the principle developed earlier in this chapter, that a wage stabilization program cannot be successfully pursued without the cooperation of both management and labor.

The fundamental factor which has not been generally appreciated is that the prolonged participation of union representatives on a wage stabilization board cannot be made palatable to themselves and their constituents if the board has only wage stabilization responsibilities. Union leaders were not elected to control their members' wages and cannot afford to appear to be doing primarily that. But the NWLB, for example, was never exclusively, perhaps never even primarily, a wage control agency. Rather, it was an agency intimately concerned with the settlement of industrial disputes and also with the improvement of collective bargaining and industrial relations generally. It was, that is to say, an agency through which employer and union representatives could seek to resolve common problems with the assistance of public authorities. In 1971–72, the Pay Board had virtually no functions other than wage stabilization. It had no disputes authority; the public members did not intend to handle cases but rather to establish regulations to be applied by a staff of lawyers and economists; and the public members evidenced no interest in the improvement of collective bargaining, either in terms of its structure and methods or in the attempt to deal creatively with the problems facing employers and unions. Thus, a tripartite board had been reduced to exclusively wage control functions, and, because of this, the position of its union members became untenable.

In general, the conclusion may be offered that a wage stabilization board which has only the function of controlling wages cannot be expected to remain tripartite, and therefore cannot be effective. Successful approaches to wage stabilization require that attention be paid to dispute settlement, to the improvement of collective bargaining, and to the emerging problems confronting management and labor in collective bargaining. Only if these elements are included in a program can the interest of management and labor be retained and the participation of the unions justified to themselves. This is a fundamental lesson of the stabilization experience of the United States in this century.

The functioning of tripartite boards has long been criticized as too much akin to three-way bargaining. Instead, critics propose a more quasi-judicial process in which application is made of law and regulations regarding permissible wage increases. A stabilization board, whether it be tripartite or all-public, necessarily involves a degree of both bargaining and regulations, so that the controversy is one of emphasis, not of mutually exclusive alternatives. Some critics oppose the tripartite system itself because of their opposition to the supposed "bargaining" which occurs in such a board. Others believe that a tripartite board is compatible with a more legalistic approach and favor tripartitism. Since the advantages of tripartitism and the reasons for preferring it to an all-public board have been set forth above, our concern here is with the emphasis on bargaining versus adjudication within a tripartite board. The objections to bargaining include the following: "the public members can make decisions only by shuttling back and forth between the one side or the other, from case to case, and that thus the decisions will be a series of compromises representing no consistent principles."[27] Sumner Slichter, probably the most persuasive advocate of a judicial approach, described his objections to a bargaining approach as follows:

> But is not bargaining an inevitable and inherent characteristic of tripartite bodies? Many people believe that it is. I do not agree. The best operation of tripartite bodies, it is true, requires a certain breadth of view and independence on the part of representatives of labor and industry . . . but . . . a wage stabilization body should be a quasi-judicial body not a bargaining one.[28]

Unfortunately, members of tripartite boards have sometimes given credence to these charges of too much bargaining by stressing the compromise aspects of a board's activities above its regulatory ones. For example, Rocco Siciliano, a business representative on the Pay Board (and later a public member), said of the board in an interview, "what we've got here in a sense is a Government-endorsed collective bargaining session."[29]

In fact, the distinction between bargaining, or compromise, and adjudication is probably far less meaningful than might be imagined. Underlying principles are necessary as the foundation upon which opposing interests can base compromise. A board which often abandoned those principles (including, for example, its own wage standards) in the interests of expediency would soon find itself unable to agree on anything, as each side attempted to bluff or in some way coerce the others to accept its views, and compromise would be impossible. On the other hand, the value of bargaining, or compromise, in determining solutions to policy or case problems is that it contributes to improving the practical application of general principles in specific situations.

5. The Impact of the Interrelationships of Wage Rates on Wage Stabilization Policy

The Need for a Theory of Wages in the Administration of a Stabilization Program

It might seem that the administration of a wage stabilization program would not require its officials to possess a theory of the process of wage inflation. This is because a stabilization program is normally pursued according to legislative provisions and regulations which may serve as a substitute for a theoretical foundation. On the contrary, however, the design of a wage control program requires a fairly specific understanding (or theory) of the inflationary process, in order to provide a framework for understanding the interrelationships of various policies involved in a stabilization effort. The purpose of this chapter is to explore the theoretical foundations of wage stabilization policy. Analytic discussions of various aspects of stabilization policy which are contained in the following chapters draw on this theoretical basis. But the significance of this chapter is broader, for it also enables us to draw several major conclusions about the nature of wage stabilization policy generally.

The most important requirement for a theory of wages which is to be useful as a framework for a stabilization program is that the theory relate increases in individual wage rates to the average rate of increase in wages in the economy. This is because a stabilization program cannot control the average rate of increase in wages directly but rather must affect the average through actions taken with respect to individual rates. Direct controls are, in essence, an intervention into some of the most minute aspects of the structure of compensation in the economy with the primary objective of restraining the rate of increase of wages in the aggregate. The degree of involvement of a stabilization program in individual wage decisions distinguishes direct controls from the management of the fiscal and monetary aggregates in the economy. In consequence, the framework of economic theory upon which monetary and fiscal policy may be based is inadequate to the requirements of direct controls. But one must return to the literature of the 1940s and early 1950s to find serious investigation into the relationships of individual wage setting and the general level of wages and rates of increase. A purpose of these pages is to revive this earlier interest in methods of directly relating the determination of individual wage rates to the general rate of increase in wages.

A theory of aggregate compensation changes suited to the study of wage policy may be very briefly described as follows. The rate of increase in a general wage (or earnings) index is dependent upon three major factors: the rate of change in the consumer price index, the long-run rate of change in output per man-hour, and the degree of distortion in the structure of wages.[1] Complicated relationships in time (involving various lag structures) relate consumer price and productivity changes to compensation. The effect of the wage structure on the rate of change in money wages arises because of the strong interrelationships of various wage rates. It is the essence of a period of inflation that wage relationships become distorted, and that money wages tend to rise in the amount necessary to reestablish appropriate differentials. The importance of distortions in the wage structure becomes very marked and may be the single largest contributor to rising money wages (a topic to which we shall return in a later section of this chapter). In a period of economic stability, on the other hand, wages on average tend to rise by that amount which reflects rising (if any) costs of living and rising productivity. In such an environment, adjustments in relative wages contribute only in a minor degreee to the aggregate rate of wage change.

The control of a wage inflation may therefore be said to involve the following elements. First, control of adjustments in compensation caused by increases in prices and productivity, either by direct controls, or indirectly through the effect of the fiscal and monetary policy on aggregate demand. Also it is necessary to control the interaction of wages on prices, as well as of prices on wages, through simultaneous actions. Second, stabilization policy must seek to control the wage structure, and thereby its influence on the rate of change in money wages. Since interrelationships of various wage rates are the essence of wage structure, the interrelationships must be understood fully and carefully managed. The task of stabilization authorities is to begin to return the structure of wages as quickly as possible (without undue effects on industrial relations or production) to one appropriate for the long-term. Yet successful completion of this task requires an understanding of both the role of wage interrelationships in the functioning of labor markets and of the connection between wage structure and the aggregate rate of wage increase. These matters are the topics of the next two sections of this chapter. The relationship of consumer prices and productivity to wage stabilization policy is explored in chapter 7.

The Interrelationships of Individual Wage Rates

Wage interrelations may be said to include the relative wages existing at any point in time and the relationships among wages as perceived by participants (e.g., workers and employers) in the labor market. The importance of wage relationships emerges on both sides of the labor market. Wage interrelationships are important on the supply side because they reflect comparisons made by persons of monetary and nonmonetary benefits and disadvantages of various employments, and also because variations in wages are important determinants of the distribution of satisfaction from employment. The first-mentioned aspect involves the function of relative wages (that is, the wage structure) in directing the flow of manpower among various employments (through affecting the volume of applicants for various jobs, the quality of applicants, the demand for training, and so on). The second aspect involves the comparison among individuals of their economic and social well-being. On the demand side of the labor market relative wages determine, in part, relative costs and thereby affect prices, profitability, and production techniques. Firms are, therefore, inevitably concerned with the structure of wages. In consequence, it is erroneous to believe that the fundamental determinants which cause behavioral relationships to exist among wage rates arise primarily in the attitudes of workers and unions. On the contrary, the concern of employers for the structure of wages is certainly not less intense than that of employees.

The Foundations of Wage Interrelationships

The Preference of Workers. The attitudes of workers toward the wages received for their labor depend, in large degree, upon their perception of the wages others receive. This phenomenon is referrred to in economic literature as the existence of interdependent utility functions among individuals. A definition has been offered by Piore: "The interdependence hypothesis is that the individuals' utility is a function not of the level of absolute income, but of the level of income *relative* to that of other individuals with whom he has social contact. (Social contact . . . includes not only direct contact, but exposure to superior goods through entertainment and advertising media.)"[2] The effect of the interdependence of utility functions is to establish behavioral relations among groups and individuals in the labor market with respect to wage rates. When a group of workers perceives a disadvantage with respect to the wages of other groups, several directions of activity are possible. The first is acceptance of the relationship, although it is undesired. It cannot be doubted that even strong preferences of workers are sometimes altered, and wage differentials accepted, although this process is often likely to be difficult. A second response is for individuals to desert the work in question for better-paying work. This certainly happens to a degree, but in most cases it is not a feasible alternative for the group as a whole. The third alternative is to attempt to have wage relationships readjusted to what are believed to be appropriate levels. This latter response is very marked in its affect on wage determination. It should also be noted that the workers' perception of a disadvantage may be either that of being behind other relevant rates or insufficiently ahead of them. The perception of a disadvantage of either sort is very largely a matter of group or individual psychology and is much affected by general social mores and attitudes (e.g., a largely competitive social atmosphere may generate strong tendencies for those with high wages to attempt to remain well ahead; a less competitive society may show less behavior of this nature).

Whatever the institutional process by which wages are determined, the concern of workers for the interrelationships of wage rates exerts considerable influence. Whether employers establish wage rates in conjunction with individual workers, or through negotiations with a union representing the work force collectively, workers find means of expressing their interest in the comparison of their own wages with those of others. Perhaps this process of wage comparisons is least visible in the situation in which an employer establishes a job-rate unilaterally, and workers are not directly consulted. Adjustments in wage rates in this situation conform primarily to the employers' perception of a need for a change in wage rates, often as a result of inability to hire workers of the characteristics desired (in skill, age, or education). Yet, even here, employers often resort to area wage surveys in conjunction with other employers as the primary information on which to base a decision to adjust wage levels. Employers by this procedure reflect the concerns of employees for the comparison of wages.

Normally, particular groups of employees are not concerned with the comparison of all wage rates, nor even of their wages with the average level of wages generally. Rather custom, existing practices, overt agreement, or the force of economic conditions direct attention to a specific rate or group of wage rates other than those of the workers involved. The dimensions of wage comparisons may include geographic, occupational, industrial, or demographic factors.

Interestingly, the element in union wage strategy which involves the comparison of wage rates is often referred to by researchers as a noneconomic (or political) element. Wage comparisons may be referred to as noneconomic only if it is desired to limit the label "economic" to the circumstances of employment, unemployment, productivity, and profitability of the firm. But in a broader sense, wage comparisons are but another economic factor in wage determination, for the roots of comparison lie in the attitudes of individuals toward their appropriate position in the distribution of society's goods and status—a matter very much economic in character, as well as sociological or political.

Functions of Wage Differentials in Production. Business enterprises are no less concerned with relative wages than the workers they employ, although many of the concerns of business are of different origin. Wage rates constitute an important part of employee compensation, which is in turn one of two elements which determine unit labor costs (the other is productivity).

Unit labor costs affect pricing and the competitive position of a firm and thereby its profitability. Other things being equal, a firm paying lower wage rates than its competitors is in a position to achieve lower prices, and higher sales and profits;[3] or, in contrast, firms paying higher wage rates are at a potential disadvantage. Conversely, in a tight labor market a firm paying lower wage scales than its competitors may be unable to attract labor. There are, therefore, in different economic circumstances varying pressures for dispersion or uniformity in the wage structure. In addition, relative wages affect the competitive positions of substitutes in the product market, so that the fortunes of whole industries depend, in part, on relative wages. It is not uncommon, therefore, to find employers essentially unconcerned with the rate of increase in money wages, so long as relative wages with competitors in the same industry and with firms producing substitute products are not altered to their disadvantage.

In many instances, the concerns of employers with relative wages go beyond comparison to the rates their competitors pay. For example, in many production processes substitutions may be made among various grades and skill levels of workers in response to alterations in wage differentials, so that the manning and hiring policies of the firm may be affected by changes in relative wages. Also, substitutions of machinery and materials for labor often result from increasing relative wages (as well as from increasing wages by comparison to machinery and materials cost). Finally, changes in relative wages across international boundaries may affect the competitiveness of various products in international markets. In consequence, employers must be deeply concerned with the structure of wages, as well as with the money level of wages or rate of increase.

Wage Structure as a Determinant of Wage Adjustments

That the attitudes of unions and employers toward relative wages are directly involved in collective bargaining has long been confirmed by participants and observers. Much attention has been devoted to analysis of the negotiations process, and we will direct our attention here to wage determination by collective bargaining. In collective bargaining the variety of circumstances and concerns of the parties can be very great. However, in many instances, perhaps most, establishment of new wage levels reduces to the decision between equal-cents-per-hour or equal percentage increases to be granted among a group of rates. Economic factors affecting the product market of the firm or industry involved may play an important role in establishing which choice is made between the two, but the basic choice is based on the relationship of the wage rates. Furthermore, once a decision has been made respecting the key rate (or rates), others are often simply adjusted to it. In some situations the key rate is determined internally; in others it is established externally (that is, by other employers and/or unions).

The most interesting cases of the determination of wages are those that involve the establishment of wage rates through other mechanisms than pattern-following. Most likely, these cases are those in which a pattern potentially exists but is disregarded to a large degree because of other influences. Often these influences are easily identifiable as economic in character (they might also be political or even personal in some situations). Because of this, models of wage determination which include only economic variables (e.g., the firm's ability to pay, unemployment among workers in the affected areas, and so on) have often been offered. But, to stress the influence of economic factors in particular situations is often not to deny a general formulation of wage theory involving rate comparisons or patterns but rather to identify the relatively greater importance in some circumstances of other influences. Furthermore, economic factors (as defined above) normally assert themselves in quite different fashion according to the various structures of product and labor markets. Most persons are familiar with the various results which the profit maximization rule will generate in monopolistic as opposed to competitive product markets. Similarly, different increases may result from similar processes in the labor market, except that the matter is made more complex by the interaction of product and labor market structures.[4] As discussed above, the interaction between product and labor markets is often related directly to the issue of wage relationships. Thus, economic models of wage determination cannot be said to exclude the influence of wage structure considerations on wage determination. Quite the contrary.

Wage Interrelationships and the Aggregate Rate of Wage Increase

The relationships between the rate of individual wage increases and the rate of change in the aggregate (or average) level of wages, as customarily measured in the United States, can be described by the following identity:

$$(1) \quad \frac{\Delta W}{W_{t-1}} \equiv \frac{(W_t - W_{t-1})}{W_{t-1}} \equiv \sum_j e_{jt} \left(\frac{\Delta W_j}{W_{jt-1}} \right),$$

where W_t = wage rate in time t, $\sum_j e_j = 1$, e_j are weights reflecting employment estimates by sector for which rates (W_j) are given.

In the most general formulation, the sectors j should be defined to represent observably distinct labor market categories, not any particular group of industrial (e.g., SIC) or occupational (e.g., census) categories.

This identity will hold in all situations, being definitionally true on an ex post basis. It can be made a useful tool of analysis if elements on the right side of the equation can be modeled. The essence of the use of the identity as an analytic tool is that it directs attention to the factors affecting separate elements or sectors of aggregate behavior. The behavior of the averages or aggregates is seen to depend on the composition and the behavior of components, rather than on other aggregate economic variables. The expression allows, therefore, for an explicit interaction of micro- and macro-level variables; that is, of individual wage rates and of the average of rates.

As a behavioral expression, equation (1) may be used to represent the summation of individual wage-rate changes occurring independently of one another, or interdependencies may be represented. Where interdependencies exist, the rate of change in the aggregate (or average) wage is seen to depend upon the structure of relative wages. For example, Akerlof has constructed a model of price and wage decisions in which adjustments depended on certain relative wages and prices; he demonstrated that inflation (in the average level of money wages and prices) rose faster the further relative wages were allowed to go apart.[5]

The variety of interdependencies which may be depicted is limitless, though those observed in the economy are presumably of a finite number. Formulation of the aggregate wage change as in (1) has the advantage of allowing the implications of various interdependencies in wages for aggregate wage behavior to be explored. An example may be useful. Most macro-wage models which relate aggregate wage changes to changes in the aggregates of profits, unemployment, or other variables seem to assume an independence of wage determination in various sectors. Although micro-models are rarely made explicit by researchers investigating macrorelationships, yet most seem to believe that at the microlevel each wage adjustment is made in terms of the economic conditions (e.g., profits and unemployment) existing in the particular labor market. Presumably, then, the behavior of the aggregate wage variable should be determined by the behavior of the causal aggregate variables, where the aggregation procedures accurately weight the various sectors. Yet consider, for discussion purposes, a circumstance in which a single major negotiation sets a pattern for a great number of other wage settlements. It is quite likely that the pattern bargain is causally dependent upon economic (and perhaps noneconomic) characteristics of the particular sector (or industry, or area, or occupation, or all of these) only—to the exclusion of concern for those sectors which follow the pattern. It may also be that, in the short run, at least, those parties which are pattern followers make none, or only small, adjustments in the established pattern in response to economic conditions in their own sector.[6] It follows, therefore, that a model of these sectors would show a change in the aggregate wage dependent upon economic conditions solely in one sector (the pattern-setting sector). Symbolically:

(2)
$$\frac{\Delta W_j}{W_{jt-1}} = \frac{\Delta W_i}{W_{it-1}},$$

for all j, $1 \ldots i$, i has only one value and

(3)
$$\frac{\Delta W_i}{W_{it-1}} = f(x_{ki}),$$

where x_{ki} represent a variety of economic variables (k) in sector i.

Then,

$$\frac{\Delta W}{W_{t-1}},$$

where

$$\frac{\Delta W}{W_{t-1}} = \sum_{j=1,\ldots i} \frac{e_j}{} \frac{\Delta W_j}{W_{jt-1}}$$

and so

$$\frac{\Delta W}{W_{t-1}} = f(x_{ki}),$$

to the exclusion of any variables x_{kj}, assumed by (2) to be of the character

$$\frac{\Delta W_j}{W_{jt-1}} \neq f(x_{kj})$$

except for sector i as specified in (3).

As a practical matter there exist in the economy, at any time, a great variety of behavioral relationships among wage rates (and of behavioral relationships among changes in wage rates) and other economic (and perhaps noneconomic) variables. In some sectors, for example, profit rates may exercise a role in determining wage increases—in others not at all (to choose a very obvious example, the nonprofit sectors of the economy). Further, while it is true that in a fully specified general model all wage rates and all economic variables are somehow related, even if only very distantly, yet there can be identified at any time some relationships of much greater importance than others. In general, wage rates will be most intimately related causally which are involved in the production of similar products, within the same geographic area, in the same or closely-related occupations, in closest physical propinquity (e.g., within a single industrial plant or workshop), closely related by the mobility of workers, with a strong historical pattern of relationships, and/or a particular institutional relationship (for example, received by members of the same union). The impact of a particular increase in a wage rate is more likely to be more pronounced (given the factors listed above) on other rates when the initial rate is relatively high, and the increase is large. Finally, the pattern effect of wage increases is likely to be generally greater the tighter labor markets generally, the more institutional arrangements favor wage comparisons (for example, a wage stabilization program tends to increase the importance, at least seemingly, of wage comparisons), and the more rapidly consumer prices are rising (since rising consumer prices generate concern among workers for their real-income position).

The Process of Wage Inflation

Understanding a period of wage inflation requires an examination of the process by which inflation proceeds. Such an examination is superior, for certain analytic and policy purposes, to an explanation of why the inflation began or who is to blame for it. In fact, the process of an inflation is quite independent (after a certain early point) of why or how it started.

It is useful analytically to compare a period of wage inflation with a more normal state. Clark Kerr, writing in 1953, defined a period of full, but not overly full, employment as an appropriate comparison.[7] Kerr suggested that in such a period wages would tend to rise by the increase in the cost-of-living plus an annual improvement trend representing increases in output per manhour and some adjustments in the wage structure. (These last-mentioned adjustments might include elimination of gross inequities, elimination of substandards, reestablishment of traditional differentials.) What distinguishes a period of inflation from a more normal state is a change in the degree of importance of these three influences. During a period of inflation, increases in wages made as a result of adjustments of wage structure become more important than the cost-of-living or productivity factors. This is so because it is the essence of a period of inflation that wage relationships become distorted and require readjustment.

Those dynamic aspects of a wage inflation which can be separated from the general influence of price increases occur in the following manner. Specific situations involving favorable economic circumstance (e.g., manpower shortages in specific industries, areas, or occupations) result in sudden increases in wage rates which exceed the rate of increase in the recent past. These increases are transmitted to other sectors through a variety of mechanisms, as described below. The result is an acceleration of the rate of wage increases in the aggregate. The mechanisms of wage transmission include, but are not limited to, the four following.[8] First, pattern-following in collective bargaining (involving any of the behavioral relationships among wage rates described above) tends to transmit new levels of wages through the economy. Second, employers seeking to prevent the pirating of men by other employers may offer or put into effect wage increases designed to reestablish previous wage relationships. As firms in certain areas or industries bid against each other for manpower, raising rates without necessarily solving the manpower problems, substantial distortions are created in the traditional structure of wages involving other employers, area, industries, or occupations. This process, occuring at the firm or industry level, is often self-defeating when done by firms generally and is a very substantial contributor to inflationary pressures. Third, it is common among large firms, especially those with many nonunion employees, to participate in groups which survey compensation practices locally. This exchange of information allows each firm to maintain its desired relationship with respect to the other firms. The wage comparison by employers, often formalized in groups which meet periodically, serves to transmit wage increases among sectors of the economy, much as does collective bargaining. Fourth, increases for certain occupations in some industries may be transmitted to other industries and other occupations by their effect on wage levels paid workers in the same occupations in other industries. John Dunlop has referred to a group of "key" jobs which affect the rates of other jobs.[9] Often these key jobs are those with external counterparts. Patterns of wage increase in other industries may be transmitted throughout an industry through the mechanism of certain strategic occupations. In no sense are these mechanisms of transmission of wage adjustments extraneous to labor market phenomena. In no sense are they autonomous influences of wage determination. These patterns of wage interrelationships are, on the contrary, integral elements of the functioning of labor markets. Once wage adjustments have begun to be transmitted through these systems, substantial off-setting influences are required to inhibit their operation, if indeed, they can be inhibited successfully.

The above description of the inflationary process suggests that a moderate wage inflation is the result of normal patterns of wage determination responding to inflationary pressures in the economic environment. In periods of moderate inflation, institutional arrangements are rarely affected, and economic forces are transmitted by traditional methods.[10] However, even the normal processes of wage determination in our economy are very complex. The aggregate effect of wage adjustments results from interactions among specific product and labor markets and between both real and monetary economic influences. The processes are, in fact, so complicated that many different results occur as circumstances vary. Different results at different periods of history suggest to some, surprised at the particular configuration of economic and institutional forces at a given time, that somehow the fundamental processes of the economy have altered.[11] On the contrary, in our economy fundamental institutional and economic processes have remained largely unaffected by recent inflationary periods. What has been lacking in most discussions has been a recognition of the full complexity of these processes.

Implications for Wage Stabilization Policy

Wage Interrelationships and the Administration of Wage Policy

There are several major reasons why stabilization authorities must concern themselves with the structure of wages. First, the failure of stabilization policy to provide for adjustments in wage structure invites the occurrence of industrial relations strife. The attitudes of workers, based in large part upon their views of the equity of existing wage structures, are a critical element in negotiations. Where workers are convinced that a proposed wage increase is inequitable by virtue of failing to restore their historic relationship to other workers' wage rates, and are thereby willing to remain on strike or go elsewhere to seek work, it becomes a very difficult task to get an agreement to resume production. There are, of course, certain circumstances in which government intervention may be successful in resolving the dispute. But where the rank-and-file of a union are themselves convinced of the justice of their demands, then public intervention against the union or even against the workers themselves will only exacerbate the worker's impression of the inequity of his situation and will embitter rather than resolve the dispute. Because relative wages occasion very strong feelings, a stabilization policy that attempts to ignore wage structure will soon founder in industrial disputes. Some procedures for allowing increases to readjust wage differentials where appropriate is a sine qua non of stabilization policy.

Second, public authorities attempting to administer a stabilization program without concern for needed adjustments in the wage structure are likely to find themselves with little employer support, especially from those employers directly involved in a particular negotiation. There are two major reasons for employers often supporting attempts by unions to restore traditional wage differentials. In one case, employers may adopt an attitude of fatalism toward demands for increases to an appropriate place in the wage structure. Employers may be of the opinion that it is useless, even with public support, to resist the union demands or that to do so successfully would be to provoke such dissatisfaction and consequent inefficiency on the job that there would be no gain, even economically, from doing so. Thus, the employer becomes, not an ally of the stabilization policy, but a neutral.

Alternatively, employers may actively support, even encourage, a union's demand for a substantial increase to restore traditional wage differentials. This is especially likely to be the case when differentials between competing employers are at issue. If the spread of wages is too broad between employers, the better workers may desert the lower-paying firms, with an adverse impact on those employers larger than the wage differential. This situation may lead to covert action by employers and unions to raise wages through subterfuge where stabilization policy does not permit overt increases. While subterfuge is always a danger in periods of stabilization associated with tight labor markets, it is well for a stabilization board to minimize it, lest others adopt the same practice.

Third, inappropriate relationships in the wage structure, if continued over time, promote the development of inefficient practices in a variety of ways. Workers may tend to move (in the short run) to higher-paying employers and areas, even though demand conditions do not warrant the flows. Firms and areas whose wages are held artificially low may find difficulty attracting workers. This may be especially serious in terms of the recruitment of new workers. Black markets in wages, conditions, and premium payments will tend to develop. The structure of demand, including derived demands for non/labor inputs, may tend to be warped in directions suggested by an unstable wage structure. In general, relative wages, more so than absolute or money wages, serve to channel the forces of demand and supply. Distortions in the structure of relative wages need to be minimized in the interests of economic efficiency.

Finally, the requirements of wage stabilization in the future include as stable a wage structure as can be achieved. Following a period of controls, a stable wage structure is far more likely to allow a resumption of moderate rates of wage increase than a structure in which distortions, perpetuated by public policies, cry for a rapid readjustment at the bargaining table.

In analyzing relative wages a stabilization program must seek to determine which readjustments are appropriate and which are not. Each wage increase may be viewed as having potentially both an equilibrium and a disequilibrium component.[12] The equilibrium component is that portion of the increase which keeps the wage rate in question in its appropriate position with respect to other rates. In a period of wage stabilization the equilibrium component might include a catch-up to related wage rates and some further advance countenanced by stabilization policy (e.g., a cost-of-living increase). The disequilibrium component of an increase involves the degree to which the total increase exceeds the requirements of traditional wage relationships (and perhaps some further increase as permitted by stabilization policy). The disequilibrium component of an increase threatens to establish a new, high level of compensation which other groups of workers or employers might seek to emulate, and should be disallowed by a stabilization board.

In conclusion, it should be noted that the comparison of wage rates which occurs in the process of wage determination is not in itself an unstabilizing influence in the economy. Quite the contrary. Wage adjustments based on preserving traditional wage relationships with other groups of workers (as opposed to efforts to take all the market will bear, or to establish new high rates of increase) are in themselves a stabilizing influence, especially if the negotiations involving pattern-setting wages can be controlled by stabilization authorities. There is, therefore, no long-run purpose for public policy to seek to discourage wage comparisons as a basis of negotiations. However, the most serious problems of stabilization occur when patterns in wage determination begin to break apart, and each adjustment as it occurs establishes a new level of money wages. Wage patterns, when they are operating, exert a stabilizing influence in many situations, in that they limit the rate of wage increase, keep the structure of relative wages in adjustment, and also allow retardation in the rate of increase as economic circumstances or controls require. When patterns collapse, or need reforming, the most difficult problems of stabilization occur.

The Effect of Distortions in Relative Wages on the Performance of a Stabilization Program

Distortions in the wage structure create a special set of problems for wage stabilization efforts. Often there is no practical choice for stabilization authorities, for the reasons given above, but to allow adjustments in the structure of wages where merited. The degree of distortion in the structure of wages, when a stabilization mechanism is imposed, is, therefore, a major determinant of the degree to which wage increases can be constrained and the period of time necessary to achieve a target rate of increase in wages on average. If there is little distortion in the wage structure, restraint can be applied across the board and the desired retardation in the average rate of wage increases achieved rapidly (presuming, of course, effective administration of the stabilization machinery). For example, this had been the situation when controls were applied during World War II. If the wage structure is highly distorted, however, a substantial volume of adjustments in relative wages may be required, limiting the degree of retardation in the rate of increase in wages which can be achieved immediately. The greater the distortion of the relative wage structure, the longer the time period that will be necessary to achieve the desired stability in the economy. There is no escape from this practical situation. It follows that the best method of controlling a wage inflation is to respond in its earliest stages, before the inevitable distortions in relative wages develop. In formulating policy, therefore, it is of critical importance to have some knowledge not only of the average magnitude of wage increases occurring, but of the structure of wages as well. The degree of maladjustment in relative wages is a primary determinant of the potential performance of a stabilization program.

It may be useful to offer an arithmetic example of the influence of wage structure on the average rate of wage increase. Imagine a two-sector economy, both sectors of the same size. For convenience in exposition, let us examine two extreme cases. In one case, wage increases in each sector were 10 percent, and the average was 10 percent. In the other case, wage increases in one sector were 20 percent, but there were no increases in the other sector so that the average was 10 percent also. This situation might result from any of a number of causes, including nonsynchronization of the timing of wage adjustments. Presume further that each sector normally had a wage level bearing some traditional cents-per-hour or percentage relationship to the other. Now, in the first case the succeeding year finds the sectors in their appropriate wage relationship; but the second case does not. Imagine that a wage stabilization program is adopted in the second year. In the first case the target level of stabilization could be fixed at whatever rate was generally acceptable to labor and management in the two sectors, the public and the government. Perhaps it might be 4 or 5 percent. But, in the second case, the sector left behind in the first year will expect an increase of 20 percent, so that even if the other sector gets no increase at all in the second year, the average increase will be very difficult to hold below 10 percent for a second year. It is in this manner that transitory distortions in wage structure directly affect the rate of increase of money wages in the aggregate.

Unfortunately, there has been little academic and public discussion of the role of relative wage adjustments in the inflationary process and of the problems distortions in the wage structure present for stabilization authorities. What little discussion has occurred has been debased by the interpretation of adjustments in wage structure as a moral issue. Because it has been customary to refer to wage structure adjustments as "equity" adjustments, observers have too often adopted a condescending attitude toward their significance. "Equity, like beauty, lies in the eye of the beholder," writes one commentator.[13] And a prominent economist has been quoted as saying that wage structure adjustments "should not be dignified as 'equity'. I don't view it as equity that, when one chicken gets out of the coop, all the others have to be let out, too."[14] But, though some may view adjustment of relative wages primarily as a matter of fairness, there are also involved substantial economic considerations, grounded in concern for the income distribution, for allocation of labor, and for productive efficiency. Furthermore, the determination of the magnitude of an "equity" adjustment is not a matter of the application of an inexact moral judgment. Rather, formal symbolic representation of the interrelationships among wage rates allows rigorous definition of wage structure adjustments. For example, if the traditional relationship between two rates is as follows:

(1) $$W_1 = \gamma W_2,$$

then, in a dynamic context,

(2) $$\Delta W_{1t} = \gamma(W_{2t} - W_{2t-1}).$$

So that the "equity" adjustment involving the wage rate identified as W_1 is quantitatively defined to be the proportion γ times the difference in the wage rate identified as W_2 between two time periods.

If wage structure adjustments are to be allowed as exceptions to the general stabilization criterion for wage increases, then the basic problem presented to stabilization authorities is the determination as to which adjustments are appropriate and which are not. If a group of workers assert that an increase, larger than generally permitted, is required to return them to some position in the wage structure, against what standards is the claim to be measured? Historically, a number of specific criteria have been established by stabilization boards for the purpose of permitting adjustments in wage structure. One of the most common criterion has been that, where a rather clearly defined wage structure exists, primary reliance is placed on historical patterns in wage relationships. It is incumbent upon the workers and employers involved to demonstrate that the wages in question have been in a particular position with respect to the wage structure generally in the firm, industry, and area, or with respect to a particular wage rate with which there is a peculiar relationship at the workplace. The matter of an alleged pattern in the wage structure is thus made a matter of historical fact to be clearly demonstrated—not simply asserted.

Where a demonstration of a historical relationship can be made, judgment must be used by stabilization authorities as to whether other factors are such as to support the claimed adjustment. Very often the evidence from the wage structure will not be conclusive in itself. Traditional wage relationships may have been distorted in some respects but not in others. Such difficult situations require careful judgment by persons expert in the matter of wage relationships and defy reduction to any simple formulas. Another issue involves how complete readjustment of traditional differentials is appropriate. The purpose of placing substantial reliance on historical data regarding the wage structure is not to return all wages to their exact position of several years past. Wage structures are evolving systems and cannot be frozen at any point nor returned to the form of a previous period without careful consideration of the economic and industrial relations consequences. Therefore, the appropriate function of stabilization authorities is to seek to allow each group of workers to assume a position in a structure of wages most conducive to efficient economic practices, industrial relations peace, and future wage stability. Again, this function requires careful judgment in individual situations.

Models of the Stabilization Process

This section provides a mathematical expression of some of the lessons for stabilization policy suggested by this chapter's analysis of wage interrelationships and wage determination. A summary of the chapter is also provided by this more formal presentation of ideas expressed above. The reader will recall that two basic conclusions emerge from the analysis of preceding pages for stabilization purposes. First, the degree of wage restraint which can be applied in a given year must be adjusted to the amount of distortion in the wage structure existing at the time controls are applied. The greater the degree of distortion, the less stringent controls can be in restraining the rate of increase of wages. Put another way, the greater the degree of distortion, the longer the period of time required to reduce the rate of wage increase to a specific target level. Second, except in circumstances with very unusual structural characteristics in the relations among wage rates, the achievement of a target average rate of increase in wages does not imply that all individual wages should increase at that rate. Stabilization would normally require that leading, or pattern-setting, rates be more tightly restrained than the average and that wages below their appropriate relationship to others be allowed increases above the average rate.

We may now give these concepts a brief mathematical formulation. In an earlier section of this chapter the relationship of individual wage adjustments to the weighted average rate of increase in wages was given as follows:

$$(1) \qquad \frac{\Delta W_t}{W_{t-1}} = \sum_i e_i \left(\frac{\Delta W_{it}}{W_{it-1}} \right).$$

Interrelationships among wages (W_i) and wage changes (ΔW_i) may be described by any of a variety of expressions, also discussed above.

Consider, for example a situation in which there were two wage rates $(W_i, i = 1, 2)$ related as in the following expression:

$$(2) \qquad \Delta W_1 = \Delta W_2$$

(i.e., a strict pattern of the same cents-per-hour increase, a not unusual pattern in wage determination) and

$$(3) \qquad \Delta W_2 = f(x_{2i}), \ x_{2i}$$

are extraneous variables specific to the sector $i = 2$. Then, from (1), by substitution,

$$\frac{\Delta W_t}{W_{t-1}} = e_1 \left(\frac{\Delta W_{1t}}{W_{1t-1}} \right) + e_2 \left(\frac{\Delta W_{2t}}{W_{2t-1}} \right),$$

and further

$$\frac{\Delta W_t}{W_{t-1}} = e_1 \left(\frac{f(x_{2i})}{W_{1t-1}} \right) + e_2 \left(\frac{f(x_{2i})}{W_{2t-1}} \right).$$

Let c be the target rate of increase for the weighted average of wage increases $\Delta W_t / W_{t-1}$, so that

$$c = e_1 \left(\frac{f(x_{2i})}{W_{1t-1}} \right) + e_2 \left(\frac{f(x_{2i})}{W_{2t-1}} \right).$$

Then, to achieve c, $f(x_{2i}) = \Delta W_2 = \Delta W_1$ must assume the value:

(4) $$f(x_{2i}) = \frac{c(W_{1t-1} W_{2t-1})}{e_1 W_{2t-1} + e_2 W_{1f-1}}$$

Whether or not this value can be assumed is, of course, a question of the values of x_{2i}. Were the equation (3) specified in detail, and were some estimate as to the probable values of the x_{2i} available, then the feasibility of the target rate of increase (c) could be evaluated and other aspects of stabilization policy adjusted as desired.

In any case, however, the resultant increase in W_1 and W_2 will not yield the same percentage increases—necessarily equal to (c) if the average rate is to be (c)—unless the condition that $W_{1t-1} = W_{2t-1}$ is met. There is, of course, no necessity for this to be so. Further, it is not required to achieve the target rate (c) for the average increase in wages that the percentage increases in the two wage rates be equal. It is, in fact, quite irrelevant.

But what are the consequences of requiring that the percentage increase in each of the two wages separately be equal? For a target rate (c) to be achieved, both rates must increase by that same percentage (c). Yet, if $W_{1t-1} \neq W_{2t-1}$, then this can be achieved only if the behavioral relationship (2) is violated. The consequences of violating behavioral relationships of this nature have been discussed above. While stabilization authorities may choose, for various reasons, to disregard some such relationships, to do so on a wholesale scale is to invite disaster. This is especially irresponsible when it is evident, even from a simple model, that stabilization does not require this approach.

What formulation of wage interrelationships is consistent with equal percentage increases in all cases? At least two instances are apparent: first, if wages follow an equal cents-per-hour pattern starting from the same base (which necessarily implies a circumstance of equal hourly wages); second, if the pattern of wage relationships is equal-percentage increases. There is, it follows, a sense in which a stabilization policy based on a simple percentage increase for all or most individual rates is simply the assertion that the stabilization authorities believe the general form of wage relationships is equal-percentage increases (which it certainly is not) or is an assertion that wage relationships should assume that form.

The introduction of much more elaborate wage models does nothing to alter these observations. Consider, for example, the following relationships

$$(5) \qquad \Delta W_1 = \gamma \Delta W_2 + f(x_{i1}),$$

and,

$$(6) \qquad \Delta W_2 = g(x_{i2}),$$

or even a simultaneous relationship:

$$(7) \qquad \Delta W_1 = \gamma \Delta W_2 + f(x_{i1}),$$

and

$$(8) \qquad \Delta W_2 = \gamma \Delta W_1 + g(x_{i2})$$

then, as before, the three equations (1), (5), (6), or (1), (7), (8), can be solved for the increases W_1 and W_2 such that a target average rate of increase (c) is achieved. Again, only under highly unusual circumstances will the resultant absolute increases in each money wage involve equal-percentage increases in each wage. The introduction of complications such as lagged relationships and/or numerous wages ($i = 1, 2, \ldots$ and various types of interrelationships among wages only serves to demonstrate further the restrictiveness of the conditions under which a policy of enunciating equal-percentage increases in all wages could be effective in achieving a target average rate of increase without violating, on a general basis, behavioral relations among wages.

The model may be put to more elaborate usages. For example, given a structure of lags in wage adjustments, stabilization authorities might seek to minimize the average rate of wage increase, subject to the constraints embodied in the structural relations in the model. Consider a simple example. Let

$$(9) \qquad \Delta W_{1t} = W_{2t} - W_{2,t-3} \equiv \Delta W_{2,t-3},$$

(10) $\Delta W_{2t} = f(x_{2it})$,

then, by substitution in (1),

$$\frac{\Delta W_t}{W_{t-1}} = e_1 \left(\frac{\Delta W_{2, t-3}}{W_{1t-1}} \right) + e_2 \left(\frac{\Delta W_{2t}}{W_{2t}} \right).$$

Now, minimize $\Delta W_t/W_{t-1}$, subject to (9), (10), by finding values for x_{2it}, such that $\Delta W_t/W_{t-1}$ is minimized ($x_{2it} - 1, 2 \ldots$ are, of course, constraints, not variables in time t). If values of x_{2it} can be achieved such that $\Delta W_{2t} = 0$, then W_{1t} will be minimized at $W_{2t-1} - W_{2t-3}$ (since $W_{2t} = W_{2t-1}$), and $\Delta W_t/W_{t-1}$ is minimized. If ΔW_{2t} can be made less than zero, a further reduction in the average rate of increase can be achieved; but rollbacks of existing wages are very difficult.

Part III The Administration
of Controls

The ability of combining facts is a much rarer gift that that of discerning them.

Louis Agassiz, "Evolution and Permanence of Type"

6. Elements in the Administration of a Stabilization Program

Organizing the Administration of Wage Stabilization

The conduct of a program of wage controls is a complex undertaking, involving the coordination of many separate elements. The design of various elements of a program and their interrelationships is the topic of this and the two following chapters. Some elements of a program are central to its overall design and operation, others to its detailed administration. In this chapter the overall design of the program is examined, and in the next two chapters the detailed administration of a wage stabilization program is considered. The topic of this chapter, the development and coordination of the major distinct elements of a stabilization program, may be referred to as the organization of the program. For analytic purposes, a program of controls should be conceived as analogous to a set of tools designed and employed by public authorities in an attempt to influence the behavior of employers and employees in directions which will contribute to the achievement of stabilization objectives. This chapter is concerned with what instruments are necessary to a successful stabilization program, how they are best designed, and how employed.

The first sections of this chapter concern the internal administrative structure of a wage control program. Included are discussions of the degree of self-administration of a program, comprehensive versus partial controls, a case-by-case versus a regulatory approach to wage stabilization, the degree and form of decentralization of the program, and the treatment of deferred increases. We begin with a discussion of the role of self-administration by business and labor of a controls program.

The Degree of Self-Administration

Self-administration essentially involves the application of the policies and regulations of a stabilization program to individual situations by the parties directly involved: the employer and, where appropriate, the union. Self-administration may take a number of forms, involving considerable oversight by stabilization authorities on the one hand, or almost none on the other. At one extreme, employers and unions may have the right to initiate wage increases within stabilization guidelines but subject to an immediate review by stabilization authorities and a possible disallowance of any increases made in excess of those permitted. At the other extreme, self-administration may involve no oversight by stabilization authorities other than that offered by general compliance or enforcement activities. Depending on the types of wage adjustments involved, it has been common in the United States to apply various degrees of self-administration. However, with respect to major aspects of the stabilization program, the degree of self-administration pursued in the different periods of wage control has been quite different.

Self-administration in varying degrees has been pursued by stabilization authorities because it appears to offer two major administrative advantages. First, self-administration lightens the administrative load on the stabilization board and its subordinate agencies. Rather than having to consider all wage and fringe benefit adjustments, the board effectively delegates to employers and unions the authority to administer aspects of its policy. Since the potential administrative load of a stabilization board in the absence of any self-administration is enormous, self-administration is necessary if the staffing and cost of a stabilization program is not to be prohibitive. During World War II, in which only minor reliance was placed on self-administration, the NWLB and its regional and industrial branches involved, at the peak of its activity in early 1945, the services of 2,613 full-time employees, 1,162 part-time or per diem employees, and 618 persons who served without compensation.[1] During the Korean period considerably greater reliance was placed on self-administration. Nevertheless, at its peak employment, in September 1952, the WSB had some 500 employees in Washington and another 1,000 in the field, and a budget for 1952 of some fifteen million dollars (including payments for services by other government agencies.)[2] During 1971–72 the Pay Board made the greatest use of self-administration attempted in the three periods. By relying on the Internal Revenue Service as a field agency, the Pay Board limited its total staff to some 250 personnel with a correspondingly limited budget. The minimization of the bureaucracy involved in the 1971–72 program was considered by the administration as a major objective, and one which was pursued with considerable success.[3] Second, self-administration of stabilization regulations eliminates delay in the processing of applications for wage increases and so promotes the public acceptance of the program.

What are the disadvantages of reliance on self-administration? First, self-administration in certain economic environments can encourage purposeful noncompliance with stabilization regulations by providing a device to disguise noncompliance. Although documented cases of noncompliance were very rare in 1971–72, yet industrial relations practitioners, stabilization authorities, and labor and management representatives often knew of various self-applications of the regulations which were extremely questionable, at best. Second, self-administration provides no check upon nonwillful but erroneous application of the regulations by private parties. Third, self-administration which is subject to later oversight by a stabilization agency places the agency in the very undesirable and difficult posture of trying to roll back a wage or benefit increase which has already taken effect. While some few such cases may be effectively handled by stabilization authorities, the capacity to return many situations to an earlier status is very restricted. Fourth, self-administration allows employers and unions to conceal aspects of their relationship from public authorities which might determine the attitudes of those authorities as to what increases are approvable, or even might suggest modification of regulations. Self-administration thereby considerably reduces the amount of information about wage rates and relationships and other aspects of industrial relations which reach the board. (Post-hoc reporting of adjustments is only a limited substitute for the arguments and evidence which can be required to accompany proposals for wage increases.) This large-scale limitation of information reaching the board is potentially dangerous; a board in substantial ignorance promises to be increasingly ineffectual as the period of stabilization extends.

Given these potential disadvantages of self-administration, what factors affect the degree of self-administration which is appropriate in a stabilization program? There are three major factors which determine an answer to this question. First, self-administration is most hazardous when the economic climate offers the greatest incentives for avoidance or noncompliance with regulations. This is not simply a matter of the aggregate economic climate but of the situation in specific sectors and subsectors of the economy as well. For even in a slack economy (and especially one in which an economic recovery is underway), some sectors will become expansive more rapidly than others. It is important that self-administration in these sectors not contribute to an emerging pattern of noncompliance. The second factor is closely related to the first. Self-administration is most dangerous when it serves as a screen to limit information reaching the board and so disguises from the board emerging pressures on wage levels in specific areas and sectors. The more a period is one of economic transformation, the greater the need of stabilization authorities for detailed information as to trends in the economy. Further, the longer the potential period in which stabilization will be pursued, the more likely will be substantial alterations in the economic environment—and the greater will be the board's need to monitor in detail what is happening in the economy. Third, self-administration is most inappropriate when it is difficult to provide specific, unambiguous regulations for application by employers and unions. During the Korean War, for example, regulations were relatively clear. The WSB adopted separate policies for general wage increases, cost-of-living increases, paid holidays, shift differentials, and so on, so that private parties could apply policies specific to each of many elements of collective bargaining or wage and salary administration in the nonunion situation. In addition, regional offices of the WSB, also tripartite and expert in industrial relations, were available to provide guidance. During 1971–72, however, regulations which attempted to encompass too many elements in a single percentage guideline figure resulted in an extraordinarily complex set of rules, often almost unintelligible to employers and unions. Further, guidance was available only from local offices of the Internal Revenue Service—a totally nonexpert agency in industrial relations.

In conclusion, self-administration can be pushed too far in the search for administrative savings and public acceptance. When pursued too far, self-administration can be destructive of the stabilization program, both by encouraging noncompliance and by insulating the stabilization board from the reality of labor and product market circumstances. As is common in failings in a stabilization program, the consequences of too great reliance on self-administration in a generally slack economic environment and in a relatively brief program (of one to two years) can often be tolerated. But the best or most appropriate degree of self-administration can only be determined by careful judgment measured against the existing and expected economic climate, patterns of wage regulations, and expected future course of the stabilization program.

Comprehensive Versus Partial Controls

Often in the United States it has been urged that controls be applied only in certain industries or to certain employers and unions. The advantages of partial controls are argued to be several, including simplicity in application and minimization of administrative machinery, costs, and delays. Two particular forms of selective controls have occasioned most experimentation: controls by industry, and controls by size of employer. Arguments for selective controls by industry have generally been unavailing, with two exceptions: in the construction industry and, more generally, among industries in a period of gradual decontrol.

Yet arguments for more extensive selective controls on an industry basis have been advanced. For example, in 1944 the Montgomery Ward Company argued the inappropriateness of the enforcement of a NWLB order against the company because the company employees were not engaged in war production. The government stressed the interrelationships of wages and industrial relations policies as justification for the jurisdiction of the NWLB over MontgomeryWard and was upheld by the courts.[4]

Further, in some situations attempts have been made by unions and/or employers to restrict wage controls to industries where price controls are also applied. For example, the Defense Production Act of 1950 exempted from controls prices of newspapers, professional services, public utility services, and insurance rates. The WSB, then chaired by George Taylor, sought an opinion from its chief counsel as to the impact of these exemptions from price controls on the wage control program. The opinion, and the policy of the board, was that wage controls were not prohibited by the exemption from price controls.[5] The board was concerned that interrelated elements of the wage stabilization program not be disrupted by purely price-related considerations.

The proposed exemption of small employers from controls has constituted a most serious problem for wage stabilization authorities in all periods of stabilization. The arguments customarily advanced for such exemption are that conformity with regulations is an unreasonably expensive burden for small companies; that the administrative burden on the stabilization program itself of monitoring and acting on the petitions of small employers is unreasonably large; and that small employers set no wage patterns in any case, and so may be safely ignored. The rejoinder to these arguments customarily includes the following points. In some industries small employers are customarily grouped in associations for the purpose of collective bargaining or establishing wages and other industrial relations policies, and these associations must be treated as if they were single, large employers; regardless of whether associations exist, in many industries or areas small employers compete with larger companies for employees and for business, and excessive increases in compensation paid to their employees may be as destabilizing to wage relationships as increases in cases involving larger employers. The destabilizing influence of small employers is especially marked in situations exhibiting any of three characteristics: considerable competition in the product market, tight labor markets (that is, competition for workers), and a strategic position for the small employer (as a subcontractor whose employees intermingle with those of larger employers). Therefore, though attempts might be made to lessen the administrative burden on small companies, an exemption from controls per se is argued to be inappropriate.

The arguments against exemptions for small employers have rarely been convincing at the outset of a stabilization program, and officials in charge of the stabilization program have normally exempted small employers from controls. During World War II, for example, General Order No. 4 of the NWLB (adopted October 9, 1942) exempted wage adjustments made by employers of not more than eight individuals. Experience under this order, however, suggested the necessity of exceptions to the exemption. Thus, the order was amended repeatedly to reintroduce controls into situations involving small employers. By August 29, 1945, when General Order No. 4 was repealed, the list of exceptions had grown to sixty-eight in number. It included such items as the tool and die industry, the shoe repair industry in California, cotton gin employees, photoengravers, the automotive repair industry in various places, machine shop workers on the West Coast, potato shippers in Maine, the jewelry industry in Albuquerque, New Mexico, and others.[6] The experience of exemption, then exception to the exemption, was repeated to a small degree in 1971-72. The Cost of Living Council wished to exempt small employers on as wide a basis as possible. Consequently, a decision of the council exempted all employees or employee units of sixty workers or less from controls.[7] Employers in construction were excluded from the original exception, but state and local government units involving small numbers of employees were not (despite a contrary recommendation by the public members of the Pay Board). Within a few months of the council's action to exempt small governmental units, it felt required to except them from the exemption because of the increasingly apparent wage interrelationships between small and larger units.

What judgments can be offered as to best procedure for handling the matter of a small-employer exemption from wage controls? Certainly, both theoretical considerations and practical experience indicate that a *general* exception for small business is inappropriate. Small business is not, by virtue of its size alone, insignificant or unimportant to national wage policy, either in the aggregate or individually. In various states of the economy (involving the position of particular industries, occupations, and areas as well as macroeconomic considerations) the potentially destabilizing impact of small business on wage patterns is very great, especially in certain industries. Hence, the wage performance of small businesses must be monitored as carefully as that of larger companies. Where experience indicates an insignificant impact, the administrative burdens of controls may be relaxed through reliance on self-administration or even limited exemptions. The error to be avoided in public policy is to presume initially that there will be no destabilizing pressures from small business, and so to relinquish controls to an unwarranted degree. Yet, because of the arguments presented above in favor of exemption for small business and the political effectiveness of small business with the Congress, the temptation to exempt small employers without careful investigation of the advisability of such a step is always present.

A Case-by-Case Versus a Regulatory Approach

At the risk of some oversimplification, a contrast may be drawn between two approaches to administration of a wage stabilization program: a case-by-case approach versus a regulatory approach. To a degree, stabilization authorities must choose between the two in establishing whatever mix of the procedures is desired. The case-by-case approach may be characterized as eschewing the establishment of specific rules or principles except in the most general sense and placing reliance instead on the adjudication of individual cases on their merits. Out of the accumulation of decisions in specific cases are developed policies applicable in other instances. Potential issues which do not come before the board in specific cases are not decided. Precedents may be utilized by the board, or, as experience accumulates, discarded. The regulatory approach, in contrast, involves the preparation of general rules designed to cover most or all foreseeable situations and the minimization of consideration of particular cases. A stabilization program necessarily involves application of both procedures, so that the choice between the two approaches is primarily one of degree of emphasis.

The major advantages of a case-by-case approach are five in number. First, considering the full record of cases which come before a board provides an unequaled opportunity for education of the members of the board and its staff in the complexities of wage patterns, practices, and interrelationships. No individual or small group of individuals in this country possesses a comprehensive understanding of existing patterns of wage relationships and the changes occurring therein, particularly in the absence of continual direct involvement in wage-setting. Further, since wage determination is only one aspect of the economic decisions confronting management and labor (changes in working rules are fully as significant to cost increases and potential impact on prices, and working-rules changes are often intimately related to wage adjustments), only a review of the entire context of wage adjustments in individual situations can convey the full range of the economic factors involved in a wage decision. Second, as a corollary of the first characteristic, a case-by-case approach allows decisions on wage adjustments to be made in the context of a full understanding of the implications of wage behavior for other economic variables, such as employment, prices, and so on. The likelihood is that the overall purpose of economic stabilization is best served by such a comprehensive review. Third, a case-by-case approach supports tripartitism. As Archibald Cox has pointed out, "Partisan [i.e., labor and management] members of a tripartite board can acquiesce in a policy developed through a series of specified decisions, some of which are favorable to one side and some to the other, even though they are unwilling to give express approval to the same policy when stated in a single document."[8]

Fourth, a case-by-case approach permits subtle shifts in policy when they become necessary, without the elaborate and often controversial task of revising or enlarging detailed regulations. This capacity of a board to shift policy is increasingly advantageous the more extended the period of controls.[9] Finally, the most often used (historically) advantage of a case-by-case approach is the capacity it affords to depart from general rules when the peculiar conditions of a specific situation require it. "The NWLB," wrote public member Edwin E. Witte, "decides every case on its own facts." In consequence, Witte added, the board may abandon what seems general policy because of the peculiar circumstances of an individual case.[10] In more recent years, both the WSB and the Pay Board similarly retained the discretion to handle some individual cases outside the automatic application of general regulations.

The advantages claimed for the regulatory approach are in some instances the reverse of those claimed for the case-by-case method—so that advantages of the one are perceived as disadvantages of the other. Four supposed advantages may be listed for the regulatory approach. First, this approach minimizes the substantial administrative task of voluminous processing.[11] Even where a board desires to proceed on a case-by-case basis, it cannot do so in a comprehensive fashion but must utilize individual cases to establish or modify policy for application to other cases. The volume of wage applications always threatens to engulf a wage board, so that a definite requirement for a substantial reliance on a regulatory approach is inevitable. Second, a regulatory procedure permits a stabilization board to avail itself of the advantage of a formal rule-making procedure which may involve a review process (e.g., including hearings) prior to the establishment of individual regulations. In contrast, a case-by-case approach is subject to the objection that, if case decisions are intended to be precedent-setting, they should be based on a survey of the problem area generally, not on the merits of particular, perhaps unusual, single case.[12] Third, the regulatory approach tends to create a relatively legalistic atmosphere in the administration of a stabilization program, as opposed to a bargaining or problem-solving approach. To some, the de jure approach is preferable. For one thing, in such an approach the cooperation among public, employer, and labor members characteristic of a tripartite board is minimized in favor of a more technical application of specific rules. For public members adverse to the difficulties of a tripartite structure, or for an administration opposed to tripartitism, a regulatory approach seems most desirable.

Fourth, a regulatory approach tends to minimize the time, effort, and specialized knowledge required of the public members of a board and its staff, as compared to a case-by-case approach. Under a regulatory procedure, decisions may be more easily delegated to staff, with decisions of policy reserved for the board; such decisions will be made in the rarefied atmosphere of abstractions, without the complexities and ambiguities of real-world situations introduced by specific cases. The demands made by such a mode of operation on the board members themselves are minimized. At the extreme, the functions of board members are reduced from a form of problem-solving in the interests of economic stabilization to one of interpretation and application of rules. Fifth, a regulatory approach tends to relieve a board of any responsibility for dispute settlement by making violation of stabilization policy a matter for after-the-fact enforcement and litigation rather than a matter of assisting collective bargaining and personnel administration to operate in a nondestabilizing fashion.

Historically, there has been from World War II to the present a steadily increasing reliance on comprehensive regulations as the preferred method of administering stabilization and a consequent reduction of the case-by-case procedure to the handling of exceptions only. What can be offered as an evaluation of the trend toward regulations as the primary focus of stabilization policy? The advantages of the regulatory approach have just been described. But has the increasing use of regulations in wage control uncovered any serious limitations on the method? There are, perhaps, two such limitations apparent in the experience of 1971-72. First, the regulatory approach engenders an excessive degree of legalism in the stabilization program. Second, regulations and the ensuing legalism become handicaps to actually affecting the decisions of employers and unions in the wage stabilization area.

Wage determination is a complex process, a point stressed repeatedly in these pages. Its complexity is never more evident than in the process of drafting regulations to attempt to restrict ways in which employers and unions can provide and increase compensation. The result of attempting to create comprehensive regulations is generally to develop so complicated a set of rules and exceptions, priorities and precedences, that the rulings of stabilization boards become almost undecipherable to persons other than lawyers (if to them), and the standards of success in stabilization become application and interpretation of the rules rather than the adjustment of actual problems in wage-setting within the context of the stabilization program's objectives. Many examples of the tendency toward excessive legalism in the 1971-72 program could be given, but let us select only one. The following is Pay Board Ruling 1972-53, "Essential Employees":

DEPARTMENT OF THE TREASURY
INTERNAL REVENUE SERVICE
Pay Board Ruling 1972-53
ESSENTIAL EMPLOYEES
   Facts: An employer pays his employees a flat rate of compensation. In addition, the employer has a written incentive plan which qualifies under the Economic Stabilization Regulations, 6 C.F.R. §201.74(a) (1972) as an "established plan."
   For the past several years, the employer has had difficulty in both retaining his old employees and recruiting new ones. Accordingly, he desires to raise his employees' salaries under the exception found in the Economic Stabilization Regulations, 6 C.F.R. §201.11(a)(2) (1972).
   Issue: Does incentive compensation paid pursuant to a §201.74(a) "established plan" constitute wages and salaries, and as such may it be increased if the Pay Board grants the employer a §201.11(a)(2) exception?

Ruling: No. Although wages and salaries are defined by the Economic Stabilization Regulations, 6 C.F.R. §201.3 (1972), to include incentive pay, 6 C.F.R. §201.71(b) (1972) states that subpart D (Executive and Variable Compensation) shall control when it is in conflict with the §201.3 definition of wages and salaries. Therefore, the revised §201.72(a) definition of wages and salaries found in subpart D controls. This definition states that the term "wages and salaries" has the same meaning "as under §201.3 except that items constituting incentive compensation*** *shall not be treated as wages and salaries****.*" (Emphasis added.) It follows that the employer may not treat incentive compensation which is paid pursuant to a §201.74(a) "established plan" as wages and salaries if he is granted an exception pursuant to §201.11(a)(2).

It hardly need be said that an employer, union representative, or employee studying such a document would have no alternative but to ask his legal counsel for an opinion as to what it means. And the reader should recall that this ruling was not one on a particular case, so that the recipients of the ruling could be expected to be familiar with the issues and points of law involved; the ruling was one issued as an explanation of Pay Board policy for the edification of and application by the public.

Thus did wage stabilization policy in the United States assume, finally, a character long urged upon it: that of a de jure proceeding involving only the most minimal concerns for the needs of collective bargaining or personnel administration generally. No longer was the board involved in settlement of collective bargaining disputes, no longer did it primarily apply general principles of stabilization to individual cases, rather the board now drafted detailed regulations and applied them on an increasingly legalistic basis, far removed in mind and spirit from the problems of wage adjustment in the workplace. Two further consequences of the increased legalism of the stabilization program should be noted. To a board very much concerned for the application of rules, and to a degree insulated from the complexities and confusions of the industrial workplace, compliance with regulations tends to carry more importance than the implications of various actions for the stabilization program. Rather than seeking to understand a problem offered by an employer or union and to resolve it in a way consistent with economic stabilization, the board and its agents too often apply narrow rules and allow the spirit (and long-run interests) of the stabilization program to be violated. In general, the letter of the stabilization regulation may come to dominate its spirit when the regulatory approach is pressed too far.[13] Finally, a legalistic stabilization program invites legal challenges. If regulations are such that only lawyers can hope to decipher them, if disputes over interpretation of narrow points can only be resolved in the courts, and if the failure to work out problems means that there is no acceptance of a decision by the affected parties, then virtually all decisions of the board invite challenges by those with the financial resources to go to court. And while litigation is an inevitable accompaniment of a stabilization program to some degree, it is best for stabilization authorities to minimize it, lest the program be picked to pieces in the courts and its policies rest in uncertainty while the delays involved in litigation continue.

Judgment must, I believe, conclude that the regulatory approach to wage stabilization has been pushed too far. If World War II represented too case-oriented a controls procedure, involving too large a bureaucracy, as many believe, then the opposite extreme has now been reached. It is time to return in the application of wage stabilization to a measured intermixture of general principles, regulations, and case-by-case actions. To a greater degree than in the Korean period and in 1971-72, stabilization policies should be established and modified on the basis of careful review of individual situations. It cannot be denied that at the outset of a stabilization program the development of policy through individual cases is a somewhat slower process, so that it is often bypassed in the rush to establish a stabilization program before a freeze expires. Consequently, it is an important function of political authorities to conduct a degree of forward planning toward the initiation of a stabilization program, so that a wage stabilization board is permitted the extra measure of time necessary to do its job well. Where little time is available, stabilization authorities are nonetheless best advised to provide as large a role for case-by-case policy development as is feasible.

Decentralization of Policy and Administration

Wage stabilization lends itself to decentralization on either policy or administrative dimensions. In addition, administrative decentralization may involve either industrial or geographic elements, or both. Historically, experiments have been conducted with all types of decentralization: policy, administrative, industrial, and geographic. As might be expected, there are both advantages and disadvantages to various types of decentralization. The issues which concern us here may be grouped into three categories. First, should there be both separate policies and administrative bodies? Second, should there be separate administrative bodies specific to separate groups? If such administrative bodies were to be established, by what means should they be coordinated? Third, should there be separate policies for separate industries or geographic areas? It will not be possible here to discuss these issues in detail. We may, however, examine briefly the merits and limitations of various arrangements and determine the factors on which the decisions as to the appropriate degree of decentralization depend. The special features of the industry most often distinguished by separate policy and administrative devices—the construction industry—will not be discussed.

The question of decentralization of policy-making and standards is much simpler to resolve than the issue of administrative decentralization. In the United States, the requirement of equal treatment for all sectors of the economy and for all geographic regions has always argued for a single national policy toward wage stabilization. The one exception has been that often some groups are exempted from stabilization requirements totally. In some instances, exemptions may be made for low-wage workers or small employers. In the most common case, fairness argues for a single stabilization policy. However, different applications may be fully consistent with a single policy. That is, applications of a single policy may require adjustments to the peculiar circumstances of individual industries, to avoid problems which might be created by application of policy uniformly in all instances. In general, there should be one overall stabilization policy with such individual applications by industry or area as are necessary to result in a similar degree of rigor in the application of controls in all instances.

The questions of decentralized administration are more difficult than separate applications of policy but are in some instances interrelated with applications of policy. Clark Kerr, summarizing his study of administration of the wage stabilization program of World War II, stated his central conclusion to be that "a chief aim of [stabilization] strategy had to be the neutralization, equalization, containment, and channeling of [wage] pressures, and that administrative organization was an important tactical weapon for these purposes."[14] In Kerr's view, separate administrative organizations for industrial sectors and geographic regions served in part to isolate the various employers and workers in each group from other groups, in order that separate policy treatment might be facilitated. In fact, truly separate policy treatment, as opposed to merely tailored applications of a single policy, could be made possible by separate administration, although it is virtually impossible in a single agency.

The principal advantages of decentralizing administration, other than providing the opportunity for separate policies, are five in number. First, establishment of industry and/or regional boards may remove much of the workload of the national board in Washington, allowing it to devote its energies to policies, to certain major cases, and to dispute settlement. On the other hand, if management of the boards is inadequate, a multiplicity of regional and industry boards can result in great confusion in Washington, where the national board must attempt to coordinate the activities of all the boards established. Second, the creation of regional or industry boards affords an opportunity for the national board to avail itself of persons expert in the wage problems of various sectors or areas. In some portions of the economy, expertise is essential to the appropriate application of policy in individual circumstances. Third, and closely related to the advantage just discussed, subordinate boards provide a means by which representatives of the public (at the board or staff level) may develop an in-depth knowledge of the economics of product and labor markets and of collective bargaining in various industries and regions. Greater benefits of this learning process accrue as the stabilization period lengthens or even after controls are ended. During stabilization, the longer the program continues the more expert private parties become in manipulating regulations and procedures in their own interests. As this situation develops, it becomes critical for the stabilization authorities to have the assistance of persons knowledgeable in the potential stratagems of each major sector. Thus, public representatives who become knowledgeable in the detailed operations of major sectors become an important resource for the entire stabilization program as the program lengthens. Further, in the years following a program, those persons knowledgeable in the behavior of sectors or regions may serve as public representatives in disputes or at other important junctures, may serve to educate Congress and the public to the merits of matters in controversy, and may, ultimately, become important in the design of a new stabilization program. In a very important sense, public representatives on the boards or staffs of stabilization bodies are the essential device of memory for the public and the government with respect to the operation of stabilization programs. Reports and studies regarding stabilization programs are generally poor substitutes for the experience of the individuals who participated in a program.

Fourth, subordinate boards permit, in a tripartite administrative structure, involvement of the leaders of unions and firms in the decisions of the stabilization program which directly affect their organizations. Not only do these leaders bring their competence to deliberations but also the capacity to do a considerable amount to secure acceptance of determinations made by the stabilization machinery. A single national board cannot include directly in its deliberations more than a few representatives of management and labor and so must deal at some distance with the leadership of unions and employers affected by its decisions. Industry or regional boards permit a much wider range of involvement in the stabilization program for management and labor. Finally, subordinate boards increase the flexibility of the stabilization program generally. Additional flexibility is the almost inevitable result of greater time and attention devoted to the problems of particular sectors or regions. The longer the period for which a stabilization program is continued, the more valuable flexibility becomes.

Unfortunately, decentralization in administration may entail substantial disadvantages as well. Foremost among these disadvantages is the difficulty of coordination of the separate boards in their relationship to one another. It is inevitable that applicants to any board will seize upon the supposed policies of other boards as justification for their own claims. It is important, therefore, that the policy of various boards be kept consistent and that apparent inconsistencies be convincingly explained to those who question them. But coordination of several boards is a very difficult task. In part, the difficulty is a result of the volume of subordinate board actions, which constitute an addition to the normal load of central board activities. In part, also, coordination is made difficult by the necessity of reconciling divergent applications of policy by the several boards. During the Korean period, the WSB attempted a program of appraising the operations of regional boards, including regular trips to the regions, screening of regional board minutes, and review of case actions. However, the program was only beginning when the WSB was terminated. In general, as we shall see below, neither the NWLB nor the WSB effectively mastered the coordination of subordinate board activities. A program might, in the end, be imperiled by the failure of coordination; though this was more likely during the Korean period than World War II. Failures of coordination inevitably create or perpetuate misunderstandings of policy. But, more important, failure of coordination, by virtue of the implication of inequitable administration of stabilization among different sectors or regions, must be studiously avoided by a stabilization effort, even at the risk of too little decentralization.

What factors, we may ask, determine the issue of separate versus single administrative responsibility? To what extent should decentralization be carried? Alternatively, one might ask, what factors affect the weighting of advantages against disadvantages of decentralization? There are three primary factors influencing such decisions. First, decentralization is the more necessary the more that the tasks included in stabilization will differ among regions or sectors of the economy. For example, in 1971–72, the general pay-control program was limited to concern for wages and fringes and possessed no jurisdiction over work stoppages or working conditions. In construction, the stabilization program had not only wage restraint responsibilities but those of dispute settlement and working rules as well. A separate agency for construction was all but required by these additional responsibilities, although wage restraint policies in construction were consistent with the general wage policies of the Pay Board. In the future it must be anticipated that wage restraint responsibilities will be coupled with concern for disputes settlement and perhaps changes in the structure of collective bargaining in certain sectors, necessitating separate administrative bodies.

Second, the problems of wage stabilization are sometimes much more difficult in certain sectors or regions. This might be a result of such factors as a much more seriously distorted wage structure, or poor collective bargaining relationships, or special problems of high demand, or even, conversely, high unemployment. In these situations, expert panels may be required to deal effectively with stabilization and related problems. Third, separate industry or regional boards are the more necessary the more that traditional wage relationships must be disrupted as a consequence of other requirements than stabilization itself. For example, during wartime it is often necessary to expand wage or earnings differentials in favor of war production industries, in order to attract or retain manpower, prevent labor disputes, and the like. The regions or sectors so affected can usefully be isolated, to a degree, from other elements of the economy through separate administrative arrangements.

Treatment of Deferred Increases

The treatment of deferred increases was in many respects the outstanding accomplishment of the wage stabilization program of 1971–72. "Deferred increases" is a short, if somewhat imprecise, term which may be used to describe wage or fringe benefit increases agreed to in collective bargaining but scheduled to take effect at a later date than the effective date of a contract (hence the term "deferred"). Deferred increases are, therefore, incremental increases which are to take effect during the term of a collective bargaining agreement. Because there has been considerable reliance on multiyear collective bargaining agreements in American industry, deferred increases are common. The periodicity of deferred increases is not limited to annual intervals. Rather, increments may be scheduled at ten-month intervals, or six-month intervals, or even quarterly. Employers often favor a series of stepped wage increments because it reduces the average cost of the increases, as opposed to a single increase at the outset of the agreement. There is no exact analogue in nonunion companies for the deferred increase, although an existing practice of an employer may be to grant an increase to the workers at some scheduled interval of less than a year. Unlike the employer party to a collective bargaining agreement, however, the nonunion employer normally retains considerable discretion over the amount of increase to be granted. In the parlance of wage stabilization, "deferred increases" has an even more specialized meaning. In that language the term refers not only to increments provided by collective bargaining agreements to take effect in the future but to those provided to take effect *after* the establishment of a stabilization program but set forth by the terms of agreements negotiated *prior* to the establishment of the stabilization machinery. For example, a contract negotiated in 1970 which provided increases to take effect after August 15, 1971, involved increases treated by the Pay Board as "deferred increases."

Deferred increases constitute a peculiar problem for a wage stabilization program. The increases are legally binding contractual commitments between two parties, management and labor. Though Congress and the federal executive branch have the legal authority to void the provisions of private contracts in the public interest, the government is reluctant to do so.[15] There are several reasons for this reluctance. Among them are an unwillingness to establish the precedent of lightly setting aside private contracts in any area of public interest and a special unwillingness to disturb collective bargaining relationships. The latter reason has often been cited in congressional debates and even in statutes. It has been common for the unions to assert that interference with the operation of agreements existing prior to the establishment of a stabilization program will do irreparable harm to the stability of industrial relations. Congress and wage stabilization administrators have often largely accepted this view. In practice, the NWLB and the WSB almost without exception permitted deferred increases to take effect. During the Second World War the relative absence of substantial multiyear agreements meant that the policy of permitting deferred increases to take effect was largely costless. During the Korean period, however, the advisability of approving the terms of the five-year automobile pact negotiated in 1950 was extensively debated. Ultimately, that agreement and similar agreements were allowed to operate without modification, and became, in part, the foundation for wage policy during the Korean period (although, in part also, the WSB attempted to isolate certain aspects of the agreement's impact on wage increases elsewhere in the economy).[16] In 1971-72 the law was similar to past statutes, but the practice was much different. The Economic Stabilization Act of 1970 was amended in December 1971 to read, "the authority conferred on the President ... shall not be exercised to limit the level of any wage or salary ... to a level below that which has been agreed to in a contract ... executed prior to August 15, 1971, unless the President determines that the increase provided in such contract is unreasonably inconsistent with the standards for wage and salary increases." But, unlike their practice in previous periods, wage stabilization authorities in 1972 began to disallow the operation of deferred increases in a substantial number of instances (the Pay Board in a few cases, the Construction Industry Stabilization Committee on an almost wholesale basis).[17]

There were two major reasons for the change in policy. First, there were in 1972 a substantial number of deferred increments scheduled to take effect, in many cases involving very substantial increases (especially in the construction industry). The problem presented by these increases to stabilization authorities concerned with the interrelationships of wages was very great. Often deferred increases threatened to establish new high levels of wages which would create inequities with respect to substantial numbers of other workers. Second, experience with interrupting a limited number of deferred increases in the fall of 1971 indicated that in many instances workers and unions were prepared to accept such governmental action without initiation of industrial disputes. It appeared that in many instances the pressures of unemployment and changed economic expectations were such as to cause workers and their representatives to accept, often without serious protests, reductions in scheduled increases. The inflation of the 1965–70 period had involved, in construction especially, so much distortion of traditional wage relationships that governmental intervention was accepted as merited by the requirements of equitable administration of stabilization. Furthermore, action by stabilization authorities in a limited number of cases inevitably led to the need to act in related situations, so that what began as an experiment limited to a few instances, grew, in the atmosphere of 1972, to a large undertaking involving hundreds of collective bargaining agreements.

However, the circumstances of 1972 were unusual and cannot reasonably be expected to be repeated in the future. What general lessons may be offered for the relationship of wage stabilization policy to deferred increases? First, the standards of criteria applied to the review of deferred increases have always been formulated as an extreme degree of the standards applied to newly negotiated wage adjustments. In the Korean period, for example, the standard for disapproval of a deferred increase was that it not have an "unstabilizing effect." During 1971–72 the standard was that a deferred increase should not be approved if "unreasonably inconsistent" with the criteria for approval of increases generally. These standards leave much to the judgment of stabilization boards and presume a relatively limited employment of the standards to deny increases. This policy of moderation and deliberation in reviewing deferred increases remains appropriate. It is, in fact, a hazardous policy for government to interfere on an after-the-fact basis with the extremely complex interactions involved in a collective bargaining agreement. Often wage increases have been offered by the employer in return for concessions by the union on other issues. For stabilization authorities to deny wage increases without offsetting adjustments against the employer can create a very undesirable industrial relations climate. It can also, if pursued too strongly, invite employers to make irresponsible wage bargains, involving large increases in future years, in the hope that government action will prohibit the operation of the agreement at a later date, leaving them to enjoy whatever short-run benefits may be gained from agreeing to large future wage increases.

Such a policy by employers is, of course, ultimately destructive both of wage stability and of good industrial relations. It ought not, therefore, to be encouraged by stabilization policy to any greater degree than necessary. For these several reasons—the uniqueness of a situation in which the unions will accept such a policy, the unusual character of the economic situation in which it is necessary, and the potential economic and industrial relations danger of such a policy—the future is likely to see much less attention to deferred increases in periods of stabilization than in 1971–72. In fact, it may be suggested that the need to restrain deferred increases in 1972 on the magnitude accomplished was itself a good measure of the extent to which controls had been late in application. During World War II and the Korean War, controls were applied closer to the onset of a major inflation, so that the unique problems and hazards of applying stabilization policy to deferred increases on a large-scale basis were avoided (as they will be in the future, it may be hoped).

The Relationship of Wage and Price Controls

It is rare, but not unknown, in American history for a wage control program to be established separately when there are no price controls, or vice versa. In general, however, the two are applied simultaneously because of the objection by unions to wage restraint if prices are uncontrolled and the objection by businesses to price controls if wages are unrestrained. The relationship between wage and price controls is uniquely the concern of the president and his advisors, for by its very nature the matter is not subject to determination by wage or price stabilization authorities alone.

The relationship of wage and price controls, in fact, involves several distinct issues. First, how are wage and price control authorities to be coordinated? What administrative arrangements can provide the necessary coordination of the two agencies? Second, several questions of policy arise. Should a distinction be made in procedure and standards for approval between wage increases with price consequences (those increases which tend to raise prices) and those without? Should approved wage increases be accepted as the basis for price increases? Should increases in consumer prices determine, in whole or in part, allowable wage increases? This section considers each of these issues and examples with the exception of the last, that is, the importance of price increases for allowable wage increases, which is discussed in chapter 7.

The administrative arrangements for coordination of the wage and price stabilization agencies have differed considerably among periods, as have the policies regarding wage and price criteria. During World War II, the Office of Economic Stabilization not only served to coordinate the activities of the wage and price stabilization bodies but also exercised general authority over actions of the wage stabilization machinery which had price consequences.[18] To effectuate wage-price coordination, applicants to the NWLB for wage increases were required to state if the increases, if approved, were to be the basis of an application for a price increase. Where a price application was intended, copies of the wage application were sent to the Office of Price Administration for its review. OPA objections to NWLB decisions would be channeled through OES. As a practical matter, the director of economic stabilization (and, through his office, the OPA) never refused a wage increase (which was permissible on wage criteria) because of its price consequences. The lack of formal action by the director probably represented less a policy of accepting whatever action the NWLB chose to take than it did a degree of careful cooperation in working out problems among the various stabilization agencies in advance. Furthermore, the general oversight of stabilization policy exercised by the Office of Economic Stabilization was important with respect to NWLB policy toward fringe benefits. One observer has commented that the NWLB policy of liberal approval of fringes "might have gotten out of hand . . . in the absence of an agency such as OES to establish general limitations on the extent to which the process could go."[19]

During the Korean War, coordination between the Office of Price Stability and the WSB was the responsibility of the Economic Stabilization Agency. However, close coordination of activities was infrequent and was generally at a policy level (not also at the case level, as in World War II). All regulations issued by the WSB were reviewed by and subject to approval of the director of economic stabilization. Price standards permitted the pass-through to price increases of approved wage increases, except that the OPS had established an "industry earnings standard" which was intended to require a reasonable degree of cost absorption by business.[20]

During 1971–72, no counterpart was established to the Economic Stabilization Agency of earlier periods. Rather, the Cost of Living Council, a cabinet-level committee, assumed general responsibility for the stabilization program and attempted, through its staff, to coordinate the actions and policies of the Pay Board and Price Commission. To an unprecedented degree, the policies of the two bodies were contradictory, and in some cases extreme conflicts required resolution by a ruling of the council against one or the other agency. Never, during 1971–72, was relatively careful and effective coordination developed of the type achieved in World War II.[21]

The issue of policy in the relationships between wage and price controls— an issue that has tended to overshadow others—is the question of the degree to which approved wage increases are to be accepted by price stabilization authorities as grounds for price increases. Commentators often insist, for example, that the price stabilization authorities can strengthen the position of the wage board by refusing to permit wage increases to be passed on to consumers in price increases. And it is alleged that in many instances the knowledge that price relief will not be forthcoming strengthens management's resolve, in collective bargaining, not to make wage concessions. In some cases, this may occur. However, in general what is important is not that *no* price pass-through be available but that it *not* be automatic. Rather, price relief for wage increases is appropriate only when the wage increases are approved by the wage board and when cost absorption by the company is impossible (as determined by price stabilization authorities). Any more rigid program is inequitable and often impractical.

The problem of establishing appropriate pricing standards for wage increases has been approached in various ways in the past. During the Second World War, the Economic Stabilization Agency had the authority to approve or disapprove wage increases with price consequences. This procedure has been referred to by one student of the NWLB as "a divided or shared jurisdictional situation." For, if the OPA had reason to be concerned that a wage increase would require a price ceiling change, "the wage increase could become effective only if also approved by the Economic Stabilization Director."[22] As a practical matter, as we have seen, the director's authority was not used to override any decision of the NWLB. During the Korean period, wage adjustments and price consequences were argued separately, first before the WSB and then before the OPS. As described by Michael V. diSalle, director, OPS,

> In OPS we never told anyone in advance whether or not they could obtain a price increase if a wage increase was approved. That meant they had to fight the battle on the wage line. Then, if they felt they could justify a price increase, sometimes they might be able to obtain one, but many, many times they couldn't. Or maybe they would secure a partial increase to offset the hardship.[23]

During 1971–72, in contrast, the Price Commission first publicly indicated its displeasure with the Pay Board's approval of the wage increases in the 1971 bituminous coal pact, then announced it would approve for cost pass-through no more than a 5.5 percent increase in wages and fringe benefits (excluding those, such as Social Security, required by law). Although the commission later supplemented this policy with exceptions for small and low-profit firms, it did not relax the position entirely. In retrospect, the World War II program had the advantage of formality and close coordination; the Korean program involved a degree of uncertainty for business as to what was allowable as a cost pass-through, though the standards of OPS provided for a measure of fairness in the final resolution of the issue.[24] In 1971–72 a tough-sounding policy was adopted but one which was practically unworkable in industries where profits and overhead were too thin to absorb wage increases above 5.5 percent. In consequence, the Price Commission chose to ignore violations of its pass-through regulations, and the Cost of Living Council struggled for many months with complaints from employers (supported by the Pay Board and Construction Industry Stabilization Committee) against the Price Commission's policy.

In conclusion, what can be offered in judgment with respect to the three issues raised at the start of this subsection? First, wage and price controls should continue to be kept apart, for they involve different skills, different knowledge, and different problems. Second, a degree of coordination of wage and price controls is important. The degree of coordination in the World War II program was perhaps too elaborate. The somewhat more distant coordination involved in the Korean program is probably more appropriate to a limited stabilization program, such as that of the Korean period and of 1971–72. But the loose and inconclusive relationship of 1971–72 is clearly inadequate to the requirements of a successful stabilization program.

Third, price consequences have been offered as a criterion for wage adjustments and were so employed in the post–World War II stabilization program. But the immediate consequences for prices cannot serve as a reliable guide to wage adjustments. For one thing, it is almost impossible in many cases to determine whether a wage increase will require a price increase. To adopt such a criterion as the primary wage standard (as opposed to a supplemental standard applied by a coordinating body such as an economic stabilization agency), is to invite disputes between labor and management as to whether a wage increase does require price relief. The technicalities of such an issue and, often, its indeterminateness suggest the avoidance of such a standard. Further, such a standard cannot serve as a guide to collective bargaining representatives. As George Taylor commented,

> Whether or not a certain union wage demand could be met without a price increase was not easily answered in economic terms. It was even harder to arrive at an answer in collective bargaining.[25]

Finally, such a price-based wage standard could easily result in anomalies in wage approvals which would seriously distort relative wages, simply on the basis of differences in company profitability (and therefore the capacity to absorb wage increases without price increases) or in product lines.

The most difficult policy question—one which involves the appropriate treatment, for pricing purposes, of approved wage increases—requires, not a single response, but one tailored to the circumstances. Whether or not a wage increase should be the basis for a price increase must be determined on a case-by-case basis, in which the desired degree of cost absorption by producers, wholesalers, and retailers is measured against profit levels for the firms at varying degrees of permissible cost pass-through. In his evaluation of the World War II program, John Dunlop suggested that high profit-levels at the outset of the war allowed absorption of substantial wage increases without price increases, and so permitted the separation of wage and price stabilization.[26] The 1971–72 program, which established separate wage and price control agencies in a period of initially depressed profits, demonstrated that high cost-absorption is not a precondition for separation of wage and price controls. Rather cost absorption in some industries can be high, depending on the state of profits.[27] In other industries, profits are so small in proportion to total sales, and wages so high, and pricing so competitive, that virtually any substantial degree of cost absorption is impossible (for example, in many service industries, construction, and others). The basic issue, then, is the cost absorptive capacity of industry in individual cases. No single formula can substitute for determinations made in each major case. This function requires a high level of expertise and care on the part of the price authorities.

Relationship to Congress

No aspect of the environment of a stabilization program is of greater potential importance to a wage stabilization board than the opinion of Congress. At any moment Congress is capable of restraining, harassing, or altering a wage control program. The means at the disposal of Congress are several, including hearings, budgetary limitations and enacting legislation. Because of the importance of Congress, the public members of a stabilization board have a special responsibility to keep careful watch on Congressional opinion. And since Congress has a long record of generally unfortunate interventions into the operations of stabilization programs, stabilization authorities have every reason to be wary of congressional opinion. Yet, since the dangers of congressional action are so clear from the historical record, the administrators of wage stabilization can have no excuse for failure to act carefully to protect the integrity of a program from congressional action.

Interventions by Congress in the conduct of the wage stabilization program of the Second World War were less extensive than during the Korean period. Nevertheless, there were several areas of intervention during the program of the 1940s, and the NWLB spent considerable effort opposing such involvements by Congress, sometimes successfully. Two examples may be cited of congressional interventions, through the legislative process. The first, and the more important of the two, involved the passage in June 1943, of the War Labor Disputes Act (Smith-Connally Act). The act was intended to strengthen the government's capacity to meet strikes against the wage stabilization program but had, in actual practice, a contrary effect. The public members of the NWLB opposed the act but were unable to stop its enactment. The second example involved the attachment to the Public Debt Act of 1943 of provisions regarding the relationship of the wage stabilization program to the minimum wage legislation (Fair Labor Standards Act) and to the National Labor Relations Act. There was also appended a prohibition against reducing wage rates below the highest paid for the affected work between January 1, 1942, and September 15, 1942 (the date of initiation of the comprehensive controls program). Congress also rescinded regulations of the economic stabilization director and provisions of Executive Order No. 9250 of the president which were inconsistent with its instructions in the Public Debt Act. These actions demonstrated the capacity of Congress to amend detailed provisions of a stabilization program and to use nonstabilization legislation as a vehicle to complete its purposes.

The wage stabilization program in the Korean period experienced continuing difficulties with Congress—difficulties which in the end proved debilitating to a substantial degree. Archibald Cox, one of the later chairmen of the WSB, and John Dunlop described the general thrust of congressional action as follows:

> It appears to be a valid summary of Korean and World War II experience that price and wage control *statutes* come to have an increasing number of exceptions and special provisions concerning strong interest or industrial groups. Some groups which do not like the price or wage standards used by administrative agencies are able to secure special legislative provisions. The initial statutes are likely to provide for more effective and tighter controls. As time passes and the initial crisis passes, the legislative influence of particular groups ... seems able to secure specific statutory standards or exceptions.[28]

To recount the sequence of events, briefly. In 1950 Congress authorized controls in the Defense Production Act. In June 1951, Representative Lucas proposed to alter the WSB by increasing the number of public members to outnumber the labor and management members and by removing virtually all disputes-settlement functions. There were extensive hearings and debates, but the amendments were not passed. On April 24, 1952, the House passed Resolution No. 532 calling for an investigation of the WSB. Hearings were held in May and June. A report critical of the board was issued. The Senate, however, also reviewed the board's actions and released a generally favorable report. Legislation was ultimately passed by Congress and signed by the president (June 30, 1952), amending the Defense Production Act. The WSB was abolished and a new tripartite board (created not by executive order of the president but by statute) was established. Generally, the statutory board had the functions of the previous board, but it was denied jurisdiction over any disputes case not involving a wage stabilization question and over any noneconomic issue. Furthermore, the 1952 amendments exempted from price and wage controls a list of items, including wages of $1.00 per hour or less, earnings of architects, engineers, and accountants, small business (involving eight employees or less, but Congress permitted the WSB to make exceptions to this exemption), bowling alleys, and the wages of agricultural labor.[29] Also, in 1952, Congress applied substantial reductions to the budget of the stabilization program, requiring large cuts in the operations and staff of the board, its regional offices, and the investigatory staff of the Wages and Hours Division of the Department of Labor.[30] As if these direct interventions in the activities of the board were not enough, Congress had originally so framed the economic stabilization program generally as to place wage controls in a difficult posture. For the 1950 act allowed the operation of agricultural price increases below parity, so that arguments for a wage policy based on cost-of-living increases were, in part, justified by the act.[31]

The overt and detailed intervention of Congress in the administration of a wage control program, which had increased from World War II to the Korean period, increased further in 1971. So substantial did this intervention become in December 1971, that it is important to recount it briefly here. As the Pay Board met to develop policies for application upon expiration of the freeze (November 14, 1971), Congress was considering extension of the ESA of 1970 beyond its two-year period. On four major issues Congress wrote into the extension reversals of Pay Board policy. First, it separated certain major fringe benefits from the 5.5 percent general pay standard of the board, which had included them.[32] Second, Congress allowed, generally, retroactive payment of wage increases due during the freeze. Third, Congress established standards for the substandards exemption which, though not setting a cents-per-hour figure, did permit legal suits to overturn the standard which was established by the Cost of Living Council. Fourth, Congress mandated, in the amendments to the act, a 5.5 percent pay increase for many federal employees on January 1, 1972, not July 1972, as requested by the president.[33] This was the second major increase for federal employees within a period of less than one year. When the Pay Board hesitated to revise its regulations to reflect these amendments, Chairman Patman of the House Banking and Currency Committee threatened to hold oversight hearings. On March 3, 1972, the Pay Board announced it had completed the revision of its regulations to reflect the congressional actions.

There was little in this conflict between the stabilization authorities and Congress to reflect credit on either party. The wage stabilization authorities had developed a program with insufficient flexibility and so opaque a group of regulations as to be unintelligible to most persons. Congress, however, did not direct its attention to the real shortcomings of the program, but rather developed a statute which made all but impossible even a far better-structured program than that which had been developed. Historical experience thus indicates five potential problems for a stabilization program which are inherent in the relationship to Congress. First, it is inevitable that certain organizations and individuals with cases pending before the stabilization board will seek assistance in expediting the handling of their case or even its favorable treatment from their congressional representatives. All regulatory agencies of the federal government are subject to such requests from congressmen (or senators) on behalf of their constituents, but a special problem exists for a wage board in this regard. Where the board is tripartite, representatives of the business and labor communities have a special role of liaison for their groups. Public members and staff of a wage board must, in consequence, always be very cautious of two extremes. On the one hand, it is important not to undermine the position of labor or management representatives by acceding to a congressman's requests in behalf of his labor or business constituents which the national labor or business representatives have been unable or unwilling to obtain for local groups. But, on the other hand, stabilization authorities must attempt not to offend congressmen by refusing any consideration of their requests. In general, public authorities are wise to inform labor and management representatives on the board of congressional requests in behalf of local union or business interests, and to work out appropriate responses to the congressmen. Overtly political requests from Congress which are without merit for the policies or procedures of the board must, of course, be refused, lest the integrity of the entire program be undermined.

Second, since congressional interest in a wage stabilization program is often the result of complaints by parties aggrieved by actions of the board, no better defense against congressional action is available than for public members in a tripartite board to work out as large a degree of consensus as possible among labor and management on each major issue. Decisions in which labor and management each had a role are not generally decisions they wish to overturn or can seek to do so without violating standards of good faith. An all-public board lacks this internal capacity both to develop policies which management and labor can jointly accept and to minimize the degree of dissatisfaction with its actions. An all-public board is, therefore, without resources to head off appeals by labor or management (or both) to Congress against its activities (although the board may try to rely on political resources within the administration to counteract congressional assaults).

Third, a wage board should attempt to minimize politically partisan interpretations of its operations. This is difficult because the administration is generally responsible for economic and industrial relations policy and therefore wishes to receive any credit (as it takes the blame) for the actions of a wage board. Yet too great an identification of the board with the administration's economic policies, particularly if they are highly controversial, invites partisan attack in Congress. Wage boards in the United States have gained some measure of defense against partisanship through the concept of the "public" member as opposed to the representative of government. Public members have often been men of high standing and respect in the nation; for example, educators or professional persons without ties to any particular political party. With such men on a wage board, there exists a capacity to stand above, to a limited but important degree, narrowly partisan political isues—and thereby to be insulated, in part, from congressional interference.

Fourth, since it is inevitable that some aspects of wage stabilization policy will become the vortex of congressional dispute, the board must be prepared to defend its actions. There are two important principles involved here. One is that in decisions or policies which may become the subject of a congressional inquiry, the board had best have its positions carefully worked out and well supported. Too often boards have been unable to provide reasons for certain policies and/or decisions, other than that the policies and decisions are arbitrary interpretations of the provisions of legislation or of a presidential directive. The second principle of defense is that policies which are structured to allow for case-by-case consideration and exceptions where appropriate are very difficult to challenge in Congress. For Congress is not likely to act where remedies for seeking exceptions to a policy exist within the board and requests for exceptions are given a full hearing.

Fifth, there is a degree to which a wage board can seek a constructive, though arm's-length, relationship with Congress. Congressional opinion provides one of the barometers of the public status of the wage control program. In some ways it is a particularly sensitive barometer—not to public opinion generally so much as to the opinion of major interest-groups. No wage board can hope to have well represented in its structure all important elements among employers and labor. Congress is, however, in its peculiar fashion, often through individual members, quite responsive to a great many constituents. A wage board may, by careful observation of congressional opinion, be better informed as to the acceptance, and often the practical consequences, of its policies and decisions on various groups.

In general, Congress has been content to write broad legislation authorizing controls, leaving to the executive branch the development of a program in detail. Congress has then sought to pick the program to pieces by hearings and amendments, rejecting any overall responsibility for it, until a much weakened program is simply allowed to lapse. Much of the responsibility for this dismal record is due to the inadequate care with which wage boards have conducted their activities. But a great deal of the responsibility for the failure of constructive congressional action rests directly and exclusively with Congress.

7. Standards for Wage Stabilization: Criteria for a General Standard

The Uses of a General Standard

Functions

A general standard for wage increases is defined as one which permits adjustments for all groups of workers in the economy. It is thereby distinguished from standards (referred to in this volume as "exceptions") which permit adjustments in situations involving certain characteristics of a nongeneral nature. The general standard, like all elements of a wage stabilization program, has certain functions to perform in the context of the program. The most important functions relate to the impact of the general standard in limiting compensation increases and in adjusting relative wages. Each element of a stabilization program, the general standard included, must be applied to the achievement of both wage restraint and adjustment of the wage structure. This section explores the role of a general standard in these two areas of stabilization activities.

Unfortunately, it appears that since World War II there has occurred a steady erosion in the understanding among the public, government officials, and even many economists and industrial relations specialists of the function of a general standard. This erosion culminated in 1971 in the establishment of a general pay standard on a very different theoretical basis than that of earlier periods. In contrast to practice during World War II, for example, recent applications of a general standard have been directed solely at the rate of increase in compensation. But the Little Steel formula of the Second World War and (to a lesser degree) General Regulation 6 of the Korean period were directed at other related objectives as well, including the establishment of a desired general level of wages and the readjustment of the structure of wage rates and earnings.

The reader will recall from chapter 2 that the so-called Little Steel formula (adopted in July 1942 by the National War Labor Board) served as the standard for general wage increases in World War II. It provided for wage increases for groups of employees equal to the rise in the cost-of-living between January 1941 and May 1942. The formula as just described, simple though it seems, was in fact a very sophisticated standard involving at least three elements. First, the formula permitted those wage rates which had lagged behind others in the period since January 1941 to be adjusted to the generally higher level prevailing in May 1942. The adjustment was made by reference to the increased cost of living during the fifteenth-month period involved and permitted increases of up to 15 percent for workers who had received no increase since January 1941. The result of this policy was that real wages were restored to the levels prevailing in January 1941. Second, the formula provided that increases beyond the 15 percent maximum permitted in the formula were to be approved only on the basis of such criteria as substandards of living and inequalities, as set forth in a message of President Roosevelt (April 27, 1942). No further general wage increases resulting from increases in the cost-of-living, in managements' ability to pay, in rising productivity, or from other factors were to be permitted. The formula broke the connection between general wage adjustments and increases in the cost-of-living and other factors after April 1942. Third, the formula was designed in such a manner that a structure of wage rates among industries, occupations, and regions, which was appropriate in the view of the board, was created.[1] Wage structure considerations were especially important in the selection of a base date from which the 15 percent permitted increase would be measured. Thus, George Taylor noted in the opinion he wrote for the board on wage aspects of the Little Steel case that "for several years prior to January 1, 1941, wages and costs of living were, in general, relatively stable. . . . The National War Labor Board has the responsibility . . . to eradicate the inequities in wages which developed during the race between wages and cost-of-living from January 1, 1941, to April 27, 1942."[2] Under the Little Steel formula workers were entitled after April 27, 1942, to an increase which represented the difference between what they had already received since January 1, 1941, and 15 percent above the January 1, 1941, level of rates.[3] Thus, upon the exhaustion of the increases allowable under the Little Steel formula, rates would have returned generally to their relative (percentage) position in January 1941. The board in the Little Steel case explicitly refused to grant the steelworkers an increase based on a standard which would use as a starting point (or base date) the rates provided by their last contract with the steel companies. As it happened, when the Little Steel case came to the board, the workers had already received an 11.8 percent increase above January 1941 levels. The board charged this 11.8 percent increase against the Little Steel formula's 15 percent and awarded the steelworkers a 3.2 percent increase under the formula (a further special increase of 2.3 percent reflecting special equities was also permitted).[4] The board noted that to take the final rates under the steelworkers' existing contract as the base for approval of a general increase (as opposed to some uniform base date applicable to all American workers) would simply be to build into the wage structure those distortions which had been introduced by the onset of inflation in 1941. Whatever rates had gotten ahead would be permitted, by such a standard, to remain ahead; those that had lagged would continue to lag.

The board also stated its purpose as one of allowing the completion of the "wage round" which had begun in American industry in 1941 and the prevention of any new round. "The big question before the Nation," George Taylor wrote, was "whether or not there would be another round."[5] The concept of a wage round clearly involved the adjustment of wage rates to each other, to a point where comparable rates had increased by the same amount.[6] And, in rare instances, the board even denied approval of increases within the amount provided by the Little Steel formula in order to prevent destabilizing effects on the structure of wage rates. For example, increases were denied in two Lever Brothers plants where the existing rates were above those in comparable plants, so that approval of a Little Steel adjustment would have simply created inequities. And in a case involving printers in New York City, Little Steel increases were denied these high-wage workers because approval "would have unstabilizing influences of far-reaching effect."[7]

Thus, in the Little Steel formula a single standard was, in part, due to the happenstance of the existence of a recent period of stable wages and prices; the standard was at once a device to preserve real wages (up to the date of April 1942 only) and one to return the wage structure to a position of relative stability. In a similar fashion, General Regulation 6 of the Korean period's Wage Stabilization Board permitted increases of up to 10 percent above the level of rates prevailing in January 1950 (the regulation was adopted in March 1951).

In contrast, in 1971 the Pay Board established a much less sophisticated form of a general pay standard. Abandoning concern for wage structure, the board agreed to permit increases of at least 5.5 percent for any group of workers above their base payroll-period compensation.[8] The base payroll period was defined as the one-to four-week period immediately proceeding the proposed increase, and the base compensation rate as that rate which was in effect just prior to the increase. Thus, the Pay Board accepted the wage structure as it was in the latter part of 1971, including substantial distortions introduced by some six years of inflation in the 1965–71 period. In response to the unions' demands for some standards of comparability of rates, the board established "catch-up" and "tandem" criteria, but attempted to limit increases thereunder to a maximum of 7 percent (including increases under the general standard).

There is no doubt that the development of a more sophisticated general standard (like the Little Steel formula) would have been somewhat difficult in 1971. Attempting to reference increases from a base period with a fairly stable wage structure would have required establishing a base date several years back (not simply some eighteen months, as in World War II) and would have produced very high permissible increases (the cost of living had risen approximately 30 percent between 1965 and August 1971, for example), even though these permissible increases had been fully exhausted by many workers as of November 1971. An alternative formulation would have been to establish a relatively low general standard for increases and rest considerable weight on wage structure adjustments. That is, rather than seek to have every group of workers receive an increase as close to the general standard as possible, each group would have received an increase appropriate to its position in the wage structure. A period of about two years would have sufficed to realign relative wages, while also constraining the average rate of increase in the economy generally.

Let us reiterate the argument of this section with regard to the functions of a general standard. The role of a general standard in a wage control program is not simply to establish a target rate of increase for all workers. Rather, it has several functions, each very different from setting a general norm. First, it must allow a degree of readjustment of wage structure distortions which may have developed. Second, as we shall see below, it should provide an adjustment of wages to increases in the cost-of-living and/or productivity over some appropriate period. Third, it must strictly limit any adjustments beyond those permissible under the first two aspects, lest those adjustments become a force for increases generally in the economy. In this regard, the general standard should serve to establish limits on wages beyond which increases are permitted only on the basis of exceptional considerations (inequities, substandards, and the like). With respect to this third function, a general standard need not be set at no increase (as was effectively the case from 1943 to 1945, when the Little Steel formula, exhausted in most instances, was continued unchanged). Rather, increases in rates generally might be permitted in step with rising cost-of-living, productivity gains, and so on. The use of various criteria as a basis for establishing a general standard of greater than zero is discussed in the next section.

The Combination of a General Standard and Exceptions

As the preceding pages have indicated, various combinations are possible of a general standard with exceptions in order to achieve a requisite degree of wage restraint and adjustment of wage structure. Formally, we may think of the percentage increase in wages generally in some time period (twelve months, for example), as a resultant of the rate of increase allowed by a general standard (for example, reflecting the increase in consumer prices and the trend rate of productivity advance), and adjustments in the wage structure.

Thus:

$$\Delta\bar{\omega} = G + \lambda S, \text{where } G = Y\Delta CPI + \delta\Delta P$$

so that,

$$\Delta\bar{\omega} = Y\Delta CPI + \delta\Delta P + \lambda S,$$

where,

$\Delta\bar{\omega}$ = percentage increase in wages on average
G = the general standard
ΔCPI = percentage increase in consumer prices
ΔP = trend (percentage) increase in productivity
S = a measure of wage structure distortion

In some states of the economy, wage structure adjustments would not be a major contributor to the overall average rate of increase. However, if a period of inflation has introduced major distortions into relative wages, readjustments may become very substantial in their total impact on the average rate of change in wages. A general problem of stabilization policy is, of course, to minimize the average rate of increase. Minimization is accomplished by affecting the various factors contributing to wage adjustments. Any stabilization program may be described by the terms of this model. For example, in World War II the stabilization program involved the following elements: first, allowing wages to reflect consumer price increases until May 1942 but thereafter denying wage increases based on cost-of-living increases; second, denying at all times, from January 1941, wage increases reflecting productivity improvements; third, allowing wage increases based upon inequities in the wage structure but, over time, eliminating most inequities so that the impact of readjustments on the average rate of wage increase was minimized. Thus, in terms of the equation given above, the factors affecting wage increases were reduced to the wage structure adjustments only, that is, $\Delta\bar{\omega} = \lambda S$, because $Y = 0$, and $\delta = 0$; but the inequities (S) were successively eliminated so that $S \rightarrow 0$. By the later years of the war a very tight stabilization program had been created. To repeat, prices and productivity were denied as standards for wages, and though inequities were still permissible reasons for increases, inequities were few, so that, symbolically:

$\Delta\omega \rightarrow 0$, because
$Y = 0, \delta = 0$ and $S = 0$, although
$\Delta CPI \neq 0, \Delta P \neq 0$, and $\lambda \neq 0$

In the Korean period, General Wage Regulation 6 provided for adjustments in step with the increase in the cost of living from January 1, 1950, to the spring of 1951; this provision was largely analogous to the Little Steel formula. But General Regulation 8 allowed further adjustments as the cost of living rose (that is, $\gamma = 1$). Several resolutions of the WSB permitted productivity increases to be reflected in wage adjustments in some industries (so that $\delta > 0$). Finally, various provisions for the readjustment of inequities provided than $\lambda \neq 0$. For a variety of reasons, the WSB was less successful in minimizing structural distortions that the NWLB had been in World War II. In consequence, the program of the WSB could be formally described as follows:

$$\Delta\omega = \Delta CPI + \delta\Delta P + \lambda S,$$

where

$$\gamma = 1, \delta > 0, \text{ and } S > 0.$$

The Korean stabilization program was, obviously, a far less rigorous one than that of World War II.

The stabilization program of 1971 may also be described in this fashion. A limited attempt was made to break the connection between prices and productivity and wages. The general standard provided for an effect of prices and productivity on wages of 5.5 percent (plus .7 percent additional on fringes), so that $\gamma\Delta CPI + \delta\Delta P$ was limited to not more than 6.2 percent. Also, a limited allowance was made for readjustment of relative wages, although no comprehensive attempt was made by the Pay Board to minimize structural maladjustments. Failure to make careful readjustment of a distorted wage structure invited continued pressure for wage increases, work stoppages, and noncompliance with the stabilization program. In consequence, a substantial tightening of the controls program in 1972–73 would have invited considerable industrial unrest, and probably widespread attempts at evasion of stabilization standards. The foundation for an increasingly rigorous program of controls (so carefully established in World War II) was neglected in 1971–72. The program of 1971–72 was of an intermediate severity as compared to those of World War II and Korea. Symbolically, $\Delta\bar{\omega} = [\gamma\Delta CPI + \delta\Delta P] + \lambda S$ where $[\gamma\Delta CPI + \delta\Delta P] \leqslant 6.2$, $\lambda S \leqslant .8$, (by self-administration) or without limit (by board approval).

At the extremes, two opposite policies with respect to stabilization are identifiable. On the one hand, a general standard permitting a general wage round based on productivity and price increases (that is, γ and $\delta = 1$) might be established, and wage structure adjustments denied (that is, $\lambda = 0$). On the other hand, a general standard of no increase (that is, γ and $\delta = 0$) might be established, with full allowance for readjustment of the wage structure (that, is $\lambda = 1$).[9] Upon what factors does the choice between the two policies rest? Let us assume, in order to answer this question, that the desired degree of aggregate wage restraint is attainable under either type of policy. Then, it appears that economic conditions should suggest an approach. Thus, when the wage structure is little distorted, a policy resting primary emphasis on a general standard is appropriate. This argument suggests a major failure of the World War II stabilization policy. In the last two years of World War II, in such an economic situation, the opposite tack was taken. Following the "hold-the-line" order in 1943, general wage adjustments were denied and the brackets policy was introduced to permit wage adjustments in circumstances involving wage inequities. An ultimate result of this policy was, as we have seen, the wage explosion of the immediate postwar period. On the other hand, in a circumstance involving considerable wage distortion, the best policy is probably that which affords the least significance to a general standard and the greatest importance to readjustment of wage relationships.

Presumably, the latter was the economic condition which confronted the Pay Board upon its establishment in the fall of 1971. The inflation of the late 1960s generated substantial wage distortions; the correction of the distortions in 1971 resulted in substantial negotiated wage increases in some industries despite an economic recession. In this situation our analysis suggests that the Pay Board should have established a stabilization program with little reliance on a general standard but considerable reliance upon structural readjustments. Unfortunately, the board determined to do precisely the opposite. It established a general standard based on national aggregate price and productivity targets (see below, in the next section, for a more complete discussion of the basis of the general standard of 1971–72) and announced strictly limited standards for approval of adjustments necessary to reestablish appropriate wage relationships. Fortunately, however, the board paid little attention in practice to its own philosophy, instead applying a general provision of its regulations (Section 201.11d) permitting it to approve adjustments of any size necessary to the needs of the "equitable position of the employees concerned." The board applied this standard in a series of major cases (involving, e.g., coal, aerospace, and longshoring) to permit wage increases well above the general standard in order to readjust wage differentials.

The Approach of the Single Wage Standard: A Critique

Briefly, those who favor a single-standard wage policy suggest a percentage figure which should apply to virtually all adjustments in compensation. In this view, the general standard should be established as a percentage increase above existing rates, and exceptions to the standard should be excluded. It is implicit in the suggestion that considerations of wage interrelationships should be of little importance. While the intellectual origins of the single-standard approach to wage stabilization are indistinct, the idea was current in both World War II and the Korean period. Yet, it was not adopted fully as the rationale of a comprehensive stabilization program until 1971.[10]

Furthermore, there has developed a theory of wage determination which appears to lend further support to the single standard as a device for stabilization. This theory is one which assigns a primary role in the determination of wages to expectations of future inflation. When there are expectations of rapid inflation, so the argument goes, wages are adjusted upward in response. In consequence, factors which limit expectations of future inflation tend to reduce wage settlements. In 1972 this expectational theory gained substantial credence among public officials, and great stress was place upon the supposed "psychological" aspects of wage inflation. Because wage and price increases were believed to be largely discretionary with unions and management, it seemed important for the government to articulate policy which would imply a future reduction of inflationary pressures and so create expectations of a lessening inflation. In response, unions and employers were expected to moderate wage and price increases. The general standard of a stabilization program was believed to play an important role in this strategy. By establishing a norm for increases, inflationary expectations would be curbed.[11]

While it is likely that expectations regarding future inflation do have a role, along with other factors, in wage determination, the evidence for any special or quantitatively dominant role is sparse. For example, an econometric study of expectations in an aggregate wage model found that employers and unions apparently discounted their own expectations highly in establishing wage increases.[12] Furthermore, a simple comparison of first- and future-year negotiated wage changes included in multiyear agreements negotiated in the 1966-72 period, indicates no greater differences between first- and future-year changes in the 1966-68 period than in 1968-72. This admittedly crude measure suggests no difference in expectations of the rate of future inflation, which is unlikely in view of the very different economic environment in the two periods. Either expectations were unaffected by substantial change in the economic environment, or the influence of expectations in wage determination was overshadowed by other factors. Whatever the evidence for the importance of expectations in wage determination, however, even less convincing is the assertion that a government-specified target rate of wage increase can affect expectations of future inflation and thereby affect the rate of increase in wage adjustments.

Those who propose a single standard appear to believe that it will be effective because it is not only simple but unambiguous. However, a thorough familiarity with the process of wage determination suggests that no single figure can be applied unambiguously (even conceptually) to all situations. Let us offer a very common example of the difficulty of applying a single standard. In the course of a two-year period in a single plant, variations will occur in the timing of wage increments and in the distribution of increases among job classifications (accompanied, inevitably, by changes in distributions of workers among classifications). These variations will result in differences of opinion as to the correct application of any established criterion. What is the appropriate base from which to measure the new increase? How should one treat expected changes in employment among wage classifications? Thus, a general standard involving a stated percentage increase over existing wage rates (or earnings) is not unambiguous but, in fact, often quite confusing, unless it can be applied on a case-by-case basis by stabilization authorities. There is therefore no substitute for a review process to determine the applicability of the single-percentage standard in individual situations. When such a standard is combined with extensive reliance of self-administration, a more difficult situation arises. Self-administration invites both manipulation of the standard and disagreements about its interpretation. For example, in some instances, various groups will tend to interpret the guideline according to their own needs, sometimes with very destabilizing results.[13] Furthermore, some groups will understandably view economic adjustments by other parties based on interpretations different from their own (regardless of the actual merit of the interpretations involved) as noncompliance with the stabilization program. The single standard, with its false impression of precision, is thus likely to result in chaos. And, publicity for the general standard which is intended to affect discretionary wage increases will be increasingly ineffectual as the evidence of actual practice, and confusion, increases. For these reasons the policy of establishing a single norm for wage adjustments possesses few of the advantages claimed for it and may engender special problems.

Criteria for Establishing a General Standard

The criteria most commonly proposed as the basis for a general standard are increases in cost-of-living or in labor productivity (that is, output per manhour), or both. In this section we investigate these criteria in depth, including the historical experience which has accumulated as to their application to wage stabilization. How are the criteria to be interpreted, and how applied? What are the advantages and disadvantages of each as the basis for a general standard? What factors affect the advisability of establishing a particular form of general standard?

Before proceeding to a discussion of cost-of-living and productivity as stabilization standards, we should note that these are not the only criteria for general standards which have been proposed. Another criterion which has received considerable discussion is the ability of firms to pay proposed wage adjustments. This issue normally arises in the context of a stabilization program in the following way. An application may be made by a union and management for a wage increase in which management certifies that it will not make approval of the proposed wage increases grounds for requesting approval of a price increase. If the full wage-adjustment cannot be approved on wage criteria alone, then does the fact that no price consequences would follow from full approval suggest that the increase should be allowed? Stabilization boards have always refused to permit wage adjustments on such grounds.

George Taylor has described the factors which, during World War II, persuaded the NWLB to deny ability to pay as a standard for wage increases: "Allowing wage increases on the ground of ability to pay would have evoked an irresistible demand for matching adjustments by other companies that lacked an ability to pay at existing prices. Such companies would generally have to raise wages if they wanted employees to work for them."[14] Thus, the primary consideration which caused the NWLB to deny ability-to-pay as a general standard for increases was the interrelationship of wage rates. At the end of the war, the NWLB adopted a policy of permitting wage increases where there were no direct price consequences. Experience was not favorable to the standard.[15] During the Korean period, the Defense Production Act of 1950 included a section (402 b[5]) which provided that wage criteria would reflect price consequences, apparently with the intent of allowing wage increases which would be paid out of profits.[16] The WSB recognized the same difficulties with such a standard as had the NWLB and largely ignored this provision of the act.[17] In 1971–72 there was no legislative mandate for a wage standard based on ability to pay (except insofar as retroactivity during the freeze and the review of deferred increases were concerned), and the Pay Board did not adopt such a standard. There can be little doubt that a wage standard which would permit whatever increases can be paid by an employer without the necessity for direct price increases is not a reasonable basis for wage stabilization and should continue to be rejected by stabilization boards in the future.[18]

There is, however, one sense in which ability to pay (or at least employer willingness to pay) is almost always considered, implicitly, by a stabilization program, and the union representatives are understandably quick to point it out. It is a fundamental characteristic of wage stabilization programs in the United States that employers are not required to pay wage increases allowable under stabilization policies unless they agree to do so unilaterally or in collective bargaining.[19] For example, a general standard of some percentage increase does not automatically entitle the worker to such an increase unless his employer agrees. If collective bargaining results in an agreed upon increase of less than the percentage standard (perhaps because of the employer's inability to pay more), the stabilization board will certainly not award a larger increase to the workers.

Increases in Cost-of-Living as a Wage Standard

The importance of cost-of-living increases as a potential wage criterion arises from the impact of rising prices on living standards. Price increases threaten to erode purchasing power, so that earnings must be increased in order to maintain their real purchasing power. In order to limit the hardship imposed by a stabilization program, it is often suggested that wages be permitted to rise in step with consumer prices in order to maintain living standards. Unfortunately, the use of consumer price increases as a wage criterion is not without considerable problems. In part, these problems arise from characteristics of the measurements of consumer prices. Let us examine several of these problems.

First, comparative levels of consumer prices and their rate of change vary considerably among areas in the United States. It is inevitable, therefore, that disputes will arise in the application of indices of consumer price increase to proposed wage increases. During the Korean War stabilization program, much attention was devoted to various measures of cost-of-living. Ultimately, the WSB recognized for wage criteria eight other cost-of-living indices than the national Bureau of Labor Statistics Index ("the" Consumer Price Index).[20] The reader can imagine that this multiplicity of indices threatened to create substantial confusion in the stabilization program, especially where uniform national wage rates or wage relationships might be affected by varying cost-of-living indices. Furthermore, regardless of whether separate indices are approved for use as wage criteria, any single national index, if disaggregated, may be expected to exhibit substantially different behavior in various areas, causing those in areas of relatively rapid price increases to demand special consideration by a wage board. Second, there always exists a potential range of disputes over the degree of appropriateness of the composition of any price index. For example, some persons may question the items which are included or excluded in a consumer price index and the relative importance of each item. Also, adjustments for quality changes in certain types of products may affect the behavior of the index (indices).[21] Once a price index has been established as a wage standard, its definitional limitations, its degree of subjectivity to manipulation, its degree of alleged bias, and other characteristics become a field upon which issues of wage stabilization may be contested. Unfortunately, consumer price indices are rarely so complete and reliable as to withstand such careful attention by contending parties. The result is to force a wage board relying on price indices to adopt somewhat arbitrary conventions as to their interpretation and application to proposed wage adjustments. The problem of defending the indices is made worse by the tendency of price controls to cause concealment of actual price increases by black market practices, such as creating false new products, multiple wholesaling, and other stratagems.[22] Third, consumer price indices normally include items such as food, interest rates, second-hand items, and the like, which are quite volatile in price. Acceptance of the CPI as a wage standard would threaten to base irreversible wage adjustments, to a degree, upon reversible price increases.

Fourth, taxes constitute a significant portion of the CPI and normally contribute to its rise. For example, between December 1965 and December 1970 increases in state and local sales taxes, residential property taxes, auto registration and licensing fees, and Federal excise taxes contributed 1.7 percentage points of a total increase nationally in the CPI of 24.8 points. In some years the contribution of tax increases was as much as 0.4 points of a total of 5.5 points. Thus, the use of the CPI as a wage standard tends to involve government in the anomalous position of permitting wage increases in order to offset the impact of rising taxes, and at a time when wage and price restraint is required by a program of direct controls. Fifth, a difficult problem involves whether a price standard should apply to wage rates or to earnings. Earnings may increase more rapidly than wage rates for many reasons, including longer hours of work, additional premium pay, and others. Where earnings are rising more rapidly than wage rates, should the cost-of-living standard be applied differently than in cases where wages and earnings rise at the same rate? And if so, how is such a policy to be applied to individual situations?

Since it has been shown that the application of cost-of-living increases as a wage standard is an administratively difficult matter, we may ask if the advantages of a prices-based standard outweigh its complexities. The answer to this question turns, in large part, on the type of cost-of-living standard developed. There are two distinct ways in which a cost-of-living standard can be stated. On one hand, the standard may simply permit increases in wages commensurate with increases in the cost-of-living (by approval of cost-of-living escalator clauses, for example). But such a standard is undesirable in that, ignoring the structure of wages, it permits an increase in wages in addition to whatever are the existing rates.[23] In contrast, a base date may be selected and increases in wages approved equal to the cost-of-living increase since that date. In this formulation, any given group of workers receives only the difference between the allowable wage increase and any increase the workers might already have received since the base date. Such a standard can be periodically updated, as required, to permit wage adjustments to keep in step with cost-of-living increases, if such a policy is desired. This formulation of a cost-of-living wage criterion, by choice of an appropriate base date, tends to remove wage distortions. (A third type of standard needs no extended discussion here, although it is commonly employed in a stabilization program. Under this policy, cost-of-living escalators are permitted to operate so long as the increases provided fall within permissible limits established by other standards. Clearly, this standard is not in reality a cost-of-living standard at all but one utilizing other standards.)

It has been demonstrated, in previous pages, that the second alternative (involving measurement of the allowable wage change from a base date chosen to establish a desirable structure of wage relationships) is preferable for a general standard. But what additional advantages does this procedure possess? One such advantage is that a price criterion which allows a given percentage adjustment in wages from a base date is more amenable to a decision to abandon a cost-of-living wage criterion, if necesary. This is because a wage standard measured between dates tends to become exhausted unless the termination date is extended. And should stabilization policy appear to require severe wage restraint involving a divorce between wage increases and cost-of-living increases, it may be easily achieved by not permitting further wage increases in response to price changes.

Are there disadvantages in pursuing a cost-of-living-based wage policy involving base and expiration dates? There seem to be few or none. The policy can be made consistent with any degree of desired wage restraint and even eliminated if necessary, so the degree of restraint involved is not at question here. As chapter 4 pointed out, the question as to whether real wage levels must be maintained during a stabilization program is dependent on numerous economic and political considerations. There is no general principle requiring maintenance of real wages. However, any degree of *general* wage adjustment permitted, no matter how small, is perhaps usefully described in wage criteria as an adjustment to rising costs-of-living. In fact, there are disadvantages to eschewing a cost-of-living wage policy. First, denying requests for wage adjustments based on rising prices contributes to making business and agricultural leaders less concerned with the effects of price increases, since there are no wage consequences. Second, a stabilization program which refuses to take any explicit account of the implications of rising prices for wage policy is likely to be vulnerable to political attack or demagoguery by union leadership.

There has been an interesting variety of historical experience in the United States with wage policy based on cost-of-living increases. The various stabilization programs have struggled with the issue of the relationship of wages and/or earnings and consumer prices, and have come to very different policy choices, at least in principle. In actual result, there has been much less difference between periods in the comparative paths of earnings and price increases. Table 7.1 demonstrates that, in each period except the Civil War, increases in hourly earnings have outdistanced cost-of-living increases, sometimes quite substantially. There were different reasons, however, for the somewhat similar behavior of earnings and consumer prices in each period.

It may be concluded that the actual relationship between increases in earnings and increases in the cost-of-living during a stabilization program is

TABLE 7.1
Increases in Earnings and Consumer Prices in Major Inflationary Periods

	Percentage Change In	
	Average Hourly Earnings Nonagricultural Industries	Cost of Living
Civil War (1861–65)	54.4	149.3
First World War		
1914–20 (annual averages)	142.0	100.0
1917–20 (annual averages)	72.9	48.4
Second World War		
1939–47 (annual averages)	67.5	52.0
1941–45 (annual averages)	40.2	22.5
Korean War		
January 1951–January 1953	11.8*	4.7
1951–53 (annual averages)	11.3*	3.0
1971–1972		
August 1971–December 1972	4.3	2.9
1971–72 (annual averages)		

*Manufacturing Only

SOURCES: Data for the Civil War, First and Second World Wars from John T. Dunlop, "An Appraisal of Wage Stabilization Policies," in Bureau of Labor Statistics, *Problems and Policies of Dispute Settlement and Wage Stabilization During World War II*, bulletin 1009 (Washington, D.C.: Government Printing Office, 1950), p. 170. Data for the Korean War from various issues of Bureau of Labor Statistics, *Monthly Labor Review*, 1950–1954. Average hourly earnings data is not available for the nonagricultural economy as a whole for January 1951 to January 1953. Data for 1971–72 from Bureau of Labor Statistics, *Employment and Earnings*, various issues.

not determined by the type of general standard adopted by the wage stabilization authorities. Rather, the relationship between earnings and price increases is determined by the interaction of a number of factors including economic circumstances (e.g., the degree of increase in hours and overtime worked, if any) and the overall impact of the application of the administrative standards for wage adjustments, however they might be formulated. In consequence, a stabilization program, such as that of World War II, which officially eschews a cost-of-living policy for wages may yet experience rising real-earnings levels, just as if a more explicit cost-of-living policy had been pursued. In general, the relationship between earnings and cost-of-living is best understood not as a wage criterion but as an indication of the progress of the stabilization program. However, when circumstances do suggest adoption of a regulation involving an explicit, formula-type, relationship between prices and wages, it should be one utilizing base dates chosen with careful consideration of issues of wage structure. It is always an error to make a percentage allowance above existing wage rates available to all groups of workers, whatever their relative position at the moment in the structure of wages. This procedure threatens to accelerate, rather than restrain, a wage-price spiral and is certain to generate disputes over the definition and application of the cost-of-living index, or indices, itself.

Productivity and Wage Standards

Productivity as a General Standard for Wage Increases. Productivity improvements have long been suggested as a standard for wage increases. In some instances the productivity standard proposed is a national average figure applicable to all wage increases; in others, productivity increases in certain firms or industries are proposed as standards for wage adjustments on a selective basis. There is, of course, a certain plausibility to arguments that wage increases should reflect increases in productivity, but there are also major limitations to these proposals. Like so many formulas for wage adjustments, the productivity standard is much simpler in the abstract than in its application to actual situations. At one extreme, a productivity standard, when applied uniformly in the economy, is no different from any other general standard for wage increases. At the other extreme, the standard, when applied on a selective basis, becomes extraordinarily complex to administer and subject to significant potential abuse.

It is sometimes argued, in support of a national wages policy which utilizes the average productivity increase as a general wage standard, that with substantial aggregate unemployment (e.g., more than 5 or 6 percent of the labor force unemployed) and slack aggregate demand, prices tend to rise only because of increases in unit labor costs.[24] Other possible causes of price increases are not, it is suggested, significant in this economic environment. But, for several reasons, this argument is not fully convincing. Many consumer prices respond less to aggregate economic influences than to variations in demand and supply for particular products (as in the case of food products) or locations (as in the case of real property). The dynamics of product market events may cause prices in these and other important areas to rise or fall quite independently of more general influences. A slack aggregate economy may nevertheless contain substantial maladjustments in particular sectors, so that prices may be rising in certain sectors despite stable labor costs and considerable unemployment in the economy generally. When the condition of the economy is such that price pressures in important sectors are independent of aggregate unemployment and labor costs circumstances, then wages policy based on aggregate productivity increases is insufficient to control price inflation. In general, it would be an unusually stable and quiescent economy in which unchanging unit labor costs would serve to insure price stability. In the more common case, other circumstances would generate some rise in the price level. Depending on the rate of increase in productivity and, therefore (if there is a productivity-based wage standard), in wages, wages might rise more rapidly than prices, at the same rate, or less rapidly. The relationship between the rate of wage change and the actual increase in prices becomes especially significant, however, when a productivity-based wage policy is pursued by the government, because of an implicit (if not explicit) commitment by the government to the workers that prices will not increase more rapidly than wages.

The customary formulation of the productivity guideline for wages in the United States (and in Western Europe as well) is that wages should rise at the same rate as output per man-hour has risen historically. This rate of wage increase is, it is generally said, consistent with general price stability in the economy, and this consistency is often argued to be the economic justification of a productivity-based wages policy. Implicit in this formulation are two implications of great interest to workers and unions: that prices should remain stable (or at least reasonably so) and that real wages should rise, in consequence, by the same amount as long-run productivity.[25] Even should these points not be explicit commitments of the government, workers might be pardoned, if they, like other citizens, presumed that the rationale offered for a public policy implied its goals (that prices should be stabilized) and that the government was responsible for its success or failure to reach its implied goals. Unfortunately, it is often quite impossible for the government to guarantee price stability.[26] The likelihood is, therefore, in most (but not all) circumstances, that the implicit pledges of price stability and rising real incomes will not be met.[27] The result of such failure by the government is to develop a situation in which workers and the unions are determined to rectify past injustices through their own actions (e.g., through collective bargaining), at the expense of wage and price stability if need be. Since the government so often is not able to achieve its implicit promises of price stability and rising real incomes, it is best advised not to make them. The failure of the government to insure that real wages rise in step with productivity may have, as we have seen, very unfortunate political and industrial relations consequences.

Major disadvantages of a national wages policy based on the long-term rate of increase in productivity have now been set forth. The disadvantages include the inadequacy of the policy to insure price stability in most conditions of the economy, and potentially undesirable political and industrial relations consequences of the productivity standard.[28] But what, then, is the appropriate role of productivity considerations in determining a general standard for wage increases? Over long periods, the rate of increase in productivity largely determines the rate of increase in real compensation per worker. In its internal planning for economic policy, the government must consider the state of the economy and the applicability of this relationship of real wages and productivity in the instant situation. If the wage structure is in a generally good order (relative wages are little distorted), and if real wages may be permitted to rise (if military necessities, for example, do not prevent this), and if the economy is growing and has high employment, then an increase in money wages on average equal to the long-term rate of increase in productivity will tend to keep labor costs constant. If aggregate demand and profits can be controlled so as to keep prices stable (and if there are only minor pressures on food, real property, and other such prices), then a general wage standard based on productivity is a responsible position for the government. Whether the government and the private sector choose to make the rationale for such a standard public is another question. After all, a percentage standard for increases is simply a percentage, regardless of its rationale. And, therefore, to tie a general standard too closely to a single justification or economic argument is only to invite problems in its application and its public acceptance.

Productivity as a Criterion for Exceptions to a General Wage Standard. The use of productivity improvements as a standard for wage increases is not limited to a general standard, however. Productivity increases may also be applied, in individual instances, as a standard for wage increases in excess, or in exception to, those permitted under a general formula. In fact, one reason for eschewing a productivity-based general wage standard (at least publicly) is that such a general policy might foreclose the application of a productivity standard in individual situations. In some cases, it is appropriate that wage adjustments be allowed which reflect extraordinary productivity improvements. But, the application of a productivity standard on a case-by-case basis must be considered in the context of wage interrelationships and other potential problems involved.

There are two general types of circumstances in which productivity improvements may be argued to constitute an argument for wage adjustments beyond those allowable under a general standard. The first is a situation in which compensation for the individual worker or a group of workers is made to depend directly on the rate of output (or cost of output). Incentive plans, and cost-savings sharing plans (such as the Scanlon Plan) are examples of such types of compensation. A second type of circumstance involves an effort by an employer to obtain from a union acceptance of new technology or relaxations of existing work rules in return for a wage increase. There are numerous places in American industry where wage adjustments might be given in return for more efficient working practices. Collective bargaining in which wage increases are predicated on productivity improvements, often involving relaxation of working rules, has lately been referred to as "productivity bargaining."[29] In some instances the net cost of "productivity" agreements to the employer may be nil, or may even result in cost-savings and lower prices to consumers. Since this may be the case, it seems at first glance that a wage stabilization policy should favor such arrangements. Unfortunately, there are considerable hazards to a stabilization program in encouraging wage increases for purposes of productivity increases.

The major limitation of productivity bargaining in a period of wage controls is that allowances above the general standard, made available to some groups of workers in return for concessions on work rules, tend to be obtained by other workers without any such concessions. This is especially likely when one employer or employer association bargains with several unions; but separate employers and unions may show a similar result because of pattern bargaining. For several reasons wage increases in collective bargaining tend to be generalized without productivity improvements. One reason is that an employer may appear to some unions to reveal what he is willing to agree to in wage adjustments when he makes an agreement with another union, whatever the elements of the entire agreement. Thus, other unions may strike to obtain wage increases received by the first union only as a result of certain concessions. Alternatively, one group of workers may feel that they are being penalized for not having established costly work rules in past negotiations, for otherwise they would have had the rules to "sell" in return for larger wage increases. These groups may demand that they receive the same wage increase as if they had restrictive conditions to trade away. But, the reader may ask, cannot a wage stabilization board judge which agreements contain valuable productivity concessions by the unions, and so deserve additional wages, and deny the others? The answer is that the board may attempt to do so but will discover the process to be extraordinarily difficult. It is, in fact, very difficult for any person outside a firm or industry to evaluate the potential value of changes in the collective bargaining agreement supposedly directed at productivity improvements.

There is also an unfortunate dynamic process which tends to develop over time and to undermine the usefulness of productivity improvements as a criterion for wage adjustments above the general standard. This process operates in the following manner. No matter how careful a stabilization board is to allow wage increases only in return for identified work-rule concessions, other employers and unions will resent those who benefit from the policy by getting higher increases. This is especially true when historical wage differentials or patterns in wage determination are allowed to be altered in favor of the group making productivity improvements. Those unions not able to trade off rules for wage increases are then encouraged to *seek* restrictive rules with the ultimate objective of trading them, at a later date, for wage increases. A stabilization board could halt this practice only by including all adjustments in agreements with any economic significance in the coverage of the policy (not only wages and fringe benefits) and by rejecting increases which are beyond some standard which is developed. This policy is possible, but is very complex and difficult to administer.[30] Rather than attempt to administer so difficult and comprehensive a stabilization policy, a wage board is likely to find itself unwittingly encouraging the development of noneconomic practices in certain instances as a result of a policy which is intended to encourage their elimination in other situations.

After this extensive review of a most complex subject the reader might well ask for a general judgment: what is the best policy for a wage stabilization program with respect to increasing productivity? Obviously, the answer depends to a degree on the nature of particular circumstances, but some generalizations are in order. First, a stabilization program should attempt to encourage productivity improvements, both at the aggregate and microlevel, as much as possible, and to discourage improvements as little as possible. The paradox, as described above, is that a wage stabilization program may best encourage productivity improvements by rigidly limiting its efforts to encourage them. Second, long-term aggregate productivity increases may be examined as an element to be considered in establishing a general wage standard. Certainly, in the long run, rising output-per-man-hour causes workers to expect rising real wages, so that unless there are special reasons for holding or reducing real wages (as, perhaps, in a major war), the nation might hope to have both wage controls and rising real wages. But, the real wages-productivity relationship should not be made a single rationale for wage increases or applied in a mechanistic fashion (that is, without regard to other considerations). Third, attempts to apply a productivity increase criterion to individual wage adjustments are appropriate where differences in output-per-man-hour (and in rates of change therein) among firms, plants, occupations, and industries tend to affect appropriate wage differentials.[31] In judging issues of wage structure, a wage board should include in its considerations the progress of productivity over time among groups of workers. A board may wish to apply other criteria to the review of proposed wage adjustments in each situation, but the impact of productivity changes on wage differentials must be an element of informed judgment of stabilization issues, lest undesired wage anomalies result.

Fourth, and last, in some instances stabilization authorities may wish to permit employers to "buy out," with wage increases larger than generally permitted, certain extraordinarily expensive work practices. Examples of such practices might have included, in recent times, manning requirements in the railways; restrictions on handling of containerized cargoes on the docks; requirements for special manning on small compressors at construction sites by various locals of the operating engineers, and so on. (No implication that these practices are solely the result of union activity or that they might not serve some useful purposes is intended here. However, it is important to recognize that reduction of such practices may have a substantial economic impact which it is in the broader interests of the public to encourage, if management and labor can agree on terms for the modification or elimination of the practices.) But, if a wage board is to allow wage increases for relaxation of noneconomic practices, there are several aspects in which it must take great care. The board must satisfy itself that the proposed productivity increases are significant and will be forthcoming in the future. The board must attempt to distinguish each situation in which it makes an approval on productivity grounds from other cases, and should seek to inform and persuade other workers and employers as to the general gain to the economy resulting from the changed practices and the approved wage increases. And the board must be prepared to limit approvals under the productivity policy to one-time adjustments, few in number and not to be repeated. Finally, the additional wage increase above generally allowable standards should be as small as possible and definitely need not be commensurate with the productivity gains in the individual case. After all, development of more efficient practices is not only a matter of public concern but is the responsibility and often in the long-term best interests of both management and labor. This group of qualifications to the application of a productivity criterion to individual cases is required in order to minimize the possibly disruptive effect of a loose policy regarding changes in work practices on the stabilization program and on economic practices in industry generally.

The Prices-Plus-Productivity Standard

In recent years much attention has been given to a formulation of a general standard for wage increases that includes the influence of increases in both consumer prices and productivity. The rationale most often given for such a standard is that real wages should rise in step with productivity, requiring that money wages also be adjusted upward to compensate for changes in the price level. The notion that price and productivity increases constitute an appropriate standard for wage increases is an old one. One source of this suggestion is that price and productivity changes have long been elements of some economic models of aggregate wage changes. Another source has been the inclusion in certain significant collective bargaining agreements (especially several in the automobile manufacturing industry) of wage adjustments based on these two factors. It is not surprising, therefore, that a prices-plus-productivity standard has been suggested frequently as a general criterion for wage increases during a stabilization program. And, finally in 1971 a form of this proposed standard was adopted by the Pay Board as the central policy of the wage stabilization program.

There are, however, several significant variants of the prices-plus-productivity standard. Three of the more important variations are described here. First, allowable wage increases may be *simultaneously* dependent on price and productivity increases. That is, in the current year, wages would be permitted to rise by the same amount as prices and productivity combined. A second variant is both *prospective* and short-run in character. The wage board would, in this formulation, establish a general standard equal to desired price and productivity increases in the current year. That is, a wage standard would be established consistent with the price and productivity objectives of the government for the current year. A third variant relates the wage standard to the long-term average annual increase in productivity and to the target for price increases in the current year. In both the second and third variant, unlike in the first, it is essential to the function of the standard as an element of price restraint to specify a quantitative figure for the general standard. This figure, which is the standard itself, is determined by a technical process involving both the estimation of the short- or long-term increase in productivity and the selection of a target price increase for the future year.[32] Unfortunately, these variants have become hopelessly inter-mingled in public discourse, and there has been little public discussion of the problems associated with each.

Let us consider briefly several of the limitations, both practical and logical, of each proposed criterion. First, the *simultaneous* standard is largely inoperable because of the difficulty of foreseeing the actual course of price and productivity increase in a given year. Yet many citizens understand the standard to imply they should receive, in wage increases, the sum of price increases and productivity increases, and will either seek to obtain an increase equal to their expectations of the increase in prices and productivity or will believe themselves ill-treated if they receive less.

Second, the prospective short-run prices and productivity standard is subject to the difficulty that it will almost certainly work quite differently in different states of the economy. The essence of the standard is to establish a rate of increase for compensation per man-hour consistent with a desired rate of price increase. It is argued by the proponents of such a standard that, if the rate of productivity increase can be estimated for the coming year, and a target rate of price increase selected, then the appropriate wage standard is their sum.[33] Unfortunately, price adjustments reflect many factors in addition to increases in unit labor costs. When other factors are favorable to price stability, wages may rise less rapidly than a prospective prices-plus-productivity standard implies. When other factors are unfavorable, prices may rise more rapidly than the standard suggests. Furthermore, the actual course of productivity increase during a year may depart from its projected growth, possibly distorting further the ultimate (or ex post) relationship of prices-and-productivity and compensation increases. A distortion of the relationship between the implied increase in prices and the actual increase, in either direction, creates problems for a wage board, especially in establishing policies for a further year of controls. If compensation-per-man-hour were not to rise as rapidly as prices-and-productivity in fact rose, unions and workers would argue for making up the difference in a further year. If compensation were to rise more rapidly than prices-and-productivity, business would argue for lessened compensation standards and/or increased prices in the following year.

Third, the compensation standard based on the long-run productivity and target price increases in the current year is subject to each of the practical problems just described plus a logical inconsistency in its formulation. The inconsistency arises as follows: if prices in the short-run are related to unit-labor-cost increases, then certainly the appropriate productivity component of a wage standard is the short-run increase in productivity, not the long-term rate. In fact, the summation of the long-term rate of increase in productivity with a short-term target price increase is an addition of noncomparable items, unless it is anticipated that the short-term rate of productivity increase will equal the long-term rate (a coincidence which reduces the third type of standard to a special case of the second type). Where it is not expected that the short-term rate of productivity increase will equal the long-term rate, then the use of the long-term rate to establish a wage criterion can have no intended relationship to short-term price consequences.

The implication of these criticisms of the various prices-plus-productivity standards is that the standards are generally imprecise in formulation, often failing to be related causally to the consequences predicted and likely to generate future difficulties for the stabilization program by creating unwarranted expectations on the part of labor and business.

Paradoxically, however, the prices-plus-productivity standard may be so interpreted and applied that it may serve usefully as a general standard in some circumstances. Such an interpretation is to allow wage increases to average an amount equal to the long-term gain in productivity and to partially (but only partially) offset expected price increases. The purpose of such a standard is to restrain compensation increases in order to exert a limiting influence on price increases over the time necessary to wind-down price pressures. Because such a wage policy is more restrictive than those normally referred to as price-plus-productivity standards, it should probably be accompanied, for acceptability to labor, by restrictions on other forms of income, so that the burden of reducing price pressures is shared among elements of the society. The important additional element added by this interpretation is the desire to sever directly the connection between price and compensation increases.

Against the background of various proposed standards, what may one conclude in general, as to the determination of the general wage standard? Four comments which constitute a fairly comprehensive judgment are in order. First, much of the discussion of the elements of a general standard and its formulation has assumed the aspects of a purely theoretical dispute which is both unresolvable and largely irrelevant to practical problems of stabilization policy. Representatives of union, management, and the government may each be expected to offer somewhat different views as to how a general standard should be constructed and what forces should be influential in determining it.

Second, whatever the rationale in advance for a wage standard, its effect in practice depends on the course of the economy during the application of the standard. Therefore, an interpretation of the standard based on the actual experience is possibly quite different from a theoretical interpretation.

Third, a general standard expressed as a quantitative limit (as in 1971-72) functions independently of any particular rationale used in its construction. Hence, the rationale used in its development becomes merely a matter of historical interest, significant in a practical sense only when an adjustment of the general standard is contemplated. However, a standard which has no quantitative limit and which is based on cost-of-living and productivity increases is a very much different matter. In fact, a stabilization program which permitted wages to rise in step with productivity and cost-of-living, without limit, can hardly be referred to as wage stabilization at all. This is because there would be normally no independent restraint exerted on wages or prices by wage control.

Fourth, we may conclude that the prices and/or productivity rationales for a general standard have no particular importance to a stabilization program as compared to other factors which would influence wage policy. The general trend of productivity and the consequences of rising prices for real wages are elements of the economic environment to be considered by labor, management, and government in establishing a stabilization program generally. But other factors, including considerations of wage relationships, the expected volume and composition of output in the economy, industrial relations situations, political considerations, and matters of the income distribution certainly carry no less weight in these considerations than prices and productivity increases. It is, therefore, an error for stabilization authorities to dwell too strongly on these two factors as elements of the determination of an appropriate stabilization policy or to publicize them as the fundamental determinants of appropriate wage adjustments.

Administration of a General Standard

Application of a General Standard

In this section we shall explore the careful definition of a general standard required for its *application* to individual groups of workers and firms. To what types of compensation adjustments should the general standard apply?

How should increases be measured? The answer to the first of these two questions depends on a variety of factors, and different stabilization boards have approached it in various ways. The most basic issue is whether a stabilization program will attempt to regulate earnings or wage rates, or both. Generally, stabilization programs have eschewed any attempt to regulate the annual earnings of individuals or workers. However, programs have differed in the treatment to be made of wage and piece rates versus average gross or straight-time hourly earnings. In some instances, involving small units of workers in a single occupation, average straight-time hourly earnings and occupational wage rates may coincide. The important issues arise when they do not. In such an instance, which is by no means uncommon in the economy, should the board consider wage rates in preference to average hourly earnings, or vice versa?

The Little Steel formula, for example, generally applied to wage rates or piece rates (with average straight-time earnings used as an equivalent of time rates in most cases) in a plant or bargaining unit. The formula explicitly did not apply to gross average hourly earnings for reasons largely associated with the desire to encourage additional production. Nor did the formula apply to various fringe benefits, including holidays, and pensions or health plans. During the Korean period the WSB initially intended the General Wage Regulation No. 6 to apply to all adjustments, wage rates and fringe benefits included. The board was unable, however, to maintain this position against opposition, largely from the unions.[34]

In 1971–72, the Pay Board attempted to go even further than the WSB by attempting to control total compensation. The general pay standard was defined in such a manner as to apply to gross compensation, including the cost to the employer of all fringe benefits (including overtime and other premiums, described by the term "roll-up," as well as pension and health benefit plans). Although congressional action forced important modifications in this definition, the general standard of the Pay Board remained broader than its historical predecessors. The Pay Board adopted a broad definition of the applicability of the general standard because of certain advantages. First, the broad definition allows direct comparability between the general standard and several of the major economic aggregates with which a wage stabilization program is concerned, such as increases in prices and productivity. Second, a broad definition of the standard often appears to provide a criterion which is simple for labor and management to apply, and one therefore consistent with a considerable reliance on self-administration in the program.

However, there are also substantial disadvantages involved in the board definition. First, there are major limitations of the all-inclusive definition which offset its supposed advantages for self-administration. On one hand a general standard, broadly defined, which approximates the intended degree of wage restraint for the stabilization program, is, paradoxically, one which cannot be made public without imperiling the success of the program. And since it cannot safely be made public, the standard is poorly conceived as a device for self-administration. Why cannot the general standard, broadly defined and commensurate with the stabilization goal, be made public? On the one hand, if made public, the general goal tends to become a minimum, not average, rate of increase. The enunciation of a single standard by federal authorities suggests that anyone ought to be entitled to that rate of increase. The result tends to be that virtually all negotiated settlements are at the announced level but that many, sometimes justifiably, go beyond. The average degree of wage restraint tends, thereby, to rise above the target level. One qualification should be offered. The intensity of this tendency for the norm to become the minimum is affected by economic conditions. In an expansive economy the tendency may be irresistible.[35] In a slack economy, however, if the norm is sufficiently high, employers and unions, and especially nonunion employers generally, in stagnant product markets may resist the tendency to award earnings increases equal to the norm.

Second, the consequence of providing such a standard for self-administration of compensation by employers and unions in the economy generally can be undesirable. For example, consider a general standard which is made to apply to gross hourly earnings (including sick leave, vacation pay, overtime, and the like). Then a possible, indeed frequent, *mis*interpretation of the standard would be to increase wage rates by the allowable amount. Arithmetically, let the average wage rate be $2.50 per hour, and the average gross hourly earnings be $3.00 (a not unusual relationship between the two in the United States in 1972, for example). Let the general standard apply to gross hourly earnings and be 6.0 percent. Then, 6.0 percent of $3.00 is $ .18. But this $ .18 is not intended to apply to wages (where it would mean an increase of 7.0 percent) but to the future average gross hourly earnings, including the effect of any increase in the wage rate on overtime (usually time and a half or double time), paid vacations, and so on. What is actually allowable as a wage increase is indeterminate until the question of any other changes in the package (such as an increase from time and a half to double time for overtime) is settled. If no changes are made except in wages, the allowable increase is 6.0 percent in wages. The essence of this limitation of the all-inclusive general standard is that it is not defined in categories intelligible to employers, unions, and workers generally and therefore is essentially irrelevant to the actual processes of decision-making in the economy. Reliance on self-administration by a stabilization board in such a situation is at the risk of substantial errors of application.

Third, a broad definition of the applicability of a general standard, while comparable to the prices and productivity measures, invites in practice the introduction of substantial distortions in the national structure of compensation. This is because the interrelationships of wages and compensation practices so important in particular labor and product markets often extend not only to total compensation packages but specifically to wage rates, piece rates, particular fringe benefits, and so on.[36] A stabilization board which ignores the comparison among these items invites the establishment of severe distortions. For an example let us return to the Pay Board's consideration in 1971 of the aerospace cases. The traditional pattern of bargaining in aerospace is that the companies follow a pattern of increases in wage rates, but each company has very different standards and experience with respect to such matters as overtime and severance pay.[37] The application of the Pay Board's broad earnings standard (excluding, however, pensions and health and welfare plans) generated different approvable increases in various companies. Rather than distort totally the bargaining traditions of the industry and the competitive positions of the various companies, the board modified considerably the application of its formula.

Fourth, an all-inclusive standard may treat employers differently according to the degree of shift in the occupational (or pay grade) composition of their labor force. One formulation of a comprehensive standard for a unit of workers may be described symbolically as follows.

$$\gamma \left(\frac{\sum_j W_{tj}}{\sum_j M_{tj}} \right),$$

where $\gamma = 1.0 + x$, where x is the general standard, e.g., 6.0 percent, W_{tj} = wage bill of the company for pay grade (or occupation)$_j$ at time t, and M_{tj} = man-hours worked in pay grade (or occupation)$_j$ at time t. Note that the distribution of a company's employees among job classifications and therefore wage rates affects its wage bill. How is a stabilization authority to require a company to estimate an effect of change in the composition of its labor force? Should it require the company to hold the distribution of employees constant prospectively, even though the company may not intend to do so in practice during the ensuing year? And how will the board act in the second year of controls; will it require the distribution of employees to remain unchanged (for the purposes of calculation) from two years back? Yet, if the board does not follow some such procedure for standardization, it is liable to permit wage adjustments by companies with many occupations which can be very different from those permitted companies with few. In effect, the average-hourly-earnings standard abandons all direct concern for wages at the occupational (or job classification) level, except for such limited regulation as can be applied through adopting conventions for estimating the impact of employment changes on allowable earnings adjustments. Where labor shortages exist in certain occupations, providing a free hand for some large companies to raise the rates they pay in these occupations can have a substantial impact on other employers. And, it cannot be expected that employers who might lose skilled people to another firm can be effectively prevented from raising their own rates of pay. Clearly such dangers will be greater in an expansive economy than in one which is relatively slack. But even in generally slack labor and product markets, some such problems arise. The greater danger, however, in relying on control of average compensation in a slack economy is that should the economy expand, the stabilization program must either be substantially modified or be eliminated if substantial problems are to be avoided.

In conclusion, what may be said about the definition of a general standard? First, that the long-run best interests of the economy and the stabilization program suggest a standard narrowly defined, that is, limited to wage and piece-rate adjustments. Standards for other elements of compensation should be provided specifically. This is the only method by which the complex interactions of elements of compensation can be adequately addressed by a stabilization board. Thus, broad definitions of a general standard which ignore the question of occupational wage rates (both within and among occupations, and both internal and external to single employers) should be avoided. A stabilization program cannot avoid establishing some form of standards for occupational rates by industry and by community. Second, the arguments favorable to a comprehensive general standard have been stated above. We have seen that they are, to a degree, illusory. Still, a stabilization program which involves only the quasi-judicial application of a single formula to all compensation adjustments may well be, administratively, the most simple for federal officials to apply. But such a program should be understood for what it is. It is a grossly limited program, and one which involves the danger of creating substantial distortions, with destabilizing consequences, in the very economy it is intended to assist in stabilizing.

The Measurement of Compensation Increases

The application of a general standard for wage increases to individual situations requires that a method (or methods) of measuring the magnitude of the proposed compensation increases be adopted. This is because there are, in fact, many potential statistical measures of wage adjustments.[38] One set of problems in measurement arises from the need to estimate certain costs in compensation packages which cannot always be exactly determined in advance because they depend on occurrences in the future (for example, the cost of a change in a late-shift premium, or in health benefits to be provided). Numerous conventions for making estimates of the value of such provisions have been developed over the years, and though these conventions may be subject to some dispute, they provide a basis for the application of stabilization criteria and need not concern us here. A second set of problems of measurement arises from the common practice in industry of spacing wage or fringe benefit increments over time in the course of a year (or of a contract's duration, if different from a year). There are important issues involved in a stabilization board's handling of the measurement of stepped increments, and these issues will be examined here.

There are a surprisingly large number of possible measures of the value of wage and benefit increments which are spaced over time. Types of measurement differ among themselves and with the circumstances attending a contract. For example, when management and labor shift from a single increment per year to multiple increments, special transitional measurement problems are created. These situations we shall ignore, however. Rather, we will focus our attention on patterns of providing increases which are unchanged. Here too, several different measures are possible. However, some are superior to others. For example, one direct method is to take a given time period, generally twelve months, sum the total value of increments over the entire period, and, if a percentage estimate is desired, compare this sum to the base value of wages and fringes (the value at the outset of the twelve-month period). Symbolically, using, for convenience, time periods of one month and a measurement period of one year:

$$k = \frac{\sum_i 12}{P_{(t-12)}},$$

where k = percentage value of the increase, $\sum_i$ = sum of all increments over 12 months, and $P_{(t-12)}$ = value of the wage and fringe benefit package in the previous time period. This method (k) may be called an "end-to-end" measurement of the increase, as it involves no consideration of whether the increments were spaced out over the months of the agreement. But, as every employer and employee understands, a wage increment awarded at the start of a year involves a larger payment to the employee in the course of a year than one occurring at the mid-point of the twelve-month period. Another measure of the value of the total increase may be made, therefore, which involves weighting each increment by the length of time it is in effect.

Symbolically:

$$k(1) = \cfrac{\dfrac{\sum i_m (12 - m)}{12}}{P_{(t-12)}} ,$$

where $k(1)$ is the newly defined measure, i and $P_{(t-12)}$ are as above, and $m =$ the number of months before the increase goes into effect. This measure $k(1)$ may be called the "time-weighted" value of the increase. Let us take a simple example. Presume that the final value of wages and fringe benefits in a collective bargaining agreement is \$4.00. Suppose, first, that an increase of \$.40 is negotiated and placed into effect at the outset of the new agreement, and there is no further adjustment for one year. Then both measures—k and $k(1)$—show an increase of 10 percent. But suppose, instead, that the \$.40 increase is divided into two increments, \$.20 at the outset of the new agreement and \$.20 six months later. Then the "end-to-end method (k) still shows an increase of \$.40, or 10 percent. But the time-weighted method—$k(1)$—shows an increase of \$.30, or 7.5 percent. Which measure is appropriate for use in a stabilization program?

Incidentally, there are numerous other measures which may be defined. For example, one might shift the base each time an increment occurs. That is,

$$k(2) = \cfrac{i_m}{\dfrac{P_{(t-12)} + \sum\limits_{m} i_m}{M}} ,$$

where $i_m, m, P_{(t-12)}$ are as above and $M =$ total number of increments. This measure is one, in essence, of averaging the percentage changes. Another measure, the "sum of the percentage method," was initially used by the Pay Board:

$$k(3) = \sum_{M} \left(\frac{i_m}{P_{t-12}} \right) ,$$

where i_m, M, and P_{t-12} are as above. In our second example, this measure would show

$$k(3) = \frac{\$.20}{4.00} + \frac{.20}{4.00} = \frac{\$.40}{4.00} = 10 \text{ percent},$$

and is, in fact, identical to k, the "end-to-end" measure. (Other measures are also available, but, like these two, are not of major significance in stabilization.)

The basic issue in the application of wage standards involves the determination of the appropriate uses to be made of the "end-to-end" and the time-weighted measures. Stabilization boards normally favor the "end-to-end" measure because it more clearly reflects what is happening to the level of wage rates and is not subject to the degree of manipulation possible with the time-weighted measure. For example, suppose that the $.40 increase in our example were due at the end of the eleventh month of the agreement. Then the time-weighted increase would be only $.033, or .08 percent. Should the $.40 increase be delayed until the final day of the twelve-month period, it would be a negligible increase in both cents-per-hour and percentage terms. Clearly, no stabilization board could permit the potential increases in the level of rates which a time-weighted standard would allow to those willing to postpone increments. However, to adopt exclusively the "end-to-end" measure also has a disadvantage, for it suggests to workers and to the unions that the most sensible arrangement (the one which maximizes their allowable compensation adjustment) is an agreement with all wage and benefit increases at the outset of the new twelve-month period. Yet, there are reasons why a board may wish to avoid this seeming rigidity. For example, it may make dispute settlement difficult. If a company has cash-flow problems, it may need to postpone wage adjustments, and a stabilization program should not unnecessarily prevent it from attempting to negotiate such an agreement. Furthermore, sometimes large wage increases are warranted—when, for example, a group of workers has not had an increase for several years and has fallen behind rates paid to comparable groups of workers. In such a situation, it may be important for the board to attempt to space out the total increase, not only to lessen the impact of large increases on the companies and prices, but also to reduce the impact of large single increases (no matter how well merited) on other units of wage earners.

In general, a stabilization board should utilize both measures. It should give preference to the "end-to-end" measure as the alternative best reflecting the impact of a compensation adjustment on the long-term level and structure of wage rates. But the board should also be aware of the effect of the spacing of increments on the immediate cost of an agreement to the employer and, possibly, on the price charged consumers. Where no issue of wage structure or interrelationships is involved, some special consideration might usefully be given to agreements which space out increments to reduce immediate cost increases. A board should never blind itself to aspects of pay adjustment simply in order to apply a single measure of the value of agreements. The best principle, as always, is for the board to preserve as much flexibility in its application of its criteria, including the form of measurement of compensation increases, as is consistent with its overall stabilization responsibilities.

8. Standards for Wage Stabilization: Criteria for Exceptions to a General Standard

The Purposes Which Exceptions Serve

Stabilization boards have always provided exceptions of many sorts to a general wage standard. There are several purposes which provisions for exceptions serve, some of which are integral to the operation of a stabilization program and others of which are somewhat incidental (although not necessarily unimportant) to its operations. Among the various purposes for exceptions which are integral to a stabilization program, five of considerable importance may be distinguished. First, exceptions are necessary to prevent undue hardships to groups of workers or employers which might arise from the application of general standards. A common exception for this purpose has been the special treatment awarded proposed increases for low-paid workers (the substandards exceptions). Second, exceptions may be necessary to permit needed reallocations of manpower. This exception has been especially important in wartime. Third, exceptions may be provided in order to further objectives of public policy not narrowly related to stabilization itself. For example, adjustments in wages necessary to eliminate discrimination by race or sex in compensation (to establish "equal pay for equal work") may be permitted regardless of general standards. Fourth, provisions for the establishment of exceptions provide an important degree of flexibility in a program. For example, the establishment of certain exceptions may be necessary to lessen anomalies created in unusual circumstances by the application of general policies to unforeseen circumstances. Fifth, and perhaps most important quantitatively, exceptions to a general standard are necessary to adjust wage relationships.

Exceptions may also be necessary for several purposes which may be described as incidental to the operation of a stabilization program. These purposes relate primarily to the ability of stabilization authorities to employ exceptions as a safety valve for pressures on the stabilization program which cannot be fully contained by general policies. Exceptions for these purposes are incidental in the sense that they are occasional, and the instances in which they will be needed are often quite unpredictable. But they may be quite important, because the inability to encompass occasional and unexpected pressures within a stabilization program by some device may very well destroy it. There are essentially three types of pressures involved in the need to provide such exceptions. First, the problems of dispute settlement may require special arrangements in the framework of stabilization policy. The application of exceptions in dispute cases is, however, generally a very hazardous operation and one which often subjects a stabilization board to great criticism. Yet, as Clark Kerr has described the matter after World War II:

> Economic and political power varied greatly from industry to industry and union to union. Some recognition, on occasion, had to be given to this unequal distribution of power—whether morally justified or not—when the groups with power were unwilling to have this power unrecognized and unrewarded even in a period of national emergency. Some lions demanded a lion's share.[1]

Second, changing economic conditions may generate pressures for wage adjustments too strong to be constrained by the existing general standards. When this occurs, careful use of exceptions may allow increases adequate to permit continuation of the stabilization program without major modifications or the occurrence of crisis situations. World War II provides a classic example of the employment of exceptions by a board as a device to permit increases without altering a rigorous general standard. The application of exceptions on a case-by-case basis permitted delay in allowing individual increases, prevented a general round of wage increases, and yet permitted, over time, many limited adjustments the net effect of which was to relieve much pressure for a relaxation of the Little Steel formula. Third, exceptions may be necessary to accommodate new developments in collective bargaining. For example, until World War II employers and unions had only limited experience with fringe benefit programs, but under the pressure of wartime wage restraint, employers and unions turned to bargaining about fringes. The NWLB used exceptions as a method of incorporating standards for fringe benefit increases in the stabilization program. During the Korean War the operation of annual improvement wage increases (e.g., in the United Automobile Workers-General Motors agreement of 1948) were accommodated in a similar manner.

It should be emphasized that a stabilization board should provide that exceptions to a general standard should operate in a constraining as well as a liberalizing direction. For in the same way that application of a general standard to the proposed increase for a particular group of workers may result in a wage rate or a compensation package which is inadequate by comparative standards, so application of a general formula may also yield a rate too high by comparative standards. A stabilization board should always preserve its option to deny the full amount allowable under a general standard when comparative relationships would thereby be distorted.

A recent example of the results of failure to make provision for exceptions to limit an increase otherwise available under a general standard is illustrative. The Pay Board initially denied itself any opportunity to limit a wage increase to less than 5.5 percent. Early in its operation the board refused to approve in total the aerospace agreements of 1971. Following the Pay Board's action, the affected unions, those of the automobile workers and the machinists, filed suit in federal court challenging the board's decision. The basis for the suit by the unions was that, of the total increase provided by the agreement, a substantial proportion had been agreed to under the old contract as a deferred cost-of-living adjustment. Thus, they argued, of the 51-cent adjustment due in 1971, only 17 cents was "new money," and the 17 cents was clearly within the Pay Board's 5.5 percent general standard and under the board's regulations could not be denied to the workers. The unions argued before the court that "there is no exception [in Pay Board regulations] cutting down on the 5.5 except in connection with some retroactivity problems which are not involved here." The judge, sensing the inadequacy of an unqualified general standard, asked the lawyers, "you mean, this 5.5 is automatic regardless of protection [against cost-of-living increases] or the adequacy of the wage or anything else?"[2] The answer was "yes," the 5.5 percent was automatic, regardless. Thus, with an automatic 5.5 percent general standard regardless of the level of the wage rate, the determination as to whether the money was agreed to prior to 1971 and the stabilization program assumed great importance. The court found for the unions and remanded the aerospace agreements to the government for further consideration. In its recodification of its regulations in the fall of 1972, the board, profiting from its experience, included in its regulations permission for it to deny the full amount allowable under the general pay standard where "necessary to preserve ongoing collective bargaining relationships" and other purposes.

We now turn our attention to various types of criteria proposed as the basis for exceptions permitting increases above a general standard. There are, of course, an unlimited variety of potential exceptions. In the following pages we will consider those most often employed in stabilization programs. The exceptions discussed are also chosen because they represent fundamental types. Several fairly common forms are not reviewed, however, because of both space limitations and the complexity of the subject. Included in the topics not treated in detail below are exceptions from a general standard for incentive plans, bonuses, stock options, and certain other specialized forms of compensation. Also, because there is enough material regarding stabilization standards to fill many volumes, this limited survey must have a central focus. One aspect of this focus is the contribution to the overall success of a stabilization policy of the particular criterion. Equally important, however, is the question as to what behavior by industry and labor the special standards and exceptions which are examined have been intended to encourage. Have the exceptions been so designed that the long-run impact of their application was favorable not only to economic stability but also to other aspects of public policy—for example, good industrial relations and greater equity in the distribution of income?

Exceptions for Low-Wage Workers

Wage stabilization programs in the United States generally have provided for preferential treatment for low-wage workers. There are two major reasons for this. First, it is generally recognized that some workers earn rates of pay which are so low as to constitute a problem with respect to the living standard which they can maintain (hence the term "substandards"), and public policy is often concerned to attempt to cause an increase in their rates of earnings. Unfortunately, application of a general standard for wage increases in these instances might have the effect of requiring low-wage workers to remain at a poverty-level of income. Where this is the case, it has often seemed inappropriate to attempt a rigorous stabilization of low wage rates as an element of a program of economic controls. Second, the application of a general standard to the wage increases which employers are prepared to make for low-wage workers (either unilaterally or as a result of collective bargaining) may appear to result in anomalies. A percentage standard, especially, normally would allow very low cents-per-hour increases for low-wage workers, and would permit high-wage workers to widen the cents-per-hour differentials. In consequence, to avoid a particularly stringent impact of controls on low-wage workers, an exception seems appropriate. Establishing an exception (or *exemption*) for low-wage workers implies a comparative standard (low-wage as compared to what?), but it has been common practice to express the exception as a minimum cents-per-hour wage rate below which the general standard does not apply. Two major issues arise with respect to this practice. First, at what level should the exception be established? It must not be so high as to emasculate the wage stabilization program generally, or so low as to be ineffectual. Second, what standards should be established for the adjustment of rates which are above the low-wage threshold but which are closely related to the substandard rates? For a stabilization program to provide an exception for rates below a certain level and to apply rigorously the general standard to rates above that level would threaten unduly to compress the structure of wage rates in many instances.

What factors influence a wage stabilization board in its determination of an appropriate level of substandard wages? In addition to the objectives of setting the level neither too high nor too low, a board normally considers four other factors. First, Congress may have expressed a view regarding the issue in the legislation enabling the president to establish an economic stabilization program. Further, in the absence of agreement within a wage board as to the appropriate level of a substandards exception, Congress has sometimes legislated a level. For example, in June 1952, Congress amended the Defense Production Act by a provision that excepted wages of $1.00 per hour or less from wage control, resolving a dispute which had not been settled within the WSB during a year and a half of operation.[3] Second, because Congress has customarily required that wage boards not disapprove increases required under the Fair Labor Standards Act, the federal minimum wage has become another major factor which a wage board must consider in establishing a substandards exception. Because the federal minimum wage does not cover all industries or establishments and because, on the other hand, it is often believed not to be adequate as a standard for an appropriate wage level, wage boards are not normally able to simply adopt the minimum wage as the substandards level. In a tripartite board, employers may argue that the federal minimum wage is too high for a national standard covering virtually all industries and establishments; while labor representatives will argue that it is too low. A third factor affecting the determination of a substandards level is the group of estimates of living costs and standards of living in the United States. The Bureau of Labor Statistics (U.S. Department of Labor) and other agencies periodically survey living costs in various cities for adequate and modest standards of living. It is inevitable that these surveys become an important element in the determination of substandards exceptions in a stabilization program. Because low-wage workers in this country so often earn below what is required, according to these surveys, for an adequate or modest standard of living, it is common for labor representatives to argue for a substandards exception based on the information contained in these surveys.

Fourth, the establishment of a substandards level depends partially on the functions of the wage board itself. Boards which have dispute functions, in addition to wage stabilization responsibilities, confront a particular problem. Whereas a substandards criterion used as a stabilization standard is permissive (an employer is permitted to pay up to the level of the substandards criterion), a substandards level applied in a disputes-settlement function may be mandatory. Thus, a board may order an employer to pay the wage level established for definition of substandards in a decision in a labor disputes case. Clearly, in such a circumstance, a board cannot simply apply a substandards criterion regardless of other considerations (as it can in the context of stabilization alone). The major supplementary considerations in disputes cases involving substandards were set forth by George Taylor for the NWLB in the textile cases of 1944–45:

In dispute cases over substandard rates, the War Labor Board problem is to determine the extent to which standards of living can be improved without creating a loss of employment and unstable employment conditions.[4]

In the absense of dispute cases, a stabilization board may leave these issues to the determination of the employer and the union (that is, to voluntary wage adjustments).

The question of what level to establish as the threshold for substandard cases is not unrelated to the method of determining the level. The NWLB, for example, resisted any single calculation, or set of calculations, as a basis for making this determination. The board solicited the recommendations of the regional boards as to the basis for substandards criteria,[5] but never accepted any specific formulation.[6] In the Korean period, the WSB resisted a single number until Congress enacted one into law in 1952, as we have seen above. In the 1971–72 period, however, the Cost of Living Council, acting when the Pay Board had reached an impasse, adopted a rationale for the $1.90 initial substandards level which was based on a Bureau of Labor Statistics estimate for the urban family minimum budget, adjusted for number of wage earners, and so on. This publicly stated rationale, supplemented by the general language of the Economic Stabilization Act amendments of December 1971, dealing with substandards, permitted a successful federal court suit by several unions which forced the Cost of Living Council to revise substantially upward its $1.90 figure (to $2.75).[7] Thus, like other aspects of stabilization, the determination of the substandards level is not a purely arithmetic matter but one requiring judgment in the balancing of opposing objectives. The attempt in 1971–72 to utilize a formula approach in determining a substandards level resulted in too high a level (an ironic result of an attempt to set too low a level) and demonstrated again the futility of a mechanical approach.

A final issue in the treatment of substandards is the manner of adjustment of nonsubstandard but related wages. To allow increases of any magnitude below the substandard level, but to restrain those above, threatens too great a compression of wage differentials in certain plants and industries. But to allow the same percentage or cents-per-hour increases for rates above the substandard level as for those below threatens the entire wage stabilization program. How are these two dangers to be avoided? Historically, the NWLB and the WSB attempted to resolve the dilemma by adopting a principle of "tapering" for related but nonsubstandard wages. In general, the tapering principle required that increases on rates above substandard be progressively less than the increases provided for the substandard rates. Whether percentage or cents-per-hour tapering was appropriate depended on whether percentage or cents-per-hour differentials traditionally characterized the plant or industry involved. This policy was not easily applied, however. As described by Dunlop, the NWLB "insisted upon 'tapered increases' under which successively smaller increases were applied, and finally no increases at all, proceeding up the wage-rate scale. This policy resulted in the dislocation of normal wage-rate relationships between job classifications. In some cases, such as the cotton textile and railroad industries, these changes proved so impracticable that subsequent increases had to be granted to higher-paid employees to restore the differentials between job classifications."[8] During the Korean period, the WSB advanced the tapering principle after Congress established a substandards level of $1.00 in June 1952. A tapering formula for increases on rates above $1.00 was advanced by a special tripartite subcommittee of the board. The formula provided for either the same percentage or cents-per-hour (depending on past practice) increases in related classifications as for those earning less than $1.00 per hour, provided that no higher group received more than the group just below it and that there was a maximum limit on the cents-per-hour increase that could be made in any situation.[9] The board never acted on the subcommittee's recommendation but handled each case on its individual merits, generally applying, however, the subcommittee's proposed policy.

In 1971–72, in contrast, the Pay Board abandoned the tapering principle per se in favor of a general constraint. "Workers within a unit already earning in excess of $2.75 are permitted increases of 5.5 percent above the average base of *their own pay*. However, if low-wage (i.e., below $2.75 per hour) employees who receive at least 5.5 percent to reach the exemption level (i.e., $2.75) are granted even greater raises, the portion of their raises which exceed $2.75 are charged against the permissible 5.5 percent available to those already making more than $2.75."[10] That is, regardless of the cents-per-hour or percentage increase granted low-wage employees, higher-paid workers could receive no more than 5.5 percent, and if low-wage workers received more than a 5.5 percent increase, and a final rate greater than $2.75, higher-wage workers would receive a corresponding reduction in allowable adjustments. Again, the Pay Board disregarded virtually all issues regarding appropriate plant or industry wage structures in its attempt to cause all unit-wide pay adjustments to be as close to 5.5 percent as possible.

The tapering principle, although superior to the Pay Board's approach, was not entirely satisfactory, as we have just noted. In practice, it has proven virtually impossible to require tapering at higher wage levels, since undesired compression of the wage structure may be bitterly resisted, both by workers and employers. It is, therefore, probably necessary to conclude that tapering as a procedure for limiting wage and cost increases for that purpose alone cannot be effective. However, of greater importance to a stabilization program is the need to prevent pressure on differentials between substandard and higher wage rates from raising higher rates in some plants and industries. Judgments as to which rates are such key rates and the degree to which they may be adjusted, if at all, in consequence of increases in substandard rates is a most important function of a stabilization board.

Exceptions Based on Interplant and Interoccupational Wage Relationships

Exceptions to a general standard for wage increases have often been made on the basis of traditional relationships between wage rates. Among the most important of these comparisons between rates are those which involve interplant, interoccupational, or geographic dimensions. Of the differentials existing at the outset of a stabilization program (or proposed to be established by management and/or labor) some are appropriate and others are not. Differentials which are existing but are not appropriate (historically or, in the case of changing circumstances, economically or institutionally) have been given the generic term in stabilization policy of "interplant" inequities, where the term is not limited to comparisons between plants, but also includes comparisons among occupations and regions. Wage stabilization programs have been prepared to permit the adjustment of interplant inequities for two major reasons, fairness to workers and the promotion of economic efficiency in production. Stabilization programs have also attempted to resist the creation of differentials (or their elimination) where the result is to establish an inequity for workers other than those directly involved.

In a period of stabilization, the application of standards to cases involving alleged interplant inequities involves primarily the comparison of wage rates. If the proposed adjustment of differentials meets certain standards of past practice, economic efficiency, or institutional necessity, then the adjustment may be approved by a stabilization board, even though the increases exceed the general standard. Conversely, increases in rates that distort wage relationships and create inequities for other groups of workers should be denied, even though the increases proposed would not exceed the general standard.

The reliance on wage comparisons as a criterion for wage adjustments has both advantages and disadvantages. The major advantages of a comparative standard, beyond the obvious value of responding to the needs for fairness and economic realism in a stabilization program, is its impact on individual employers and unions. These advantages may be highlighted by comparison with stabilization boards which attempt to adjudicate proposed increases solely on the basis of a formula which measures increases in cost rather than using a comparative criterion. No stabilization board can produce better estimates than the immediate parties of the true cost of proposed wage and fringe benefits adjustments, so that the board is necessarily largely dependent on the costing done by the parties. Furthermore, local parties often resent a national board attempting to judge these matters separately from their own evaluations. Yet, local parties are often blinded by their own self-interest to how stabilization criteria are intended to apply to their own situations. Therefore, because a stabilization board cannot readily oversee the internal operations of individual employers and unions, and because the parties are often tempted to misapply wage criteria, problems in the application of a formula to individual agreements arise.

In contrast, reliance by a stabilization board on wage comparisons with other units of workers as a criterion for evaluation of proposed increases has clear advantages. First, the wage board can be as expert in applying a comparative criterion as the local parties. Second, misapplication of the criterion by private parties is more readily discernible by a board. Third, the attention of individual employers and unions is directed outward by the wage standards at the impact of their proposed pay adjustments on other employers and workers, not inward at their own problems. Since stabilization policy is, in its essence, the application of concern for the general welfare to the activities of individual employers and unions, use of a comparative standard forces private parties to confront directly the impact of their own internal dealings on other groups in the economy. However, a stabilization board may find it extraordinarily difficult to apply a comparative criterion correctly because of the many complex issues involved in wage interrelations. A brief list of the problems involved in applying a standard of comparability of wage rates would include the following: (1) job titles which are identical among firms often actually involve different job duties; (2) methods of wage payment differ (e.g., piece v. time rates), and complicate pay comparisons; (3) the definition of the geographic area in which comparisons are appropriate may be difficult; and (4) the regularity of employment differs among jobs and firms.[11] With so many factors influencing comparisons, inappropriate judgments regarding relative adjustments in wages are easily made. Unfortunately, errors in application of a comparative criterion can be very damaging to a stabilization program, because they tend to create inequities for other workers, leading to a broad upward movement of interconnected rates.

Avoiding the unfortunate consequences of misapplication of a comparative criterion depends upon a wage board's response to the two fundamental issues involved in the adjustment of interplant inequities: which wage comparisons are appropriate and which rates are to be taken as fixed for stabilization purposes. What factors determine appropriate relationships? A board normally considers two fundamental sets: institutional and labor market-related factors. Administratively, boards often employ historical patterns as a surrogate measure of the influence of these two sets of factors. Historical patterns may normally be altered with board approval only in the case of compelling evidence of changing institutional or economic circumstances.

It may be surprising to some readers that institutional factors generally seem to take a degree of precedence over labor market factors in establishing wage differentials in an uncontrolled economy. That is, the employment of workers by a single firm, or their membership in a single labor organization, constitute powerful forces tending in the direction of wage uniformity among plants, occupations, and regions.[12] Two of the most careful students of the American wage structure have concluded that "the main positive factor accounting for inter-plant differentials, in short, is the substantial variation in the wage-paying ability of various firms, combined with refusal of the more profitable firms to maximize profits by paying as low wages as they could pay. The labor market imperfections which have been revealed so fully by recent research appear to have only a passive or permissive effect."[13] Other institutional factors than the boundaries of a single firm have less significance, however. Reflecting the practice of employers and unions, stabilization boards have accepted institutional practices which can be demonstrated from historical information as standards for wage adjustment.

Labor market factors such as shortages or surpluses of manpower are also often significant in determining relative wages and have been applied by stabilization boards as a principal standard of evaluation of interplant inequities. Different labor markets exist for different industries and occupations, of course, so that the board must determine not only the relationship of wage rates, but also the labor market area from which to draw rates of comparison. The appropriate definition of the labor market area is the geographic area in which a particular group of workers moves among employers and occupations, in response, in part, to influences exerted by wage differentials.

In order to prevent wage distortions from developing, stabilization boards have sometimes established a hierarchy of wage comparisons. For example, the WSB during the Korean period applied various comparisons in the following priority: firms applying for approval of a wage adjustment under the interplant inequity criterion were required to demonstrate that the proposed rates were "not in excess of rates for the same or comparable jobs in (1) the same industry in the same labor market area, or, if none, (2) in a comparable industry in the same area, or, if none, (3) in the same industry in the most nearly comparable area."[14] But comparisons alone should not always determine the approvability of a proposed increase, that is, an inequity, by comparative standards, which exists should not require approval for an increase regardless of other considerations. The reasons for the inequity may also be significant. For example, rates in a particular plant or employee unit might have lagged behind increases in closely related rates because of relatively low skill or low productivity. Let us consider a particular case. Suppose that new equipment or a new process is tried out by a company in several plants and is finally placed in one plant because of the capacity of workers there to do the new jobs involved. Wage rates might be raised in that plant accordingly. In this situation, for a stabilization board to ignore the reasons for which differentials are widening and to permit an upward readjustment of wages in other plants to restore the old differentials, would be profoundly destabilizing. Thus, it may be seen that some changes in differentials are required by economic or institutional factors, so that in reviewing interplant inequity cases a stabilization board must not apply a comparative criterion without regard to such factors.

The discussion thus far has assumed that the wage rates to be compared can be identified. This is not always a simple matter. For example, precisely what elements of compensation are to be compared among various units of workers? The possibilities include:

1. Hourly rates for workers actually paid on time basis.
2. Hourly minimum rates for workers paid on a piece-rate or other incentive basis.
3. Piece rates per unit of output.
4. Earnings per unit of skill and effort required....[15]

Often labor and management, faced with such a set of varying possibilities, seek to create uniformity of unit labor costs among various competing firms. In other instances, identical wage rates are established, with unit labor costs varying among firms because of nonwage factors. A stabilization board risks creating havoc in an industry when it substitutes one measure of comparison for that traditionally employed. For example, historically the practice of unions and management in the western lumber industry has been to establish common wages rates and fringe benefits for various classifications of workers who are employed by many firms, large and small, in the industry. Individual firms either negotiate with the union through an employer association or operate as independents. Furthermore, unit labor costs vary considerably among firms, in consequence of the size and characteristics of the firms. As a result, average wages might be as much as four times higher in a logging operation than in a box plant. How have stabilization boards handled such an industry? In 1952, the WSB issued a resolution permitting a standard cents-per-hour increase in the western lumber industry in each occupational classification.[16] However, in 1972, the Pay Board applied its wage criteria to the associations of lumber firms as a unit, not to each wage classification, and reduced the wage increases which had been negotiated. The board permitted uniform increases among the employers who were members of the associations. But many independents, because of varying labor costs due to a different composition of employment by classifications, were allowed to place the increases into effect. The threatened result was the establishment of different wage rates in the same occupational classifications in the industry, a result without merit as an element of stabilization policy.[17]

The application of a comparative criterion is also hampered by the difficulty in many situations of defining an occupation, so that wage-rate comparisons can be made between plants and areas. Many semiskilled occupations, particularly, are quite specialized and confined to a single firm or industry. In fact, most semiskilled workers are not hired on an occupational basis, and the range of variation in wage rates resulting from the capacity of various industries and/or employers to pay is very great.[18] In such situations, characteristic of many manufacturing and service industries, the application of a comparative criterion for wage increases is particularly difficult. Further, however, employers and unions are usually handicapped in demonstrating the existence of interplant inequities. In general, recourse must be had to either summary statistics, such as average hourly earnings, or to the rate of key occupations for comparisons. Generally, approvals of adjustments based on interplant inequities should be minimized in the area of semiskilled workers in manufacturing and service industries.

We now turn to the question of the determination of stabilized rates—those rates which are not to be changed except as a result of the application of a general standard (that is, as part of a general adjustment of wage rates in the economy). As indicated above, the failure to hold certain key comparative rates stable (except for general changes) threatens a process of readjustment of other rates through the application of the exception for interplant inequities. The identification of stabilized rates is critical, therefore, to the application of an inequities criterion. It is not possible to discuss in detail the determination of stabilized rates in individual circumstances. However, as a general rule, it may be offered that stabilized rates are those which are in their appropriate position with respect to both the internal wage structure of an establishment and with respect to comparable plants, occupations, and industries.

Several types of realignment of wage rates have been approved by stabilization boards. Boards have traditionally provided for approval of certain very close wage patterns called "tandem relationships." Tandem situations exist where one group of workers has historically received the same increase as that provided for another group. Approval of increases for the leading group may thereafter be used as an argument for approval of the same increase for the followers. A board must always be careful, however, to distinguish true tandem relationships from those which are merely alleged. The failure to do so can permit a round of wage increases to occur which are generally destabilizing. Wage boards have approached this problem differently, however. Tandem relationships were given a narrow definition and close scrutiny on a case-by-case basis by the NWLB and later by the Pay Board. The WSB of the Korean period, however, followed a more liberal course. For example, in November 1952, the WSB approved increases in the rubber manufacturing industry above those permitted by the general standard, citing as a tandem relationship the close similarity of general wage movements in rubber to those in automobiles in the post–World War II period.[19] In general, whether a board rigidly limits tandem approvals or is more flexible, it must always seek to be aware of three factors. First, it should attempt to foresee, in each case which comes before it, the potential generalization of the increases approved to other workers and plants via the existence of tandem relationships, however defined. It is important, that is, that the board act in as full knowledge of the secondary impact of its action as possible. If the potential secondary impact is undesirable, the initial action of the board should attempt to minimize secondary impacts. Second, the application of a tandem criterion always involves the potential problem that the grounds on which the leader's increase is approved (e.g., productivity increases), may not be applicable to the followers. For this reason, tandem relationships must be investigated carefully by a board and should not automatically receive approval. Third, tandem relationships should always be required to reflect actual leadership conditions in labor and product markets and in institutional arrangements, not simply chronological precedence. For example, small units should not be permitted to set patterns on a tandem basis for major units, unless there are other circumstances than the dating of agreements which suggest that this constitutes appropriate board policy.

The tandem relationship is a special case of interplant wage comparisons. Less rigid relationships have normally been considered by stabilization boards on a case-by-case basis, often without well-defined standards. Yet the absence of standards reached an extreme in 1971–72 when the Pay Board allowed itself to approve exceptions of virtually any amount to the general standard, if required, in the board's judgment, by the "equitable position of the employees involved." The board did in fact apply this criterion often, but never attempted to define it carefully either in general or in individual cases. Thus, the board provided no guidance to labor and management as to what was permissible under this standard. In consequence, the practice of the application of interplant inequity standards in a stabilization program cannot be said to have been advanced at all by the Pay Board. An example will illustrate the point. In approving an increase of 9.7 percent for more than one thousand nonunion production workers at Maidenform, Inc., plants in New Jersey and West Virginia, the board said only that the increase was justified "under regulations relating to the tandem qualification, the 'catch-up' exception, and the avoidance of gross inequities exception."[20] This statement of the basis of the board's decision was purely formalistic and provided no guidance as to what wage relationships were considered significant in determining the permissibility of an exception. Such formalistic statements of the reasons for decisions were common Pay Board practice.

Before concluding this discussion of interplant inequities, we should examine more carefully the so-called "brackets" policy of World War II. No more sophisticated effort directed at the readjustment and stabilization wage relationships has even been made by a government program in the United

States or abroad, to this author's knowledge. The effort was not entirely successful and was certainly not without major limitations, but a great deal is to be learned from a study of the experience. The brackets policy began with a directive of the Director of Economic Stabilization to the NWLB on May 12, 1943, authorizing the board "to establish as rapidly as possible, by occupational groups and labor market areas, the wage-rate brackets embracing all those various rates found to be sound and tested going rates. All the rates within these brackets are to be regarded as stabilized rates, not subject to change save as permitted by the Little Steel formula. Except in rare and unusual cases in which the critical needs of war production require the setting of a wage at some point above the minimum of the going wage bracket, the minimum of the going rates within the brackets will be the point beyond which the adjustments mentioned above may be made."[21] The NWLB proceeded to direct its regional bodies to create tripartite panels for the purpose of establishing the brackets, and it provided instructions regarding the procedures to be used, modifying them periodically as experience suggested. For example, on April 11, 1944, the NWLB instructed the regional boards to establish a bracket for each major job classification. "Each bracket should be for jobs which are comparable as to type of work performed," it said. But "similarity of names [i.e., job titles] is no guarantee of comparability of jobs. . . . It may be found necessary to determine separate brackets, with respect to the same-named jobs, for different general types of establishments." In order to establish the brackets, sample surveys of plants and employees were to be conducted on a local labor-market basis, although "there is no hard and fast rule with respect to geographic or industry coverage." Rather, since "there is no automatic, statistical way of determining the wage rate brackets," the "use of sound judgment and discretion by the tripartite boards is necessary."[22] Thus, the regional wage stabilization boards of the World War II period set out to reduce the wage structure of the American economy to a set of brackets of industrial and occupational classifications on a geographic area basis.

In order to apply the brackets to individual cases, however, the boards had to determine the "minimum" rates of the various brackets. The NWLB provided instructions regarding various procedures. "If the basic [wage] data [for a classification] are presented in the form of a frequency distribution of single rates, a minimum may be determined by finding the first substantial and representative cluster . . . of rates." If, however, the basic data were not single rates, but rate ranges, a more complex procedure was suggested to determine an "allowable rate range which is the minimum of the bracket."[23] The "minimum" did not mean, the reader will notice, the selection of the lowest individual rate which could be found for a single job classification, but rather a cluster or range of rates at the lower end of the bracket of "sound and tested going rates." Yet another method of determining the minimum was also used, the "strict 10 percent method." That is, "the weighted coverage of all the rates in an occupation in an industry in an area is computed and the point 10 percent below the [weighted] average is set as the minimum of the bracket."[24]

Several uses were made by the NWLB and its regional offices of the brackets. The most common use was in the administration of interplant inequity cases. An example of the application of the brackets is as follows: a regional board might have established the minimum of the bracket for a certain job classification in a certain area at $ .72 per hour. An application by an employer and union to raise the rate of pay of persons employed in that classification from $. 67 per hour to $. 74 per hour might then by judged to be an excessive increase, and an increase to only $. 72 per hour might be permitted.[25] But the brackets were also used to set wage rates for newly established plants and in the review of cases involving intraplant inequities.

The elaborate systemization and extensive effort which went into the brackets policy did not prevent a variety of problems from developing. First, the use of the minimum of the brackets as a standard for interplant inequities and other types of cases afforded to the wage structure generally and to the economic stabilization program an undesirable rigidity. This rigidity became increasingly important as the stabilization program lengthened. Second, the brackets intentionally accorded a certain primacy to local geographic comparisons in wage relationships, as opposed to industrial comparisons among localities.[26] As time passed, considerable pressures developed against this emphasis in certain industrial settings. In general, John Dunlop concluded, "the experience of the bracket program clearly demonstrated that there were large areas of the wage structure which had to be handled upon an industry rather than a locality basis. Industry influences predominate in many sectors of the economy, such as coal, railroads, and basic steel. The locality approach to wage stabilization can in fact be applied only to a portion of all wage rates."[27] For those communities in which were located a number of plants within a single industry, the brackets provided an effective technique of stabilization.

The reader will recognize that no effort of a stabilization agency has involved the extent of study of the American wage structure which was undertaken in the context of the brackets program of World War II. However, it cannot be doubted that such an extensive effort is required of a rigorous program of wage restraint in the context of an overfull employment economy. While a less ambitious program of wage comparisons may suffice for the incomes policies of recent years, the fundamental standard against which all effective stabilization must be measured is some sort of brackets policy, albeit perhaps improved by a more careful attention to the requirements of industrial, as opposed to geographic, structures. And in any industry in which rigorous wage restraint must confront over-full employment, some approximation to the detailed study of wage structure represented by the brackets policy is necessary to provide for the correction of interplant inequities without the risk of stimulating progressive upward adjustments of interdependent wage rates.

Exceptions Based on Intra-Plant Wage Relationships

Pay adjustments above those allowed by a general standard may be required not only for the readjustment of wage relationships among plants, occupations, and areas but also within individual establishments. Adjustments based on the structure of wage rates internal to an establishment have traditionally been referred to in stabilization programs as "intraplant" inequities.[28] The need for intraplant adjustments of wage rates may occur for three major reasons: distortions in the internal wage structure which have developed prior to the stabilization program from a variety of causes;[29] the introduction of new technological processes requiring an altered structure of wage rates; changes in the economic environment. Not all three influences are equally important at different periods, however. For example, in the 1940s the needs of conversion to a wartime economy and, later, of reconversion to a peacetime economy, emphasized the impact of changes in the economic environment on internal wage structures to a degree not matched since. Furthermore, the distortions in internal wage structures inherited by the World War II period from the depression of the 1930s were much more extreme than those which confronted stabilization authorities in later periods. So insignificant were these two factors (changing economic circumstances and distortions in the internal wage structure), in later years, that the Pay Board in the 1970s essentially ignored them, adapting its policies with respect to intraplant inequities primarily to the problems created by substantial technological change.

The interests of a stabilization program in the internal wage structure of individual plants has its source in three factors. The first is the necessity for restraint on the average level of wage adjustments made. For a stabilization program to permit internal wage adjustments without limitation would, in many instances, invite evasion of the wage restraint objectives of a stabilization program. Second, in circumstances in which avoidance of interruptions of production due to strikes or lockouts is of importance to stabilization authorities, establishment of well-ordered internal wage structures provides an affirmative influence in the direction of industrial peace. Third, there often exists an extensive intermingling of intraplant and interplant aspects of wage structure. That is, approvals of readjustment of rates of pay for some job classifications on an intraplant inequities basis may have a substantial impact on the interplant structure of wage rates, potentially requiring readjustments of wage rates in other plants. In general, of the various types of intraplant wage adjustments which are common, two types often have interplant consequences, while a third does not. The introduction of formal or informal job evaluation plans, which provide a systematic method of establishing job classifications and wage differentials within a plant, have the potential for affecting the external (to the plant) wage structure. Also, wage adjustments covering broad groups of workers (for example, all hourly-paid workers, or all workers exempt from overtime), often threaten to have an impact on wage relationships with other plants. However, minor adjustments of the wage rates of small groups or individuals which are out of line with others in a plant do not normally have an impact external to the plant. Where intraplant adjustments do threaten a destabilizing impact on interplant wage relationships, a stabilization board must attempt to avoid creating interplant inequities by approvals of wage adjustments based on a standard reflecting intraplant inequities.[30]

Briefly, therefore, wage stabilization policy may be said to have three objectives with respect to the internal wage structure of an establishment: to permit necessary readjustments of rates where merited by certain standards; to exercise restraint over the magnitude of the wage adjustments directly and indirectly involved (through, for example, the creation of interplant inequities); and to favor the establishment of appropriate internal wage structures as a contribution to industrial peace and to high levels of production efficiency. We will first consider the restraint aspects of stabilization programs.

Generally, stabilization programs have been prepared to permit minor adjustments in wage-rate relationships among individuals or small groups of workers within a plant. In some instances these adjustments have been required to be within the allowance of a general standard (as in 1971-72), or in others to be made as exceptions additional to the allowance of the general standard (as during the Korean period). Adjustments involving large units of workers have normally not been allowed at any time as exceptions to a general standard, with a few exceptions during the World War II period. However, changes in technology, pace of production, and other influences sometimes have tended to cause the average earnings of pieceworkers to rise relative to those of hourly workers. A readjustment to traditional differentials for the hourly workers was considered by the NWLB to be an intraplant inequity exception.[31] In the Korean period and in the 1970s, adjustments for such large groups were, except in special circumstances which are described below, required to be included within the allowance of the general standards (which were, of course, generous compared to those of World War II).

With respect to more limited intraplant adjustments, there have been varying degrees of attempts by control boards to restrain destabilizing adjustments. During both the Korean period and 1971-72, stabilization boards relinquished the detailed supervision of internal wage adjustments conducted by the NWLB and dealt with intraplant inequities in two ways. First, companies were allowed to make such internal adjustments of rates as were included within the general standard. Further, appeals to the boards for additional increases on an intraplant inequity basis were heard on their individual merits. In the case of the WSB, most were probably approved.[32] In the case of the Pay Board, most were probably denied. Yet, in neither period did the stabilization boards (the WSB and the Pay Board) have solid criteria for their actions in these instances. For only through the use of a brackets policy, or similar method of obtaining comparative wage-rate information, could a board intelligently appraise the potential impact of a proposed internal wage readjustment on the external wage structure. As Livernash described the experience of the Korean period: "From a stabilization point of view, a job (and the attached wage rate) is critical if there is danger of . . . spiral increases. Such (initial) increases are unstabilizing even though involving only a small immediate increase in total average earnings." But how is a board to determine these situations? Unfortunately, Livernash notes, "the burden of proof to deny (a proposed intra-plant wage adjustment) is virtually upon the stabilization agency."[33] In the absence of detailed data on the interplant wage structure, a board is largely without resources, unless other unions and managements call a potentially destabilizing action to its attention. Faced with this impotence, the WSB tended, as we have said, to approve increases above the general standard, the Pay Board to disallow them. But neither board was able to limit increases in key rates which were *within* the general standard but were destabilizing—an opportunity the brackets policy permitted the NWLB. In general, in handling questions of the internal wage structure of firms both the WSB and the Pay Board abandoned any careful concern for the impact of internal wage adjustments on external wage relationships.

The failure of stabilization boards to consider carefully questions of intraplant wage structure may have other serious implications than those for interplant wage relationships. For example, suppose one establishment normally distributes the increase allowable under a general standard among its job classifications in such a way as to retain reasonable internal differentials. Another establishment, however, may provide a distribution of increases which substantially narrows differentials. Probably no serious situation will arise within a single year. But if controls continue for two or three years, the second establishment may seek relief from its compressed wage structure on an intraplant inequities basis.[34] A stabilization program will be tempted to deny the request, of course, but that course of action does not resolve the problem that has been created within the plant. The general conclusion which is to be derived from this discussion is that a stabilization program can afford to ignore the intraplant structure of wage rates in approving general wage adjustments only if it expects to have a brief existence. If stabilization policy is continued for a period of years, the internal wage-rate structure becomes of substantial importance to the potential success of a program of wage restraint.

The third reason cited above for stabilization boards to have an interest in the internal wage structure of establishments is the desire to encourage good practice in internal wage administration as an element of increasing production efficiency and encouraging industrial peace. All stabilization programs have pursued this policy to a degree. The most marked efforts in this direction were made in World War II. The NWLB encouraged various plants to conduct job evaluations, and certain major industries, including airframe manufacture, West Coast shipbuilding, and basic steel, employed job evaluation as a fundamental element of the wage stabilization process.[35] The public members of the NWLB intended to improve, through job evaluation, the industrial relations practice of American management. There was no evidence, in the Korean period or 1971–72, of any such desire on the part of wage stabilization authorities to improve the long-run practice of personnel management and industrial relations in American industry. During the 1971–72 period, for example, the Pay Board defined its intraunit inequity exception to apply only to "an inequitable pay situation within an appropriate employee unit resulting from the introduction of new or changed technology, and affecting not less than 10 percent of the job classifications and not less than 25 percent of the employees in the appropriate employee unit." The board then, by indirection, recommended the use of a formal job-evaluation plan to establish the altered wage structure resulting from the changed technology. Probably, the general practice of American management with respect to internal wage policy has improved since the 1930s, in part because of the influence of the NWLB, and this practice is, in the 1970s, less chaotic and inequitable than before. However, substantial opportunities exist in many sectors of the economy for improvements in the design of jobs, the structure and form of wage payments, and so on. It is appropriate for wage stabilization boards to encourage better practices, since improvement in personnel management and industrial relations contribute to the efficiency of American industry and thereby to underlying stabilization objectives.

Exceptions Reflecting Patterns of Wage Administration

At this point it is useful for analytic purposes to distinguish three types of wage adjustments. First, there are general adjustments in most or all rates in an establishment or industry. Adjustments of this nature have been subject to a general standard for wage increases and to criteria for interplant inequities. Second, adjustments may be made in the rates of individual jobs or classifications. In periods of wage control, such increases have been normally subject to standards based on wage comparisons, including those relating to interplant and intraplant inequities. Third, adjustments may be made in the rates paid to individual *workers*. Primarily, adjustments of this type result from promotions, merit plans, or rewards for length of service. The stabilization standards which apply to these type of increases are discussed here. Further, three special types of changes which may have an impact on compensation are also reviewed here: that is, changes in the scheduled hours of work and the establishment or modification of incentive plans.

Increases in compensation for individual employees which result from promotions, performance reviews (i.e., merit increases), or length of service would ordinarily be of little interest to a stabilization program for several reasons. First, in normal circumstances these increases amount to little aggregate increase in compensation; second, they often reflect increased output per worker and so have little impact on unit costs; third, they do not generally affect job rates and have little or no consequence for the relationship of wage rates. Furthermore, these practices provide a necessary element of flexibility in the compensation policy of a firm and thereby contribute to good personnel relations. For these reasons stabilization boards are reluctant to interfere with such practices. Yet, in a period of stabilization, a board must be careful that the elements of wage administration internal to an establishment are not utilized to subvert wage controls. This could occur in a number of ways. Promotions might not be made to more responsible or skilled jobs but rather to jobs merely renamed in order to provide a cover for a wage increase. Similarly, so-called "merit" increases might be granted on a large-scale basis without regard to performance, and longevity increases might be awarded at intervals so frequent as to serve merely to raise rates generally.[36] Stabilization boards have customarily sought to provide standards and procedures which permit bonafide promotions, merit review, and longevity increases to operate without interruption, while constraining potential abuses.

Employers may sometimes offer, or collective bargaining agreements provide for, reductions in the standard hours of work (e.g., from a forty-hour to a thirty-six-hour week) with no change in the hourly rate of pay. It is common for those affected to argue that such adjustments in the hours of work should be of no interest to stabilization authorities. In many instances they are correct. But in some circumstances, a stabilization issue may be involved. For example, an hours reduction may have the effect of requiring overtime at a premium rate of pay. In some instances guaranteed overtime may be required by a collective bargaining agreement; in others it may be the result of a verbal agreement. In still other situations, it may be the necessary result of a shortage of workers. Whatever the reason, guaranteed overtime may have a substantial impact on average hourly earnings. For example, an adjustment from a forty-hour to a thirty-six-hour week, with four additional hours at time-and-a-half is equivalent to a 5 percent increase in average hourly pay on a forty-hour week basis. (If the premium rate is double time, the adjustment is equivalent to a 10 percent pay increase.) This circumstance is relatively straightforward, and stabilization boards have, at least in World War II and the Korean period, examined proposed changes in the hours of work for their stabilization consequences.[37] In 1952, for example, the WSB permitted the New York Stock Exchange to reduce the standard work week of its employees upon a finding that the net effect on hours worked per employee was unclear and probably was not destabilizing.[38] A more indirect impact on stabilization policy of a change in the standard hours of work may result from interdependencies in production processes. For example, in industries in which workers are organized on craft lines, and work together, a change in the hours of work for one craft might have the effect of increasing production costs, though not earnings to workers, because of premature cessation of work by one craft. Alternatively, the employer might be obligated to provide overtime for the craft which has negotiated the shorter week—a situation akin to the one just discussed. In either instance, the impact of the hours change is unfavorable to the stabilization program. In general, hours reductions must be evaluated by a stabilization board on the grounds of their general effect on stabilization policy, broadly defined. Such cases are normally few and often involve unique circumstances. An ad hoc, case-by-case approach to these situations is best. The most generally applicable standard for approval or disapproval of proposed adjustments in hours is existing practice regarding the length of the work week in comparable occupations and industries.

Incentive plans have been the source of some problems for stabilization programs also. Generally, existing incentive plans have been allowed to operate in industry subject to the general standards and exceptions provided, with special arrangements made for the technical problems of adjustments in incentive rates. But boards have carefully examined proposed changes in plans or in proposals by employers to establish new plans. In general, the problem for a stabilization board is to prevent incentives from being used as a subterfuge for an otherwise nonapprovable wage increase. How has this problem been addressed in the past? During World War II, the NWLB issued no specific instructions with respect to incentive programs and referred their provisions to collective bargaining wherever possible. The board did attempt to provide guidance for itself and for management and labor in developing incentive schemes. In the Korean period, the WSB was prepared to approve incentive plans on a case-by-case basis where unit labor costs were increased, then the plans were shown not to be destabilizing or creating intraplant inequities. Furthermore, to protect against the erosion of incentive standards which commonly results from the introduction of new technology and new processes, the board required that adequate provisions be made for correcting and maintaining the standards of the plan. These policies of the board proved especially applicable to incentive plans directed at individual initiatives but were inadequate for plant-wide schemes. To handle these types of plans, the board applied two other criteria: that the percentage increase in earnings not exceed the percentage increase in output per man-hour, and that the incentive-output relationship not be affected by normal changes in operation. The intent of the board was to base earning increases solely on increased productivity.[39] Finally, during the 1971-72 period the Pay Board sought to permit the establishment of new plans without prior approval only when the aggregate amount of compensation in the employee unit was not increased above what would have occurred in the absence of the new plan. Plans which would tend to increase total compensation could be approved by the Pay Board "under such terms and conditions as may be imposed by the Pay Board." The board failed to specify the factors determining those terms and conditions. This review of historical experience suggests that, because incentive plans are very much specific to individual plants and industries, boards should handle them largely on a case-by-case basis. On this basis, however, boards have always been prepared to approve virtually unlimited increases in compensation through incentives, if higher earnings are generated by increased production so that there is no increase in unit labor costs.

Policies Regarding Fringe Benefits

In the years during and since World War II fringe benefits have become an important element of employee compensation in American industry. Fringe benefits have, therefore, been of increasing concern to stabilization authorities. This section examines the problems which fringes pose for a wage control board. The several attempts which have been made to develop relatively simple administrative devices for regulating the growth of fringes are described. But it is demonstrated that no satisfactory method for regulating fringes has been found. In fact, if anything, the difficulties of regulating fringe benefits is growing and poses a special problem of great importance for the future. In some important instances fringe benefits have become a virtually uncontrollable engine for inflationary pressures. The inflationary impact of fringes on total compensation increases can be seen in aggregate statistics. In the late 1960s and early 1970s, for example, increases negotiated in fringe benefits exceeded those in wages, causing the package increase (wages plus benefits) to be above that in wages, even at the high rates of wage increase occurring in those years. How this situation has come about and its implications for stabilization policy are explored below.

There are actually two main types of fringe benefits which can be distinguished, and these types should be discussed separately.[40] There are, on the one hand, provisions for health care and pensions normally provided through insurance funds. On the other hand, there are benefits such as paid holidays, paid vacations, sick leave, maternity benefits, overtime premiums, shift premiums, and so on. Because of the peculiar circumstances which attend the operation and cost of insurance plans, these two types of benefits have for many years been distinguished in public discussion and in stabilization policies. In general, the relative importance of both types of fringes has been increasing in the total compensation package. For example, the cost of health, welfare, pension, and similar benefits (excluding Social Security and other payments required by law) in a sample of 146 companies in the United States rose from 6.5 percent of total payroll in 1949 to 10.9 percent in 1969. Payments for time not worked (e.g., overtime premiums, vacations, holidays, paid lunch periods, and so on) rose from 5.8 percent in 1949 to 10.6 percent in 1969.[41] We will now discuss, in turn, the major issues of stabilization policy with respect to insurance plans and other fringe benefits.

Health, Welfare, and Pension Plans

There is a long-standing myth that employer contributions to social welfare plans such as health insurance or pension plans are not inflationary and therefore are of no interest to stabilization authorities. During the Korean period, when fringes were of less relative significance as an element of compensation than later, this view was expressed even by representatives of government. This argument, that insurance (and pension) plans do not add to purchasing power and therefore cannot be inflationary, is deficient in several respects because it ignores other economic consequences of increases in nonwage compensation. First, increases in prices may be required because of increased employer expenses for insurance programs. Second, inflationary pressures may be exerted in the medical industry by increased health insurance programs.[42] Third, the impact of an increase in insurance costs on the total compensation package of one group of workers may be transmitted by earnings comparisons to other workers, and translated into either increased fringe benefits or higher wages. Thus, regardless of the impact of insurance programs on purchasing power, other potential consequences of their increase require the attention of stabilization authorities.[43]

What types of standards were applied in the past by stabilization programs to insurance plans? During all periods a distinction has been drawn between cost increases for employers which are required to maintain existing benefit levels and those which may be sought to improve benefit levels. Increases required to maintain benefit levels have usually been exempted from controls. Increases to support new benefit programs or improved benefits have been subject to various types of standards. For example, during World War II the NWLB alternatively granted approval to "reasonable" insurance plans or indicated that no approval was required. In disputes cases the board sometimes ordered the establishment of plans and in other cases did not, relying largely on industry practice.[44] In the Korean period health insurance programs were subjected to rather detailed standards regarding benefits and employee contributions.[45] Pensions, on the contrary, were approvable if meeting certain very general requirements and if they were not otherwise unstabilizing.[46] Within a few months the flexible policy applied to pensions was extended to health insurance. Petitions regarding insurance programs were submitted to a tripartite national panel, which processed some forty thousand cases in a single year.[47] The Pay Board in 1971 established special standards for these fringes based exclusively on the magnitude of increased employer costs. The board permitted 0.7 percent additional increase in the base compensation rate to be applied to "qualified" fringe benefits.

Thus, history suggests three methods of regulating plans in a period of stabilization: blanket approval, flexible and broad general standards of both benefit and cost nature, and a formula approach to costs exclusively. None is satisfactory with respect to insurance plans in the 1970s. Perhaps in no other area of compensation does past experience provide so little guidance for the future. What explains this unusual situation? The fundamental cause is that insurance plans have become, in important instances, highly complex features of the economic environment. There has developed a bewildering variety of plans, benefits, costs, and administrative devices,[48] so that characteristics of a plan may serve as a target for other groups of workers, contributing thereby to economic instability. Several examples may help to clarify the point. First, the cost of maintaining benefit levels has in some circumstances become so high as to exert a destabilizing influence on other wage and benefit packages. This has been especially important in industries characterized by numerous small employee units and multiple employers, where the costs of maintaining pension coverage comparable to that provided in plans covering many workers has sometimes become very expensive. Second, in some instances, benefit levels have been negotiated which both parties know will have extreme cost consequences in the future. Such plans are potentially unstabilizing in their effect on costs and prices in the establishments directly involved and, through comparisons in bargaining, exert unstabilizing influences on compensation in other employee units. A stabilization program which allows cost increases in this situation simply because benefits were previously agreed to by the parties is also an inadequate stabilization effort.

What, then, should be the elements of a future stabilization policy with respect to insurance plans? First, insurance and pension costs cannot be simply subsumed within a general standard; practical realities will not permit this for several reasons. A stabilization board must deal directly on insurance plans with parties other than labor and management—medical societies, insurance companies, cooperative health plans, and others. These parties, if they are not satisfied with the board's policies, may appeal, very likely successfully, to Congress for relief. Furthermore, insurance plans raise complicated issues of the interaction between social and economic policy which are not answered simply by noting that benefits do cost money.[49] In consequence, a board will be required to develop policies explicitly related to insurance programs. (The need for detailed policies, as we have said above, is less severe the shorter the duration of a period of controls is expected to be.) In addition, boards must also be prepared to set relatively precise standards for what is encouraged.

Second, a somewhat ironic situation has now developed which complicates the control of insurance plans. There are two distinct types of insurance plans with respect to the method of determination of costs and benefits. These methods are presented by the Bureau of Labor Statistics in tabular form, as follows:[50]

	Type of Plan	
	Multiemployer	*Single Employer*
Benefits	Set by trustees	Collective bargaining
Costs	Collective bargaining	Employer purchase from insurer

Originally, single-employer plans were controlled through benefit standards, while cost standards were applied to multiemployer plans. That is, the matters negotiated in collective bargaining were those for which standards were prepared. But, during the Korean period, a first attempt to control single-employer plans by cost alone was made—a policy which was later adopted on a general basis by the Pay Board. Regulation of benefits was abandoned for single-employer plans, as it had always been for multi-employer plans. This cost-only procedure of control has not worked well. Hence, it is now certain that, as a result of the large volume of money involved, the interrelationships of benefits and costs, and the potentially destabilizing aspects of insurance plans, it will be necessary for stabilization boards to resume regulation of benefits in single-employer plans and to extend regulation for the first time to benefits provided by multiemployer plans.

Third, the structural problems in collective bargaining which generate unreasonably high costs or benefit levels, or both, in individual situations, and which may become pattern setting and thereby destabilizing, must be addressed by a stabilization board directly. These structural problems cannot simply be repressed or constrained—they have become too significant quantitatively. Rather, the regulatory leverage and the influence of stabilization authorities should be employed to reform, where necessary, medical and pension coverage, to restructure benefits provided, and to improve the administration of insurance plans.

Fourth, and the most difficult of the measures thus far proposed, a stabilization board must be prepared to abandon the policy of permitting whatever cost increases are necessary to maintain previously established benefit levels under insurance programs. Not only have benefits in many instances become too costly simply to ignore, but such a policy encourages local parties to establish unreasonably high benefit levels in the certainty that the employer contribution increases which are required in the future will be approved under stabilization regulations. In place of this permissive policy of the past, boards must be prepared to act on an ad hoc basis to deny increased contributions to funds and to require structural changes in the funds or reductions in the benefits provided, as the circumstances require. The standards which should be established to determine whether benefit levels or costs are excessive in fringe benefit plans are those which are based on industry or area practice. It is the extreme situations which are potentially destabilizing.[51]

Other Fringe Benefits

Fringe benefits other than insurance or pension plans more closely approximate wage increases in their direct economic impact on earnings and purchasing power of workers. In some instances the effect of these fringes is to increase the weekly or annual earnings of workers; in others, weekly or annual earnings are not affected. But in all cases, these fringes increase the average compensation paid by employers per hour worked. Stabilization authorities have been concerned with the impact of changes in these benefits on both the relative earnings of workers and on the costs of production. In the former case, the danger is that fringe benefit increases may be used by employers and unions as a subterfuge for wage increases. In the latter case, increases in fringes, although so distributed among workers that relative earnings are not distorted (e.g., as pay for time not worked), may cumulate to substantial cost increases with a corresponding impact on product prices. Since these potential nonstabilizing consequences of changes in noninsurance fringes have been more apparent than the consequences of increases for insurance plans, stabilization boards have dealt more explicitly and firmly with them than with insurance plans.

Noninsurance fringes, like insurance plans, may be regulated either through the benefits provided or the costs incurred (or both). Past stabilization boards have attempted one or the other method, not both. Control of benefits is, generally, the more complicated and administratively difficult method but is also potentially the more effective contribution to stabilization objectives. Regulation of *both* benefits and costs, a yet more difficult and potentially more effective approach, may be required in the future, as is the case with respect to insurance plans. What has been the historical experience with respect to noninsurance fringes? During World War II, these fringes were reviewed on a case-by-case basis, resulting in the establishment of standards for the level of benefits, especially with respect to overtime premiums and shift differentials. In the case of other fringes, the board would permit establishment or improvement, if justified by area or industry practice, but would not award them in disputes cases. During the Korean period the WSB, following an abortive attempt to include all fringes on a cost basis in the general wage standard, adopted a special policy applicable initially to five types of noninsurance fringes: paid vacations, premium pay for days and hours of work, paid holidays, shift differentials, and call-in (or reporting) pay.[52] These so-called "major" fringes were to be approved by the board on the basis of area or industry practice.[53]

The WSB's experience with the administration of industry or area practice as a standard for fringe benefit increases was not a happy one. Two basic problems developed. First, employers and/or unions petitioning for an increase in fringes tended to give data on industry or area practice which was favorable to their proposal, and the government was often unable to verify the information without its own survey mechanism. Second, the passage of time tended to require government approval of the petition in the absence of evidence as to its unacceptability, despite the government's suspicion that the proposed changes were unwarranted.[54] In response to these difficulties, the WSB established specific standards for certain benefits, regardless of industry or area practice, but failed to announce them publicly. Rather, the WSB applied such standards internally. A further observation from the experience of the NWLB and WSB is appropriate. Both boards attempted to apply inequity criteria to noninsurance fringes, including both inter- and intraplant standards. Employers, particularly, objected to the application of intraplant standards, arguing against the extension of benefits granted a few workers in an establishment to all workers. Most likely, the employer members were correct. Benefits of a noninsurance nature are important elements of the differentials which constitute an internal wage structure, and if intraplant comparative standards are to be applied to fringes, care must be exercised to preserve appropriate differentials among workers.

The Pay Board in 1971 abandoned all efforts to regulate benefits. Rather, the board shifted to a totally cost-oriented standard, effectively including noninsurance fringes in the general pay standard. The logic of the board's shift in policy from previous periods was twofold. First, it wished to control total compensation with a view toward constraining unit labor costs of production; there are often substantial secondary (as well as direct) impacts on employer costs occasioned through existing levels of fringes. Second, the

Pay Board wished to grant as much flexibility as possible to local parties in the allocation of the permissible pay increases among wages and fringes. No comparative standards for benefits were included, therefore, except insofar as a catch-up exception was permissible—but here again the standard was a percentage increase in cost (not to exceed 7 percent in total of the base compensation package). Despite a certain logical consistency in the board's policies, considerable confusion was created. In consequence, the board moved even further in the direction of a formula approach to noninsurance fringes. After one year of operation, the board adopted a figure of 7 percent for estimating the value of noninsurance fringes by smaller employers (employee units of one thousand or fewer). Rather than estimate the cost of noninsurance fringes as part of the compensation package, smaller employers simply multiplied straight-time hourly earnings by 1.07 to obtain a surrogate measure of straight-time plus noninsurance benefits. The 7 percent figure was derived from a Bureau of Labor Statistics study of average practice in American industry.[55] Pay Board regulations regarding increases in wages and noninsurance fringes were applied to the estimated wage-plus-noninsurance-fringe-benefits base. Thus, the board had not only abandoned any effort to discover and regulate benefit levels, it had in much of the economy abandoned any effort to discover and regulate actual costs of noninsurance benefits as well.

Was Pay Board practice an improvement on past stabilization policies? Probably not. Yet, the consequences of an exclusively cost-based policy for fringe benefits depend on the economic environment and the duration of the stabilization program. In an expansive economy it invites the building of substantial distortions in the benefits provided to different groups of workers. By ignoring comparative factors, the cost-oriented policy invites great difficulties for stabilization authorities in the second and third years of a stabilization program. Furthermore, at the expiration of a stabilization program, the distortion of comparative relationships invites a surge of bargaining to obtain for some workers what others have already received. That is, the same sort of leapfrog bargaining which has become familiar in wage negotiations can equally well operate with respect to fringes. The advantage of comparative benefit standards for fringes is that they provide a method of constraining the possibility of this form of distortion and readjustment of the structure of fringe benefits.

Exceptions for Manpower Purposes

Manpower shortages are a common cause of decisions by employers to raise wage rates. When the economy is expanding, increases in wages which are necessary to attract labor may seem very *inexpensive* to employers compared with the costs of attempting to increase production with an existing work force or compared to the loss of the additional business altogether. Yet, a stabilization board exists to restrain wage increases, and so potentially comes into conflict with employers seeking to raise wages to retain or attract labor. These circumstances are often especially difficult for a stabilization board because employers seeking manpower may be even more insistent on making wage increases than the union or the workers themselves are to receive the increases. In such circumstances, the public members of a board may come under great pressure if they attempt to deny increases. The basic issue for stabilization policy is, of course, to what degree wage increases are to be permitted as a means of attracting or motivating labor to increase production. Since wage adjustments may affect manpower flows among occupations, regions, and industries in a variety of ways, the interaction between wage policies and manpower needs can be quite complex.[56] It may be surprising, in light of the importance and complexity of this relationship, that there has been substantial unity of policy in all periods of stabilization on this issue.

In general, stabilization boards have refused to permit employers to grant wage increases on a broad scale for the purpose of retaining or attracting labor. The boards have apparently felt that such increases would be unlikely to be effective in attracting labor and would tend to result in an undesired general increase in the wage level. Boards have, therefore, favored other devices than wage increases to accomplish the needed recruitment and distribution of manpower. Yet, while rejecting widespread exceptions to a general standard for manpower purposes, the approvals made of increases under substandards and inequity exceptions have often had a significant manpower impact. In some situations boards have been cognizant of this impact, and have, in fact, granted inequity and substandards exceptions, in part because of their manpower implications.[57] For this reason, a study of the manpower impact of stabilization policy would be required to focus on intended and unintended (or incidental) effects resulting from the overall, nonmanpower-related, policies pursued. We are not here concerned with that analytic task but rather with the more limited review of the direct use of manpower-related criteria in the administration of a wage stabilization program. While eschewing manpower criteria broadly as a base for wage policy, boards in all periods have, nevertheless, been prepared to make exceptions in certain circumstances to the general policy, in order to allow increases for manpower purposes. But the explicit nature of the exceptions allowed, the types of problems which arose, and the applications of the standards provided have differed among stabilization periods.

In fact, historical evidence confirms what would be expected on theoretical grounds: that the problems of wage stabilization related to manpower flows have been most pronounced and have received, correspondingly, the greatest attention in periods of large-scale military conflict. In such periods, unique combinations of wage standards have been created to make wage approvals for manpower purposes, and the need for coordination of wage stabilization and manpower agencies has been perceived. There was a beginning of such coordination in World War II, but many problems remained unsolved at its termination.[58] There has been no practical experience with this problem since, and little or no attention has been given the problem, outside of planning for national emergencies by the federal government. Alternatively, wage controls have not been applied in this country in peacetime periods which involved substantial labor market tightness, such as the late 1920s and the late 1960s. The peculiar problems of peacetime controls and tight labor markets are, therefore, largely unexplored.

It appears, however, that the past policy of narrowly restricting approval of wage adjustments based on labor shortages should be continued in future stabilization programs, and other means of directing the flow of labor than wage increases should receive the primary reliance of public policy.[59] In part, this is because wage adjustments are a slow and unresponsive device for many of the emergency situations in which the need for additional manpower arises. Furthermore, manpower requirements often fluctuate. Can it be imagined that wages would first be raised, then lowered, in step with manpower needs? Not at all. A money wage-rate once established would be very difficult to reduce. In consequence, such devices as increased overtime pay, longer days and weeks of work, special premiums for various types of work, travel pay, and the like, which are available to increase compensation in the short run without distorting wage differentials for the long run, may be preferable to wage increases as a means of alleviating labor shortages in specific instances. (Overtime and other premiums employed on a broad scale in industry to avoid wage increases may have undesirable consequences in later years, however, by stimulating among workers higher earnings expectations than can be accommodated in the long run.)

Part IV   Additional Aspects of
                           Stabilization Policy

Men who are very difficult to drive
are sometimes very easy to lead.

T. E. Lawrence, quoted by Liddell Hart
in Colonel Lawrence

9. Controls and Collective Bargaining

Collective Bargaining and Inflation

What should be the relationship between an economic stabilization program and collective bargaining? Is collective bargaining such a source of wage inflation that it must be suspended in order to gain wage and price stability? Or, is collective bargaining incompatible with wage controls for administrative reasons? Conversely, should wage control authorities attempt to preserve, or even strengthen, collective bargaining? And, should they wish to sustain collective bargaining, are they able to do so? These questions constitute the subject matter of this chapter. We begin with a consideration of the relationship between collective bargaining and inflation.

Aspects of Collective Bargaining Unfavorable to Economic Stability

Collective bargaining is a complex and multifaceted process, so it should not be surprising that it has both favorable and unfavorable aspects for economic stabilization. In the short run there are four potential consequences of collective bargaining as a wage-setting device which are threatening to wage and price stability.

First, collective bargaining may operate to increase wages generally beyond what is reasonable in terms of adjustments to changing economic conditions (including, for example, rising prices, rising profits, and labor shortages). This is the so-called "cost-push" inflation. Further, cost-push is said to make it doubly difficult to achieve full employment because it raises wages beyond the equilibrium level in various labor markets, thereby causing unemployment. But demonstration that cost-push from collective bargaining is a significant autonomous contributor to general inflation is difficult. Still, in some situations, collective bargaining may generate important inflationary pressures. It may, in individual instances, increase compensation beyond what is merited by economic circumstances. This may occur because of the conversion into wage increases of adjustments made in noneconomic issues, or because of political circumstances internal to a union or company which generate large increases. In the absence of collective bargaining it is less likely that such matters would have an impact on wage adjustments. Furthermore, in a stable economy, most such influences would be temporary in nature, and the impact of unreasonable settlements on other situations would dissipate rapidly so that they would be of limited concern. However, in an expanding economy, and especially when future economic circumstances are uncertain, large settlements, whatever their cause, may have unstabilizing effects on a broad group of other situations, especially in the same industry or in closely related industries. Collective bargaining, by generating some such settlements, may serve to be destabilizing.

There is a common view that the inflationary impact of a collective bargaining settlement depends, in some important ways, on the size of the unit of workers involved. Two types of arguments are advanced in support of this view. One suggests that wage adjustments which affect small groups have little economic impact and so may be ignored. But this argument neglects the secondary impact of wage adjustments for small groups of key workers upon those received, or demanded, by other groups of workers. Often small groups set important patterns in wage determination which affect much larger numbers ultimately. A second argument is that only large employee units establish wage patterns. This assertion is without empirical foundation.

Second, collective bargaining tends to respond to a wider range of economic factors than do other wage-setting mechanisms, and in some economic circumstances this may be destabilizing. It is well established that *all* methods of determining compensation (including unilateral determination by employers) respond rapidly to labor shortages by increasing pay, but collective bargaining may also respond to increasing profits and prices (to cite only two other factors) with an alacrity and to a degree which other wage-setting mechanisms do not.

Third, collective bargaining structures may in some industries and areas contribute to an inflationary spiral by permitting closely interrelated wage rates to become distorted, requiring readjustments in the structure of wage rates, sometimes to the detriment of wage-price stability. Inflationary pressures deriving from such distortions are especially likely in industries with multiple bargaining units, e.g., construction, printing, the public sector, and maritime.

Fourth, collective bargaining tends to put a floor under money wage rates, so that decreases in going rates are exceedingly unlikely except in major depressions (although in isolated instances involving very unfavorable economic circumstances, decreases in wages are sometimes agreed to, whatever the more general economic conditions). This downward rigidity in wages contributes to an upward bias of the general level of wages.

Aspects of Collective Bargaining Favorable to Economic Stability

Against these unfavorable aspects of collective bargaining should be balanced a series of aspects favorable to economic stability. Surprisingly, some of these potential contributions to economic stability are simply the other side of the coin, so to speak, of those "unfavorable" aspects just listed.

First, collective bargaining in the United States normally entails fixed-term contracts, so that wage rates and fringes are established with a degree of certainty for a period of from several months (though, in normal times, rarely less than one year) to several years (though, in normal times, rarely more than three years). In inflationary booms, the practice of fixed-term agreements imparts great initial resistance to a wage-price spiral. It is not likely that any other wage-setting mechanism could be so desirably inflexible in the short run.[1] (Although in some instances wage increases which anticipate an inflation could be destabilizing.) In part, this is because American labor organizations are well-disciplined internally, so that the wildcat strikes and payment of wages above negotiated levels common abroad do not commonly occur in this country.

Second, collective bargaining may in some instances prevent noneconomic practices from entering the industrial workplace during business expansions, by directing the careful attention of managers at each negotiation to what high sales volume and ready-cash availability are doing to loosen production standards in their plants. Effective general management is, as a result, in a better position to control costs than otherwise.[2]

Third, the process of collective bargaining itself and the grievance machinery of unionized plants permit a comparatively orderly approach to the resolution of production and industrial relations problems which commonly develop in a period of business expansion. Through the grievance procedure, especially, such problems are often resolved at their origin or, in the case of unresolved grievances, by private, voluntary, binding arbitration during the term of an agreement, thereby reducing greatly the likelihood of work stoppages, strikes, or other disruptions. Such disruptions, whatever their cause, are not only expensive themselves but often become the occasion for demands for wage or benefit increases.

The fundamental point of these examples is that business expansions and booms bring with them industrial relations problems which collective bargaining may serve as a mechanism to resolve, thereby containing economic pressures. On the other hand, the collective bargaining process, in making new agreements, is also amenable to translating economic pressures into compensation increases. Labor and management have the responsibility for the actual result of the bargaining process.

The Net Impact of Collective Bargaining on Inflation

But, the reader might object, surely it is possible to conclude more about the *net* impact of collective bargaining on wage inflation than what has been said above. For example, there have been many efforts to establish the impact of unionization (and thence collective bargaining) on wages. Evidence suggests that unionization in the United States tends to increase, to a limited degree, the relative (that is, comparative) wages of unionized employees versus nonunionized employees.[3] But the impact of collective bargaining on the general rate of increase of wages is more conjectural. Probably the most sophisticated exposition of this question has been made by Sumner Slichter. He concluded that unions tend to impart a small inflationary bias to the economy, but his most interesting analysis related to the more general and long-term consequences of the inflationary bias in wages. The tendency of collective bargaining to place sustained upward pressure on wages, Slichter argued, induces considerable technological progress as employers seek less labor-intensive methods of production. It also results in either increasing unemployment or price increases. But unions are, in Slichter's view, a major device for generating additional consumer income and spending, an outcome which increases employment, diminishes susceptibility to economic recessions (contributing to the long-run preservation of capitalism), and reinforces the tendency of prices to rise in booms. Because of the income-generation effect of wage increases, Slichter observed, increasing wages do not generally result in increased unemployment (though there might be such effects in certain industries or areas on a limited basis). Were the public to choose to attempt to minimize the income-creation effect of collective bargaining in order to eliminate even moderate inflation, concluded Slichter, it would have to sacrifice a rapid rate of industrial growth and accept the increased likelihood of more numerous and more severe recessions.[4] This analysis remains, in the present author's view, the most plausible and complete understanding of the aggregate impact of collective bargaining in our economy.

But increasing wages is not the only method through which collective bargaining may have an impact on inflation. Changes in working rules and working conditions can also have considerable impact on labor costs and thereby on prices. And condition changes may be negotiated which have either favorable or unfavorable effects—that is, which decrease or increase unit labor costs. It is unfortunate that we have virtually no data which apply directly to the additional costs or savings from rules and conditions changes. Historical experience suggests that periods of high economic activity generate the growth of noneconomic practices in private business, both in the union and nonunion sectors. There is even reason to think that this process operated in the public sector as well, in the late 1960s. But we have little evidence of the independent impact of collective bargaining on the growth of noneconomic practices in inflationary periods (though recent experience suggests it may be large). In periods of economic decline, improvements in working practices, either by formal agreement or informally, may be used to slow or even reverse the increase in unit labor costs, although wages continue to climb. Finally, and alternatively, when wage rates are restrained by controls, changes in conditions may be resorted to as a device to increase earnings or leisure. It is unfortunate that in 1971-72 the wage stabilization program (except in construction) ignored working condition changes and thereby permitted, in some important instances, very great increases in unit labor costs to occur despite constraints on wages. In the long run, the economy may be better served by the negotiation of somewhat higher wage levels than by the creation of increasingly noneconomic practices.

Factors Affecting the Relationship
of Collective Bargaining and Economic Stability

Whatever the net impact of collective bargaining on economic stability, it is certain that its impact is not the same in all industries or in all types of inflationary circumstances. Business expansions are rarely distributed evenly across the economy. In those sectors experiencing rapid growth, collective bargaining may prove to be an additional destabilizing influence. In the decade just passed, growth was, for a period at least, especially strong in contract construction, health services, food retailing, and state and local government services. Unfortunately, these were sectors of the economy characterized by highly decentralized collective bargaining and, in health and government services, relatively recent union organization and consequently nascent collective bargaining. These characteristics caused collective bargaining to be, not a stabilizing or even a neutral influence in these sectors, but rather a contributor to the inflationary pressures. Negotiations in these sectors, often accompanied by strikes, led to high wage increases for certain groups of workers, which were then equalled or excelled by others. Simultaneously, the pressures of declining output upon certain sectors also generated inflationary pressures, especially in railway and maritime transportation.[5] In other sectors of the economy (particularly manufacturing) the impact of collective bargaining was more stabilizing. For example, in the automobile agreement of 1970 and the steel agreement of 1971 (both three years in term), large settlements were negotiated at a time of low production activity in the two industries. But the agreements provided predictable costs and continued production during the rapid expansion of 1972-73, without the development of the crazy-quilt pattern of wage relationships and pressures for further increases which decentralized bargaining created in other industries.

Collective bargaining does not respond uniformly to different types of inflationary pressures. For example, in the boom occasioned by the consumer goods shortage at the end of World War II, collective bargaining, despite serious strikes, offered little or no independent inflationary pressures.[6] Even the decentralized bargaining system in construction operated to adjust wage levels to varying economic circumstances in the country, rather than to distort wage rates and lever them upward. During the speculative boom of 1950–51 collective bargaining agreements in major manufacturing reinforced a wage-price spiral but one which was likely to have occurred anyway. On the positive side, the multiple-year term of some agreements provided a stabilizing influence prior to the application of controls. In the late 1950s, the end of the post-World War II period of high production in manufacturing was not reflected by a retardation in wage increases negotiated in collective bargaining, and large settlements continued to be negotiated. These settlements were in part responsible for the moderate inflation of 1956–59.[7] The role of collective bargaining in the inflation of 1965–70 has been described above as being dominated by generalized demand pressures and by the undesirable consequences of decentralized bargaining and rapid growth in output in a few sectors of the economy.

We have, therefore, a complex picture of the relationship between collective bargaining and inflation—a picture in which the source of inflationary pressures and their differential impact on various sectors interacts with the varying structures of collective bargaining and timing of agreements. Whether collective bargaining serves as a constraint upon inflationary pressures or exacerbates them depends on the factors listed above, and the net effect is often difficult to estimate, even after the fact. Public policy should seek to lessen the unfavorable consequences of collective bargaining and to emphasize those consequences which are favorable to economic policy. There would seem to be no justification for an approach to stabilization policy which either by design or accident is generally destructive of collective bargaining.

Wage Controls as a Threat to Collective Bargaining

The advent of a program of wage controls has usually been accompanied by announcements of the permanent end of collective bargaining. For example, during World War II a management spokesman offered his judgment that:

> The principal impact on collective bargaining derives from the wage controls, the price controls and the labor disputes procedure. The effect of these three combined has been profoundly to weaken management's ability to bargain effectively, and to deal great blows at the institution of private bargaining from which it may never be able to fully recover.[8]

Collective bargaining in the United States did recover, of course, but historical experience did not still further predictions of disaster, either in the United States or abroad. A prominent British economist, for instance, made a judgment similar to the one just quoted with respect to the impact of an incomes policy on collective bargaining in Great Britain:

The establishment of an incomes policy is such a traumatic shock to traditional wage and price determination procedures that things can never be the same again.[9]

This prediction was also too extreme, of course. Yet it is, as a practical matter, impossible for the government to intervene in the process of wage determination under the guise of an economic stabilization program without simultaneously affecting industrial relations generally, including collective bargaining, union organization, and other matters. Controls do *tend* to cause collective bargaining to atrophy, with the consequence that, in many situations, employers and unions fail to make progress in solving their joint problems. Industrial relations may decay generally, with resulting high costs in increased industrial strife and increased inefficiency at the workplace. What are the sources of these dangers?

Removing the Wage and Fringe-Benefit Package Increase from Negotiations

The development of criteria for wage increases by a stabilization board provides a convenient excuse for either management or labor, or both, to avoid the responsibility for true collective bargaining. Employers, for example, sometimes choose to adopt a rigid interpretation of the application of stabilization criteria to their own situation and refuse to discuss with the union any other interpretation. Employers have accused unions of refusing to bargain because the unions refused to accept the employers' view of what was an approvable increase under the stabilization rules.[10] In some instances employers have been so adamant regarding what was a permissible increase as to provoke a finding by the NLRB of an unfair labor practice. For example, in the fall of 1971, upon announcement by the Pay Board of the 5.5 percent general pay standard, a company retracted a larger offer it had made to the union during previous negotiations and attempted to place into effect a 5.5 percent increase without union agreement. This action elicited a complaint to the NLRB and a finding of an unfair labor practice by virtue of a refusal to bargain.[11] In many instances, however, companies simply attempted to utilize the regulations as a method of avoiding the requirements of serious negotiations, though without the extreme position which might have resulted in a citation for refusal to bargain by the NLRB. So pronounced was suspicion of management behavior in 1972, for example, that Senator Proxmire charged that "business wants to rely on the government to set prices for them, and more important, to protect them from the demands of labor unions.... Your [i.e., business's] support of these price and wage controls makes me wonder if the controls aren't really becoming a shield for business to rely on instead of their own initiative in negotiating with labor."[12] However, unions also sometimes use the stabilization policies as a subterfuge to avoid negotiations. For example, unions may refuse to negotiate with employers except to obtain the maximum increase allowable under stabilization policies, indicating explicitly an unwillingness to discuss any other issues of interest to the employer (modifications in working conditions, grievance machinery changes, and so on). In this respect, the unions have sometimes assumed a position like that taken by some managements, as cited above: an adamant refusal to conduct negotiations other than to "rubber-stamp" an allowable wage increase. In situations where one side has refused to participate in this limited proceeding, insisting instead on actual collective bargaining about a range of issues, the other has sometimes pressed negotiations to an impasse and demanded the intervention of stabilization authorities in support of its position. In these instances collective bargaining may be said to have broken down by virtue of an insistence to limit negotiations to the application of stabilization regulations alone.

Wage controls sometimes have had a seemingly opposite effect upon collective bargaining, but one which has also been somewhat damaging. Where both parties might agree upon the amount of an allowable wage increase, one side might seek to pursue other bargaining goals to the exclusion of agreement on the wage issue. In some instances this stratagem was an understandable attempt by management or labor to resolve long-disputed issues which in the past had too often been neglected as the parties concentrated on wage issues.[13] However, in other instances, bargaining power was simply redirected from wages to other issues, sometimes frivolous in nature. When negotiations came to an impasse and work stoppages occurred in such circumstances, collective bargaining had degenerated to a marked degree. In general, wage and fringe benefit issues are so important an aspect of collective bargaining, so often at its very heart, that their removal from negotiations whether by agreement or at the insistence of one party only, tends profoundly to distort the collective bargaining process in ways which are often destructive.[14]

Undercutting the Bargaining Relationship

A program of wage controls affords either management or labor a tempting variety of opportunities for subterfuges, dishonest actions, and double-crosses which may be employed against the other. The utilization of such tactics tends, in many instances, to disturb or destroy the previous collective bargaining relationship and may have undesirable consequences upon industrial relations long after the termination of the controls program. In some further instances it is the stabilization board that, in its rejection of a negotiated agreement, tends to destroy the collective bargaining relationship by introducing suspicions of double-dealing where none had existed.

For some employers a stabilization program presents an almost irresistible opportunity for manipulating collective bargaining to their own short-term benefit. For example, the employer might agree to substantial wage increases in negotiations with a union in return for concessions in nonwage items or to avoid a strike. He then might lobby through employer representatives on a stablization board against the wage provisions of the agreement which he had negotiated, hoping to be relieved of his obligation to pay the increase negotiated. This course of action might seem to promise the employer that no work stoppages need occur, no substantial wage increase need be paid, and some gains in noneconomic areas might result. In some extreme situations the stabilization board might be faced with a dispute over the negotiated wage increase with the union involved, while the employer might overtly encourage the union (thereby standing by his agreement) but covertly encourage the board's objections to the increase. Stabilization boards in the United States and industrial relations itself have been fortunate that most American management has not availed itself of the opportunity for such practices. Unfortunately, the government has, in some instances, actually encouraged them. The most recent, and historically the most flagrant, example is the Pay Board's policy of permitting *only* employers signatory to a collective bargaining agreement negotiated prior to the stabilization program to challenge its terms. The board actually invited those bound by such agreements to seek their repudiation by the government. A policy more destructive of industrial relations harmony can hardly be imagined.

Labor unions also were sometimes guilty of deceptive practices involving stabilization boards. In some instances, union leaders encouraged management to agree to large increases in order to prevent supposed dissatisfaction by the workers, with the guarantee that the increase would be denied by the government. The union then lobbied for the agreement strongly with the stabilization board and insisted that management, as evidence of its good faith in signing the agreement, also lobby for its approval. In consequence, some employers, in important instances, have found themselves with far larger increases approved by a board than they had anticipated or would have agreed to had they not been persuaded by the unions to rely on the board to disallow the terms of the agreement.

In yet other instances, board proceedings may be employed by one party as an element of its bargaining strategy against the other. Such instances are common with respect to NLRB proceedings. In some negotiations, each party, almost as a matter of custom, charges the other with various unfair labor practices, hoping thereby to gain some limited advantage in the negotiations. Similar ruses may be employed at the expense of a stabilization program. For example, an employer may seek to have the stabilization board challenge the validity of wage adjustments in situations closely related to his own negotiations. In other cases, bargaining may be reduced to a discussion of what subterfuges for wage increases may exist and how the union and the company may best employ them. These devices reduce the value of collective bargaining as a method of resolving real disputes and contribute to the erosion of good industrial relations.

Finally, stabilization boards may themselves contribute to the collapse of effective bargaining by refusing to study an agreement completely, instead applying some formula or rule of thumb to judge its provisions. Where local parties have seriously attempted in negotiations to apply stabilization policies to their own peculiar circumstances, a rejection of their solutions by a board, without adequate or persuasive reasons can convince both parties that their effort was in vain, and that serious negotiations in a period of stabilization are not fruitful. Unfortunately, the impact of stabilization policy on responsible bargaining relationships is all too often of this nature.

Stabilization Boards as a Substitute for Collective Bargaining

Where a formal disputes-machinery is attached to a stabilization board, further unfavorable impacts on collective bargaining may occur. These impacts are of two major types. First, the weaker party in negotiations may choose to thwart negotiations, preferring to take its chances with a determination of the issues by the stabilization board (or whatever agency of dispute settlement is available). Second, either party might choose to take unusual or technical issues to the board by bringing negotiations to an impasse with those issues unresolved.

The most common instance of the weaker party resorting to a disputes machinery in preference to collective bargaining involves employers, of course. In the high employment economy which so often accompanies a stabilization program, employers would often be compelled to grant increases above allowable levels, or to incur work stoppages, where there was no resort to alternative machinery. But, in many instances, the employer may nevertheless find himself in a very difficult position which appears to cause collective bargaining to have become a trap. For stabilization policies may appear to guarantee the union a minimum increase which it desires to obtain without any concessions to the employer. Further, a strike for a greater increase is often not a strike against the employer at all, who might willingly grant it, but against the policies of the stabilization program. The employer is thus caught in the middle, so to speak, in a dispute between the union and the government.

Weak unions also may make use of the disputes machinery to avoid the consequences of true collective bargaining. During World War II, for example, the textile workers union carried two major rounds of negotiations (1942 and 1945) to the NWLB. In essence, the union had little power to compel increases in the unionized sector of the industry (concentrated in the northeastern states) through collective bargaining because it had very little of the southern textile industry organized. Rather, the union preferred to argue its position before the NWLB, and twice obtained substantial wage increases from the board. The employers, of course, objected strongly to the board's allowing itself to be used in this fashion.[15]

The existence of a quasi-arbitration machinery for disputes settlement also tempts both parties in a negotiation to put all issues to the machinery, rather than to do much bargaining between themselves. During World War II, disputes cases sometimes arrived at the regional boards with hundreds of unresolved issues, often regarding trivial matters. So common did resort to the board become that, during its existence, the NWLB processed more than 20,692 disputes cases. "It would appear," observed one student of the board's activities, "that hundreds of cases and thousands of minor issues were tossed into the lap of the Board for final determination that might have been bargained out between the parties."[16]

How Strong a Threat to Collective Bargaining?

Despite the various pitfalls which a stabilization program creates for collective bargaining, the institution has proven to be remarkably resilient in past periods of controls. Even during World War II, for example, a great majority of agreements were negotiated by the parties without disruption. To a degree this experience is surprising and testifies to the stubborn strength of private institutions when endangered by government policies and administrative actions. But collective bargaining has been supported also by numerous and extensive efforts of the stabilization boards to protect its integrity. We will consider below these methods of preserving collective bargaining in a period of controls. Before proceeding to that topic, however, we might ask what factors affect the degree to which collective bargaining is endangered by a stabilization program.

There are three primary factors, of which only the first two are related to the wage restraint function of a stabilization board. Collective bargaining will be the more threatened by a stabilization effort, the more restrictive are wage restraint policies (that is, the greater the divergence between the allowable rate of increase in compensation and that rate which unconstrained collective bargaining would yield) and the longer is the duration of controls. Conversely, a controls program which is brief in duration and relatively liberal with respect to approval increases, need have little general impact on collective bargaining. The final factor affecting the degree of interference between a controls program and collective bargaining is the character of a disputes machinery, if any. Where a comprehensive disputes-settlement machinery exists, collective bargaining is most likely to be foresaken by one or both parties in favor of resort to the government's machinery.

Methods of Preserving Collective Bargaining

There are a number of methods by which a stabilization board may seek to minimize its unfavorable impact upon private negotiations. These include tripartite administration, the leaving of considerable discretion to the negotiating parties, the preservation of private arbitration, concern for other aspects of collective bargaining than economic issues, and certain administrative devices. Each of these methods will be discussed below. More important than such specific methods, however, is the general attitude of stabilization authorities to collective bargaining. Historically, bargaining has been strongly supported by stabilization boards in some periods and weakly supported, at best, in others. For example, during World War II Nathan Feinsinger, a public member of the NWLB, put the philosophy of the NWLB as follows:

> First, granted that governmental intervention in collective bargaining is inevitable in time of war, such interference should be limited to the narrowest possible scope. Second, to the extent that such interference is inevitable, the Board should follow the best practices developed by voluntary collective bargaining. Third, the government should withdraw from the field of collective bargaining at the earliest moment that the war effort will permit.[17]

One of the lessons of World War II was that such support for collective bargaining rebounded in some important ways to the advantage of the stabilization authorities. In contrast, in 1971 the Pay Board maintained a scrupulous detachment from collective bargaining, evidencing little support for or interest in the institution itself. The result of the board's policy was an increasing conviction by many companies and unions that the board was irrelevant to important aspects of their joint problems. It is instructive, as evidence of the continued validity of the World War II lesson, that collective bargaining in 1971-72 survived the board's neglect with little difficulty, while the Pay Board itself became, to a large degree, a casualty of the indifference or outright antagonism of the private parties whose behavior it had sought to regulate.

Tripartite administration of a stabilization agency serves in several ways to preserve collective bargaining during a period of controls. First, much of the content of local negotiations is simply shifted to a different forum, that of the board itself, and from a bipartite to a tripartite framework (that is, one which includes representatives of the public). Individual companies and unions are represented by their national leadership on the tripartite board, however, so that the views of local-level negotiations often remain influential in the ultimate disposition of the issues involved in the negotiations. Second, tripartitism provides negotiating parties with a privileged and trusted line of communication to the stabilization program, so that local negotiations may be better informed of the issues important in the view of stabilization authorities. This communication helps insure that local parties may, if they desire, develop solutions in their own unique circumstances within the policy framework of the stabilization program, rather than negotiate an agreement on one basis, only to have it reviewed by a stabilization board on another. Third, union and management representatives on a stabilization board often insist that a greater degree of deference be given to the agreements of local parties than would be likely from an all-government board.

Stabilization boards may also encourage collective bargaining by leaving a range of discretion to local parties in the application of stabilization criteria. There are many means by which this may be accomplished. For example, local parties may be allowed to retain some discretion over the distribution among wages and fringes of an approved economic increase. Furthermore, a board might choose to set certain key wage rates, leaving the parties to establish other rates within the established framework. The NWLB, for instance, in the Little Steel decision, returned to the companies and union for negotiating any changes in incentive tonnage or piecework rates required as a result of its general directive in the case. Similarly, in the 1945 textile cases, the board specified a number of occupational rates and assigned to collective bargaining "the task of completing a properly aligned and balanced wage structure."[18] These elements of discretion left to local negotiations by the NWLB were, it is apparent, real and important but, nevertheless, not very broad.[19] The board in the Korean period, on the other hand, encouraged wide discretion in collective bargaining, reserving, however, the option to review and disallow the agreements reached in negotiations. In the words of a management representative, the WSB told unions and employers that:

> The Board told unions and employers, in a statement issued last September 21, that, while it placed a responsibility upon the parties to respect wage stabilization policies in their negotiations, they were free to make such wage agreements as they might desire and to seek Board approval on the basis of special facts or equities which might justify an exception to usual policies, or on the basis that there were reasonable grounds for modification of existing policies.[20]

And, in 1971-72, the Pay Board granted local negotiations virtually unlimited authority as to the form and distribution of the approved amount of compensation increase.

A third method of preserving local collective bargaining which has been followed to a degree in all periods of stabilization involves the treatment accorded by a wage board to private arbitration proceedings and decisions. Generally, boards have encouraged private arbitration of grievances, even where economic issues were involved. Boards have not, however, felt compelled to allow the implementation of an arbitrator's award where there might have been undesirable consequences for stabilization. Rather, boards have normally accepted an arbitrator's interpretations of the terms of a collective bargaining agreement as the proper interpretation but have then reviewed the agreement, so interpreted, to determine its consistency with stabilization policies. Where the placing into effect of the arbitrator's award would prove destabilizing, boards have denied approval. There is no conflict inherent in this procedure between the arbitrator's function and that of the stabilization board. Rather, the arbitrator rules on what the agreement requires in the instant situation, and the board reviews the decision to see if it is consistent with stabilization policy. Encouragement of private arbitration, subject only to review, also tends to relieve the board of much potential business for its own disputes-settling machinery.

We have described a few methods by which a stabilization board may assist in the preservation of collective bargaining in the short run, that is, during the term of a stabilization program. These methods will help to offset, in part, the disruption which a stabilization program will ordinarily cause collective bargaining. There are also, however, important contributions which a board may make to the long-run health of collective bargaining. Among these contributions are encouragement of what may be termed "best" practice in various areas of industrial relations and also the direction of attention at fundamental aspects of bargaining, such as its structure in various industries and the institutions which assist negotiating parties.

The degree of encouragement of "best" practice in industrial relations provided by a stabilization program has varied in the past. In World War I, for example, Felix Frankfurter chaired a War Labor Policies Board composed of representatives of government agencies. The board made recommendations for wage standardization and for the inclusion of dispute-settlement clauses in contracts for war production. U.S. participation in the war was brief, however, and little was accomplished.[21] A major effort to encourage better practice in industrial relations occurred during World War II and took many forms. For example, the NWLB encouraged the establishment of carefully designed job classifications and wage-rate schedules (including, in some instances, incentive schemes and bonus arrangements),[22] and went on record as "strongly favoring the establishment by the parties themselves of grievance machinery which provides for the final determination of day-by-day differences over the application and administration of collective agreements."[23] The board also encouraged improved methods of dispute settlement at the termination of agreements.[24] Finally, NWLB chairman William H. Davis went so far as to provide a general blueprint to industry and labor for their conduct with respect to each other.[25] The board was, it is apparent, attempting to provide leadership for industry and labor in many forms but directed always at the long-term improvement of collective bargaining and industrial relations.[26] Both the WSB and the Pay Board were less ambitious. Perhaps this was to be expected, for the optimism which existed for the future of collective bargaining in the late 1930s and early 1940s evaporated to a large degree in the strikes of 1946–47. The opinion of national leadership and the public with respect to the value of collective bargaining has since been more reserved.

Yet it is ironic that the controls program of 1971–72 was largely justified by its proponents as educational in purpose. That is, the function of the general pay standard was asserted to be, in part, to assist parties in collective bargaining to more fully understand what responsible wage behavior involved. This objective was surely laudable. But how did the Pay Board attempt to achieve it? First, a simple formula was established which was supposed to cover a myriad of differing circumstances. Second, the formula was set forth in concepts (e.g., average productivity, roll-up, base compensation rate, excludable fringe benefits) largely alien to the practice of collective bargaining or personnel administration. There was no real attempt by the Pay Board to engage in a dialogue with the private sector, that is, with management and labor. What was stated to be largely an educational process was pursued in practice as a regulatory one. Rather than discussion, which is a fundamental element of the learning process, the private sector received from the government only exhortations and regulations couched in an often unintelligible jargon. In consequence, as an educational effort which was intended to improve the wage determination process in this country, the standards of 1971–72 were largely futile.

In the future, stabilization boards may be called upon to excercise leadership with respect to what will then be current problems of collective bargaining. While it is difficult to imagine precisely what future problems will be, some are, nonetheless, already evident. Among the major problems for collective bargaining in the coming decades will be (1) developing methods of resolving disputes during contract negotiations without resort to strikes in industries in which work stoppages are especially inconvenient to the public or damaging to the parties; (2) making adjustments in compensation and productivity to the changing economic fortunes of various industries; (3) providing means of controlling the increasing costs and complexity of provisions for health, welfare, and pension benefits; (4) making certain required adjustments in the structure of collective bargaining in several industries; and (5) insuring that manpower availability is commensurate with future needs in expanding industries. A stabilization board should assist private parties in approaching these problems. Furthermore, it would be disastrous to the country in the long run were stabilization boards to be seized as an excuse by unions and employers to escape their responsibility for the tremendous problems involved in resolving the dissatisfaction at the workplace of individual employees or groups of employees regarding the character of their jobs and their compensation. No central or bureaucratic device can resolve such problems of the workplace efficiently. A stabilization board can, however, urge that the parties in collective bargaining deal with these issues, and it may assist them in some ways.

Contributions of Collective Bargaining to Stabilization

An Economic Barometer

The continued operation of collective bargaining during a period of controls provides a useful barometer for a board of what economic adjustments would be in its absence. Where virtually all negotiated increases are above those permitted by stabilization policies, it is clear that the "market level" of wages, to use Arthur Ross's distinction, is well above the "stabilization level."[27] Alternatively, where the two levels converge, the stabilization board may wish to adjust its policies, for example, to permit greater self-administration of its standards. The results of collective bargaining are particularly useful in indicating not only the general, or average, market level of increases, but the varying circumstances of particular sectors. A stabilization board may wish to adjust its specific policies to respond to especially inflationary sectors, as revealed, in part, by the continuing results of bargaining. However, it might be objected that collective bargaining settlement levels are not a perfect barometer of labor market forces. Rather, particular increases may represent the effects of maldistributions of power between the unions and employers or even a fictitious level of increases designed to be reduced by the stabilization board. Because of these possibilities, settlement levels must be considered by the board with circumspection and in the context of other sorts of information. Nonetheless, the results of bargaining are often a separate and useful measure of labor market forces for a board.

Determining the Timing of Wage Decisions

Collective bargaining agreements, which virtually always in the United States operate for a fixed term, serve to focus the wage adjustment problems of particular industries at particular points in time. The sequence of contract expirations and renegotiations allows a board both to concentrate its limited resources upon problems in succession and to influence later settlements by its actions in previous situations. In the absence of some such organization in time of wage decisions, a board would be subject to unexpected and multiple pressures at any given time through demands for unscheduled compensation increases. Collective bargaining, by organizing the forces of the labor market for discrete wage decisions, provides a very great service to a stabilization program.

Collective bargaining agreements also provide a device for extending the impact of stabilization decisions beyond the life of a board itself. An example may help to clarify this very important point. Consider an agreement reached between a union and an employer which provides that as of a given date the straight-time hourly rate of pay of certain employees shall rise from $4.20 to $5.00, an increase of $.80 or 19 percent, to be in effect for twelve months. Suppose that this agreement is submitted to a stabilization board, and an increase of $.30, or 7 percent, is approved. At this point a board should insist, by administrative methods if not by legal regulation, that the collective bargaining agreement be amended to reflect the board's decision, that is, to show the rate of $4.50, not $5.00. To fail to have this done involves the likelihood that, should controls be lifted, the rate of wages paid would jump to $5.00, as provided by the agreement. A board may restrict this effect, to a degree, by establishing a time duration for its orders, so that the rate of $4.50 would be required to be in effect for twelve months, regardless of the board's continued existence. But at the expiration of the board's order, the rate would tend to go to $5.00 and any additional increase negotiated would be from the $5.00, not the $4.50, base. Where the agreement has been modified, however, the final rate in the old agreement, and the base from which new negotiations begin, would be $4.50.

The controls program of 1971–72 had a mixed experience with this issue. The Pay Board did not require modification of agreements to reflect its reduction of negotiated amounts but did establish a time duration for its decisions. As time passed, the board became increasingly concerned with the implications of the unamended contracts for wage levels should controls be lifted. When the board was abolished on January 11, 1973, it was apparent that, within a year, unless some form of controls was maintained, virtually all actions of the board on collective bargaining agreements would have been eliminated and the original wage rates would have been back in effect. This problem the board labeled the wage "bubble" or "spring." It was necessary, therefore, to retain wage controls in a substantial form in 1973 in order to prevent the evaporation of the Pay Board's actions in 1972. In contrast, however, the Construction Industry Stabilization Committee had persuaded local parties, in most cases, to amend agreements to reflect the committee's decisions, so that there was no problem of rapid evaporation of the stabilized wage levels due to the terms of existing bargaining agreements. The contrast between the practices of the two agencies in this respect clearly demonstrates the capacity of a board (in this case, the construction committee) to use collective bargaining agreements as an asset to the long-term stabilization effort.

10. Dispute Settlement

Types of Disputes

The settlement of labor disputes is a matter both critical to the success of a stabilization program yet also tangential. Dispute settlement does not involve the structure of a program, or its administration, or the standards for wage adjustments—matters which have been the topic of earlier chapters. Rather, dispute settlement involves the protection of the program from assaults upon it. Yet, this matter is of as great importance as any other, for the effort expended upon the development and administration of a wage stabilization program is futile unless the program can be defended from those who seek to disrupt it. Since a program which involves significant wage restraint is almost certain to invite challenges, the importance of a method or methods of response to challenges can hardly be overrated. The fundamental problem is to find a method of settling labor disputes within the context of the stabilization policy. Since it is unlikely that overt challenges (such as a strike against the program) can be entirely avoided, a secondary objective is to minimize challenges, so that the government has a chance to confront successfully those which do occur. An important aspect of defeating overt challenges is for the government to mobilize, in advance, support which will deter some adversaries and be effective in constraining others.

The lessons of history are very important in this area. During World War II strikes in the bituminous coal industry and on the railways repeatedly challenged the NWLB, with some success for the unions involved, but did not destroy the program. In retrospect, the unions no-strike pledge of December 1941, has been adjudged the single major factor in preserving the stabilization effort. In contrast, the stabilization board of the reconversion period disappeared in a wave of strikes in 1946. During the Korean period, a nationwide steel strike in 1952 seriously undermined the entire stabilization program (both wages and prices) and prepared the way for a bituminous coal dispute to topple the WSB in the fall of 1952. In 1966, the machinists (IAM), in a dispute with major airlines, administered the coup de grace to the guideposts. In 1971-72, the Pay Board avoided a serious threat to the controls program by two stratagems: first, by establishing controls after the major negotiations of 1971 were completed and, second, by administering a very flexible program of limited wage restraint. But, faced with a number of negotiations in 1973, the board's lack of any disputes-settlement machinery became a causal factor in its abolition.

There are, of course, many types of labor disputes, not all of which involve stabilization issues. Jurisdictional strikes or those over workers' grievances may be of concern in a wartime period when continued production is a public objective in itself but of little or no importance with respect to stabilization policies. Those industrial disputes which may involve stabilization issues, however, are actually of three distinct types, each of which has traditionally been handled differently. The most frequent type of work stoppage (or threatened stoppage) is that which occurs in the process of contract negotiations between an employer and a union and is common in the absence of controls. A second type of work stoppage is unique to a stabilization period. In this type of dispute, a union or employer may prolong a work stoppage that occurs in the context of negotiations in order to obtain guarantees of the approval of the proposed settlement by stabilization authorities prior to conclusion of the agreement between management and labor. A third type of dispute is also unique to a stabilization period and involves the stoppage employed as a weapon against a decision by the wage board. Stabilization authorities are potentially involved in all three types of disputes, although to varying degrees.

The industrial disputes which may threaten a stabilization program are not of a single type with respect to the characteristics of the work stoppages which are threatened or which actually occur. In some few instances, employers may lock out their employees in a dispute, confronting government authorities with a work stoppage caused by management. In most situations, though, it is the union which precipitates a work stoppage. The unions have, at times, shown great ingenuity in developing various kinds of stoppages or pressures. For example, unions sometimes call a single, large strike, shutting down an industry nationally or in a major geographic area. Examples of the single big strike might include the coal and steel disputes described above, threatened national railway stoppages, and so on.[1] But this is not the only tactic of the unions. They might also initiate small or partial strikes, or brief but repeated strikes in an industry. A union might, in preference to a strike against an entire industry or all the plants of a large employer, strike selectively certain companies or facilities and, if it appears useful, alternate in some fashion the companies or plants which are struck. If the targets chosen are strategic, great leverage can be obtained by the union in this fashion. Finally, in particularly bitter disputes, where avenues of overt protest, such as the strike, are denied to workers, resort may be had to industrial sabotage. This may be a particularly difficult action to prevent or suppress and one potentially extraordinarily expensive to the employer. Surprisingly, perhaps, there were important cases of industrial sabotage in labor disputes even during the patriotic fervor of World War II. For example, troops were stationed inside the Cities Service oil refinery at Lake Charles, Louisiana, in 1945, to attempt to prevent recurrence of damage to equipment which had taken place in a labor dispute.[2] Where government has gone to the extreme of seizing industrial facilities in the attempt to have production continued, the unions have sometimes sought for alternative methods of applying pressure. Blackman notes, for example, that:

> In an effort to cope with the unusual problems of seizure cases, the striking unions have developed the following major techniques: extending the strikes to the unseized firms of the same region or industry, or to the unseized plants of the same company; confining the strikes to only a small portion of the seized industry or firm; refusing to call off strikes ordered before seizure but avoiding any overt acts in their support during government possession; calling new strikes during government possession but disguising them as "spontaneous" cessations of work by individual employees; postponing the strikes to other specific dates.[3]

Nor can it be certain that this list exhausts the imagination of union membership and leadership in response to governmental initiatives to restrain work stoppages. Rather, it is to be expected that the future will provide new and unusual types of tactics in disputes.

The variations which may occur in the relationships between a wage board and a labor dispute are many, all involving peculiar problems for a stabilization program. In some instances the problem is to achieve settlements within the criteria propounded by the board. In other instances the problem is to prevent a union from compelling an employer to disregard a stabilization board's directives. In yet other circumstances, a board may be required to assist in the resolution of a dispute occasioned by the application of its policies. It is characteristic of industrial disputes, however, that any strike involving the policies of a board, no matter what the strike's origin, may become profoundly threatening to the existence of a wage stabilization program if the dispute cannot somehow be resolved.

Methods of Government Intervention

Labor disputes may often pose a serious threat to the effectiveness of a stabilization policy. How, then, should the government respond to actual or threatened work stoppages? The simple answer which most readily comes to the minds of many persons is to outlaw strikes against a stabilization program. Variants of this approach have been attempted but less successfully than might be imagined. Making an action illegal does not necessarily cause it to disappear but rather provides either a deterrent or a legal weapon against those who defy the prohibition. The legal weapon may be more or less successful in ending disputes, depending on the environment and how well the weapon is employed. But there are other devices for responding to labor disputes than strictly legal ones. For example, an agreement by the unions not to employ the strike during a period of stabilization, the so-called "no-strike pledge," may be an effective tool for lessening disputes. Such a pledge is not ordinarily obtainable, however, except in periods of the most threatening military emergency. Where a no-strike pledge is not available, then the government must seek, at the minimum, an agreement by the unions to resolve disputes, including those involving work stoppages, within the stabilization criteria. The absence of such an agreement effectively makes the stabilization program hostage to the threat of the strike by any labor organization which is cohesive and strategically placed in the economy.

A pledge not to strike, or to settle disputes within a stabilization framework, will not itself guarantee that no stoppages occur, though it may help to lessen their number and, perhaps, importance. But what should be the government's response to an actual or threatened stoppage? There are, potentially, various forms of response, including mediation of the dispute, arbitration (if possible), the use of legislation, and any number of coercive measures. In the pages below we will examine, in turn, each of these alternatives. The reader, as he considers the various governmental responses possible in a strike situation, might wonder if there are any general principles of the successful application of measures to restrain the successful use of work stoppages against a stabilization program. Archibald Cox, discussing the value of various methods for government responses to so-called "emergency disputes," listed three standards which may be formulated to apply specifically to a stabilization period. Cox suggested that a method of responding to a work stoppage should: first, lead to a continuation (or resumption) of production; second, look to a settlement of the underlying dispute within the stabilization criteria; and, third, avoid, or at least delay, the necessity for a choice by public officials between the first two objectives.[4] The last point deserves emphasis. The fundamental objective of a work stoppage by a union or employer is to force the government to make a choice between attaining a resumption of production or compliance with stabilization policy. The purpose of the government's response must be to avoid having to make such a choice. The maneuvers of the various parties to a dispute, and of the government in response, are to be understood most clearly as being directed at this matter. Such a struggle necessarily involves elements of threat, deception, feints, and other stratagems commonly employed in conflicts, and success normally requires a flexibility on the part of the government which is inconsistent with an automatic or mechanical response to the challenge.

The No-Strike Pledge

A pledge by the unions not to strike confers two advantages on a stabilization program. First, to the extent it is observed, it reduces the potential number of stoppages. Second, it provides a degree of moral leverage for the government in attempting to bring an end to strikes which do occur. Both are significant advantages, so that a no-strike pledge should be sought by the government in each period of stabilization, and some form of pledge should be obtained, if possible. At the outset of World War II the unions gave an unqualified no-strike pledge for the duration of the war, subject only the the establishment of a tripartite war labor board to make recommendations in disputes situations. Virtually all commentators have recognized the substantial importance of the no-strike pledge to the stabilization program of that period. "Any careful study of the wartime handling of labor disputes," said Edwin Witte, "must lead to the conclusion, shared by all the members of all three sides of the War Labor Board—management, labor, and the public—that the mainstay in the government's policy was the no-strike pledge rather than any law or executive order."[5] Further, the disputes policy was itself critical to the success of the wage stabilization program. The most convincing demonstration of this occurred at the end of World War II. The government abandoned the disputes-settlement machinery, and the no-strike pledge ended, but a form of stabilization program was continued. The stabilization effort failed. Why? John Dunlop offered the following judgment:

> The critical mistake . . . was the combination of the decisions on wage stabilization and the abandonment of disputes machinery. Had the dispute-settling machinery been extended to set the key-wage patterns, free collective bargaining could probably have settled a tolerable proportion of other disputes and made the adjustments to a peacetime economy on a day-to-day basis more smoothly.[6]

How effective was the no-strike pledge of World War II? Certainly, the pledge did not prevent numerous strikes from occurring. There were some fifteen thousand strikes and lockouts during the term of the no-strike pledge. Of these, some eight thousand occurred in the last two and one-half years of the war, after passage of the War Labor Disputes Act supposedly strengthened the government's hand in responding to stoppages. The average length of stoppages during the war was five to six days (compared with twenty-three days in 1936–39), and the percent of available working time lost due to strikes was lower than prior to or following the war.[7] The no-strike pledge did not, therefore, eliminate strikes, but it was useful nonetheless. It limited the number of stoppages; it served as a pretext for national union and employer leadership to intervene in local disputes to obtain a resumption of production; and it prevented the occurrence in World War II of a major dispute which could have crippled the stabilization program, as, for example, the coal strike of 1952.

A no-strike pledge is useful not only in limiting the number of stoppages but also in providing a mechanism through which those that do occur may be isolated and resolved within the stabilization framework. Finally, since this latter advantage of the pledge depends essentially on the employment of the good offices of the national union officers to assist in settling disputes, it may be, in some instances, adequate for the government to seek only such good offices when a comprehensive no-strike pledge may be unattainable. In peacetime, this policy is particularly appropriate for two reasons. First, work stoppages per se do not constitute the same problem as in wartime when the continuation of production is an end in itself. Second, the likelihood is greater in peacetime of a strike against a stabilization program receiving the support of national officers and of other unions, and thereby being successful. Since the government in peacetime is better able to tolerate stoppages, but still requires the cooperation of national union officials and other labor organizations in resolving disputes within stabilization criteria, the appropriate policy is to seek, not a no-strike pledge, but an agreement to cooperate in dispute settlement within the principles of the stabilization program.

The Use of Mediation

When a labor dispute threatens to result in a work stoppage, and when stabilization issues are involved, it is common for the government to request the parties to agree to mediation of the dispute. Acceptance of mediation does not entail agreement by either party to make concessions in order to settle the dispute. In consequence, it is unlikely that either party can fail to agree to meet with mediators and with each other. As George Taylor pointed out, "a suggestion to mediate seems so reasonable on its face, especially when the public interest is at stake, that refusal of the relatively strong party to go along can easily result in adverse public opinion."[8] Mediation often serves, therefore, as a means for entrance of public authorities into a dispute, although it provides no guarantee of a settlement of the issues. Yet, the mere fact of discussions with the parties may be of great value. To quote George Taylor once more, "economic warfare turns on unforeseeable happenings and surprising personal reactions. What both parties 'deep down' are willing to settle for, instead of taking their chances on a strike or lockout, is the real key that a mediation board seeks to discover."[9] Mediation may also, by its very informality, serve to assist in the settlement of a dispute. As Dunlop and Hill described the value of informality in World War II proceedings, "many a difficult and highly controversial case . . . was promptly settled over a drink. . . . These informal sessions promoted harmony and understanding . . . that never could have been achieved in a [formal proceeding]."[10] A further advantage of mediation is that it has a less serious impact on collective bargaining than procedures which remove responsibility for agreement from the parties.

Mediation is not, however, a unitary process—there are several variations. One of the unhappy aspects of the present state of understanding of dispute resolution in the United States is that the single term "mediation" is now used to describe a variety of procedures, which in previous and more sophisticated times were separately identified. For example, several decades ago the distinction between conciliation and mediation was widely understood. The job of a conciliator was to attempt to promote harmonious relationships between the parties to a dispute, trusting that a less bitter atmosphere would assist in the settlement of the issues. Mediation, however, involved a more complicated process. A mediator not only sought to reconcile the parties but to develop an independent judgment of the matters in dispute and to provide suggested solutions at the request of either or both parties. Recently, in the public sector at least, there has been some additional development of "mediation" procedures, including, especially, reliance on fact-finding procedures.[11] It is important that the government have potentially available as wide a range of procedures for mediation as might conceivably be useful in responding to various disputes.

The United States in 1917 institutionalized the mediation function by establishing the United States Conciliation Service. This service was abolished in 1947, and an agency of similar function, the Federal Mediation and Conciliation Service, was established. The existence of this independent federal agency (whose director is a presidential appointee) has been the source of both advantage and, in some instances, difficulties to stabilization authorities. The value of the mediation service is that it provides a staff of professionals who are often of substantial assistance in the resolution of disputes, and may in addition provide considerable useful information to a stabilization board when a policy of coordination and cooperation among the agencies can be developed. However, the disputes-responsibilities of a wage stabilization board do raise certain issues of jurisdiction between the board and the FMCS. Generally speaking, these matters have been successfully resolved in the past and may continue to be so in the future. In the guideposts period of the mid-1960s, however, considerable strain developed between the Council of Economic Advisors, which was pursuing the guideposts policy, and the FMCS. The council felt that the mediation service was not willing enough to attempt to get parties to settle agreements within the guideposts and was rather pursuing a policy of peace at any price in terms of the level of economic adjustments. In consequence, there developed the view that a major element of future successful incomes policy was to subordinate the activities of the mediation service more completely to stabilization objectives.

To a degree, the suspicions of the council members as to the FMCS's behavior were justified. As described by the director of the FMCS in the mid-1960s, William E. Simkin, the service sometimes "openly gave active support to seeming deviations from the [guideposts] where the facts of a specific case suggested that the simplistic percentage application was not an adequate criterion. And if the two parties to a dispute decided to ignore the formula, we did not 'blow the whistle.' "[12] But, as Simkin said, the source of the difficulties between the council and the service lay less in the unwillingness of the service to assist in the stabilization effort than in the undue rigidity of the guideposts. There was a similar experience in 1971–72, resulting from the 5.5 percent standard. But the abandonment of the single standard in 1973 provided the basis for closer cooperation between the mediation service and the stabilization program.

Arbitration

Arbitration is a process by which an impartial panel decides a dispute for the parties involved. There are many forms of arbitration, as there are of mediation. In the United States the generic term "arbitration" has come in common usage to identify what may more accurately be called voluntary binding arbitration—arbitration in which the parties have voluntarily agreed to accept an arbitrator's decisions regarding the issues in dispute. There may also be compulsory binding arbitration, or even compulsory nonbinding arbitration. Nonbinding arbitration differs from mediation only in that it tends to be preceded by a more formally judicial process than the recommendations of a mediator. The various forms of arbitration each may be useful in various circumstances involving disputes and a stabilization program. Historically, a number of different arrangements have been employed, the more important aspects of which are explored below.

During World War I there were established in the shipbuilding, marine and longshore industries joint adjustment boards, which were, in fact, methods of voluntary binding arbitration of labor disputes. The adjustment boards were created by agreement between the president of the United States and the presidents of the American Federation of Labor and of the national unions involved. The boards included a public member, a labor member, and the representatives of a federal defense agency, representing, in essence, the employer interests.[13] This adjustment-board model was followed in World War II in the establishment of the Wage Adjustment Board by agreement of the government and of the construction unions (two years later the employers were included in the board). The aspects of this model which involved its industry-specific orientation and the *bi*-partite labor and government composition have since largely been abandoned, in part because of the shift of emphasis in national boards from disputes settlement to wage stabilization responsibilities.

During World War II, the National War Labor Board represented a complex and subtle intermingling of mediation and compulsory and voluntary arbitration. The board was the custodian, so to speak, of the unions' no-strike pledge, in that it was to decide disputes as an alternative to open economic conflict. Decisions of the board possessed status, not because the board was a regulatory agency of government, but because the parties had agreed to accept its determinations in lieu of strikes or lockouts.[14] In this sense the board was not an agency of compulsory arbitration but one of voluntary arbitration.[15] Furthermore, its decisions in disputes cases were not automatically binding on the parties but rather were enforceable at the discretion of the president. In this manner, the board's directives in disputes cases were akin to recommendations, not to directives. The board has provided some data for evaluation of its success in settling disputes. For example, in 1944 in only 8 percent of disputes cases was there a strike after a decision had been issued by the board.[16] Generally these strikes were brief and were settled by acceptance of the board's award.

During the Korean period the WSB exercised a limited arbitration-like function upon receipt of a dispute certified to it by the president. The board's recommendations were not binding upon the parties, nor were they obliged to participate in its proceedings. Furthermore, the board was prohibited by Title V of the Defense Production Act of 1951 from issuing a recommendation without a majority vote of its members. This provision prevented the public members of the board from making a recommendation in a disputes case on their own authority. In the 1952 steel case, however, as we have seen above, the joint recommendation of the public members and the labor members was ineffective in settling the dispute. Enarson concluded that "a public member recommendation, standing alone, might have been appropriate."[17]

We now turn to the last point in our review of historical experience in the use of arbitration as a device in settling disputes involving a stabilization program. During both World War II and the Korean War, stabilization boards were generally quite independent of other stabilization agencies in their disposition of disputes cases, though they were bound, of course, by interpretations of stabilization policies. While certain types of rulings on voluntary applications by both the NWLB and the WSB were subject to approval of a director of economic stabilization, there was no such practice respecting disputes cases. Dunlop said:

The NWLB as a matter of policy, refrained from consulting with the Director of Economic Stabilization regarding particular cases prior to the decision of the Board. . . .

Such conferences on particular cases tended to destroy confidence in the Board as a dispute-settling agency of the last resort and to shift responsibility to the Stabilization Director. The public members of the Board did, however, thereafter continue to consult with the Director on issues of stabilization policy.[18]

And Enarson complained that:

> For all the elaborate hierarchy of bosses, the WSB proved to be virtually autonomous....
>
> In dispute cases, neither ESA [Economic Stabilization Agency] nor ODM [Office of Defense Mobilization] had policy control, though the Board was bound by existing wage policies and standards.[19]

What may be learned from this historical experience involving the use of arbitration in disputes involving stabilization issues? There are three major lessons. First, there must be provided as much voluntarism as it may prove possible to obtain in the arbitration function, whether conducted by a stabilization board or by an ad hoc panel. The provisions for voluntarism may result in peculiar administrative or legal arrangements, the nature of which cannot be predicted in advance. But organizational simplicity and clarity should, in this area, be sacrificed to obtain the contribution to the successful resolution of disputes which a degree of voluntarism supplies. The government should *not*, therefore, establish by legislation or executive order a general arbitration machinery but rather should provide for the possible establishment of such machinery upon whatever basis may elicit an important degree of voluntary consent from the parties generally. Second, the board should have considerable flexibility in its application of arbitration or mediation formats. In some instances, an informal proceeding is to be preferred to a formal one. In some instances the board may wish to make no award of the issues in disputes, while in others it may decide to employ a recommendation of the public members only. There is no advantage to be gained from establishing an invariant procedure, and much to be gained by flexibility. Third, for a board to be an effective arbitration mechanism in settling disputes, it must have considerable discretion in its actions and be subject to appeal only in the courts. Any other arrangement will cause disputing parties to go to whatever higher level of government holds the actual authority to rule on the merits of their dispute. Coincident with this necessary independence is, however, a special responsibility of the public members of a disputes panel to coordinate their actions with other elements of the stabilization program and to persuade them of the necessity and legitimacy of the decisions in disputes cases. This is required because the officials in charge of a stabilization program cannot be expected to permit a degree of independence to a wage board which they fear will result in decisions inconsistent with the requirements of the general stabilization program.

Legislative Action

The Congress of the United States is periodically subjected to pressures to become involved in the settlement of labor disputes. Generally, the impetus to congressional intervention during stabilization periods has not been the preservation of stabilization policies but the need for resumption of operations in industries where work stoppages imperil or seriously inconvenience the public. For this reason there has been little or no congressional intervention in many work stoppages which have threatened the stabilization program without creating large-scale public inconvenience. The 1971–72 stabilization program, in which numerous strikes occurred with potential stabilization consequences but which provoked little congressional concern, is the most recent evidence of this. However, when Congress becomes concerned with a dispute which has stabilization aspects, it may or may not deal directly with the stabilization issues involved. Congressional response to disputes may assume any (or all) of three forms: first, Congress may legislate the terms of settlement of the dispute; second, Congress may establish a forum by which the dispute is to be settled; and, third, Congress may simply provide penalties for initiating or continuing a work stoppage. Characteristically, in periods of stabilization, Congress has not chosen to legislate the terms of a settlement, preferring to leave that function in the hands of stabilization authorities. Rather, Congress has established both a procedure for settlement of the dispute (an arbitration-like proceeding by a stabilization board)[20] and penalties for those who undertake a work stoppage instead.

How effective has congressional action been in limiting work stoppages and preserving a stabilization program? The most interesting congressional action with respect to disputes during a period of stabilization involved the enactment of the War Labor Disputes Act (the Smith-Connally Act) in 1943. First proposed in 1941, final passage of the act was provoked by the series of coal strikes in 1943 which prompted President Roosevelt to ask Congress for legislation permitting seizure of the mines and penalties for work stoppages. Congress responded with a bill of general application—the War Labor Disputes Act. The act officially recognized the NWLB as a panel to settle disputes and authorized the president to take possession of industrial facilities to prevent any stoppage of production; it also provided penalties for any person who interfered with the operation of seized facilities by strike. lockout, and so on. The act also required the unions to follow a set of procedures established by the act for giving notice to the government of labor disputes "which threaten seriously to interrupt war production" and required continuance of production for not less than thirty days following such notice. On the thirtieth day the National Labor Relations Board was to conduct an election among the employees to see if they wished to interrupt war production for the reasons given in the notice, with the board to announce the results of the election. There the procedure terminated. A strike was, by inference, legal at this point. In fact, never in World War I, World War II, or the Korean War were strikes per se outlawed because of defense requirements. Such a prohibition speaks too strongly of enforced servitude or compulsory labor to have been acceptable in this country.

The president and the NWLB were dissatisfied with the act, and the president vetoed it. Congress thereupon passed the legislation over his veto. The difficulty with the act was that it implied the legality of strikes following exhaustion of the procedures provided, despite the unions' no-strike pledge. It threatened, therefore, not to strengthen the government's hand against stoppages, but to weaken it. In the outcome, the act apparently had little effect on the frequency of strikes,[21] but the experience indicates the sometimes unexpected but potentially disruptive impact of legislation. Three characteristics of congressional behavior stand out in this, the single major instance of disputes legislation by Congress during a period of stabilization. First, the legislation was very narrow in conception. Congressional action was induced by the mineworkers dispute, and little cognizance was taken by Congress of the broader impact of legislation. Second, the motivation of the legislation was almost exclusively political (directed at John L. Lewis and the mineworkers), without regard to nonpolitical considerations, especially the status and needs of the stabilization program. Third, the complex method of legislative enactment, with its often peculiar results, was demonstrated once again. The proponents of an antistrike law obtained only a set of procedures which had to be followed before a strike could occur. The opponents of any legislation at all were also partially unsuccessful, getting a piece of law at best innocuous, at worst, damaging to the stabilization effort.

Since World War II there has been legislation providing for disputes-settlement procedures in so-called national emergency strikes (the Taft-Hartley Act, 1947) which has complicated the procedures for handling disputes in a stabilization period. Conflict between the provisions of Taft-Hartley and procedures preferred by the president and the WSB developed in the Korean period, especially in the steel case of 1952. There has been no further legislation with respect to dispute settlement since the Korean period, though proposals for legislation with respect to disputes in various transportation industries have been given some prominence. In general, the realtionship between provisions for dispute settlement that exist now (especially in Taft-Hartley and the Railway Labor Act) or might in the future and the special problems of dispute settlement in a period of stabilization has not been worked out and may be expected to be a problem in the future. The unfortunate aspect of the legislation which is generally applicable is that it is often too automatic and too rigid in procedure for the special problems of a period of stabilization.

Coercive Measures

Even when public officials actively seek to avoid confrontations, some situations requiring compulsion will certainly occur. What types of coercion are available to the government in responding to challenges to a stabilization program? And what factors will determine the success or failure of the coercion applied?

Perhaps it is best to begin our discussion with the second question: upon what does the success or failure of government coercion to end a strike depend? There are four major factors which influence the success or failure of compulsion. First, there is the body of opinion of those external to the dispute itself. "Public opinion," the term customarily used to identify this factor, is too broad a label and should be separated into two elements. There is, on the one hand, public opinion broadly conceived, as developed largely by the press and telecommunications media. This public opinion (which we may designate "mass" opinion for convenience of exposition), for whose support parties to a labor dispute often contend and whose influence is so often touted by the casual observer, is, in reality, generally of very little assistance in ending a strike. (Mass opinion is particularly effective in influencing politicians, however, and may, through that means, sometimes be of use in resolving a dispute.) Another and more significant form of public opinion is that of the community most closely related to the striking workers. This community may be composed of the relatives, friends and/or fellow workers (the peers) of the strikers. These are the individuals whose support sustains a walkout and whose enmity can often cause it to be ended. Where this community supports a stoppage, it is very difficult for mass opinion to exercise any effective influence on the strikers. Furthermore, in some industries in which workers are largely isolated from other persons (coal or maritime) adverse public opinion of either sort may be largely ineffectual in influencing strikers to return to work. In consequence, public opinion favorable to the termination of a strike may be of assistance in supporting compulsion to end a dispute, or it may strengthen the workers against the government, or it may be of no importance either way.

Second, and most important among those factors affecting the ability of government to end a strike by compulsion, is the availability of replacements for the strikers. Workers who cannot, by virtue of skill, location, or the unpleasant character of their jobs, be replaced are unlikely to be successful targets for compulsion to resume work in a dispute. If the employers are required by the factors just listed to rehire the striking men, the power of strikers to compel a settlement desirable to themselves is very substantial.

Third, many matters internal to a union affect its ability to withstand government coercion to end a strike. Among the more important matters is the degree of dissonance between the leadership and the workers, if any.

When there is suspicion or lack of confidence, it is possible to break up the striking organization and thereby achieve a return to work. In many situations, however, the leadership, no matter how unreasonable its demands may sound to public opinion, is voicing the convictions of the workers themselves, so that compulsion directed against the leadership will be ineffectual in persuading the members to return to work. Furthermore, the degree of commitment which the workers have to the issues in question is an important aspect of the environment in which coercion operates. If the membership is not deeply attached to the issues in dispute, compulsion may more easily end the strike. Where there is strong membership concern for the matters in dispute, coercion may only engender militancy and a sense of being unjustly treated.

Fourth, physical violence against strikers carries its own inherent dangers. It is most likely to be effective when employed defensively—to protect private property or nonstrikers. But even in these circumstances, police or military action which threatens to provoke a labor insurrection (as in the UAW-Chrysler dispute of 1937 or the coal strike of 1943) may be repudiated by various public officials at the last moment. In summary, coercion is most likely to succeed against a strike when mass opinion and, especially, community opinion can be mobilized against the strike, the strikers are replaceable, the union is internally divided and the commitment of the workers involved is weak, and any physical violence against strikers is defensive in nature and of limited scope. When these four factors (or any combination) are unfavorable, coercion may be unsuccessful. Employed in an unfavorable environment, compulsion may be counterproductive. It may, for example, create solidarity in a striking union rather than divide it; in other instances, it may drive away irreplaceable workers, defeating the objective of resuming production; and, in still other instances, it may remove the leadership of a strike, leaving no one with whom to negotiate a settlement but without causing the strike to end.

The employment of coercion by the federal government to end work stoppages which involve economic stabilization issues began in the railway shopmen's and bituminous coal disputes of 1919. President Wilson then urged the parties to agree on terms which would not add to the cost of living. The president's plea failed in the coal dispute, and he supported it with a revival of wartime price controls and an antistrike injunction.[22] There have been several instances since of compulsion applied in disputes with stabilization consequences. In most major instances, the president has first called upon the parties to settle the dispute peaceably, as did President Wilson. Often such an appeal is without success. As Blackman puts the matter, there has often been a "willingness of those who have created labor-dispute emergencies to pursue their economic goals to the bitter end, to turn their economic weapons against the President in an effort to obtain his aid against their opponents, and to interfere deliberately with presidential measures to maintain uninterrupted production under terms consistent with the nation's emergency policies."[23] We may anticipate that there will be similar instances of the willingness to employ private economic power against a stabilization program in the future. The government possesses a variety of methods of coercion with which to respond to such challenges, some of which involve administrative penalties, some criminal penalties, and others raw force. We will consider, in turn, six of these methods.[24]

As a practical matter, most threatened or actual violations of wage stabilization regulations are committed by labor unions, so that the discussion below is necessarily primarily directed at the unions. However, in some instances management opposition to particular decisions results in a lockout. And in other instances nonunion employees may quit work in violation of stabilization regulations.[25] Wherever appropriate, the discussion below explicitly includes mention of management, though the possibility of application to nonorganized workers is implicit only.

Administrative Penalties

The procedures of the NLRB, which administers the rights and obligations established for workers, unions, and employers under federal law, has sometimes served as a convenient vehicle for the imposition of administrative penalties on striking unions.[26] For example, one administrative penalty developed in World War II has been used repeatedly. Normally, employees who strike to compel their employer to grant increased wages and to improve working conditions are engaged in concerted activity protected by the Labor-Management Relations Act (Taft-Hartley) and so may not be discharged, though the employer may replace the strikers temporarily (that is, during the strike) or even permanently. However, during World War II, the NLRB held that a union striking to compel an employer to pay an increase without approval by the National War Labor Board was not engaged in protected activity, so that the employer was free to discharge the strikers should he desire to do so.[27] This precedent was followed in the Korean period and in 1971–72 as well. For example, when employees struck an employer in 1972 to compel payment of an agreed-upon wage increase despite the freeze, the NLRB upheld their discharge by the employer.[28] This administrative device is useful only, of course, when the employer is prepared to discharge and replace the strikers. Wage stabilization boards also have certain administrative methods for response to a union striking in defiance of stabilization policies. It has been standard practice in all periods of stabilization for a board to refuse to handle a case while the employees were striking to compel a favorable decision (although, as a practical matter, boards have sometimes failed to successfully apply this rule).[29] Furthermore, boards have sometimes denied full retroactivity of an approved increase to a striking union. And, during World War II, the NWLB, in some instances, denied the maintenance-of-membership provision to "irresponsible" (striking) unions.[30] The problems inherent in providing penalties against strikes were highlighted, however, by NWLB experience with employers who, by various devices, provoked certain unions to strike in order to have maintenance-of-membership denied by the NWLB on that basis.[31]

Presidential Intervention

A federal action which is coercive only in the mildest sense involves an appeal by the president to the parties to a dispute to resume work while the issues in the dispute are submitted to mediation or some similar procedure. The device is sometimes effective but often not so.[32] It is coercive in the sense that it is intended to place the refusing parties in an undesirable public posture and to prepare the way for more overtly coercive actions, if they are needed and the authority for their use is available. A presidential request is most likely to be effective in ending a stoppage when there has already been a private agreement by the union to return to work, so that the request essentially provides only a convenient occasion for the action.

The Use of Troops to Perform Strikers' Work

In some cases military units may be successfully used to replace strikers at their jobs. Blackman lists nine instances in which workers have been temporarily replaced by soldiers or civilians (under military auspices) to keep production going. For example, during tugboat strikes in New York harbor, military personnel and equipment have been substituted for private boats. In the lumber industry strike in 1917–19 the army rented the labor of ten thousand soldiers to private logging firms under government contracts. In two New York longshore disputes the army hired nonstriking civilian dockworkers as temporary government personnel.[33] The success of the government in replacing strikers with military or civilian personnel depends upon the capacity of the replacements to perform the work involved. In an increasingly mechanized society, employers are often reluctant to entrust expensive equipment to the hands of partially competent personnel, so that even where there is an apparent possibility of replacing strikers with soldiers, the employers involved may prevent it.

Compulsion of Individual Workers

Compulsory or forced labor has been, as a general matter, abhorrent to the American tradition since the Civil War ended slavery. However, periods of wartime or stabilization have repeatedly included the threat, and sometimes the actuality, of penalties against individual workers for participating in a work stoppage against the policies of the government in an emergency period. During World War I collective bargaining agreements in coal included a penalty clause at the insistence of the federal fuel administrator. In the event of a strike the miners participating in the stoppage were to be fined $1.00 per day if the dispute were not submitted to the Fuel Administration for resolution and production resumed. The fine was to be deducted by the employer from the men's pay and contributed to the Red Cross. In the event of a lockout, the employer was to be fined $1.00 per day for every employee put out of work.[34] During World War II a more substantial application of compulsion to individual workers occurred in San Francisco. Lodge 68 of the machinists (IAM) refused to agree to work overtime beyond forty-eight hours per week (or eight hours in each of six days). The refusal was overcome in the end by the citation of fifty-eight machinists of draft age to their draft boards and the discharge of several older men without the right of referral to other defense-related employment. The refusal to work overtime ended, and the draft boards suspended the induction process.[35]

Coercion of individual workers has not been practiced in more recent periods of stabilization and is unlikely to be resumed unless there should be another major military conflict. In the absence of such a conflict the procedure speaks too strongly of totalitarianism to be of much use in this country. However, in periods of national emergency, coercion of individuals may be effective in some instances in causing a return to work, especially when, as in World War I, labor and management might be persuaded in one fashion or another to agree to it in advance.

Coercion of Union and Employer Leadership

More common than the coercion of individual workers has been the provision of penalties against union leadership or company officials for strikes or lockouts in certain situations. The measures involved may be fines or even jail terms. In some instances the penalties are prescribed by law for certain activities; in others they may be assessed by a court pursuant to the violation of a court order. As pointed out above, never in this century have strikes or lockouts in ordinary collective bargaining been made illegal. However, strikes or lockouts for certain purposes, or in defiance of special requirements of a procedural nature, have normally been prohibited. For example, in 1971–72, the Economic Stabilization Act provided fines for officers of unions or companies who violated the act of up to $5,000 for each violation and civil penalties of up to $2,500 for each violation.

Provisions for penalties may, in some instances, serve as a useful purpose of deterrence or even punishment for offenses. They do not of themselves prevent all violations, or even, in some cases, major violations. Furthermore, the leadership of unions may often be fairly insensitive to fines or jail sentences, having little money to lose in fines and knowing that a jail sentence may increase the leaders' political standing with the membership of the union. Thus, as is the case regarding most sanctions, a stabilization board is better advised to employ threatened penalties as a device for seeking an accommodation to settle a work stoppage than to apply sanctions at the first opportunity, thereby risking their failure.

Sanctions Against Organizations

The type of fines and civil penalties described above have been applicable not only to union or corporation officers for violations of the stabilization regulations but also to their organizations. Sanctions under a stabilization program are normally divided in the following manner: for violating procedural rules (that is, until the board has ruled on the approvability of a proposed compensation adjustment)[36] and thereafter for failure to accept the ruling (as expressed in the form of a work stoppage, a refusal to pay the increase, or the like). When a union strikes in violation of a procedural requirement or against a board decision, the first legal recourse of the government is normally to seek a court order to end the walkout. Injunctions are an important and often effective tool in controlling work stoppages. Failure to obey an injunction to return to work threatens a union and its leadership with contempt of court proceedings and with penalties ranging from fines to imprisonment. An injunction does not, however, ordinarily settle the issues in a dispute, but merely postpones a work stoppage for a time. It provides time for a stabilization board to examine a dispute and attempt to start a process of resolution of the issues. However, injunctions, like other forms of government coercion, are not invariably successful. Their use may, in some instances, embitter a dispute rather than resolve it and make it even more difficult to prevent later work stoppages.

Seizure

A major resort of government policy when faced with a work stoppage has been seizure of the industrial facilities involved. Practically, seizure involves the taking over of control of the company by the government for a period. It may or may not involve the substitution of government officials (civilian or military) for the private management of the firm. The workers are, however, declared to be the employees of the government, and a work stoppage is thereby made illegal. Seizure has been used for two primary reasons: to keep production going while a dispute is resolved, or to enforce a decision of a public (or tripartite) board as to the terms of resolution of a dispute. The former of these objectives has involved perhaps the most important historical instances of the use of seizure, particularly in various bituminous coal and steel industry disputes. Seizure has been used in these cases to remove the immediate provocation for a strike by substituting the government for the private company as the employer.

Seizure, however, involves many problems of its own. First, the government must be able to operate the seized facility—a not inconsequential matter should management fail to be cooperative.[37] Second, seizure raises the issue of what terms and conditions of employment are to apply during the government's operation of the facility. In some instances the government would prefer to retain the previously existing conditions while negotiations take place, in others it might wish to negotiate new terms with the union and place them into effect; in still other instances it might wish to place into effect the recommendations of a disputes panel regarding changes in the conditions of employment. This flexibility of approach is vital to successful use of the seizure technique. However, during World War II corporations became adept at delaying, by legal challenges, the placing into effect of a NWLB order enforced by seizure.[38] And in 1952, in the most recent case of seizure in a labor dispute (involving the basic steel industry), the Supreme Court prevented the government from placing into effect the terms of settlement recommended by the WSB, agreeing with the companies' contention that to do so would cause irreparable harm to managements' bargaining position in the dispute. The result of this and previous court decisions has probably been to greatly reduce the value of seizure as a method of resolving disputes. There has been no test of the status of seizure since the 1952 steel dispute, but Blackman has concluded, "if the interim order [of the Supreme court] in the steel-seizure case becomes a precedent, private employers could convert any seizure into the equivalent of an old-time [antistrike] injunction by bringing an equity suit against the seizing agency and requesting an interim [court] order enforcing the status quo [in terms of wages and conditions of work]."[39] Third, and in part as a consequence of the legal developments just cited, seizure does not itself settle the dispute but merely assists in preventing a work stoppage. Once a seized facility is again in operation, the government must still attempt to bring the parties to some settlement, lest a strike occur when it relinquishes the seized facility. Fourth, unions in some instances may actively oppose seizure. In the 1942–52 period considerable effort was devoted by several unions to developing techniques of resistance to government seizure of facilities. The responses of the unions included striking unseized facilities and avoiding cooperation with government officials at the job sites. Yet, for the unions, like management, resistance to or acceptance of seizure remains primarily a question of whose side the government's intervention appears to favor.

In general, seizure is an extreme, but sometimes successful, method of avoiding a work stoppage. Its ultimate value rests, however, on the ability of the government to resolve the basic dispute between management and labor during the term of the seizure.

The Statutory Strike

In recent years there has been considerable effort devoted to research for alternatives to the work stoppage as a means of compelling parties to a dispute to reach a settlement. One proposal in particular has received attention—the so-called "statutory strike." Under this proposal legally imposed penalties of a financial nature would be assessed against management and labor involved in a dispute as a means of encouraging each to desire to reach agreement, but a work stoppage would be prohibited. The proponents of this plan argue that its advantages would be to minimize disruption to the public by keeping production going, without allowing either side to profit from a refusal to reach agreement.[40] The idea has merit, particularly in the context of a military conflict or when a particularly disruptive dispute might threaten a stabilization program. In fact, such an arrangement was employed to help settle a dispute at the Jenkins Company valve plant in Bridgeport, Connecticut, during World War II. The Navy seized the facility to prevent a work stoppage but, in order to assist in resolving the dispute itself, ordered all the company's receipts paid to a navy "comptroller." A wage increase ordered by the NWLB was placed into escrow. Thus, neither the company nor the workers were able to benefit immediately from the government's action to continue production.

Perhaps in the future, stabilization boards, exercising disputes responsibilities, may again experiment with the development of means of promoting the resolution of disputes. Legislation to permit exploration of this area would be useful, although the enactment into law of any specific procedure or arrangement would now be premature. Within a stabilization framework there is no effective substitute in the settlement of disputes for careful and patient discussion, negotiation, and persuasion involving only limited use of enforcement powers.

The Effectiveness of Coercion in Labor Disputes

What general conclusions may be drawn from this brief survey of the alternative means of coercion available to the government in a labor dispute? First, considerable flexibility is required in the government's response to different types of labor disputes. While work stoppages by major unions affecting whole industries (coal, railroads, steel) have received most public attention, strikes by small units of employees in essential facilities have been as important and as difficult to handle. During World War II, Blackman concluded, "the threat of a few hundred machinists [at Hughes Tool Company] to strike was a greater problem for the War Department than . . . the strike of . . [14,500] truck drivers in Chicago."[41] More recently, the Long Island Railway strike of December 1972 and January 1973, arising in part from an action by the Pay Board, presented very difficult problems of settlement, mitigated only by the tactical mistakes of several of the unions involved in dealing with their own national organizations.

Second, it is apparent that coercion may sometimes be successful in terminating a work stoppage and sometimes unsuccessful. The degree of success of coercion depends, as we have said above, on a group of factors which largely constitute the environment of the dispute. But success also turns in part on the manner in which the government conducts its intervention and how effectively the union is able to respond. In a serious confrontation, government officials must expect their actions to compel an end to the strike to be challenged on the picket lines, in the courts, and in Congress. To prevail in the application of compulsion to a labor dispute often requires the government to be successful in these three forums and then to be successful in imposing approved wages and conditions (under the stabilization program) at the workplace. This is a tall order. Clearly, the government has only a limited capacity to engage in and prevail in such disputes. A stabilization program is well-advised to use coercion as sparingly as possible, conserving its resources for critical situations. This again suggests the importance of obtaining the degree of cooperation from labor and management in a stabilization program necessary to the avoidance of open conflict.

A third lesson involves a more subtle point than the issue of success or failure of government efforts. It is the question of what constitutes success or failure. Elected public officials are adept at attempting to present to the public a favorable picture of government efforts. Union and management leaders are often prepared to allow public officials to have public relations victories, involving the appearance of success of some overt act of coercion, so long as the reality of the matter is favorable to the private interests involved. Thus, a failure of a stabilization program to contain a threat to its policies may be made to appear, in the short run, a dramatic success. Careful observers must always attempt to distinguish between appearance and reality, measuring the success of the stabilization program's response to work stoppages by the longer-term effectiveness of the program.

Evaluation of Government Action in Labor Disputes

We turn finally to three rather fundamental issues of governmental involvement in labor disputes in the context of a stabilization program. First, in what circumstances is government intervention most likely to successfully terminate disputes within the framework of a stabilization program? Second, what has been the balance of government intervention—has it been favorable to management or to labor, and with what effect on their tolerance for government involvement? Third, should stabilization boards be involved in dispute settlement at all? Is there an alternative?

The discussion in the previous pages suggests that the most favorable condition for government intervention in disputes is one in which national leadership of employers and unions have agreed in advance to assist the government in the settlement of disputes within the stabilization criteria. In wartime this agreement may take the extreme form of a no-strike pledge by the unions and joint agreement to utilize the services of a tripartite panel as an arbitrator of disputes. In less dangerous times, there may be an agreement limited to cooperation on an ad hoc basis to settle such disputes as might arise. However, it may be offered as a general principle that, if national leaders of labor and/or management encourage challenges, a stabilization program will be sore beset and probably will not survive.

Second, has the balance of government intervention, by whatever means, been favorable to management or labor? Does the resistance of much of American management to a disputes-settlement function for a stabilization board represent a position justified by previous experience—or is it simply a selfish desire to have wage stabilization and perhaps a limitation of strikes without any necessity for a presentation of issues in disputes to a panel of neutrals? The most careful study of the experience of management and labor during wholesale government intervention in disputes during World War II concluded that there was no discernible advantage to either side, on balance.[42] The experience of more recent years does not require that this judgment be modified. However, it cannot be denied that some elements of American business have fared far worse than others under the disputes authority of various stabilization boards, particularly with respect to non-economic issues. This is especially true of industries weakly organized by the unions.

How practical is the attempt to keep stabilization boards fully out of disputes settlement? Are there alternatives which are viable in the long run? This chapter has demonstrated that a stabilization program cannot simply ignore labor disputes and hope to maintain an effective stabilization program. A board may, with some luck and some adroit sidestepping of confrontations, survive without some disputes mechanism for a brief period (the Pay Board lasted a little more than a year) but not for a prolonged one. However, it does not follow that the board itself need be the agency to be involved in disputes. Have the critics offered any alternative? Sumner Slichter, responding to the WSB's recommendation in the steel dispute of 1952, made a suggestion. The WSB, he said, had sought to resolve the basic steel dispute by bargaining with the two sides (by mediation) instead of giving a quasi-judicial opinion on the issues or, even better, remaining detached from the dispute until an agreement was reached and submitted to the board for its review. Slichter expressed outrage that the rejection by the steel companies of the WSB's recommendation had resulted in the seizure by the president of their property. "Rejection by the employers of bargains made between the public and the union representatives is not," said Slichter, "a sound basis for seizure of the employers' property by the government."[43] But what did Slichter recommend as an alternative? Merely that the president get directly involved in the dispute at the outset and that the stabilization board retain its independence to rule, ultimately in a legalistic manner, on the stabilization issues involved. But neither the union nor the companies were prepared to settle without government guarantees of approval of both wage and price increases. For the stabilization board not to have made recommendations in advance of such government commitments would have been simply to remain uninvolved in the resolution of issues which are of substantial importance for stabilization. Nor could a stabilization board be expected to overrule, post hoc, a presidential commitment to the companies and the union, as Slichter implied. Furthermore, early involvement by a wage board tends to lessen the degree to which political considerations affect the determination by the government of the issues involved.[44] Certainly those who would prefer a less active role for stabilization boards in disputes would not favor the substitution of more partisan political considerations in the government's handling of a dispute, were the choice to be put to them in that fashion.

11. Conclusions
and Prospects
for the Future

Summary

A Comparison of Program Elements

This section attempts to encapsule much of the subject matter of previous chapters in the form of two tables. In table 11.1 the five major elements of a comprehensive wage stabilization program are arranged against a listing of seven periods in which formal stabilization efforts have been attempted in the United States. It is immediately apparent from the table that only the stabilization program of the Second World War was comprehensive, in that it included each of the five policy elements listed. In contrast, the most limited of the programs was the guideposts effort of the 1960s. The cells in the table note for each period the existence and the degree of development of the various elements of policy. A comparison of the World War II and the guideposts programs by reference to the table will help make clear the meaning of the cell entries. For example, during World War II the program included a complete administrative arrangement (the NWLB and its regional offices), complete standards for wage increases (including the Little Steel formula and the brackets policy for interplant and intraplant inequities), a complete disputes mechanism (involving a no-strike pledge by the unions and the use of the NWLB as a body to award decisions in disputes), a legislative basis in several congressional acts, and an extensive and ongoing arrangement among management, labor, and government for the duration of the war. The guideposts period was very different. The arrangement for administering the stabilization policy was limited to the staff of the President's Council of Economic Advisors, a small body inexpert in stabilization matters and one with other duties to perform. The guideposts were a limited set of wage criteria at best. The program included no disputes mechanism. It had no direct legislative authorization and was not founded on any agreement among management, labor, and the government (in partial consequence of which both management and labor felt free to violate the guideposts in their own interests).

Other comparisons from the table are less dramatic but still interesting. For example, the major difference between the World War II program and its more important successors, the Korean program and that of 1971–72, are

TABLE 11.1
Stabilization Programs in the United States

Major Elements of Stabilization Policy	NWLB, World War I	NWLB, World War II	NWSB, 1946	WSB, Korean War	Guideposts 1962-66	Pay Board, 1971-72 Phase II	Cost of Living Council, 1973, Phase III
Administrative arrangement	Limited	Complete	Limited	Complete	Very limited	Complete	Limited
Standards for wage increases	Limited	Complete	Limited	Complete	Limited	Complete	Limited
Disputes mechanism	Limited	Complete	None	Complete	None	None	Limited
Legislative basis	None	Complete	Complete	Complete	None	Complete	Complete
Agreement among management, labor and government	Complete	Complete	Complete	Limited	None	Limited	Limited

shown to be the successively reduced significance of a disputes function in a stabilization program, so that in 1971–72 it disappeared entirely. Also, the agreement between labor, management, and government upon which the World War II program was based was not replicated in later programs, contributing to an important degree to their lesser relative success (that is, measured against the economic environment) in restraining inflationary pressures. For illustrative purposes, the program of partial controls which in 1973 followed the 1971–72 program is also described in the table, although previous discussion in this volume does not include the 1973 period. Two developments in the 1973 program merit attention here. First, the trend from World War II forward in the direction of the elimination of the disputes function in a stabilization program is reversed by the inclusion of a limited disputes machinery in 1973. Second, the 1973 program represented a more careful effort at decontrol than did the NWSB program in 1946, following immediately after the World War II program. In 1946 the transition period from comprehensive controls to none was made by a program lacking a disputes mechanism and without acceptance by management and labor. A consequence was the failure of the 1946 program. This experience, in part, prompted the inclusion in the 1973 program of a limited disputes mechanism and a limited agreement with management and labor as to the function and form of the stabilization effort. Thus, the table demonstrates the continuing evolution of stabilization programs in the United States.

The table is, however, limited in its capacity to reveal the full range of differences among programs. For example, some readers may object fairly that substantial differences which existed between the World War II program and that of the Korean period are not visible in the table. The important divergence of practice between the two periods with respect to the particular standards established for wage increases is not revealed by the table's description of each program as having "complete" standards. Also, the very different administrative arrangments of the two programs are not illuminated by describing each as "complete". Unfortunately, for convenience in exposition such matters as differences of practice could not be included in this table, nor are they summarized in this chapter (with some few exceptions), although the reader may find extensive discussions in earlier chapters of varying wage standards and administrative arrangements.

Lessons from the Comparison

The comparison of stabilization programs by policy elements suggests four major lessons regarding wage stabilization efforts in the United States. 1. *The development of wage stabilization policy overall has not been in a single direction but rather has been characterized by the gradual decline and later resurgence of various elements of policy.* For example, the importance of an arrangement among management, labor, and government has been differently adjudged at various periods, resulting in its inclusion in some stabilization efforts and absence in others. Similarly, the need for a disputes mechanism has been variously evaluated and has sometimes been included in programs and at other times excluded. It would be tempting to explain these cycles as the result of the conscious adaptation of policy elements to the economic, industrial relations, and political environments of various periods of stabilization, but there is little evidence that policymakers have generally operated in such a manner. Program characteristics have generally resulted from a variety of influences, only some of which have been the needs of the stabilization effort itself. In contrast, program elements have too often been established by government officials with little or no experience or knowledge of stabilization requirements. Unfortunate consequences have often resulted from the imperfect match of program structure and the requirements of stabilization policy in a particular period. These experiences have been a primary factor in causing the reintroduction of program elements in later periods. For example, the incapacity of the government to enforce the guideposts of the 1960s caused it, in 1971-72, to rely heavily on a statute to develop an excessively legalistic stabilization program. Similarly, the absence of an agreement among management, labor, and government was recognized to have so adversely affected the NWSB in 1946 that the government accepted substantial modifications from both management and labor to the stabilization program in the Korean period in the attempt to achieve some semblance of a joint effort.

A more regular and intimate cycle of inclusion and exclusion in policy involves both the form of administrative arrangements and the degree of completeness of wage standards. In all periods limited administrative arrangements have been combined with limited wage standards, and complete administrative arrangements with complete wage standards. This is not to imply that administrative arrangements and wage criteria have not differed among and within periods but that the degree of completeness involved in either has been commensurate within each period. In part this is because an extensive administrative arrangement is required by an extensive set of wage standards. Further, there is a rhythm of progress, in arrangements and standards, from limited to complete to limited. In part this pattern is the result of the succession by a decontrol period of a period of complete controls (as in 1946 and 1973). But this is only part of the story. Each period of complete controls has proven so undesirable a bureaucratic process to those who experienced it that a less complex program has all but been required to follow it. This erosion of acceptance of controls by management and labor is a point of major importance to which we shall return later. But this dynamic process of acceptance and later rejection of comprehensive controls is in part responsible for the cycle of administrative arrangements and wage standards among programs.

This discussion is not intended to suggest that there should not be an effort by the government to adjust the form and content of a stabilization program to its environment. This is, in fact, an important obligation of government, as we shall see below. Nor is the discussion above intended to imply that public officials have not made efforts to achieve some consistency between program characteristics and the requirements of a particular situation. In some instances they have done so. In general, however, the progress of stabilization policy in this country, particularly since World War II, cannot be described or understood as an intelligent adjustment of programs and policies to changing circumstances. There was some of this to be sure, but there was also considerable adjustment and readjustment of programs because of mistaken views about stabilization and because of factors quite extraneous to the needs of stabilization. The uneven progress of public policy results from these latter influences.

2. *The table also demonstrates that many combinations of program elements are possible, yielding a substantial variety of previous and potential stabilization programs.* Of the seven programs described in the table none are identical in their composition. There has been in the past and will continue to be considerable experimentation by public officials with the form and content of stabilization programs.

3. *Some program components can be substituted on a less than perfect basis for other components in the effort to maintain a wage stabilization policy.* Many of the subtleties involved in the understanding of stabilization efforts arise from this substitution, and it is certain that this factor will be of increasing importance in the future use of stabilization policy. For example, in the First World War the government sought wage restraint primarily through voluntary agreements among management, labor, and government. The less than satisfactory experience of this period suggested that the stabilization effort be strengthened in the initial months of World War II by reliance on a no-strike pledge and a disputes mechanism to constrain wage increases. By the fall of 1942 the government had imposed direct stabilization by administrative arrangement and with complete wage criteria. (This development within World War II is not described in the table.) Thus, the wage stabilization function per se was shifted first from agreement among government, labor, and management to a disputes mechanism and then to a set of rules and procedures applying to wage increases. This last device was, of course, the most direct in its stabilization effect. But the process of transference has also worked in reverse. For example, a disputes mechanism has been relied upon as a surrogate (albeit imperfect) method of wage stabilization when the government could not or did not desire to rely upon administrative arrangements and wage standards to control wage increases. Such a substitution has occurred in the following way. When complete administrative arrangements and wage standards were in existence, the primary role of a disputes mechanism has been to resolve controversies

within the framework of the stabilization criteria with minimal interruption of production. Thus, from the narrow viewpoint of a stabilization objective, the disputes machinery existed for the purpose of protecting the stabilization machinery. But in the absence of complete administrative arrangements and wage standards, a disputes machinery has served to provide government officials with some degree of stabilization impact. This is because dispute settlements require wage judgments (when the issues involved in the dispute are economic), and the disputes mechanism provides the government a method of involvement in the situation in which the strike may be used to establish new high rates of wage increase. There are historical examples of the substitution of a disputes machinery for direct wage controls. For example, in 1945, the government tried but failed to open a discussion with management and labor of wage criteria for the decontrol period under the guise of a method of settling expected disputes. In contrast, in 1973, the government was successful in a similar endeavor, contributing to the greater success of the decontrol program of 1973.

4. *Various designations have been used to describe the stabilization programs of different periods as a whole, including, for example, "voluntary" or "compulsory," but the most accurate and useful designations of programs would indicate the degree to which they are or are not comprehensive.* A comprehensive stabilization program may be said to involve in a complete fashion the five major elements of stabilization policy listed in the table. By this standard only the World War II program was truly comprehensive, and all other programs may be characterized as having been less comprehensive in various ways. Certainly a stabilization program is more likely to be a useful tool of economic policy the more fully it can be made a comprehensive program. (There is, however, no necessary connection between the proposed degree of wage restraint and the comprehensiveness of a program.) Thus comprehensiveness, as defined here, may serve as a relatively unambiguous standard of comparison among programs.

Other possible characterizations are necessarily ambiguous, however. For example, all stabilization programs involve some degree of voluntarism and some degree of compulsion. The World War II program was perhaps the most fully compulsory of any, but George Taylor, the vice-chairman of the NWLB, has demonstrated that it was in a fundamental way a voluntary program. In contrast, the guideposts were heralded as voluntary but were made operative in some instances by presidential intervention carrying implicit threats of federal action if the president was unsuccessful. Furthermore, it would be erroneous to conclude, as many have done, that the guideposts collapsed because they were voluntary, not compulsory. Rather, the collapse of the guideposts is more explicable in terms of other limitations. Lacking an agreement from management and labor to cooperate in a stabilization effort, lacking a statutory basis, and lacking any disputes mechanism, the guideposts program floundered on strikes against its wage standards and disregard of its policies by labor and management.

Influences on the Type of Stabilization Criteria Chosen

We turn now to a discussion of the factors which influence the type of compensation standards developed by a program. Perhaps the most convenient method of summarizing what has been in practice a substantial range of divergence among programs is to distinguish two major alternative approaches to the form of compensation criteria. Since these approaches are not program elements of the type described above but are intellectual biases or preferences, they are more difficult to categorize and to analyze. However, an attempt to organize these approaches to compensation criteria and to describe their relative importance to the types of compensation criteria actually employed by various programs is made in table 11.2. The two approaches are characterized as follows. The first involves the limited use of a general standard for compensation increases and relies much more heavily on specific or particularized criteria for adjustments in various types of compensation. For example, criteria for wage adjustments might involve certain types of wage comparisons. Alternatively, criteria for fringe benefits might involve the establishment of particular benefit levels for certain industries and geographic areas, specifying, for instance, the number of paid

TABLE 11.2
Relative Importance of Alternative Approaches to Compensation Criteria Employed by Wage Stabilization Programs

Alternative Approaches	Stabilization Programs				
	NWLB, World War II	WSB, Korean Period	Guideposts, 1962–66	Pay Board, 1971–72	COLC, 1973
Particularized criteria (involving limited use of a general standard and specific criteria for various types of compensation)	Strong	Strong	None	Limited	Partial
A generalized norm (involving primary reliance on a general standard expressed as a target percentage increase in total compensation)	Very limited	Limited	Strong	Strong	Partial

holidays approvable or the amount of pension benefits and certain eligibility rules. In contrast, the second approach places primary reliance on a generalized norm expressed as a percentage increase in total compensation (that is, including both the amount of a wage increase and the estimated total employer cost of fringe benefit adjustments). Specific standards other than the norm are minimized in this approach, and in their place is established a certain limited range of criteria for exceptions to the norm. Both approaches have advantages, and both have significant disadvantages.

To recapitulate briefly the conclusions of chapters 7 and 8 above, the major advantage of particularized criteria is a greater relevance to the actual operations of the labor market in determining compensation, with a consequently greater capacity to apply restraint, especially in the longer run (over a period of more than a single year). The major disadvantage of particularized criteria is substantial administrative complexity and magnitude. The merits of the generalized norm approach are in direct contrast to those of the approach of particularized criteria. The major advantage of the generalized norm is administrative simplicity; its major disadvantage is a degree of generality so great that restraint is abandoned over important aspects of the normal processes of determining compensation in the society, with potentially destabilizing consequences, especially in the longer run.

Each approach to the form of compensation criteria in a stabilization program has had and continues to have its vigorous advocates, each its detractors. No period of stabilization has escaped a debate between the partisans of these two approaches. Yet the relative degree of influence of each approach on particular stabilization programs has varied greatly. A summary of the relative influence of the two approaches is given in the accompanying table. It may be observed that the influence of the advocates of particularized criteria was especially prominent in the programs of World War II and the Korean period, although the influence of the advocates of a generalized norm gained in the Korean program. The guideposts of the 1960s were in part a reaction against the large administrative requirements involved in the approach of particularized criteria. The guideposts may be characterized as exclusively reliant upon a generalized norm. In turn, the Pay Board's program was largely a reaction against the lack of clarity and specificity of the guideposts, so that a limited element of the particularized criteria approach was reintroduced to supplement primary reliance on a generalized norm. Thus, the programs of World War II and of 1971–72 may be viewed as contrasting counterparts, each with elements of both approaches but with the emphasis reversed in 1971–72 from where it had been placed in 1942–45. By 1973 the inadequacies of the Pay Board's overreliance on a generalized norm were apparent, but the additional administrative requirements of a shift to reliance on particularized criteria were so great as to prevent that shift. A sort of hybrid program resulted, drawing its inspiration in various, and probably about equal, ways from both approaches.

Earlier chapters have discussed the factors which should affect the choice between the two approaches, including the degree of wage restraint required, the expected length of the program, the degree of distortions in the economy at the outset of the program, and the economic and industrial relations climate. That discussion need not be repeated here. However, the important point which may be added to the earlier discussion is that whatever the intrinsic merit of either approach in specific situations, proponents of each have thus far failed to demonstrate to policymakers the preferability of one or the other. Each side has had its opportunity in one or more programs to demonstrate the superiority of its approach. Neither has succeeded. The result is that the advocates of either approach remain deeply convinced of their own position, but others are uncertain. In the future it is likely that the experience of 1973 will be repeated. The advocates of each approach will press upon government officials the advisability of reliance upon one approach rather than the other. These officials, however, are likely to wish to combine the two approaches in various forms. An important question for the future effectiveness of stabilization policy is the degree to which the two approaches can be reconciled. An additional and perhaps more important question is the degree to which officials will be able to adjust the combination of the two approaches to the needs of the economy in particular periods and to modify the combination as circumstances change. Modifications of a program to meet changing circumstances will not be an easy task but will require great care and professionalism. Upon the capacity of the government to make these adjustments in ensuing years will rest much of the cause of success or failure of stabilization policy generally.

Some Lessons of Recent Stabilization Experience

Before we turn our attention to a group of conclusions about wage stabilization policy generally, we should summarize some lessons of recent experience with stabilization programs. These lessons are not of such magnitude as to be included below in the general discussion on policy, but they are important nonetheless. Therefore, in these next few pages we shall consider three of the consequences of the 1971–72 program which are most significant to an understanding of stabilization policy but which have escaped general attention.

1. *The stabilization effort in 1971–72 established that a formal program of controls could be useful even in a largely slack economy.* Prior to the 1960s it had been widely accepted that wage controls could serve no useful purpose in a slack economy, since unemployment was expected to restrain wage increases. The wide acceptance of a cost-push explanation of inflation in a slack economy had largely replaced the earlier view by 1971, so that wage controls were argued to be required as a method of restraining a generalized cost-push inflation. What had not been foreseen was the degree to which

compensation adjustments in the economy in 1972 would differ among sectors, including substantial upward pressure in some areas. The Pay Board established the usefulness of controls in a slack economy not by holding compensation adjustments in each employee unit to the level of the general wage and salary standard, an objective which was not accomplished, but by screening cases and in several important situations preventing new levels of compensation from being established. The potential secondary effects on compensation in important sectors of American industry of certain of the adjustments disapproved by the Pay Board were great. The result was that in some important respects the wage structure was kept in better order in 1972 than would have been likely in the absence of the controls program. This result was a contribution to stability in the years immediately following 1972. This accomplishment requires careful consideration because it was not what the Pay Board publicly stated its objective to be and it was what many persons (including some members of the Pay Board itself) believed was not needed.

2. *The country paid a substantial price for the operations of the Pay Board and Price Commission in 1971-72 in the erosion of support among business and labor for a stabilization program.* This judgment is especially important because it must offset, to a degree, the evaluation of the economic results of the 1971-72 program, especially those statistical studies which purport to establish that the program effectively restrained both wages and prices below otherwise expected levels. The results of the erosion of support by business and labor were quickly apparent. In the spring of 1973 rapid increases in prices stimulated demands by consumer groups and the press for a reimposition of comprehensive controls. But resistance from both management and labor to a return to the 1971-72 program was great enough to prevent Congress from legislating more vigorous controls or the administration from imposing them. (Ironically, of course, the public positions of labor and management favored action to reduce inflation; yet neither was prepared to accept the necessary additional governmental regulation of wages and prices.)

How had the stabilization authorities in 1971-72 developed such strong opposition so quickly? Perhaps, it might be thought, the program had been so vigorous in constraining price and wage increases that business and labor were driven to opposition. But there is little evidence for such an interpretation. Even the most ardent supporters of the program credit it with only a marginal contribution to increased wage and price stability in 1971-72. And during the course of the program neither management or labor suffered unduly. Corporate profits rose rapidly, and wage adjustments not only rose at a substantial rate but for the first time in several years exceeded the rate of increase in consumer prices. Thus, it was not so much the general degree of constraint applied to wages and prices which generated opposition, as the manner in which the stabilization agencies conducted their functions. To confine our remarks to the wage side, certain aspects of the operations of the wage stabilization program which engendered bitter opposition in labor, and a lesser but important degree of opposition in management, can be identified. First, the intrusion of the Internal Revenue Service as an agent of the Pay Board into collective bargaining relationships and pay practices was resented. The agency was inexpert in many compensation matters, and its role in the stabilization program was widely interpreted as an effort to intimidate private parties. Second, the Pay Board operated for much of its existence with only limited management and labor participation, and often acted on matters of substantial importance to local parties with an apparent disregard for the specific concerns of the parties. The result was an impression that the board was distant, arbitrary, and often destructive in the application of its regulations. In response to those aspects of the wage stabilization program, important leaders of management and labor supported the government's decision to terminate the controls program in January 1973, at a time when the economic, political, and industrial relations environment in the country might well have resulted in a choice by the administration to continue fairly comprehensive controls had the stabilization agencies not deeply estranged those in the economy with whose economic behavior they were concerned.

3. *The aftermath of the 1971–72 program again demonstrates the capacity of government, with the assistance of private parties, especially the press, to generate a mythology of success regarding a program which in fact had a somewhat mixed experience.* The unfortunate aspect of the substitution of a mythology of success for a clearheaded analysis of successes and failures in a program is not that undue credit is received by some public officials (for this, after all, is a fleeting matter) but that hard lessons are supplanted by myth. In the United States the shape of the mythology for the 1971–72 program is already apparent. It is that the wage-price stabilization program of 1971–72 was largely successful in restraining cost-push inflation; that the wage program was more constraining than the price program; that the entire program was abolished in a major stroke of mistaken economic policy-making in January 1973; and that the subsequent price inflation of spring 1973 was largely due to the elimination of the program. Enough has been said previously to indicate that this interpretation is erroneous in large part and that it ignores fundamental lessons of the 1971–72 experience. For example, this view ignores the increasing intolerance of business and labor for controls which developed in response to the Pay Board's procedures; the unsuitability of many of the board's regulations for stabilization in a longer time-span than a single year; and the lack of a disputes procedure in the face of a round of major negotiations in 1973. On the price side it should be said, at least, that Price Commission regulations would not have been constraining

on most of the sectors in which price pressures appeared in early 1973 even had the regulations remained in effect.[1]

Conclusions: The Most Significant Aspects of Stabilization Policy

Many aspects of stabilization policy have been discussed in preceding chapters. An attempt to repeat the conclusions drawn in those chapters with respect to each topic discussed would be unreasonably lengthy. However, a series of the most important conclusions of those chapters taken as a whole may be listed here, in order to emphasize their importance. There are conclusions of two major types: those which pertain to the requirements for a successful stabilization effort and those which involve limitations of stabilization policy. We will first consider four requirements for effective stabilization, reserving the limitations of stabilization policy for discussion in the next section.

Cooperation from Management and Labor

The single most important element in the success of a wage stabilization policy is that there be some understanding between management, labor, and the government regarding the form, content, and environment in which the program will operate. No particular type of arrangement is required. Rather, the understanding may be made to fit the circumstances of the moment. At one extreme, a national emergency may require a vigorous program of wage restraint, necessitating an extensive and specific understanding among management, labor, and the government. At the other extreme, a program of moderate restraint in a peacetime economy may require only limited arrangements developed on an ad hoc basis. In this situation, the contribution to the success of a stabilization effort of limited arrangements may be important even when there is conflict among the various groups on most economic and political matters.

What is required of any understanding, no matter how complete, is that the private parties, especially organized labor, cooperate with the government in the stabilization program. But "cooperation" used in this context need not imply overt support of the stabilization effort. Rather, cooperation requires only that private parties not seek actively to undermine the program. In some instances, cooperation of labor and management may extend to participation in the administration of the program and even, as in World War II, in its enforcement. In other instances, cooperation may extend no further than an agreement to assist the government in the settlement of labor disputes. If, however, there is *no* range of cooperation among government, labor, and management regarding a stabilization program, then it is most likely that elements of either management or labor which might seek to use economic weapons or political influence to weaken or destroy the program will be successful.

A corollary of the proposition that labor and management cooperation is necessary to the success of any stabilization effort is the recognition that government cannot pursue a stabilization policy unilaterally. This conclusion is not affected by the degree of regulatory compulsion available to the government. There is, unfortunately, a tendency in the United States to measure the potential effectiveness of a stabilization effort by the degree of compulsion mustered to support it. For example, when the 1973 stabilization program was announced, Walter Heller, former chairman of the President's Council of Economic Advisors, made the following response to a question regarding the potential success of the program. "The real question," Heller said, "is how much clout the program will have."[2] The "real question" is not this but one which might be phrased as follows: "Is the program founded upon a general agreement among government, business, and labor to cooperate in the stabilization of the economy?" Or, more colloquially, the question might be phrased, "Will management and labor go along?" Should the answer to these questions be negative, no degree of "clout," or government compulsion, will make the program successful, or guarantee it more than a very brief life. If cooperation with the program is promised by management and labor, however, then its chances of success are much improved, and the administrative characteristics of the program, including the government's enforcement powers, will become of significance in adjudging its potential for success.

Elements of Stabilization Policy Other Than Wage Restraint

Closely related to the need for cooperation from management and labor in a stabilization program is the role of elements of the program which do not involve wage restraint directly. In general, the interest or involvement of management and labor cannot be long retained by a stabilization program which is narrowly restricted to limiting wage increases. Union leadership cannot justify to its membership participation in such a program, nor can management afford to ignore other aspects of industrial relations by a narrow pursuit of wage restraint. Elements of a stabilization program in addition to wage restraint may include, for example, procedures for dispute settlement, attempts to improve the functioning of collective bargaining in various sectors or industries, and concern for the long-run improvement of industrial relations. A wage stabilization agency may deeply involve business and labor representatives in the stabilization effort in individual situations through devoting attention to problems at the workplace which may have been translated into requests for economic adjustments before the stabilization program began. In general, what is required of a stabilization agency is that it provide management and labor with an opportunity to address their common problems, which are generally broader than stabilization issues, through the mechanism of the stabilization program. This attention to the broader context of problems within a stabilization framework involves the potential for engaging substantial support of business and labor for the stabilization effort and for continuing that support over a period of several years, to a degree which a narrow attention to wage restraint alone cannot accomplish.

Understanding the Operations of Labor Markets

The policies and decisions of a stabilization effort must be based upon a thorough understanding of the operations of labor markets if the effort is to be successful. This judgment, like the preceding ones, is the more certain the longer the term of stabilization required by the government and the greater the desired degree of wage restraint. The failure of stabilization officials to understand the often diverse functionings of particular labor markets involves the risk that actions of the stabilization program will introduce inefficiencies and disruptions into the economic system, sometimes to the disadvantage of stabilization objectives.

There are many aspects of labor market operations which are potentially significant to the activities of stabilization authorities, including, for example, patterns of labor mobility, of employer competition for workers, of promotion within an employee unit, and others. But by far the most significant aspects of the behavior of labor markets for stabilization policy are the interdependencies of compensation among groups of workers, firms, and industries. The failure to recognize interdependencies results in the most important type of error to which stabilization programs are prone—that of ignoring, or being ignorant of, the secondary impact of actions in particular instances. That is, it is common in the economic system for particular groups of workers and firms to be involved in a system of compensation which includes fairly rigid interrelationships. An action of a stabilization board with respect to an element of such an interrelated system necessarily tends to require consistency in other actions. Other elements of the system, certainly those workers and firms in the particular system, will demand this. Yet stabilization authorities often find themselves in the position of attempting to resist the generalized application of an action taken by the stabilization program with no initial realization of its implications elsewhere. For example, in 1972 wage stabilization authorities reviewed a request for a substantial economic adjustment from a small paper mill in an upper midwestern state. The mill employed forty-two workers, many of whom earned relatively low wage rates. This mill appeared to be the only paper mill in the immediate geographic area involved. Applying its discretion under stabilization regulations, the Pay Board approved the entire increase. Unfortunately, it later became clear that compensation in this mill was in significant ways related to compensation in the pulp and paper industry in the entire area of the United States east of the Rocky Mountains, and the board's action in the case of this small mill created substantial problems in the later resolution of cases involving tens of thousands of workers in scores of mills. Examples of such situations from the experience of stabilization programs in this country can be listed almost without limit. In fact, it is characteristic of the process of increasing maturity in a stabilization program that its officials come to recognize that the primary determinant of the importance of a particular case is not the size of the employee unit or units directly involved but the likely extent of secondary effects of the decision in the case.

The importance of interrelationships in compensation patterns and practices is also an argument against too great reliance in a stabilization effort on formulas or other types of overly generalized wage regulations. The complexity of the economy is such that a stabilization board cannot know in advance what anomalies in individual situations may result from the application of formulas or specific rules. Too often a formula will permit different rates of compensation increase within a closely interrelated system. In such a circumstance a stabilization board is not normally able to resist pressures to permit all units in the group to obtain whatever level of increase has been allowed to other units. In practice, stabilization authorities are generally confronted with an unpalatable choice: allowing all units the highest increase permitted for any of their group or attempting to maintain differentials which the industry does not desire or, in some cases, will not tolerate. Minimizing the frequency of such situations requires a stabilization program involving qualitative standards, with considerable latitude for flexibility in application to particular instances. And there is required an understanding of the most important interrelationships in the economy.

Concern for the Long Run

It has often been alleged that the primary effect of the various periods of stabilization policy in the United States has not been to restrain inflationary pressures but merely to postpone their impact. Unfortunately, there is evidence to support this conclusion, especially from the experience of the aftermath of the World War II program. But there is no inherent reason why a wage stabilization effort must be followed by a surge of wage adjustments, if attention is provided by stabilization authorities to the potential long-run impact of stabilization policies and to the form and timing of the transition from controls to an uncontrolled economy.

There are two major factors which contribute to the likelihood of wage instability in the aftermath of a program of controls and which may be identified to be a direct result of the controls program itself. First, there inevitably exists a tendency during a stabilization program for labor and management to divert economic pressures for compensation increases into whatever avenues are the least tightly restricted by the stabilization program. Generally, the major avenues permitted for economic pressures have been increased fringe benefits, improved working conditions, and the increased provision of funds for such purposes as training or promotion. The uneven development of fringe benefits, conditions, and various other arrangements among employee units, firms, and industries during the course of a stabilization effort may result in a buildup of inflationary pressures whose magnitude becomes apparent upon the expiration of controls. This process can also operate to undermine a stabilization program within its lifetime, should the program be continued for a period of several years. Because programs of controls have generally been of limited duration in this country, the usual dynamics of this process are for wage stabilization policies to divert inflationary pressures from direct compensation into indirect forms, and for the stabilization program to expire at a time when the destabilizing influence of the improvements in indirect compensation upon labor costs are becoming apparent. The result has often been a sudden surge of increased labor costs.

Second, employees generally and labor unions in particular often view the termination of controls as a license to seek substantial wage adjustments, especially where the effect of the controls program was to deny to them wage increases which had been negotiated. This problem is particularly serious when collective bargaining agreements exist at the termination of a program which provide for substantially higher wage rates or benefit levels than permitted by the stabilization program, so that a result of the elimination of controls is to permit these agreements to go into effect.

These two factors that arise out of a stabilization effort and that generate the principal pressures for instability in the long run are generally amenable to minimization by stabilization authorities if certain policies are followed. For example, stabilization authorities need not simply ignore whatever changes unions and employers propose for noncompensation items such as working conditions, training funds, and the like, even though these items are not compensation, if that term is narrowly defined. These items almost always contribute to employer costs and often affect employee earnings and the position of various groups of workers vis-à-vis each other. Hence, it is sometimes appropriate to consider them as compensation. However, in order to apply restraint to such items, it would not be necessary for a stabilization program to develop detailed criteria for adjustments in the items. Rather, the application of general supervision over these items, in order to constrain adjustments which may have particularly unstabilizing consequences, would be adequate in most circumstances. Another example involves the problem of collective bargaining agreements which provide for nonapproved levels of compensation. These increases can be restrained in several ways. The stabilization board might persuade the parties to renegotiate collective bargaining agreements to conform to the approved level of compensation (or require renegotiation as a condition of the allowance of any wage increase). Alternatively, stabilization authorities might by regulation set the duration of approved wage adjustments to the datè of the expiration of an agreement, so the possibility that levels of compensation above those approved might go into effect by operation of a contract would be eliminated.

A major source of problems for stabilization policy in the long run is the tendency of government officials, stabilization authorities, and the public generally to view a program of controls exclusively as a device to restrain immediate or short-term increases in compensation. In consequence, rarely is any thought given to the implications of a program's policies for the future. Not only is this disregard of future consequences unfortunate in the later instability it invites, but it also represents a default of government leadership. For a stabilization program provides the opportunity for government to encourage the development of better compensation practices, improved means of dispute settlement, and generally improved industrial relations. Were stabilization authorities to seize these opportunities by emphasizing the longer-run implications of their policies, then the aftermath of a stabilization program need not be unstable by virtue of the previous controls.

Conclusions: The Limitations of Stabilization Policy

A thorough understanding of stabilization policy requires a recognition of the limitations of the policy as well as its other characteristics. There are numerous limitations of wage and price controls, many of which have been discussed in preceding chapters. Most important, it has been stressed above that the wage restraint aspect of stabilization policy cannot normally be pursued without regard to other national objectives. This is because a single-minded pursuit of the goal of limiting wage inflation is likely to be inconsistent with other social goals, including industrial peace, a reasonable distribution of income, the reduction of poverty, and productive efficiency. The potential incompatibility of various public goals is a very important matter and severely constrains the operation of a stabilization program. However, the interrelationships of various national objectives with a stabilization program have been discussed at length above and therefore need not be repeated here. Rather, we shall now explore two other aspects of stabilization policy which limit its usefulness, and we shall draw certain conclusions from the discussion.

1. *Stabilization policy is a complex group of interrelated elements which,*

if it is to be successful, must be adapted to a particular economic, political, and industrial relations environment. A stabilization program appropriate to one environment may be quite inappropriate to another. In addition, once a program is in operation it is likely that environmental circumstances will change, requiring alterations in the program. In consequence, wage controls are not a standard form of public policy which can be switched on and off as desired by the government or the public. The necessity of adapting a program to its environment is sometimes believed to be no more than the necessity to make adjustments in the criteria or standards of the program, that is, in the "tightness" or "looseness" of wage restraint. However, this is not the case. Rather, in order to maintain whatever degree of wage restraint is desired, it is likely that changing environmental factors will require substantial adjustment in the elements of the program itself, involving, for example, increased (or reduced) reliance on dispute-settlement machinery, and altered administrative arrangements. The adjustment of the elements of a program requires considerable expertise in stabilization matters and is a far more difficult task than decisions with respect to the tightening or loosening of wage standards.

The major implications of the relationship of a stabilization effort and its environment is that the operation of a stabilization policy is made thereby a very hazardous undertaking for the government. This is because, if a program is not appropriate to its environment, a number of unfortunate results are likely. First, the stabilization program may simply fail in its effort to restrain wage increases. Second, an inappropriate stabilization effort may actually work perversely in the economy to accelerate wage inflation. This effect is particularly likely to be apparent in the long run, that is, in the later years or the aftermath of a period of controls. Third, an inappropriate stabilization effort may have unfortunate consequences for industrial peace or for political stability, in either the short or the long run, or both. For instance, it has not been an unfamiliar experience in this country for a stabilization program to be swept away in a wave of strikes or to contribute to a change of political atmosphere.

Since a stabilization program may encounter difficulties in certain circumstances, it is useful to try to identify circumstances favorable to a program. Generally, of course, a stabilization effort is most likely to be successful when its structure and its policies are appropriate to its environment. Because so many unique types of environments are possible, it is difficult to refine this statement without undue specificity. In earlier chapters various economic, industrial relations, and political circumstances have been examined with regard to their implications for the type of stabilization policy appropriate. Here, at the risk of some oversimplification, we may summarize the circumstances generally most favorable to a successful stabilization effort. First, an expanding economy is helpful because it provides the possibility of increased earnings for workers through increased work opportunities and so assists in relieving pressure for wage increases. Second, a general perception of a national emergency which suggests a need for stabilization policy will normally facilitate agreement among management, labor, and government as to the content of a stabilization program and will assist in generating public acceptance of the program. Third, the possibility of a firmer degree of wage restraint is enhanced by an orderly wage structure rather than one which includes substantial relative wage distortions. This is because an orderly wage structure lessens the need for large increases to restore appropriate differentials in some instances and reduces the necessity for allowing different rates of increase among employee units (an always potentially difficult policy). Fourth, a fairly even distribution of economic activity throughout sectors of the economy is important because it makes more likely the avoidance of labor shortages in particular industries and areas, with consequent upward pressures on certain wage rates. Fifth, the potential value of a stabilization effort is enhanced by political stability and by a relatively bipartisan economic policy. A highly partisan political atmosphere, such as often accompanies approaching congressional or presidential elections, is disruptive of a stabilization effort. Sixth, a stabilization policy is facilitated by a stable industrial relations climate generally. Periods in which industrial conflict between management and labor is intense, or in which especially emotional noneconomic issues are in dispute, are greatly hazardous to a stabilization effort. In summary, these six characteristics of the environment are uniformly advantageous to a successful stabilization effort. The absence of any or all these conditions not only makes more difficult the task of a stabilization program but may imperil its success.

2. *Stabilization policy is in many ways extraordinarily vulnerable to the opposition of elements of the labor or management communities.* The opponents of a stabilization effort have several methods of attempting to alter or eliminate aspects of a program which are undesirable to them. In the first instance, union defiance of a stabilization effort may take the form of a work stoppage, a weapon not ordinarily employed by management directly against wage controls (although work stoppages with certain aspects of a lockout have been used by certain companies to compel changes in the structure of wage-price policy taken as a whole). But work stoppages, while the most dramatic form of confrontation between private groups and the government over stabilization policy, are generally less effective and less often resorted to than the exercise of influence in the Congress, or of challenge in the courts. Congress has, historically, proven rather receptive to the complaints of labor and management regarding particular aspects of stabilization policy. In consequence, in each period of wage controls in the United States the enabling legislation has been repeatedly amended to

provide relief from aspects of controls for various industries or groups of employees. An ironic aspect of this process has been that Congress is often in the public position of demanding firmer controls while quietly weakening the program in its actions on legislation. From the point of view of stabilization authorities, congressional critics often seem adept at criticizing the failure of the stabilization program to restrain wages or prices while simultaneously weakening the tools provided for stabilization authorities to use. This process is exacerbated by the local and regional geographic orientation of the American Congress. Because of this orientation many local unions or corporations exercise considerably greater influence in Congress through a strategically placed representative or senator than do national unions or employer groups, or the federal administration itself. Thus, even though national union and management leadership may cooperate with the government by not challenging a program, dissatisfied individual companies or local unions are sometimes able to obtain legislatively mandated changes in the stabilization program for their own benefit.

Stabilization policies may also be challenged in the courts, often successfully. In some instances a successful challenge may be the result of procedures or decisions of a board which are indeed inappropriate under the regulations or policies of the program. In other instances, however, successful challenges may result from the imperfect understanding which federal judges and the Justice Department (which must represent the stabilization program in court) possess of the economic and industrial relations factors which affect a stabilization program. Generally, labor and management have access to a greater fund of knowledge and experience respecting economic and industrial relations matters than the government, so that a contest in court is often extremely hazardous for stabilization authorities. Furthermore, the most significantly disadvantageous aspects of a legal challenge to an action of a stabilization board may not be the danger of an unfavorable decision but the delays involved in litigation. Pending cases which challenge major policies or decisions of a board may as effectively limit its activities as an unfavorable decision by causing other elements of management and labor not party to the suit to arrange their own behavior to be consistent with the possibility of the government's loss in the decision of the court. In summary, these three methods of response by private parties to a stabilization program (the work stoppage, congressional lobbying, and legal challenges) are in many instances of such importance and so often successful, wholly or partially, that stabilization policy must be judged to be extremely vulnerable to these parties and, thus, severely limited in its potential for success.

3. *Stabilization policy in any particular form erodes rapidly and must be adjusted substantially over relatively brief spans of time if it is to have any continuing effectiveness.* The "erosion" of stabilization policy occurs for many reasons, several of which have already been mentioned. Among these

factors are successful challenges to aspects of stabilization policy by management and labor through Congress, the courts, or by use of a work stoppage, as described above. Other factors are also significant, however. For example, a stabilization program necessarily imposes costs and frustrations upon local parties through the paperwork and consequent delays inherent in a program of controls. It is characteristic of a period of stabilization that the initial tolerance of delay which greets the outset of a program is rapidly dissipated and is replaced by an impatience to be rid of the program. Also, private organizations are exceedingly imaginative in developing methods of achieving their objectives within the letter, though not the spirit, of the formal policies and regulations of a stabilization program. In consequence, the longer a set of policies and regulations is in effect, the more likely will be the development of methods of avoiding the implications of the policies. Finally, a stabilization board inevitably creates opposition to itself through case decisions which are unfavorable to particular groups. Over a period of two or three years this opposition can become of such magnitude as to endanger aspects of the program or the program itself. Unfortunately, this process, which is ultimately inevitable, can also be made to be quite rapid, if stabilization officials conduct the program in a manner which suggests that it is arbitrary or capricious or unreasonably indecisive. Because of these many factors which contribute to the erosion of a program, through lessened public tolerance of its activities and through increasing overt opposition of disgruntled groups, the life expectancy of a particular type of stabilization arrangement can be expected to be brief. In addition, government officials wishing to maintain a general form of stabilization policy must be advised to alter its specific form and content frequently.

A Glance Into the Future

In the course of these pages it is likely that a number of questions have occurred to the reader regarding the future course of wage stabilization policy in the United States. It would be interesting to list and explore at length the many questions about the future which can be imagined, including those about the course of the immediate future. However, whatever predictions of immediate events that might be made would surely be rendered uninteresting by the passage of time even before this volume could be published. In consequence, it is preferable to look only at broad directions and substantial periods of time and to do so briefly because of limitations of space.

Probably the first inquiry which requires a response is whether controls can be expected to become a permanent feature of the American economy. The question has two aspects. First, is there likely to be a continuing need, or perception of a need, for a stabilization policy; and, second, are continuing controls a likely response? The first question is the more easily answered. Persistent inflationary tendencies in wage levels and prices may be expected to accompany the growth and evolution of the American economy and its institutions. But it is less certain that controls will be a continuing feature of the government's response. This is not to deny that many government officials and private citizens do now, and in the future will continue to, advocate controls as a response to inflationary pressures. There is an enticing simplicity to the argument that fiscal and monetary policy should be used to stimulate the economy and should be supplemented by controls to restrain inflation. This argument will always have its adherents, and in consequence it is likely that there will be experiments with direct controls. Yet experience with periods of controls will inevitably reveal the difficulties and limitations of stabilization policy, resulting in periodic abandonment of controls. What is likely to be different about the future use of controls will be a greater frequency of use than in the past, since national emergencies will be less likely to be only the occasion for their employment. Instead the government may be expected to initiate and abandon controls in an unpredictable rhythm dictated by changing political and economic circumstances.

Controls will not be permanent, but what can be expected to be a continuing characteristic of the future is a greater degree of government intervention in wage and price determination in American industry than previously. Since 1971, it is clear that the degree and pattern of peacetime intervention by the government in the economy has changed. Fiscal and monetary policy alone will probably only rarely be the sole tools of government economic policymakers in the future. Rather, direct interventions in the operation of the economy, often of a brief and experimental nature, may be expected. In large part this pattern of government intervention may be anticipated because the inflationary pressures inherent in a large, interdependent international economic system will reemerge periodically, although with differing degrees of severity. In recent years the public in the United States appears increasingly unwilling to tolerate the shifting fortunes of the economy without overt government intervention. But government intervention will be limited. We may expect in this country a halfway house between the centralized planning of the socialist states and the largely unfettered economy of our own past. A centrally planned economy is unlikely in the United States both because of the inefficiencies it would entail and for political reasons. However, a return to the substantially unregulated economy is equally unlikely in view of public concern over inflationary pressures.

The Most Probable Course of Stabilization Policy

The issue is, then, not whether there will be government efforts at wage and price stabilization but what forms these efforts will take. Enough has been said previously in this work to demonstrate that the range of options open to the government is very broad and that types of a stabilization effort which will be unique historically are by no means unlikely. Thus, let us phrase the question: what kinds of stabilization efforts can we expect in the future? In order to give an answer, however, we must make an important distinction between what public policy is likely to be in fact and what it should be. This distinction is necessary because public pressure for the government to respond to inflationary tendencies is likely to produce types of actions which have little or no merit as a response to economic problems. National administrations are, that is, likely to attempt to resolve political difficulties by ill-considered and perhaps economically damaging stabilization measures. Apparently the government in the United States, like those abroad, has discovered that the semblance of a stabilization program can be a useful political device in the short run, even though the program does not attempt to come to grips with actual economic problems. Furthermore, by issuing requests (which are likely to be unheeded) for management and labor to support such a semblance of a program, an administration might attempt to shift the blame for its instability to stem inflationary pressures to the private parties. For these reasons, the temptation for a government to establish a largely illusory program of controls is often irresistible. In consequence, stabilization policy in the future is as likely to be established in the image as in the reality. Careful students of economic policy must learn to recognize this distinction.

The problem of what type of stabilization programs may be created, as opposed to the types that are warranted, is also complicated by the variety of objectives to which stabilization may be directed. And, since it is not uncommon for a government to undertake stabilization policy for different reasons than those announced, or even in pursuit of a goal only tangentially related to economic stabilization, the circumstances which may lead to a program of controls are difficult to isolate and to predict. For example, a large stabilization program may be developed for any of the following reasons (which were explanations suggested for the establishment of the 1971–72 program) and others: to restrain pressures by labor costs or price levels; to restrain wages in order to allow expanded profits for investments in capital stock; to redistribute income from high to low wage earners; to redistribute income to the public sector (that is, to restrain growth of private consumption); to minimize industrial conflict by setting limits to disputes over wages; to provide reassurance to domestic and foreign observers that an expansionary fiscal and monetary policy will not result in unbridled inflation; to improve the structure of relative wages and compensation; or to demonstrate, for political purposes, the decisiveness of the administration. Each of these objectives may serve as the occasion for some sort of wage stabilization policy, yet each requires a different type of policy, cosmetic or more substantial. Since so many objectives may be addressed in some form by a stabilization effort, predictions of when and what form of policy may be established cannot be based on the expected occurrence of a certain set of particular circumstances in the economy.

Probably the most persistent characteristic of stabilization policy in the future will be the periodic announcement by the government of a norm, or target, rate of increase for compensation within some specified period (that is, a type of guidepost such as a single percentage figure or a simple arithmetic formula). The pressures for such a policy appear too widespread for the government to ignore, whether or not a more complete stabilization effort is conducted. Perhaps it is somewhat surprising that a guidepost policy is so much sought after, since, as we have seen above, it is quite unlikely to be successful in restraining wage increases. However, there are several reasons for the popularity of a guidepost type of policy. Government economic officers and economists and businessmen in the private sector often desire a wage guideline to be used for planning purposes directed at related economic factors (expected price increases, consumption levels, and so on). Nor do the unions particularly resist a guidepost, for it permits union leaders in economically favorable circumstances to gain political advantage with their constituents for breaching the guideposts. In fact, both management and labor may, in many instances, prefer to negotiate in the context of guideposts in order to be relieved of the difficult responsibilities of adjusting compensation changes to economic conditions. Arguments about whether to exceed a single government guidepost are often a much simpler task for management and labor representatives than is problem-solving in the context of collective bargaining. Finally, both the press and political and economic personalities generally can be expected to continue to demand in the future, as in the past, that the government comment on the so-called responsibility of particular wage settlements—a demand that will propel the government toward a guidepost policy. In consequence of these several factors, it is likely that our society will rarely be without some form of government norm for wage increases in the future, except, perhaps, when a more comprehensive stabilization program may make a single norm inappropriate.

If we are to have the persistence of some type of guidepost approach, what can be done to maximize its usefulness to the stabilization of the economy? There are, of course, many different ways in which to formulate and conduct a guidepost-type policy. Probably the least effective method would be that utilized in the mid-1960s, that is, the formulation of the guideposts by the government alone, without the involvement or cooperation of management and labor, and the administration of the policy by government officials without any expertise in the operations of the labor markets. The result, an uncritical application of the guidepost percentage to all situations without regard to economic and institutional factors, was damaging to both economic stability and industrial relations. But a guideposts-type policy can be made less damaging and more likely to be constructive in restraining inflationary pressures. For example, the government might announce a target rate of increase for average hourly earnings and unit labor costs and convene meetings with labor and management representatives, both generally and for major sectors separately, to discuss the application of the policy to their individual situations. A target rate of increase for average hourly earnings is not, of course, identical to a wage norm or standard, since numerous other factors than wage increases affect changes in average hourly earnings and unit labor costs. But concentration of public policy on average hourly earnings and unit labor costs would have two major advantages. First, average earnings and unit labor costs are in important respects more significant economic variables than wage levels, for they more directly affect price levels through consumer purchasing power and production costs, respectively. Therefore, they are more appropriately the concern of economic policymakers than are rates of compensation per se. Second, concern for restraint of the rate of increase in earnings and in unit labor costs is consistent with different rates of increase in individual wage settlements and thereby may assist in keeping the government from being called upon to intervene in every situation in which an employee unit receives more than some single guidepost increase. As we have seen in chapter 5 above, stability in the average rate of increase is not inconsistent with different rates of increase in individual situations (reflecting different economic circumstances) and should be encouraged by public policy.

Suggestions for Stabilization Policy in the Future

Having reviewed the likely future course of stabilization policy and having offered some suggestions to improve a guidepost-type policy, we may now offer several suggestions as to the most appropriate form of stabilization efforts. These suggestions fall into two general areas: the use of other types of public policy than direct controls or guideposts for stabilization purposes, and types of direct stabilization policies. Most of the discussion below will relate to the second area. The topics to be reviewed in the second area range from ad hoc interventions in particular situations to the use of comprehensive controls. This discussion is based largely upon the conclusions about stabilization policy generally which have been set forth earlier in this chapter. But those conclusions are not repeated here.

Other Types of Public Policy Than Controls. The United States, like other nations, attempts to pursue simultaneously several different, and sometimes conflicting, economic and social objectives. To achieve the desired mix of objectives at any given time, the government possesses five general sets of policy tools: monetary policy, fiscal policy, measures to increase product supplies, measures to increase industrial peace and productivity, and direct wage and price controls.[3] Each of these types of public policy may be employed for stabilization purposes, and, as we have seen above, the direction of each type of policy at any given time constitutes an important aspect of the environment of direct controls, if direct controls are utilized. In fact, it has often been pointed out that direct controls cannot unconditionally serve as a substitute for fiscal and monetary restraint in order to achieve stabilized wage and price behavior.

But there has been too great a tendency to rely solely upon macroeconomic variables as a measure of inflationary pressures and for the government to respond primarily with macroeconomic policies. This emphasis is unfortunate, because to a much greater degree than is generally realized the sources of the problem of a moderate degree of inflation are found in particular sectors of the economy. Shortages and bottlenecks in particular industries and labor markets become translated into rising prices and wages with secondary effects on the general level of prices and wages. Problems of this nature can be resolved by aggregate or macropolicy measures only at considerable cost in increased unemployment, lessened total production, and less rapid economic growth. To avoid the costs associated with macropolicy, considerably greater attention should be devoted in the United States to longer-run policies for generating balanced economic growth—balanced among sectors of the economy and over time. The failure of government to pursue policies on a sector-by-sector basis is often responsible for price-wage surges which distort the economy and contribute to periodic inflationary spirals. An appropriate concern for government economic policy in the future should be the mobilizing of public and private resources to deal with problems of imbalance of supply and particular sectors. The more common practice of concentrating public attention primarily on price and wage increases (not economic imbalances) is often futile, for it substitutes concern for symptoms of economic difficulties for attempts to treat those difficulties themselves.

The need for the management of demand and supply in particular sectors arises from the most fundamental characteristics of the wage-price process. If the government wishes to restrain wages and prices, it must provide some alternative means of allocation of materials, products, and labor among competing users. To fail to provide alternative means of allocation invites shortages, inefficiencies, and black markets. On the other hand, if the government wishes to preserve the allocation of materials, products, and labor by market mechanisms, it must accept the price and wage consequences. If we may phrase the basic public objective as greater price and wage stability at minimum cost to economic efficiency, then there are alternative methods of pursuing this objective. Either the government may control prices and wages directly and perform such allocation functions as required by the economic environment and the degree of price and wage restraint desired; or it might attempt to influence the supply and allocation of materials, products, and prices and thereby influence price and wage behavior. There has been far too little experimentation in the United States with this latter course of action. If successful in certain sectors, government action to increase supply or assist in allocation among users could lessen the need for an overt stabilization policy or facilitate the administration of direct controls. Unfortunately, the success of such policies requires a detailed knowledge of particular aspects of the economy and a degree of cooperation with private parties which is difficult for the government to develop. Happily, however, there has been an increasing consciousness of the importance of direct product and labor market policy by the government in recent years. For example, the development of input-output analysis for the American economy is only now becoming adequately advanced to permit identification of sectors with particularly significant potential price and wage problems. Input-output analysis also provides a tool which may be used to suggest patterns of response to emerging imbalance of demand and capacity in particular sectors.

Furthermore, there is increasing attention devoted to what have been termed active manpower or employment policies whose purpose is to provide a labor force adequate to the needs of an expanding economy. But considerably greater attention is required to be devoted to the skilled trades than has been the practice in recent years, since shortages in skilled trades are especially likely to result in inflationary wage increases. Numerous methods of response to labor shortages in skilled occupations are possible, depending upon economic and institutional factors. For example, encouragement of a measured pace of expansion in particular sectors might assist in the balancing of manpower demand and availability. Alternatively, increased training programs might be useful in some instances. Finally, in some circumstances it might prove useful to seek the redesign of jobs and compensation schemes in order to make better use of especially skilled manpower.

Regrettably, the current character of government efforts in the area of skilled manpower is largely hortatory and is completely inadequate to respond to expected problems. In general, the government should conduct far more experimentation with the adjustment of demand and supply of manpower, productive capacity, and materials in particular sectors than has occurred in the past. Such an emphasis would be more valuable in the long run to the country than repeated experiments with various types of programs of wage and price controls. Unfortunately, what sectors require particular attention and through what methods of public policy cannot be set forth here but must be the subject of other studies.

Restraining Wages Through Ad Hoc Interventions in Particular Wage Situations. National administrations in the United States have increasingly become involved in specific wage decisions in the private sector. This tendency may be expected to increase in the future. Two factors are primarily responsible. First, the attention of the government is often drawn, in various ways, to wage decisions which threaten to be destabilizing in their influence on prices and on other wage rates. Second, in many instances government is drawn into situations where the primary problem is not of wage-price stability but the danger of a major work stoppage. It is not uncommon, of course, for the two problems to be joined in a single situation. Government involvement in such circumstances is likely to occur regardless of explicit legislative authority for government intervention. Since most situations which threaten wage instability or work stoppages occur in sectors of American industry organized by unions, this area of public intervention involves the issue of the coordination of collective bargaining and national economic policy.

Ad hoc intervention by the government in wage decisions may assume many forms, including mediation, persuasion, and threats of legal or economic action against either or both sides in the dispute. Whatever the form taken, however, there are certain basic limitations of the ad hoc approach which constrain its usefulness. First, the government faces a much greater difficulty in obtaining accurate information regarding issues in disputes and the secondary consequences of particular wage adjustments than is generally appreciated. The government tends in many instances to get information late, in a form which is often only partially accurate, and often only at great cost and effort. Because of difficulties in obtaining information, the government often acts in a hasty, ill-designed manner which too often has consequences in direct oppostion to those intended. A fundamental prerequisite of improved intervention by the government in wage decisions is more accurate and extensive information about the economy. Second, ad hoc interventions have required the development of a method and procedure for government involvement de novo in each circumstance. For example, in each situation there must be a decision as to what level of government is to intervene, by what device, and after consultation with what other agencies of government or private groups. The necessity to make these decisions often generates a paralysis of government action. Some experimentation in the future with standard procedures for intervention would, therefore, be useful. Third, ad hoc intervention requires great judgment from public officials about the substance of particular wage decisions and their likely impact on other situations. Informed judgment regarding the economy and collective bargaining is unfortunately very rare in government. Fourth, the legal basis of ad hoc interventions is often at issue, so that a determined corporation or union may find it relatively easy to successfully challenge the government in court. The sources of the legal uncertainty of the government's position in ad hoc interventions are two. On the one hand, specific regulations about wages and prices are usually not existent when a policy of ad hoc intervention is pursued. In consequence, there is a question of the legal basis for any restraint applied to private parties by the government. Also, the government can be challenged to justify its choice of particular situations in which to intervene. In the absence of a general program of controls, defense of intervention in one situation and not in another may be difficult. These two factors complicate a policy of ad hoc intervention seriously. (Incidentally, offensive legal action by the government to enforce a stabilization program is never easy, even when formal controls exist. For example, from March 1971 to February 1973, the Justice Department initiated only nine cases involving pay standards and twenty involving price standards under Phase I and Phase II regulations. The Justice Department refused the requests by stabilization authorities to pursue many other cases, arguing, in part, that the price and wage standards of 1971–72 were not specific enough to sustain suits.)

What, then, can the government do short of a comprehensive program of controls in pursuit of stabilization objectives? A procedure which we have argued is likely to become common would involve the enunciation of a guidepost for wage increases and an attempt at enforcement through ad hoc intervention in specific situations. Yet, we have seen that a guidepost is not a particularly useful policy device and that ad hoc enforcement is subject to severe limitations. Do other alternatives exist? Possibly they do. The government might, for example, approach situations involving stabilization issues on other bases than stabilization alone. As we have emphasized before, most situations which are threatening to wage-price stability arise out of underlying factors. The government might be able, in important instances, to pursue stabilization objectives indirectly through attention to other aspects of a situation. What other aspects of a wage decision might be amenable to government intervention? We may list several. For example, many potentially destabilizing wage adjustments arise out of problems in the structure of collective bargaining in certain industries. Particularly significant in this regard are structural problems in the construction, retail food, maritime, and printing industries, and in the state and local government and health-services sectors of our economy.[4] In these and other parts of the economy, problems of industrial disputes are closely related to wage-price behavior. Government initiatives to encourage new methods of dispute settlement, better administration of fringe benefits, and other advances in industrial relations would serve not only the direct purpose of industrial peace but would help achieve wage-price stability also. In consequence, government initiatives directed at the reform of collective bargaining structure in certain industries and sectors or at encouraging improved methods of dispute settlement may have important secondary effects on economic stability. Alternatively, antitrust policies might in some instances serve to promote wage-price stability by challenging positions of unusual economic power. Perhaps what is most needed is some agency of government concerned with the impact of a broad range of private and public policies on economic stability and authorized to mobilize various aspects of government and private action to pursue stabilization objectives through other methods than a program of direct controls.

The Use of Comprehensive Controls. At last we turn to the question of how comprehensive controls should be used in the future. We have stressed above that formal wage-price controls erode rapidly and can be successfully applied only temporarily. Two implications might be drawn from this judgment. On the one hand, it might be urged that comprehensive controls be reserved for periods of national emergency, in order that their effectiveness not be dissipated in less important circumstances. Or, it might be argued that controls should be used to assist in the management of the economy, but sparingly. There are, after all, numerous forms of direct controls, so that careful adjustment of a stabilization program to the needs of the time need not preclude the usefulness of another form of program in another situation. In the aftermath of the Korean program, Arthur Ross argued for such a policy. "What is needed," he wrote, "is a law, enacted to run for a considerable number of years, empowering the President to reimpose direct controls without awaiting further [congressional] authorization.... We need to learn ... to use the right instrument at the right time. That is one of the lessons of the Korean experience."[5] There is little doubt that Professor Ross was correct in his prescription. But the twenty years which have passed since he made his suggestion have done little to inspire confidence in the capacity of Congress or the executive branch to adjust policies to economic circumstances or to resist the shifting of political forces which support or oppose stabilization efforts.

In the end, the safest course for the country is probably to experiment with limited stabilization efforts and also with indirect means of pursuing stabilization objectives. Formal and comprehensive programs of controls should be reserved for emergency situations which, one may hope, will not arise.

Notes

Chapter 1

1. John R. Hicks, *The Theory of Wages* (London: Macmillan, 1932), p. vi.

2. For the monetarists see, for example, Milton Friedman, "The Role of Monetary Policy," *American Economic Review*, 58, 1 (March 1968), pp. 1–17; and for a simple but clear statement, "Inflation and Wages," *Newsweek*, September 28, 1970, p. 77. For the other group see John M. Keynes, *The General Theory of Employment, Interest, and Money* (New York: Harcourt Brace, 1936); and, for a more simple exposition, Paul A. Samuelson, *Principles of Economics*, 7th ed. (New York: McGraw-Hill, 1967), pt. 2.

3. See Herbert Stein, *The Fiscal Revolution in America* (Chicago: University of Chicago Press, 1969), especially p. 382.

4. Charles L. Schultze, testimony before the Senate Antitrust and Monopoly Subcommittee, January 19, 1972 (mimeo).

5. See, for example, George L. Perry, *Unemployment, Money Wage Rates and Inflation* (Cambridge, Mass.: M.I.T. Press, 1966); also Perry, "Inflation vs. Unemployment: The Worsening Trade-Off," *Monthly Labor Review*, 94, 2 (February 1971), pp. 68–71; and Bent Hansen, "Excess Demand, Unemployment, Variance and Wages," *Quarterly Journal of Economics*, 84, 1 (February 1970).

6. A. W. Phillips, "The Relations Between Unemployment and the Rate of Change of Money Wage Rates in the United Kingdom, 1861–1957," *Economica*, 25 (November 1958), pp. 283–99.

7. For a rigorous theoretical critique of those theories of inflation which attribute much causal significance to the aggregate rate of unemployment see William Bowen, *The Wage Price Issue* (Princeton, New Jersey: Princeton University Press, 1960), and Edwin Kuh, "A Productivity Theory of Wage Levels: An Alternative to the Phillips Curve," *Review of Economic Studies*, 34 (October 1967), pp. 333–60. See also Daniel S. Hammersmesh, "Wage Bargains, Threshold Effects, and the Phillips Curve," *Quarterly Journal of Economics*, 84 (1970), pp. 501–17, who found that the rate of unemployment was an insignificant factor in determining the rate of negotiated wage increase in several large firms.

8. Albert Rees and Mary T. Hamilton concluded that there were so many relationships among changing unemployment rates and rates of inflation that each should be labeled, "Unstable! Apply with extreme care." (Rees and Hamilton, "The Wage-Price-Productivity Perplex," *Journal of Political Economy*, 75 [February 1967], p. 70).

9. See James Tobin, "Raising the Incomes of the Poor," in Kermit Gordon, ed., *Agenda for the Nation* (Washington, D.C.: The Brookings Institution, 1968). Some recent studies suggest not stability in the size of aggregate shares but a slowly rising share for labor as a whole. See, for example, Irving B. Kravis, "Income Distribution: Functional Share," *Encyclopedia of the Social Sciences* (New York: Macmillan, 1968), vol. 7, pp. 132–43.

10. E. Robert Livernash, "Wages and Benefits," in *A Review of Industrial Relations Research* (Madison, Wisconsin: The Industrial Relations Research Association, 1970), vol. 1, p. 86.

11. Ibid.

12. See, for example, James W. Kuhn, "The Riddle of Inflation," *The Public Interest*, 27 (Spring 1972), pp. 63–77.

13. See John T. Dunlop, *Wage Determination Under Trade Unions* (New York: Macmillan, 1944).

14. See, for example, the Carnegie Commission on Higher Education, *Institutional Aid: Federal Support to Colleges and Universities, A Report and Recommendations* (New York: McGraw-Hill, February 1972). Federal support for higher education was $3.5 billion in 1968, when the Carnegie Commission recommended that the support level should be raised to $13 billion in 1976–77, a recommendation reaffirmed in the 1972 report (p. 1).

15. For a description of federal housing programs and federal budget outlays for housing see "Federal Housing Programs" (Special Analysis M) in *Special Analyses of the United States Budget, Fiscal Year 1973,* (Washington, D.C.: Government Printing Office, 1972), pp. 202–8.

16. See "Federal Outlays Inflation Factor," *New York Times,* May 8, 1972, p. 55, in which Michael E. Levy offers a judgment that "The process of increasing the transfer of resources from the productive to the non-productive economy at such a rapid rate . . . has led both business and labor to intensify their efforts to maintain or improve their relative economic positions through higher wages and higher prices."

17. See *Statistical Abstract of the United States,* 1972, p. xvii. Also see Sar A. Levitan and Robert Taggart, III, "Has the Blue-Collar Workers' Position Worsened?" *Monthly Labor Review,* 94, 9 (September 1971), pp. 23–29; and R. J. Lampman, *Monthly Labor Review,* 60, 2 (May 1970), pp. 270–79. For a review of the competition between welfare payments and earned incomes in Massachusetts see Michael J. Piore, "Jobs and Training," in Samuel Beer and R. Barringer, eds., *The State and the Poor,* (Cambridge, Mass.: Winthrop, 1970), pp. 66–69.

18. Not all groups were successful in protecting their interests, of course. Particularly in import-sensitive industries, wages often fell behind. Other groups were successful in improving their position substantially, including, for example, public employees and construction workers.

19. See Roy Harrod's testimony before the Banking and Currency Committee, United States House of Representatives, cited in Bureau of National Affairs, *Daily Labor Report,* no. 39 (February 26, 1971), pp. A8–A10.

20. Economic groups, rather than being well-defined and separable, often overlap in membership, creating a crazy-quilt pattern of interrelationships and creating for the economic system (and its analysts and expositors) a situation of the utmost complexity and one in which generalizations as to the general (or net) behavior of the system in a changing environment are especially hazardous.

21. J. K. Galbraith, *The New Industrial State* (Boston: Houghton Mifflin, 1967), pp. 397, 268, and 260 respectively. So firmly did Galbraith come to accept the need for controls that he hailed their imposition in 1971 by the Nixon administration and several months later continued to defend the Pay Board and Price Commission against criticism as to the substance of their policies (see, for example, Robert D. Hershey, "Economic Shift in U.S. Perceived by Galbraith," *New York Times,* December 16, 1971, p. 93).

22. Robert Lekachman, testimony to House Banking and Currency Committee, quoted in Bureau of National Affairs, *Daily Labor Report,* no. 39 (February 26, 1971), p. A10.

23. See, for example, Hobart Rowan, "'Believer' Who Talks Tough Makes Price Board Work," *Boston Globe,* June 4, 1972, p. 64.

24. "Controls cannot deal with the causes of inflation . . . they may mask the inflation temporarily but at the same time they create distortions in the market and the economy which are potentially damaging. The only real answer to inflation is a fundamental attack through combined recognition by all instruments of government . . . that fiscal and monetary restraint is vital" (editorial, *Wall Street Journal,* June 23, 1972, p. 8).

25. This view was strongly held by a substantial group within the Nixon administration in 1971, with consequent internal objection to initiating a controls program. See, for example, Hendrik S. Houthakker (until mid-1971 a member of Mr. Nixon's Council of Economic Advisors), "Competition versus Controls," Statement to the Subcommittee on Antitrust and Monopoly, Antitrust Committee, U.S. Senate, January 21, 1972 (mimeo).

26. M. Friedman, letter to the editor, *New York Times*, November 24, 1971, p. 34.

27. Edwin G. Dolan, "Squeezing the Inflation Balloon," letter to the editor, *New York Times*, April 3, 1972, p. 50. See also R. G. Lipsey and J. M. Parkin, "Incomes Policy: A Reappraisal," *Economica*, 37, 146 (May 1970), pp. 115–38.

28. Griffith Johnson noticed in 1952 that "there is a widespread view that we could stop all this· inflation . . . if the government would just freeze all prices and wages and then keep them frozen . . . the same naïveté which leads to superficial conclusions of this sort would make it difficult . . . to obtain any broad understanding of a more limited role for direct controls in the total stabilization program" (G. G. Johnson, "Reflections on a Year of Price Controls," *American Economic Review*, 42, 2 [May 1952], p. 298). The same widespread view, fostered by those seeking, or seeking to retain, political office continues to create misunderstandings in the 1970s.

29. The likelihood of failure of a stabilization program is too often overlooked by its pro- ponents. For example, Michael V. diSalle commented in 1971, "If you have a price and wage pro- gram that is functioning you can pour some money into the economy and still keep inflationary pressures under check" ("Full Scale Wage-Price Controls?" *Nation's Business*, 59, 10 [October 1971], p. 34). Mr. diSalle might have added that whether or not inflationary pressures can be kept in check, and to what degree, depends on several things, including how much money is poured into the economy and in what sectors, the type of stabilization program and how artfully it is administered, and the acceptability of stabilization to various private interest groups.

30. Lester C. Thurow, "Economic Controls on the American Economy," testimony before the U.S. House of Representatives, Banking and Currency Committee, October 7, 1971, p. 1.

31. See, for example, Otto Eckstein and Roger Brinner, *The Inflation Process in the United States*, a study submitted to the Joint Economic Committee of Congress (Washington, D.C.: Government Printing Office, 1972).

32. James Duesenberry has said of incomes policy, "It's not an all-or-nothing proposition. . . . It is a matter of getting people to change their behavior by a modest amount, to change prices a little bit more slowly or a little bit less" (quoted in *On Incomes Policy*, Papers and Proceedings from a conference in honor of Erik Lundberg [Stockholm: Industrial Council of Social and Economic Studies, 1969], p. 114).

33. Clark Kerr, himself a prominent economist, has offered this judgment of the role of the economist as a policymaker in the area of wage restraints: "The economist *qua* economist is apt to care too much about the content of the [wage] settlement, although acceptability is, and by the nature of the situation must be, the ultimate reference. The general public should look to the public members [of a wage stabilization board] to mediate industrial peace and to the President and Congress . . . to stabilize the economy" (Kerr, "Governmental Wage Restraints; Their Limits and Uses in a Mobilized Economy," *American Economic Review*, 42, 2 [May 1952], p. 384).

Chapter 2

1. U.S. Bureau of Labor Statistics, *Monthly Labor Review*, 10, 6 (June 1920), p. 1385.

2. John A. Fitch, *The Causes of Industrial Unrest* (New York: Harper & Brothers, 1924), pp. 40 and 13. Incidentally, this record of wage and price changes was not due to any particular stabilization efforts in this period, as the reader will discover below.

3. The council was established in 1916 to centralize control over problems of production which developed because of the war. It consisted of the secretaries of six federal departments. Subordinate to the council was the Advisory Commission, composed of seven representatives of business, the professions, and organized labor (the labor representative was Samuel Gompers).

4. U.S. Bureau of Labor Statistics, *National War Labor Board*, bulletin no. 287 (Washington, D.C.: 1922), p. 9.

5. Ibid., p. 10.

6. Ibid., p. 35.

7. Ibid., pp. 24–25. Other dispute settlement agencies included the Shipbuilding Labor

Adjustment Board, the Emergency Construction Commission, the National Adjustment Commission for the Longshoremen, and the President's Mediation Commission.

8. Alexander M. Bing, *War-Time Strikes and Their Adjustment* (New York: E. P. Dutton, 1921), p. 159.

9. Ibid., p. 154.

10. U.S. Bureau of Labor Statistics, *National War Labor Board*, p. 24.

11. Ibid., p. 52.

12. Ibid.

13. Ibid., pp. 52–53.

14. Ibid., p. 65.

15. Ibid., p. 58.

16. Bing, *War-Time Strikes*, p. 161.

17. Abraham L. Gitlow, *Wage Determination under National Board*, (New York: Prentice-Hall, 1953), p. 101.

18. Bing, *War-Time Strikes*, pp. 195–203.

19. The minimum subsistence level was established at $1,500 a year for a family of five in December 1918. However, the board set minimum rates considerably lower than would have been necessary to earn $1,500.

20. Gitlow, *Wage Determination*, pp. 107–9.

21. George W. Taylor, *Government Regulation of Industrial Relations* (New York: Prentice-Hall, 1948), p. 97.

22. U.S. Bureau of Labor Statistics, *Report on the Work of the National Defense Mediation Board: March 19, 1941–January 12, 1942*, bulletin no. 714 (Washington, D.C.: Government Printing Office, 1942), pp. 39–40.

23. U.S. Bureau of Labor Statistics, *Problems and Policies of Dispute Settlement and Wage Stabilization During World War II*, bulletin 1009 (Washington, D.C.: Government Printing Office, 1950), p. 21 (pp. 1–25 are an introduction to a further group of articles in the volume).

24. Ibid., p. 21.

25. Howard S. Kaltenborn, *Governmental Regulation of Labor Disputes* (Chicago: Foundation Press, 1943), p. 93.

26. Kaltenborn, *Governmental Regulation*, pp. 99–102.

27. U.S. Department of Labor, *The Termination Report of the National War Labor Board*, vol. 2 (Washington, D.C.: Government Printing Office, 1947), pp. 1038–44 (hereafter cited as *Termination Report*).

28. Ibid., vol. 1, pp. 12–16. Industry geographic agencies included the New York Metropolitan Milk Distributors Commission, the West Coast Lumber Commission, the Automotive Section (under the Detroit Regional Board), the War Shipping Panel, and the National Air Frame Panel. The Wage Adjustment Board for the construction industry had been established previous to the NWLB by order of the secretary of labor following an agreement between government agencies and the building-trades unions.

29. William H. Davis, formerly chairman of the NDMB, served as chairman of the NWLB until March 8, 1945; George Taylor, vice chairman of the NWLB under Davis, served as chairman from March 9, 1945, until October 15, 1945; Lloyd K. Garrison was chairman from October 16, 1945, until December 13, 1945. Nathan Feinsinger served as chairman of the NWSB, the successor to the NWLB.

30. *Termination Report*, vol. 1, pp. 45–51.

31. Ibid., vol. 1, pp. 7–10.

32. Ibid., vol. 1, pp. 10–11.

33. This description was given by George Taylor, vice chairman of the NWLB, in an address to the National Industrial Conference Board, New York City, September 23, 1943. The text of the speech is reprinted in ibid., vol. 2, pp. 516–21.

34. See ibid., vol. 1, p. 88, for the precise wording.

35. Ibid., vol. 1, pp. 93-95, 101-2, 66-67.

36. U.S. Department of Labor, Division of Labor Standards, *The President's National Labor-Management Conference, November 5-30, 1945,* bulletin no. 77 (Washington, D.C.: Government Printing Office, 1946), pp. 38-39.

37. *Termination Report,* vol. 1, p. 466. The new National Wage Stabilization Board consisted of W. Willard Wirtz, chairman, and Sylvester Garrett, public members; Earl. N. Cannon and R. Randall Irwin, industry members; and Robert J. Watt, AFL, and Carl J. Shipley, CIO, labor members.

38. Ibid., vol. 1, pp. 464-65.

39. Morris A. Horowitz, "Wage Structure Changes During the Wage Stabilization Period," mimeo (1954), p. 4.

40. "Wage Policies of the WSB: A Symposium," *Industrial and Labor Relations Review,* 7, 2 (January 1954), p. 175 (editor's introduction).

41. Horowitz, "Wage Structure Changes," p. 6. Eighteen percent was only a partial mobilization. In World War II, the defense budget was 42 percent of national production (Arthur M. Ross, "The Lessons of Price and Wage Controls," Institute of Industrial Relations reprint no. 46 [Berkeley: University of California, 1953], reprinted from *The Commercial and Financial Chronicle* [January 1, 1953], p. 2).

42. See U.S. Wage Stabilization Board, *Wage Stabilization Program, 1950-1953,* mimeo (1953), pp. 7-23, for a discussion of the passage of the act and its provisions (cited hereafter as WSB).

43. U.S. House, Committee on Education and Labor, *Disputes Functions of Wage Stabilization Board,* Hearings on H. Res. 73, May 28-June 15, 1951, 82nd Congress, 1st session, pp. 73-74.

44. John T. Dunlop and Archibald Cox, "The Decision to Invoke Direct Controls," manuscript (1954), p. 12.

45. Bruno Stein, "Labor Participation in Stabilization Agencies: The Korean War Period as a Case Study" (Ph.D. thesis, New York University, 1959), pp. 42-45. Much of Stein's study of this period is based on Thomas Holland, "A Chapter on the Earlier History of the Wage Stabilization Board," Executive Office of the President, Office of Defense Mobilization, Washington, D.C., mimeo (1953).

46. General Wage Regulation 1, issued by the Economic Stabilization Agency.

47. WSB, *Wage Stabilization Program,* p. 70.

48. See Stein, "Labor Participation," pp. 82-88, for a discussion of the issues leading to the labor walkout.

49. See WSB, vol. 2, pp. 27-34, for a discussion of the passage of the amendment and its provisions.

50. John T. Dunlop and Archibald Cox, "Strikes Against Wage Stabilization: The Bituminous Coal Case," mimeo (1954), pp. 42-44.

51. Morris A. Horowitz, "Administrative Problems of the Wage Stabilization Board," *Industrial and Labor Relations Review,* 7, 3 (April 1954), pp. 396-99.

52. Bruno Stein, "Wage Stabilization in the Korean War Period: The Role of the Subsidiary Wage Boards," *Labor History,* 4 (Spring 1963), p. 163.

53. Horowitz, "Administrative Problems," pp. 394-97.

54. Stein, "Wage Stabilization," p. 174.

55. WSB Resolution 64, January 24, 1952.

56. Gitlow, *Wage Determination,* pp. 198-200.

57. See the arguments of the board's official historians and their statistical evidence in WSB, vol. 2, pp. 443-44, and vol. 3, pp. 423-26.

58. It was necessary for public members of the WSB to reply carefully to the facile criticism that the board was not a wage stabilization board at all but a "wage *stimulation* board." This

allegation was in part the impetus to Clark Kerr's article, "Governmental Wage Restraints."

59. Arthur M. Ross, "Productivity and Wage Control," *Industrial and Labor Relations Review*, 7, 21 (January 1954), p. 189.

60. Hugh Clegg, a member of the British National Board for Prices and Incomes in 1966-67, has summed up the experience of the British incomes policies in the 1960s as "a colossal failure." Clegg has written a very interesting review of British experience entitled *How to Run An Incomes Policy—And Why We Made Such a Mess of the Last One* (London: Heinemann, 1971).

61. See Daniel J. B. Mitchell, "Incomes Policy and the Labor Market in France," *Industrial and Labor Relations Review*, 25, 3 (April 1972), pp. 315-35.

62. Bernard D. Nossiter, "Discontent in Western Europe," *Boston Globe*, July 16, 1972, editorial page.

63. See Murray Edelman and R. W. Fleming, *The Politics of Wage-Price Decisions: A Four-Country Analysis* (Urbana: University of Illinois Press, 1965), pp. 308-9.

64. H. A. Turner, "Collective Bargaining and the Eclipse of Incomes Policy: Retrospect, Prospect and Possibilities," *British Journal of Industrial Relations*, 8, 2 (July 1970), pp. 197-212.

65. Ibid., p. 202.

66. Lloyd Ulman and Robert V. Flanagan, *Wage Restraint: A Study of Incomes Policies in Western Europe* (Berkeley: University of California Press, 1971), p. 230.

67. Derek Bok and John T. Dunlop, *Labor and the American Community* (New York: Simon and Schuster, 1970), pp. 304-5.

68. According to Turner, "incomes policy has certainly done something; but there is uncertainty as to exactly what that is" ("Collective Bargaining," pp. 199-200). See also Walter Galenson, ed., *Incomes Policy: What Can We Learn From Europe?* (Ithaca: New York State School of Industrial and Labor Relations, Cornell University, 1973).

69. There is, however, considerable differentiation of union organization and behavior and of collective bargaining procedures and structure among European nations. See, for example, Walter Galenson, ed., *Comparative Labor Movements* (New York: Prentice-Hall, 1952); Everett M. Kassalow, *Trade Unions and Industrial Relations: An International Comparison* (New York: Random House, 1969); Bruno Stein, "Incomes Policies in Western Europe: A Summary," *Labor Law Journal*, 16, 11, (November 1966), pp. 717-24.

70. Albert Rees, "Wage-Price Policy" (New York: General Learning Press, 1971), p. 9.

71. J. Pen, "The Strange Adventures of Dutch Wage Policy," *British Journal of Industrial Relations*, 1, 3 (October 1963), pp. 318-30.

72. See *On Incomes Policy*, pp. 95-110.

73. In World War II, for example, British wage stabilization policy was entirely based on extragovernmental, voluntary action of unions and employers. See John T. Dunlop, "An Appraisal of Wage Stabilization Policies," in Bureau of Labor Statistics, *Problems and Policies*.

74. Joseph J. Walka, "Wage and Price Policies in War and Peace," (Ph.D. thesis, Harvard University, 1969), p. 93. Mr. Walka served with the Council of Economic Advisers during much of the guidelines period.

75. Ibid., p. 196.

76. Albert Rees has referred to this dispute as "a dramatic instance of government helping to breach its own wage policy," "Wage-Price Policy," p. 9. See also John Sheahan, *The Wage Price Guideposts* (Washington, D.C.: The Brookings Institution, 1967), pp. 57-60.

77. C. L. Schultze, testimony, U.S. Congress, House of Representatives, Committee on the Post Office and Civil Service, Federal Salaries and Fringe Benefits, Hearings, 89th Congress, 2d sess., 1966, p. 4.

78. Joseph J. Walka, "The Origins of the Wage-Price Guideposts: An Exercise in Presidential Staff Initiative," *Public Policy*, 16 (1967), pp. 293-315.

79. Walter W. Heller, *New Dimensions in Political Economy* (Cambridge: Harvard University Press, 1966), pp. 21-26, 42-47.

80. Walka, "Wage and Price Policies," p. 189.

81. Gardner Ackley (then chairman of the Council of Economic Advisers), "The Contribution of Guidelines," in George P. Shultz and Robert Z. Aliber, eds., *Guidelines, Informal Controls and the Market Place* (Chicago: University of Chicago Press, 1966), pp. 71, 75.

82. Sheahan, *Guideposts*, p. 196 (the period in question is 1962–66. After 1966 the guideposts were clearly ineffective); George L. Perry, *Unemployment*.

83. Eckstein and Brinner, "The Inflation Process."

84. S. W. Black and H. H. Kelejian, "A Macro Model of the U.S. Labor Market," *Review of Economics and Statistics*, 38, 5 (September 1970), pp. 712–41.

85. Robert J. Gordon, "The Recent Acceleration of Inflation and Its Lessons for the Future," *Brookings Papers on Economic Activity* (1970 [1]), p. 17.

86. John T. Dunlop, "Guideposts, Wages and Collective Bargaining," in Shultz and Aliber, *Guidelines*, p. 84.

87. Ibid., p. 89.

88. "Report of the Vice President's Task Force on Inflation: Policy Against Inflation," in Bureau of National Affairs, *Daily Labor Report*, no. 203 (October 16, 1968), p. X-3. Otto Eckstein, a member of the CEA during the Johnson administration, served as chairman of Mr. Humphrey's "Task Force."

89. Gardner Ackley, testimony before the Joint Economic Committee of Congress, August 31, 1971. Also, Ackley, "An Incomes Policy for the 1970's," *Review of Economics and Statistics*, 54, 3 (August 1972), pp. 218–23.

90. "Report of the Vice President's Task Force on Inflation," p. X-7.

Chapter 3

1. Michael V. diSalle reported that on the day President Johnson announced a large-scale escalation in Viet Nam, he said that he had almost instituted controls that morning. DiSalle added, "Definitely, they should have had price and wage controls that same day" ("Full-scale Wage-Price Controls?" p. 37).

2. See *Business Week,* June 17, 1972, p. 101. The data cited are from the Opinion Research Corporation of Princeton, New Jersey.

3. See, for example, Secretary of Labor James D. Hodgson, "A Bit of Perspective on Collective Bargaining and Economic Controls," an address to the National Industrial Conference Board, June 3, 1971 (printed in Bureau of National Affairs, *Daily Labor Report*, no. 107 (June 3, 1971), pp. E-1–E-3); also, Edwin Dale, "Nixon's Economic Plan," *New York Times,* June 30, 1971, p. 22.

4. See *Report of the President's Council of Economic Advisers* (Washington, D.C.: Government Printing Office, 1972), especially pp. 65–72.

5. Only Mr. George Meany, president of the AFL-CIO, has chosen, perhaps inadvisably, to put these administration fumblings on public record, though others experienced them as well. See Meany's report of November 18, 1971, in *Proceedings of the Ninth Constitutional Convention of the AFL-CIO.* Meany said, for example, that an administration source phoned him on one occasion to ask what he thought of Judge George Boldt as a possible chairman of the Pay Board; called again to say Boldt had been determined by the administration to be "totally and completely unfit for this job"; and phoned yet a final time to confirm that Boldt would indeed be appointed chairman of the Pay Board, on which Meany was to serve (ibid., pp. 21–22). Meany's comments to his convention were the immediate background to his celebrated battle (or nonbattle, as the case may have been) with the president when Mr. Nixon spoke to the AFL-CIO convention the following day.

6. *Report of the President's Council of Economic Advisers*, p. 96. It is interesting that in 1968 the "Report of the Vice President's Task Force on Inflation" proposed a program to "get the rate of inflation down to 2–2½ percent in twelve months" (p. X-5).

7. Pay Board Order No. 1, November 13, 1971.

8. The board created a tripartite Cases and Appeals Panel (which began work on March 31,

1972) with power to act for the full board on cases pending before it. As described by the board itself (Pay Board News Release No. 67, March 31, 1972) the panel would "hear all cases which cannot be decided by the Internal Revenue Service or the staff of the Pay Board. These include requests of increases in excess of 7 percent in Category I [5,000 or more employees] and appeals from previous decisions by the Internal Revenue Service and the staff of the Pay Board." The full board continued to hear cases which at least two of its members wanted brought before the board.

9. Order No. 2 of the Pay Board, issued November 14, 1971, exempted the construction industry from the unit-size classification and required notification of prior approval by the Construction Industry Stabilization Committee of all adjustments made through collective bargaining agreements in construction.

10. Cost of Living Council, *First Quarterly Report on the Economic Stabilization Program, Covering the Period August 15–December 31, 1971* (Washington, D.C.: Government Printing Office, 1972), p. 6.

11. See, for example, Philip Shabecoff, "Senate Rebuffs Pay Unit, Backs Retroactive Raises," *New York Times*, December 2, 1971, pp. 1 and 33.

12. The phrase "unreasonably inconsistent" first appeared in Section 3(b) of Executive Order No. 11588 (March 29, 1971) establishing the Construction Industry Stabilization Committee, where it was applied to the matter of approval of increases provided by agreements negotiated before March 29, 1971, the date of initiation of the stabilization program in construction (so-called "deferred increases"). As interpreted by the CISC, the phrase related primarily to the effect of an increase for one group of workers on increases for other groups. A deferred increase was unreasonably inconsistent with stabilization objectives when its implementation would, through patterns of wage comparison, make it difficult or impossible to settle newly negotiated collective bargaining agreements within stabilization criteria. The phrase was thus a judgmental criterion intended for application in the dynamic context of determining wage adjustments. The phrase was not intended to be translated into a simple formula or percentage guideline.

13. The House formulation was, in fact, originally adopted by the board itself and included in its November 8, 1971, statement. Its inclusion in the act without modification or supplement would presumably not have affected the board's intention to deny retroactivity during the freeze in most cases.

14. Conference Report, House of Representatives and the Senate, 92d Cong., 1st Sess., 1971 (Report 92-745), p. 21.

15. In contrast, the standards of the Construction Industry Stabilization Committee as developed by the CISC and the Pay Board explicitly denied an automatic approval of 5.5 percent in all cases.

16. Pay Board Ruling 1972-6, February 16, 1972.

17. See Pay Board News Release No. 10, December 2, 1971.

18. Hours worked may differ from hours paid for because of premium pay for overtime, holiday pay, or other fringe benefits.

19. See Bureau of National Affairs, *Daily Labor Report,* no. 73 (April 13, 1972), p. A-1.

20. See, for example, "Simplified Guide to Pay Board Regulations," prepared by the Pay Board staff and circulated to the public, September 1972.

21. Economic Stabilization Act as Amended, Section 203(b)(2).

22. See, for example, Testimony of Pay Board chairman George Boldt to the Economic Committee of Congress, November 13, 1972. See also, Herbert Messer, "Fringes in Phase II," excerpts from a speech to the American Society of Pension Actuaries, in Jack McKinley, ed., *The Prototype Planner* (New York: Kew Gardens, December 1972).

23. This provision expired in summer 1972, with some few exceptions.

24. Pay Board resolution regarding "Intra-Plant Inequities," Pay Board Press Release No. 79, April 26, 1972.

25. For example, in Chicago the Truckdrivers' Independent Union (not affiliated with the International Brotherhood of Teamsters) negotiated a group of agreements covering small numbers of workers and providing larger than percentage-equivalent wage adjustments (measured by comparison of the final rates of wages, not on a time-payment basis) for increases in the consumer price index. The board then disapproved this practice.

26. Perhaps no area of Pay Board regulations generated such confusion as its policies on merit increases. Initially the board exempted only merit plans provided in collective bargaining agreements. An outcry from the nonunion sector caused the board to extend the exception to all such plans but to carefully define what was a qualified plan. The initial policy on merit increases was issued in December 1971; the final policy on March 22, 1972.

27. The so-called "Percy Amendment," after Senator Charles Percy, Republican of Illinois (Section 203.f3).

28. The chairman of the board was a retired federal judge. Another public member was an attorney. The other public members were strongly concerned with legal procedures. For example, see Arnold R. Weber, "A Wage-Price Freeze as an Instrument of Incomes Policy: or the Blizzard of '71," *Proceedings of the Industrial Relations Research Association* (December 1971), p. 161.

29. Originally, a challenge required sponsorship of five members of the then tripartite board. The employer members proposed to challenge *all* deferred increases, but the board required that each challenge identify a proposed increase in writing to the chairman of the Pay Board. (Pay Board Press Release No. 36, January 11, 1972.)

30. A "party at interest" was defined as an employer or his representatives "who could be required to pay the wages and salaries in question" or his employees or their representatives. Thus, the only private parties who could formally challenge an increase were the employers who had negotiated it—an extension of the legal concept of "interest" which had the effect of undermining the industrial relations concept of good-faith negotiations.

31. For example, the commercial printing industry in New York City had challenged deferred increases due its employees during the freeze (see Damon Stetson, "Industry Challenges Raise Due Printers," *New York Times,* November 24, 1971, p. 15).

32. Pay Board Press Release No. 94, June 7, 1972. The increases involved were provided by collective bargaining agreements between the Amalgamated Meatcutters and Butcherworkmen's union and retail food chains in the Philadelphia area.

33. Philip Shabecoff, "Defining of Poor is a Phase II Issue," *New York Times,* January 17, 1972, p. 49.

34. Philip Shabecoff, "Controls Ended for Wages up to $1.90," *New York Times,* January 30, 1972, p. 1.

35. "Judge Hears Challenge to $1.90 Pay Controls," *AFL-CIO News,* June 24, 1972, p. 2.

36. *Jennings* v. *Connally,* U.S. District Court of the District of Columbia, Civil Action No. 226-72, July 14, 1972; in Bureau of National Affairs, *Daily Labor Report,* no. 137 (July 14, 1972), pp. G-1/G-6.

37. *AFL-CIO News,* May 13, 1972, p. 3.

38. Statement of the business members, *New York Times,* November 20, 1971, p. 16c.

39. Ibid., statement of the public members.

40. See text of Pay Board decision, *New York Times,* December 10, 1971, p. 71.

41. Walter Rugaber, "Pay Board Backs a Rise of 46% Over 42 Months," *New York Times,* December 10, 1971, p. 1.

42. The union refused to announce ratification prior to Pay Board action (Brooks Jackson, "Dividend Pay Board OK's 10% Railroad Wage Hike," *Houston Chronicle,* January 26, 1972, p. 8).

43. Philip Shabecoff, "Pay Board Staff Backs Coast Dock Raise," *New York Times,* March 14, 1972, pp. 1 and 28.

44. Pay Board Press Release No. 61, including the text of the resolution adopted by the board, March 16, 1972.

45. Ibid.

46. Statement of the executive council of the AFL-CIO, November 18, 1971 (text printed in *New York Times,* November 19, 1971, p. 28).

47. Some of the rather bizarre internal operations of the board found their way into the press. See, for example, James L. Rowe, "Pay Board Criticized," *Washington Post,* December 7, 1971 ("Meetings are often so confused that members are not always aware of what they are voting on.... Labor members often ridicule Boldt in the meetings and, sources said, are particularly fond of calling public member Arnold R. Weber an Administration 'hatchet man.' According to reports, Weber 'goes through the ceiling' at the continued needling.")

48. Statement of the AFL-CIO Executive Council (mimeo), Washington, D.C., August 19, 1971.

49. Mr. Meany denied any political intent in the resignation of the union members. See the transcript of a National Broadcasting Company interview with him (Bureau of National Affairs, *Daily Labor Report,* no. 61 [March 28, 1972], p. A-3).

50. Meany's testimony to the Joint Economic Committee of Congress, Bureau of National Affairs, *Daily Labor Report,* no. 78 (April 20, 1972), p. A-17.

51. Ibid.

52. *Teamsters News Service,* March 22, 1972.

53. Pay Board Press Release No. 94, June 7, 1972. The name of the union is incorrect in the Pay Board Press Release but is quoted as printed.

54. Bureau of National Affairs, *Daily Labor Report,* no. 126 (June 28, 1972), p. A-12.

55. See, for example, the comments of a panel of economists as reported by the *New York Times,* January 7, 1973, p. F-37.

56. See Arnold R. Weber, "After Phase II," speech to a symposium at Catholic University, Washington, D.C., as reported in the Bureau of National Affairs, *Daily Labor Report,* no. 63 (April 2, 1973), pp. A-4/A-6.

57. Statement by the president, August 16, 1945, text in *Termination Report,* vol. 3, p. 577.

58. There was also considerable overt dissatisfaction with the Pay Board within the business community. For example, Malcolm Denise, vice president for labor relations of Ford Motor Company, described his company's experience under the board's regulations as follows: "Our first 'control year' under Phase II regulations covered the period November 14, 1971, to September 14, 1972, which occurred during the second year of our UAW contract. For purposes of applying Pay Board regulations, the rate of hourly labor cost at Ford rose 5.7 percent during this period. In point of fact, it rose 9 percent—well over half again as much" (remarks to the Detroit Auto Writers Group, text in Bureau of National Affairs, *Daily Labor Report,* no. 37 [February 23, 1973], p. G-1).

59. Many unions had developed considerable bitterness against the Pay Board because of administrative delays and apparent arbitrariness in the handling of cases. See, for example, Patrick E. Gorman (general secretary-treasurer of the Amalgamated Meatcutters and Butcherworkmen), Statement to the Committee on Banking, Housing and Urban Affairs, U.S. Senate, February 6, 1973; printed and circulated by the Meatcutters.

60. See, for example, Arnold R. Weber, *In Pursuit of Price Stability: The Wage-Price Freeze of 1971* (Washington, D.C.: The Brookings Institution, 1973).

61. Ibid.

62. See Joel Popkin, "Prices in 1972," *Monthly Labor Review,* 96, 2 (February 1973), pp. 16–23.

63. See Neil Jacoby, "After Phase II What?" *Center Report,* 5, 4 (Santa Barbara, California: Center for the Study of Democratic Institutions, October 1972), pp. 10–12. Also, Arnold R. Weber and Daniel J. B. Mitchell, "Wages and the Pay Board," *Proceedings of the Industrial Relations Research Association* (December 1973).

64. It had been noted previously that the guideposts of the mid-1960s had also apparently had a disproportionate effect on nonunionized employees (see Frank L. Bernbach, "National Incomes Policy and Its Impact on Labor-Management Relations," in *National Incomes Policy and Manpower Problems* [Berkeley: Institute of Industrial Relations, University of California], pp. 55–56).

65. Considerable confusion was introduced into the evaluation of the progress of the stabilization program by the Pay Board's procedure for compiling statistical data. The board issued a weekly statistical release in which a percentage was given as "the combined weighted [by number of employees] average of increases effective after November 13, 1971, for Categories I and II" (those units of more than one thousand employees which were required to report increases to the board). Throughout the spring and summer of 1972 this figure was 4 to 5 percent. The figure was widely taken to represent the level of increases in new collective bargaining agreements, a misinterpretation the Pay Board made no effort to correct.

66. Bureau of Labor Statistics, *Current Wage Developments*, various issues.

67. Chairman George H. Boldt, address to the National Press Club, Washington, June 30, 1972 (Pay Board Press Release No. 103). The statistical evidence regarding the impact of the Phase II program led almost immediately to disputes among economists regarding its effectiveness. See, for example, Barry Bosworth, "Phase II: The U.S. Experiment with an Incomes Policy," *Brookings Papers on Economic Activity* (1972 [2]), p. 375, and Robert J. Gordon, "Wage-Price Controls and the Shifting Phillips Curve," *Brookings Papers on Economic Activity* (1972 [2]), pp. 417–18.

68. D. Q. Mills, "Explaining Average Earnings Increases in Construction: 1953-1972," *Industrial Relations*, 13, 2 (May 1973).

Chapter 4

1. See Ulman and Flanagan, *Wage Restraint*; also Daniel J. B. Mitchell, "Incomes Policy and the Labor Market in France," pp. 315–35; and B. C. Roberts, *National Wages Policy in War and Peace* (London: Allen and Unwin), 1958.

2. See Dunlop, "An Appraisal."

3. Lester C. Thurow, "Analyzing the American Income Distribution," *American Economic Review*, 60, 2 (May 1970), pp. 261–69. Also, Thurow and R. E. B. Lucas, "The American Distribution of Income: A Structural Problem," a study prepared for the Joint Economic Committee of Congress, March 17, 1972 (Washington, D.C.: Government Printing Office, 1972).

4. See, for example, "Beyond Phase 2," *Wall Street Journal*, April 26, 1972, p. 16. The *Journal's* editorial writer quoted Under Secretary of the Treasury Charles E. Walker to the effect that "The prospects for getting representatives of labor, business and government to sit down at the table and attempt to agree on wage and price policies . . . look pretty good to me." Responded the *Journal*, "We would be happier with a government that tried . . . attacking excessive [private] power . . . than we would be with one that left our fate to a . . . group of power brokers."

5. Archibald Cox, last chairman of the WSB of the Korean period, has commented, "Wage stabilization was more than writing a few regulations; it required the continuing consent of the people to whom the regulations applied if industrial output was to be increased and industrial peace maintained" (Dunlop and Cox, "The Bituminous Coal Case," p. 12).

6. John T. Dunlop and Archibald Cox commented, "It appears to be a valid summary of Korean and World War II experience that price and wage control *statutes* come to have an increasing number of exceptions and special provisions concerning strong interest or industrial groups. Some groups which do not like the price or wage standards used by the Administrative agencies are able to secure special legislative provisions. The initial statutes are likely to provide for more effective and tighter controls. . . . The statutory standards get diluted" ("The Decision to Invoice Direct Controls," manuscript [1954], p. 7).

7. Apparently both AFL and CIO leadership favored extension of controls under certain

conditions, but John L. Lewis of the United Mine Workers prevailed, with the support of elements of management, against the two federations and the administration.

This interpretation is implied (and has been confirmed by the author through private conversation) in Taylor, *Government Regulation*, pp. 221ff. See also *President's Labor-Management Conference, 1945*, pp. 12–13.

8. However, in the process of reforming the WSB in the spring of 1951, after the unions' withdrawal, the president created a National Advisory Board on Mobilization Policy. This board paralleled a similar group which was active in World War II. The board was quadra-partite, including representatives of labor, management, government, and agricultural interests. The board, in 1951, served as a device for consultation regarding the future of the stabilization program and recommended (the industry members dissenting) the reformation of the WSB with dispute-settlement functions (see Harold L. Enarson, "The Politics of an Emergency Dispute: Steel, 1952," in Bernstein et al., *Emergency Disputes and National Policy* [New York: Harper & Row, 1955], p. 52).

9. President Roosevelt in his April 27, 1942, message said, "We can face the fact that there must be a drastic reduction in our standard of living." In fact, the anticipated general decline in real wage levels during the war did not occur.

10. See, for example, Secretary of Labor James D. Hodgson's address to the twenty-eighth convention of the Amalgamated Clothing Workers of America (mimeo), Miami Beach, May 30, 1972.

11. The public posture of the unions prior to and during the period of controls was quite different. The AFL-CIO continued to insist that high profits were a major cause of inflation, and there was congressional support for its position. Senator George McGovern, a Democratic presidential hopeful, proposed an excess profits tax of 82 percent (the Korean War level).

12. It should be added that the union leadership in some cases has been remarkably patient with government in these matters. For example, construction wages were once subject to controls for sixteen months (1971–72) before the administration finally imposed any degree of effective controls on profits or prices. See D. Q. Mills, "Construction Wage Stabilization: A Historic Perspective," *Industrial Relations*, 11, 3 (October 1972), pp. 350–65.

13. For a discussion of the history of union security disputes in World War II see Derber, "The Principles of Dispute Settlement," in Bureau of Labor Statistics, *Problems and Policies*, pp. 72–103.

14. George Taylor, "The War Labor Board's Role in the Democratic Process," address at Swarthmore College, December 6, 1942; text in *Termination Report*, vol. 2, p. 502.

15. See WSB, vol. 1, pp. 20–21, and Bruno Stein, "Labor Participation in Stabilization Agencies," pp. 74–75.

16. WSB, vol. 1, p. 20.

17. During both World War II and the Korean War there were tripartite regional boards established, as well as a national board. This discussion is limited to national boards; though many aspects of the discussion apply to regional boards as well, some do not. There is, of necessity, far less of a policy-making function exercised in the regional boards than at the national level. The role of public members of the regional boards should be far from different from that of the members of the national board, concluded Clark Kerr: "The public members of the regional boards . . . are not to mediate between the [labor and management] parties before them but to enforce in individual cases . . . national wage restraint" (Kerr, "Governmental Wage Restraint," p. 375).

18. Ran V. Morley, associate public member of the NWLB, commented to a meeting of the Printers' National Association, October 1, 1943, that "if there is irritation against the War Labor Board, it is very understandable. There are two classic ways of being unpopular. One is to interfere in a domestic quarrel . . . that, in the beginning was the first task [i.e., dispute settlement] laid upon the Board. The other is to interfere with a man's pocketbook . . . that now is the second of our obnoxious tasks" (text in *Termination Report*, p. 524).

19. Benjamin Aaron, "Enforcement," in Bureau of Labor Statistics, *Problems and Policies*, p. 359.

20. Evidence that a board has gone too far in the direction of the position of either side is not difficult to obtain, since the side benefiting will normally announce its pleasure with the board's policy. For example, the statement of the business members of the Pay Board upon the announcement of its initial policies, said, in part: "The Pay Board program is simple and understandable, with a single pay standard of 5.5 percent annually. It is equitable and fair to all, requring almost every American to make some sacrifice" (text in Bureau of National Affairs, *Daily Labor Report*, no. 216 [November 9, 1971], p. AA-8). This was high praise, and was a harbinger of difficulties ahead with the labor members.

21. William E. Simkin, *Mediation and the Dynamics of Collective Bargaining* (Washington, D.C.: Bureau of National Affairs, 1971), pp. 123, 132.

22. "The public representatives," reported Lloyd Garrison, an alternate public member of the NWLB, 'have learned and are constantly learning from the industry and labor representatives facts and viewpoints which no books could ever contain.... One man's mind contains little wisdom. One man's viewpoint is always distorted. It is only out of the interpenetration of differing minds and viewpoints that sound judgments spring" ("The Impact of the War on Labor Relations," address to the Industrial Relations Association of Wisconsin, January 12, 1944 (text in *Termination Report*, vol. 2, p. 531).

23. Speaking of the NWLB of World War II, Dexter Keezer said, "It is axiomatic that the true inwardness of a labor dispute often bears little or no relationship to what is being proclaimed about it—a fact which makes it possible to have a complete documentary record of the dispute and still have no idea of what it is really about. Their Labor and Industry colleagues could and did give the Public members crucially important help in overcoming this difficulty by letting them know, in those rather subtle ways developed by people who work closely and continuously together, the real significance of the dispute involved and what would suffice, if not be satisfactory, as a remedy" ("Observations on the Operation of the NWLB," *American Economic Review*, 36, 3 [June 1946], p. 48).

24. See McPherson, "Tripartitism," in Bureau of Labor Statistics, *Problems and Policies*, for a rather more narrow discussion of the contributions of partisan members to a stabilization program (especially pp. 238-39).

25. For example, see Garrison's comments on the World War II experience, in "Labor Relations," p. 531. Also, Witte, "Wartime Handling of Labor Disputes," *Harvard Business Review*, 25, 1 (Autumn 1946), p. 187.

26. Witte, "Labor Disputes."

27. Garrison, "Labor Relations," p. 532. The quotation in the text is Garrison's paraphrase of views he did *not* share.

28. Sumner Slichter, "Wage Stabilization and Emergency Disputes," *The Commercial and Financial Chronicle*, 185, 5110 (April 24, 1952), p. 53.

29. *New York Times Magazine*, December 12, 1971, p. F-3.

Chapter 5

1. The term "wage structure" refers to the relationship of various wage rates, including both straight-time earnings and fringe benefits. See Cynthia Taft and Lloyd Reynolds, *The Evolution of Wage Structure* (New Haven: Yale University Press, 1956), p. 9.

2. Michael J. Piore, "Interdependent and Irreversible Utility Functions and Wage Behavior," manuscript, February 9, 1968, p. 9.

3. Of course, other things are not always equal, so that high-wage firms may be competitive by virtue of greater productivity, sales effort, or even be protected by a monopoly position. This in no way, however, deprives relative wages of an important role in the competitive positions of various firms.

4. John T. Dunlop (*Wage Determination*) has explored the interaction of product and labor

market structures in detail. See also, Martin Segal, "The Relation Between Union Wage Impact and Market Structure," *Quarterly Journal of Economics*, 78, 1 (May 1964), pp. 95–114.

5. George A. Akerlof, "Relative Wages and the Rate of Inflation," *Quarterly Journal of Economics*, 83, 3 (August 1969), pp. 353–74.

6. In the long run such a situation could lead to substantial inefficiencies or anomalies, but situations of this nature are nonetheless common in our economy.

7. Clark Kerr, "Government Wage Restraints."

8. Dunlop, *Wage Determination*, pp. 122–30.

9. John T. Dunlop, "The Task of Contemporary Wage Theory," in *The Theory of Wage Determination: Proceedings of a Conference*, ed. J. T. Dunlop (London: Macmillan, 1957), pp. 3–27.

10. On the other hand, periods of hyperinflation are characterized not only by distortion of traditional wage relationships but also by destruction of traditional institutions of wage determination (such an institution, for example, would be the fixed-term contract characteristic of collective bargaining in the United States). See, for descriptions of the collapse of economic institutions in hyperinflation, Chang Kia-Ngan, *The Inflationary Spiral: The Experience of China, 1939–50* (New York: Technology Press & Wiley & Sons, 1958); and Brescrani-Turroni, *The Economics of Inflation* (London: Allen and Unwin, 1937).

11. See, for example, Lewis Beman, "The Emerging Debate about Inflation," *Fortune*, 85, 3 (March 1972), pp. 50ff.

12. See James Tobin, "Unemployment and Inflation," *American Economic Review*, 42, 1 (March 1972), p. 9.

13. Lindley H. Clark, Jr., "Speaking of Business: Constructive Ideas," *Wall Street Journal*, February 23, 1972, p. 14.

14. Arthur Okun, commenting on a paper by Albert Rees ("The Construction Industry Stabilization Committee: Implications for Phase II," *Brookings Economic Papers*, no. 3, 1971).

Chapter 6

1. Taylor, *Government Regulation*, p. 178, n. 48. These figures do not include employees of other agencies assigned to wage stabilization duties, as, for example, those of the U.S. Department of Labor, Division of Wages and Hours.

2. WSB, vol. 3, pp. 421ff.

3. See also the testimony of Pay Board Chairman Boldt to the Joint Economic Committee of Congress, November 13, 1972, mimeo, p. 7.

4. John L. Blackman, *Presidential Seizure in Labor Disputes* (Cambridge: Harvard University Press, 1967), p. 137.

5. The text of this memorandum (dated August 1, 1951) is in WSB, vol. 3, pp. 57–66.

6. See *Termination Report*, vol. 2, pp. 164–69.

7. One reason for the exemption was to reduce the administrative burden of the stabilization program on the Internal Revenue Service, which largely administered it. See Philip Shabecoff, *New York Times*, June 5, 1972, p. 29.

8. Dunlop and Cox, "The Bituminous Case," p. 13.

9. During World War II the NWLB developed a succession of stabilized limits reflecting the shift in the focus of employer and union applications as avenues for wage adjustments were exhausted. "It would have been difficult, if not impossible, in advance to formulate a comprehensive system of stabilized limits" (Dunlop, "An Appraisal," p. 160).

10. Supplementary opinion of Edwin E. Witte, public member in the case of Melville Shoe Corp., NWLB No. 111-6642-D (August 23, 1945), text in *Termination Report*, vol. 2, p. 401.

11. "Only enough of a bureaucracy is needed," opined Federal Reserve Board member Sherman J. Maisel, "to devise reasonably equitable rules of the game, keep them current, and explain them" (*New York Times*, November 24, 1971, p. 57).

12. There is considerable literature regarding the comparative merits of case-adjudication versus rule-making by government administrative agencies. See, for example, David L. Shapiro, "The Choice of Rule-Making or Adjudication in the Development of Administrative Policy," *Harvard Law Review*, 78 (1964); and Glen O. Robinson, "The Making of Administrative Policy: Another Look at Rule-Making and Adjudication and Administrative Procedure Reform," *University of Pennsylvania Law Review*, 118 (1970).

13. To the credit of the Pay Board's staff, there often seemed a greater concern for the long-run interests of stabilization as opposed to narrow application of rules (especially where some proposed economic adjustment was approvable under the rules but in a particular context was clearly destabilizing) evidenced at the staff level than at the level of the board itself.

14. C. Kerr, "Distribution of Authority," in Bureau of Labor Statistics, *Problems and Policies*, p. 291.

15. For example, in Norman v. Baltimore and Ohio Railroad (294 U.S. 240), the Supreme Court said that private "contracts must be understood as having been made in reference to the possible exercise of the rightful authority of the Government, and that no obligation of a contract can extend to the deficit [citing Knox v. Lee] of that authority" (text in Paul Freund, et al., *Constitutional Law* [Boston: Little Brown, 1961], vol. 1, p. 291).

16. See WSB, vol. 1, pp. 189–99.

17. The Pay Board disallowed some 200 deferred increases scheduled to take effect in 1972 (affecting only a relatively small number of workers); the CISC disallowed some 1,400 (affecting about 250,000 construction workers).

18. Bowles stresses the importance of the OPA's statement in the Air-Frame Industrial Wage Conference of July 1942, in convincing the administration to establish by executive order in the fall of 1942 the comprehensive stabilization program described in the text (*Promises to Keep: My Years in Public Service* [New York: Harper and Row], 1971, p. 58).

19. Douty, "Development of Wage-Price Policies," in Bureau of Labor Statistics, *Problems and Policies*, p. 142.

20. WSB, vol. 1, pp. 13–18.

21. The incorporation of the Price Commission and the Pay Board into the Cost of Living Council in 1973 established effective coordination of the wage and price function but at the cost of flexibility in policy formulation and administration.

22. Jack G. Gray, "Jurisdiction," in Bureau of Labor Statistics, *Problems and Policies*, p. 281.

23. DiSalle, "Full Scale Wage-Price Controls?" p. 35.

24. For example, in addition to the Industry Earnings Standard, other standards for price relief included product, individual company, and essential product relief. See WSB, vol. 1, p. 14.

25. Taylor, *Government Regulation*, p. 215.

26. Dunlop, "An Appraisal," p. 181.

27. For example, Dunlop and Cox reported: "The steel case of 1952 was to highlight the large cost absorptive capacity of that industry under the industry earnings standard and to involve the issue of the extent to which wage rate increases should be absorbed under price stabilization" (John T. Dunlop and Archibald Cox, "The Wage Level and the Cost of Living," manuscript [1954], p. 17).

28. Dunlop and Cox, "The Decision to Invoke Direct Controls," p. 7.

29. For a discussion of the legislative developments of 1952, see WSB, vol. 3, pp. 27–34.

30. See WSB, vol. 2, p. 175.

31. Dunlop and Cox, "The Wage Level and the Cost of Living," p. 17.

32. The Internal Revenue Service, acting as the Pay Board's agent, was ruling in 1971 that all fringe benefits were included in the general standard of 5.5. See, for example, an arbitration award in which Pay Board standards were an issue: Bureau of National Affairs, *Daily Labor Report*, no. 79, April 21, 1972, p. A-1.

33. See *Washington Post*, December 23, 1972, p. 1.

Chapter 7

1. "In developing the Little Steel formula the Board was impressed with the wage inequities between different groups of workers which arose from the disparities in amounts of general wage increases previously made by various plants and in different industries" (George Taylor, "The Wage Stabilization Policy of the National War Labor Board" in NWLB Report to the President, February 22, 1945, in *Termination Report*, vol. 3, p. 893).

2. George W. Taylor, Opinion of the National War Labor Board in the Little Steel case, July 16, 1942; text in *Termination Report*, vol. 2 pp. 293–99.

3. The NWLB was prepared to hear arguments from workers and their employers that the base date selected (January 1941) was inappropriate as a standard for the relative wage position of a particular group of workers.

4. Taylor's opinion, *Termination Report*, vol. 2, pp. 293–99.

5. Ibid.

6. There has been criticism of the board for adopting a percentage adjustment in the Little Steel formula rather than a cents-per-hour adjustment. See, for example, John Dunlop, who argued that the Little Steel formula permitted increase in cents-per-hour wage differentials between skilled and unskilled workers (by using a percentage standard) "at a time when tightening labor markets and the demands of war production required narrowing of [cents-per-hour] skill differentials" ("An Appraisal," p. 164).

7. Lever Brothers Co., NWLB cases No. 2276 and 2303-CS-D (September 2, 1942) and New York Employing Printers Association, Inc., Case No. 111-90-R (June 25, 1943), cited in *Termination Report*, vol. 1, pp. 209–10.

8. A later qualification to this policy is discussed in chapter 8.

9. The allowance of both a general increase in wages, reflecting price and productivity increases, and readjustment of wage differentials may be viewed as the loosest wage stabilization policy, that is, the one least likely to interfere with the ordinary operation of wage determination in the economy. Clark Kerr described such a policy as the upper limit of government wage policy ("Governmental Wage Restraints," p. 377).

10. The board had considerable nonpartisan support for this view. See, for example, a statement attributed to Walter Heller, extending the concept of the single percentage wage criterion from newly determined increases to deferred increases. "Heller noted," reported the Bureau of National Affairs, "that a guideline of 5 percent to 6 percent for wage increases would be compatible with the Administration goal of a cut in the inflation rate of 2 percent or 3 percent by the end of 1972. It would be feasible, therefore, he said, to allow deferred increases nearly within this range to take effect" (*Daily Labor Report*, no. 207 [October 27, 1971], p. A-9). The reader will recognize that it is not necessary to restrict all wage settlements to 6 percent or less, in order to have all settlements average 6 percent.

11. The strategy of using controls to combat a "psychological" inflation was proposed by economists in the winter of 1971–72 and adopted by the administration in the summer and fall of 1972 as an explanation of the activities of the Pay Board and Price Commission. For example, George Perry wrote: "Although the concept lacks theoretical elegance, I am persuaded that inflation is now perpetuated to an important degree because of high "habitual" rates of wage and price increase.... If this habitual situation in wage setting is interrupted, there need be no consequence for real output and employment. I am offering a treadmill explanation of the present situation. A middle-road incomes policy is designed to get us off the treadmill, down to a lower habitual average rate of wage and price increase" ("After the Freeze," *Brookings Papers on Economic Activity* [1971 (2)], p. 446).

12. See Steven J. Turnovsky and Michael L. Wachter, "A Test of the 'Expectations Hypothesis' Using Directly Observed Wage and Price Expectations," *Review of Economic and Statistics*, 54, 1 (February 1972), pp. 47–54.

13. See, for example, the description by William E. Simkin (the former director, FMCS) of how the maritime officers' unions "observed" the guideposts in the mid-1960s: "The officer unions wrapped the flag around themselves and embraced the 3.2 percent formula. For them it was a good formula, partly because they put everything but the kitchen sink into the base. Previously, they had usually bargained percentage increases in basic rates. The 3.2 percent above total compensation ... meant about double that figure on basic rates. Subsequently, application of 'me too' clauses covering alleged inequities among these unions resulted in increases that probably equalled or exceeded the negotiated 3.2 percent" (that is, in Simkin's view the increases received by the officers' unions were approximately 6 percent on total compensation, or 12 percent on base wages) ("Effects of the Structure of Collective Bargaining in Selected Industries," in *Proceedings of the Industrial Relations Research Association* [May 8–9, 1970], p. 515).

14. Taylor, *Government Regulation*, p. 212.

15. Ibid., pp. 217–19.

16. WSB, vol. 3, p. 18.

17. WSB, vol. 1, p. 17.

18. Should an ability-to-pay standard be employed, despite the factors which argue against its use, there are several aspects of its application which are likely to be problematic. These aspects include the determination of what period should be used to measure a firm's ability to pay, the estimation of how the volume of production expected will affect ability to pay, and the question of how rate of return on investment is related to ability to pay. See John T. Dunlop, "The Economics of Wage-Dispute Settlement," *Law and Contemporary Problems*, 12, 2 (Spring 1947), pp. 290–91.

19. However, in awarding the terms of a new contract wage boards have sometimes, in disputes cases, explicitly considered arguments regarding an employer's ability to pay proposed wage increases and have awarded larger increases to the workers than the employer desired. (See, for example, the NWLB's opinion in the International Harvester Company cases, issued April 15, 1942; text in *Termination Report*, vol. 2, pp. 273–87.)

20. The eight indices so recognized were state-wide or territorial indices for Hawaii, Louisiana, Massachusetts, Michigan, New Jersey, Pennsylvania, and the National Industrial Conference Board's national index of consumer prices. See WSB, vol. 3, p. 96.

Incidentally, the Consumer Price Index is not, in actuality, a measure of changes in the cost-of-living. It is, rather, what its name suggests: an index of consumer prices. The index is periodically updated to include new products purchased by consumers, including, for example, color televisions, stereos, and so on. These items do not necessarily belong in a true cost-of-living index, which might be thought to involve more of a subsistence concept.

21. The discussion in the text is not meant to imply that the Bureau of Labor Statistics Consumer Price Index is deficient; rather, only that disputes as to its characteristics and implications as a wage standard should be expected.

22. As Milton Friedman has commented, "Whatever else a price and wage freeze or price and wage controls may do, they distort published price indexes and make them highly unreliable measures of the movement of actual prices. A major challenge to our ingenuity is to find more reliable measures" ("Have Monetary Policies Failed?" *American Economic Review*, 72, 2 (May 1972], p. 17).

23. The establishment of cost-of-living escalator clauses in collective bargaining agreements is itself an unstabilizing element in wage determination in an uncontrolled economy. See Joseph W. Garbarino, "The Economic Significance of Automatic Wage Adjustments," in H. W. Davey, ed., *New Dimensions of Collective Bargaining* (New York: Harper & Brothers, 1959), pp. 154–75.

24. See the *Report of the President's Council of Economic Advisers, 1962*, pp. 185–90, for a discussion of the theoretical basis for the wage-price guideposts. The proposition that, if wages rise at the same rate as labor productivity, prices will tend to be stable, is sometimes referred to

as "Hansen's Law," after Professor Alvin Hansen. This proposition, which is sometimes put forward as an arithmetic identity is, in fact, of very questionable validity. It depends on two relationships, both of which are oversimplifications. The first is that wage increases directly affect unit labor costs on a proportional basis. The second is that prices are proportional to unit labor costs. While both relationships are unquestionable as statements of a tendency, or as expressions of a partial connection (that is, with other influences unchanging), they are much less certain as empirical assertions. For example, if prices are proportional not to unit *labor* costs but to *total* unit costs, then the Hansen proposition becomes less general (that is, its accuracy depends upon the relationship of growth rates in the productivity of various factors of production).

25. This is not the only possible interpretation of the implicit promises of the productivity guidelines but is, I believe, the most reasonable. An alternative interpretation would be that workers are entitled only to those wage increases which reflect productivity improvement in general and that the effect of rising prices (if prices do rise) on their earnings is of no interest or consequence to policy-makers. That is, the productivity standard would fully determine money wage increases, with real wage changes (positive or negative) to be the resultant of whatever price changes occur. But this is an unlikely interpretation of the intent of public policy with respect to wages in a Western democracy (unless the expectation of possibly declining real wages is explicitly publicized—as in the United States during World War II).

26. Even were prices to rise less than wages, increased taxes might offset the gain in purchasing power. While taxes are clearly the province of government policy in a manner consumer prices are not, tax rates are not fully discretionary with public officials, since such rates must reflect many other considerations than wage policy alone.

27. For example, Al Rees has noted that "Perhaps the most serious problems of a wage policy based on productivity trends alone arise when the price level rises faster than does average productivity. Under such circumstances continued adherence to the productivity criterion produces a fall in real wages. To make workers bear this much of the burden of checking inflation is clearly unacceptable to labor organizations. On the other hand, policy makers are often unwilling to include compensation for past price increases in the wage criteria" ("Wage-Price Policy," p. 10).

28. A major qualification must be made here. As always in economic policy, what the government does is less important than how it does it, at least as regards the acceptability of government policy to the private sector. The discussion in the text relates primarily to a unilaterally determined government policy for wage increases based on productivity. The unfortunate consequences possibly resulting from such a policy are described. However, there may be states of the economy such that government, business, and labor, after consideration of the full implications of wages policy, prefer to pursue a productivity-based general wages policy. In such a circumstance, many of the unfortunate political and industrial relations consequences of a policy unilaterally suggested by the government would be minimized.

29. The British have stressed productivity bargaining strongly in the last decade. For a detailed study of an apparently successful series of agreements involving wage adjustments in return for more efficient work practices, see Ronald Edwards and R. D. V. Roberts, *Status, Productivity and Pay: A Major Experiment; A Study of the Electricity Supply Industry's Agreements and Their Outcome, 1961–71* (London: Macmillan, 1971). A foreword by E. H. Phelps Brown discusses the role of productivity bargaining in British incomes policies.

30. It was followed in construction in 1971–73, for example.

31. The process by which productivity improvements are translated into wage adjustments is neither mechanistic nor automatic and does not ordinarily depend on the expectations of workers that wage increases will be the result of increased productivity. Rather, relatively rapid productivity improvements for one group of workers vis-à-vis others probably become translated into increasing wage differentials through lessened employer resistance to larger than usual wage adjustments for the more productive workers.

32. A further variant would be to permit wage increases equal to the long-term rate of increase in productivity, plus whatever price increases occur in the next current year. I am not aware that any proposal of this sort has been put forward as a suggested wage standard.

33. This procedure was suggested, in essence, though with the desired rate of price increase established at zero, by Myron Joseph (see "Requiem for a Lightweight" [University of Pennsylvania Conference on Pricing Theories, Practices, and Policies, October 1966 (mimeo)], pp. 20–21, cited by John Sheahan, *The Wage-Price Guideposts*, p. 157).

34. The union representatives on the first WSB issued a dissenting opinion upon the adoption by the public and management members of Regulation No. 6, initially defined to include all fringe items as part of the 10 percent increase allowed by Regulation No. 6. The union representatives criticized this formulation of the general standard for wages as "unworkable" and designed to "break down the long and well established distinction between wages and non-wage forms of compensation." The dissent cited as an example an increase in rent on company-owned houses and asked if such an increase affected the general standard. See text of the union representatives statement in WSB, vol. 3, especially p. 73.

35. Some readers might expect that the impact of the norm on wage decisions is independent of how broadly it is defined. That is, a norm tends to become the minimum whether it is narrowly limited to wage rates or broadly extended to gross earnings. This is logically correct. However, a narrowly defined norm can be supplemented by other policies to achieve the net degree of desired wage restraint. A broadly defined standard (or norm) cannot, by definition, be so supplemented.

36. See, for example, the discussion of the problem of relative compensation comparisons in Reynolds and Taft, *The Evolution of Wage Structure*, chap. 1.

37. See, for example, Arthur P. Allen and B. V. H. Schneider, *Industrial Relations in the California Aircraft Industry* (Berkeley: University of California, Institute of Industrial Relations, 1956 [a pamphlet]). Also, see Bureau of National Affairs, *Collective Bargaining Negotiations and Contracts: Bargaining Techniques and Trends*, Section 18:5, "Aerospace," information service, periodically updated.

38. Much of the following discussion is based upon a memorandum prepared by Albert Rees for the Construction Industry Stabilization Committee in 1971.

Chapter 8

1. Kerr, "The Distribution of Authority," p. 293.

2. U.S. District Court for District of Columbia, *IAM and UAW* v. *George Boldt*, July 31, 1972 (transcript), p. 19.

3. WSB, vol. 1, p. 548.

4. Text of the NWLB's decision, *Termination Report*, vol. 2, p. 382.

5. See the recommendations of the regional boards in the *Termination Report*, vol. 2, pp. 659–64.

6. "After three years of experience . . . the Board still has no inflexible rule for the correction of substandards of living to apply in disputes cases. The particular circumstances of each case must be given separate consideration" (George Taylor, opinion in the 1944–45 textile cases, *Termination Report*, vol. 2, p. 382).

7. The Cost of Living Council in its determination of the $2.75 figure retreated into ambiguity. "In arriving at the $2.75 figure, the Cost of Living Council did not use just one set of calculations" (Cost of Living Council Press Release no. 127, July 25, 1972). And the Council commented, "the $2.75 per hour figure, by itself, exempts 43 percent of private non-farm employment from direct pay controls."

8. Dunlop, "An Appraisal," p. 165. The NWLB sometimes established tapering procedures specific to a single industry, as in the case of the laundry industry (see *Termination Report*, vol. 2, p. 997).

9. WSB, vol. 3, pp. 236–40.

10. Pay Board news release no. 117, August 7, 1972.

11. See Dunlop, "The Economics of Wage-Dispute Settlement," pp. 283-85.

12. Hill, "Inter-Plant Inequities," in E. Stein, ed., *Proceedings of the Fifth Annual New York University Conference on Labor* (New York: Bender and Co., 1952), p. 707. There is, of course, a degree of interaction among institutional and economic factors. For example, the Frigidaire Division of General Motors (employing several thousand workers) produces electrical appliances and has been organized by the International Union of Electrical Workers (IUE). Yet, negotiations covering these workers traditionally follow the pattern of wage rates and negotiations in the automobile industry rather than in electrical manufacturing. By 1972, the impact of the automobile pattern on the competitive position of Frigidaire vis-à-vis other electrical manufacturers was so unfavorable that large-scale layoffs were required. Under this pressure the union agreed to waive wage increases for two years and agreed to establish two separate locals reflecting varying product market conditions: one in the appliance business, the other in automobile air-conditioner manufacturing (*New York Times*, November 22, 1971, p. 1).

13. Reynolds and Taft, *The Evolution of Wage Structure*, p. 175.

14. Hill, "Inter-Plant Inequities," p. 708.

15. Reynolds and Taft, *The Evolution of Wage Structure*, p. 176.

16. WSB Resolution No. 101 (revised), July 24, 1952. For a description of collective bargaining in the western lumber industry see Paul L. Kleinsorge, "The Lumber Industry," *Monthly Labor Review*, 82, 5 (May 1959), pp. 558-63.

17. The only motivation for the board's action was apparently a desire to apply as literally as possible the terms of its regulations, including those of the Cost of Living Council which excluded small firms which were not members of associations from wage controls.

18. See, for example, Robert L. Raimon, "The Indeterminateness of Wages of Semi-skilled Workers," *Industrial and Labor Relations Review*, 6, 2 (January 1953), pp. 180-94; also, Peter B. Doeringer and Michael J. Piore, *Internal Labor Markets and Manpower Analysis* (Lexington, Massachusetts: Heath Lexington Books, 1971), especially chap. 4.

19. Opinion of Chairman Cox in the rubber cases, November 3, 1952, WSB, vol. 3, pp. 119-21.

20. Bureau of National Affairs, *Daily Labor Report*, no. 206 (October 24, 1972), p. A-4.

21. "Policy Directive of the Director of Economic Stabilization: Clarification of Executive Order No. 9328," May 12, 1943, in *Termination Report*, vol. 2, pp. 117-18.

22. *Termination Report*, vol. 2, pp. 671-72.

23. Ibid., p. 975.

24. NWLB Summary of Board Actions, May 1, 1944; text in *Termination Report*, vol. 2, p. 1176.

25. The application of the brackets was not always so simple, of course. See, for example, the NWLB's decision in the Jenkins Brothers (Bridgeport, Connecticut) case, which dragged on from 1942 to 1944 (*Termination Report*, vol. 2, pp. 353-57).

26. William H. Davis, "Some Thoughts on Industrial Relations in the Transition from War to Peace," speech at the New School for Social Research, New York, February 19, 1945; in *Termination Report*, vol. 2, p. 553.

27. Dunlop, "An Appraisal," pp. 164-65.

28. The term "intraplant" is to be understood as a generic term relating to all aspects of wage structure internal to a single establishment, whether the establishment is the only plant of a firm, or one of the plants of a multiplant firm, or not a plant at all but a shipping facility, a warehouse, a retail store, and so on.

29. It is often surprising to the casual observer that a high degree of distortion in the internal wage structure of a plant can develop in our economy, since competition is expected to weed out nonefficient producers. The process of "natural selection" in the economy may take a very long time to operate, however, and the establishment of a stabilization program unfortunately involves public officials in problems, such as distorted internal wage structures, otherwise best left to the private parties immediately concerned.

30. The discussion in the text is largely derived from E. Robert Livernash, "Stabilization of the Internal Wage Rate Structure," *Industrial and Labor Relations Review*, 7, 2 (January 1954), pp. 211–20.

31. NWLB, *Wage Stabilization Manual*, in *Termination Report*, vol. 2, p. 988.

32. See Livernash, "Stabilization of the Internal Wage Rate Structure," p. 217.

33. Ibid., pp. 217, 218.

34. Ibid., p. 215.

35. "A well-known case was that West Coast Airframe Cos. decision. Manpower utilization in this vital industry was appallingly bad. Turn-over was holding back production. Rate structures were described as 'chaotic.' New workers were sometimes paid higher than experienced personnel. New jobs were sometimes assigned rates unrelated to other job rates. The Board ordered a job evaluation plan adopted by all plants to bring about standardization and simplification. Job titles were reduced from 1,000 to less than 300. Labor grades were reduced to 10" (John B. Parrish, "Relation of Wage Control to Manpower Problems," in Bureau of Labor Statistics, *Problems and Policies*, p. 211).

36. See Sar A. Levitan, *Ingrade Wage-Rate Progression in War and Peace* (Plattsburg, New York: Clinton Press, 1950).

37. In World War II, the NWLB utilized industry and area practice to determine the approvability of shortened work weeks. See *Wage Stabilization Manual*, in *Termination Report*, vol. 2, p. 1014.

38. WSB Opinion, October 2, 1952, in WSB, vol. 3, pp. 219–21.

39. WSB, vol. 1, pp. 302–14. A Scanlon-type cost-savings sharing plan proposed by the Pfaudler Co. was approved by the WSB. For a discussion of the Scanlon Plan, see Fred G. Lesieur and Elbridge S. Puckett, "The Scanlon Plan—Past, Present and Future," *Proceedings of the Industrial Relations Research Association* (1968), pp. 71–80.

40. The introduction of the term "fringe benefits" has been attributed to a regional chairman of the NWLB. See James C. Hill, "Stabilization of Fringe Benefits," *Industrial and Labor Relations Review*, 7, 2 (January 1954), p. 221.

41. "Employee Benefits, 1969," report of a biennial survey by the United States Chamber of Commerce. Incidentally, total fringe benefit payments (including legally required contributions) were 31.7 percent of total payroll in 1969, and a study by the Institute for the Future has estimated that this proportion will rise to 50 percent by 1985. Also, the Chamber reported that in 1971, among 885 firms surveyed, pension, health and welfare, profit sharing, annuity or savings plans constituted 8.5 percent of all nonlegally required compensation (see U.S. Chamber of Commerce, *Employee Benefits, 1971* [Washington, D.C.: 1972], table 7).

42. For a study of the impact of collective bargaining about health insurance on medical costs, and a review of various types of union policies regarding medical care, see Joseph W. Garbarino, *Health Plans and Collective Bargaining* (Berkeley: University of California Press, 1960).

43. The neutrality of insurance plans with respect to purchasing power may also be disputed. However, space limitations prohibit a discussion here.

44. *Termination Report*, vol. 1, pp. 380–88.

45. Wilbur J. Cohen, "Health, Welfare and Pension Plans Under Wage Stabilization," *Industrial and Labor Relations Review*, 7, 2 (January 1954), pp. 235–45. Cohen reports, for example, that the board had a major problem trying to get parties to divert funds into other benefits than rising surgical fees (pp. 244–45).

46. Frank C. Pierson, "Pension Plans Under Wage Stabilization," in E. Stein, ed., *Proceedings of the Fifth Annual New York Conference on Labor*, pp. 775–85.

47. Cohen, "Health, Welfare and Pension Plans."

48. Bureau of Labor Statistics, *Administration of Negotiated Pension, Health, and Insurance Plans* (Washington, D.C.: Government Printing Office, May 1970), bulletin no. 1425-12.

49. See Cohen, "Health, Welfare and Pension Plans," p. 235.

50. Bureau of Labor Statistics, *Administration of Negotiated Pension Plans*, p. 3.

51. The most constructive response to the destabilizing pressures excited by medical costs, in particular, on the rate of increase in employee compensation would be to achieve a substantial moderation in the rate of increase of medical costs. A wage stabilization board cannot attempt this directly. Rather, a wage board is limited to encouraging other governmental authorities to attempt to do so. During 1971–72 the Price Commission attempted to regulate medical fees in an effort which several times changed direction and was, ultimately, without significant achievement. It is very important, however, that in the future increases in medical costs be constrained, otherwise the potential effectiveness of a stabilization program for compensation in industry generally is greatly reduced.

52. "Call-in" pay is a premium paid to workers in some industries (especially construction) who report for work at their employer's direction but are not put to work for some reason (such as nondelivery of needed materials).

53. WSB General Wage Regulation No. 13: "The Board will use as a standard for comparison the practice of that grouping of establishments most appropriate to the preservation of historical, traditional or otherwise normal patterns of adjustment." Difficulties which arose in the application of these standards because of conflicts between area, industrial, and, in some instances, single corporation (or "company")practice, are described in Hill, "Stabilization of Fringe Benefits."

54. Lloyd Bailer, "Board Policies on Fringe Benefits," in E. Stein, *Proceedings of the Fifth Annual New York University Conference on Labor*, pp. 721–34. (Bailer was a public member of the WSB.)

55. Bureau of National Affairs, *Daily Labor Report*, no. 217 (November 8, 1972), pp. AA7–AA9.

56. See Parrish, "Relation of Wage Control to Manpower Problems."

57. As John Dunlop summed up the matter from the NWLB's experience: "The point is not that wage changes were used extensively to transfer workers. Rather, wage structures which were serious impediments to desired movement were modified to permit other factors inducing movement to operate." In addition, increases for coal mining, shipbuilding, and aircraft manufacture were permitted which were well above the average rate of increase in all industry. Though "the status of [certain of] these increases under the stabilization program was subject to some uncertainty and suspicion," the increases served a useful purpose in attracting manpower to these war-related industries (Dunlop, "An Appraisal," pp. 171–72).

58. Parrish speaks of "the most striking feature of World War II wage and manpower controls, namely, the almost complete lack of coordination between them until the closing months of the war.... An overall manpower policy was never achieved. Manpower authority was dispersed through many agencies" ("Relation of Wage Control to Manpower Problems," p. 223).

59. A troublesome aspect of this policy is, of course, that stabilization boards will continue to receive, as in the past, applications for approval of wage adjustments on grounds such as substandards and inequities, where the supposedly justifying circumstances may be greatly exaggerated or even falsified for the purpose of obtaining increases necessary to retain or recruit manpower. It is said by participants in the World War II program that the subterfuges to which employers and unions sometimes resorted to obtain a wage increase were often very elaborate and extensive.

Chapter 9

1. During 1961–65, compensation under collective bargaining lagged behind compensation gains in the total private economy. See Marten Estey, "Wages and Wage Policy, 1962–1971," in William Fellner, ed., *Economic Policy and Inflation in the Sixties* (Washington, D.C.: American Enterprise Institute, 1972), p. 168.

2. See Sumner Slichter, Robert Livernash, and James Healy, *The Impact of Collective*

Bargaining on Management (Washington, D.C.: The Brookings Institution, 1960), especially chap. 31.

3. See H. Gregg Lewis, *Unionism and Relative Wages in the United States: An Empirical Inquiry* (Chicago: University of Chicago Press, 1963).

4. Sumner H. Slichter, "Do the Wage-Fixing Arrangements in the American Labor Market Have an Inflationary Bias?" *Proceedings of the American Economic Association* (May 1954), and "Economic and Collective Bargaining," in *Economics and the Policy Maker* (Washington, D.C.: The Brookings Institution, 1959)—both reprinted in John Dunlop, ed., *Potentials of the American Economy: Selected Essays of Sumner H. Slichter* (Cambridge: Harvard University Press, 1961), pp. 379–405 and 416–32 respectively.

5. See "Effects of the Structure of Collective Bargaining in Selected Industries," a group of five papers by Beatrice Burgoon, D. Q. Mills, Joseph Goldberg, William E. Simkin, and Chamberlain, in *Proceedings of the spring meeting of the Industrial Relations Research Association* (1970).

6. See, for example, Albert Rees, "Wage-Price Relations in the Basic Steel Industry, 1945–1948," *Industrial and Labor Relations Review*, 6, 2 (January 1953), pp. 195–205.

7. Derek Bok and John Dunlop list and characterize these periods without describing the role of collective bargaining in each, though they note that it was "not the same in each" (Bok and Dunlop, *Labor and the American Community*, pp. 292–93).

8. Malcolm Denise, "The Impact of the Controls Program on Collective Bargaining," in E. Stein, ed., *Proceedings of the Fifth Annual New York University Conference on Labor*, p. 348.

9. Derek Robinson, "Implementing an Incomes Policy," *Industrial Relations*, 8, 3, p. 89.

10. See, for example, the statement of the *New York Times* to its employees regarding the demands of its guards' union in 1972. The union had demanded a raise "far in excess of guidelines set by the Pay Board," and had shown "no desire to negotiate" (*New York Times*, June 13, 1972, p. 46).

11. Quarterly Report on Case Developments by the NLRB; text in Bureau of National Affairs, *Daily Labor Report*, no. 106 (May 31, 1972), p. D3. Also, *Daily Labor Report*, no. 87 (May 3, 1972), p. A7.

12. Quoted in *Washington Post*, November 15, 1972; also *New York Times*, November 15, 1972, p. 21.

13. During 1972, for example, the AFL-CIO encouraged its affiliates to press for improvements in nonwage areas such as working conditions and job security. See comments attributed to Rudolph Oswald, Bureau of National Affairs, *Daily Labor Report*, no. 41 (February 29, 1972), pp. A2-3.

14. Unfortunately, it may be offered as a general rule that wage determination by formula, whether it be by virtue of a stabilization program or by agreement of the parties, tends over time to reduce collective bargaining to bitter disputes over frivolous issues.

15. See, for example, the dissent of the industry representatives on the NWLB to the board's decision in the southern cotton textile case, March 20, 1945; text in *Termination Report*, vol. 2, pp. 391–92. Data on wage changes during World War II in textiles as opposed to other manufacturing industries may be found in *Termination Report*, vol. 1, pp. 541–42.

16. Emmett H. McNatt, "Problems of Case Processing," in Bureau of Labor Statistics, *Problems and Policies*, p. 331.

17. Nathan P. Feinsinger, "Impact of the NWLB on Collective Bargaining," in *Termination Report*, vol. 3, p. 556.

18. NWLB, opinion in the textile cases; text in *Termination Report*, pp. 384–85.

19. For example, John Dunlop concluded that the standards established by the NWLB for each fringe benefit separately, "substantially distorted the bargaining process which would have considered the package of benefits as a whole" ("An Appraisal," p. 167). However, as we have seen in chapter 8, separate standards for each major benefit serve stabilization objectives by

preventing structural distortions between fringes and wages among related employee units.

20. Malcolm Denise, "Collective Bargaining and Controls," p. 350.

21. Bing, *War-Time Strikes*, p. 126.

22. "General Order 31 prescribed a model plan for wage-rate increases to individual employees which might be adopted without specific Board approval. The objective was to get intra-plant jobs properly classified and provide orderly and systematic upgrading within the classified structure. Limitations were imposed on the rate of progression within rate ranges" (Parrish, "Relation of Wage Control to Manpower Problems," p. 212).

23. NWLB, opinion in Atlas Power Company, no. 521, December 20, 1942.

24. George Taylor pointed out that "Collective bargaining need not be looked upon as a self-effectuating process. Some procedures lead to agreement; others lead to strikes . . ." Hence the necessity for government to provide and insist upon the use of procedures designed to facilitate agreement. (Taylor, *Government Regulation*, p. 126.)

25. W. H. Davis, "Training Management and Labor for Industrial Leadership," speech to the Society for the Advancement of Management (Washington, D.C., May 18, 1944); text in *Termination Report*, vol. 2, pp. 533–36.

26. C. Wilson Randle listed twelve contributions to collective bargaining which resulted from the World War II and Korean stabilization programs. The contributions were primarily a result of the NWLB program, with some contribution by the WSB. In Randle's view, the stabilization efforts "(1) Helped to create and spread fringe issues. (2) Encouraged the acceptance of incentive systems. (3) Aided the introduction of job-evaluation plans. (4) Made popular and gained widespread acceptance for the cost-of-living wage pleas. (5) Bolstered the prevailing wage argument and [gave] it recognized status. (6) Created and made uniform a bargaining technology. (7) Brought order to previously chaotic wage structures. (8) Encouraged the introduction of wage-rate ranges and formal plans for intra-range employee progression. (9) Provided standards for contract negotiation and format. (10) Established and encouraged the use of grievance procedures. (11) [Gave] inspiration to the establishment and usage of arbitration. (12) Significantly reduced man-days lost through strikes and lockouts" (C. W. Randle, "The Impact of Wage Stabilization Upon Bargaining Practices," *Labor Law Journal*, 2, 9 [September 1951], pp. 655–58).

27. Ross, "Productivity and Wage Control," pp. 177–91.

Chapter 10

1. The general strike by unionized workers, a characteristic tactic of many labor movements abroad, has not been employed or seriously threatened in the United States during this century and is therefore omitted from this discussion.

2. Blackman, *Presidential Seizure in Labor Disputes*, p. 77.

3. Ibid., pp. 26–27.

4. Archibald Cox, "Seizure in Emergency Disputes," in Bernstein et al., *Emergency Disputes and National Policy* (New York: Harper and Brothers, 1955), p. 235.

5. Witte, "Labor Disputes," p. 180.

6. John T. Dunlop, "The Decontrol of Wages and Prices," in Colston E. Warne, ed., *Labor in Postwar America* (New York: Remson Press, 1949), p. 22.

7. *Termination Report*, vol. 1, p. 535.

8. Taylor, *Government Regulation*, p. 127.

9. Ibid., p. 107.

10. John T. Dunlop and A. D. Hill, *The Wage Adjustment Board: Wartime Stabilization in the Building and Construction Industry* (Cambridge: Harvard University Press, 1950), p. 109.

11. See, for example, Jean T. McKelvey, "Fact Finding in Public Employment Disputes: Promise or Illusion?" *Industrial and Labor Relations Review*, 22, 4 (July 1969), pp. 528–43.

12. William E. Simkin, "Can Mediation Work in a Control Climate?" remarks before

Twenty-first Conference, Association of Labor Mediation Agencies; text in Bureau of National Affairs, *Daily Labor Report*, no. 126 (June 28, 1972), p. F-1.

13. Bing, *War-Time Strikes*, p. 22.

14. Taylor, *Government Regulation*, p. 141.

15. Ibid., p. 134.

16. *Termination Report*, vol. 1, pp. 533-34.

17. Enarson, "The Politics of an Emergency Dispute," p. 57.

18. Dunlop, "An Appraisal," p. 162.

19. Enarson, "The Politics of an Emergency Dispute," p. 58.

20. For example, Title V of the Defense Production Act of 1950 provided for conferences among labor, management, government and public representatives to establish a disputes settlement procedure. This provision of the law was never invoked (WSB, vol. 3, p. 23). In April 1951, however, Executive Order 10233, provided the WSB with the limited disputes responsibility.

21. See Witte's extensive treatment of this issue in "Labor Disputes," pp. 181-83.

22. Blackman, *Presidential Seizure in Labor Disputes*, p. 15.

23. Ibid., p. 23.

24. See ibid., pp. 85-86, for a lengthy list of various coercive measures available to the government in labor disputes.

25. For example, in 1972 the nonunionized employees of ABC Prestress and Concrete left their jobs in an attempt to force the employer to pay wage increases under review by the Pay Board. See Bureau of National Affairs, *Daily Labor Report*, no. 134 (July 11, 1972), p. A-1.

26. For a detailed description of the relationships between the stabilization boards and the NLRB in World War II and the Korean period, see *Termination Report*, vol. 2, pp. 48, and 580-83, and Blackman, *Presidential Seizure in Labor Disputes*, pp. 207 and 214.

27. *American News Co., Inc.*, 55 NLRB 1302.

28. See NLRB, General Council, "Quarterly Report on Case Developments," text in Bureau of National Affairs, *Daily Labor Report*, no. 106 (May 31, 1972), p. D-3.

29. Blackman, *Presidential Seizure in Labor Disputes*, pp. 103-5. For NWLB rules on the matter of action on cases while a strike or lockout was in progress, see Section 2.6, Rules of the NWLB, text in *Termination Report*, vol. 2, p. 137.

30. See *Termination Report*, vol. 2, p. 342.

31. Ibid., p. 513.

32. See Blackman, *Presidential Seizure in Labor Disputes*, pp. 14-15.

33. Ibid., pp. 227-228.

34. Bing, *War-Time Strikes*, p. 101.

35. Blackman, *Presidential Seizure in Labor Disputes*, p. 49.

36. Thus, it is not normally illegal for a union to demand an increase which might be greater than stabilization policies might permit, or for an employer to agree to it. The increase cannot legally be placed into effect however, without approval of the board (except where self-administration is permitted and the parties believe the increase to be allowable under stabilization regulations).

37. Incidentally, Blackman concluded that in most seizure operations it has proven easier for the government to replace corporate executives than skilled labor, and his book includes speculation as to the reasons for this (*Presidential Seizure in Labor Disputes*, p. 90).

38. Ibid., p. 53.

39. Ibid., pp. 62-63.

40. See, for example, LeRoy Marceau and Richard A. Musgrave, "Strikes in Essential Industries: A Way Out," *Harvard Business Review*, 27, 3 (May 1949), pp. 287-92.

41. Blackman, *Presidential Seizure in Labor Disputes*, p. 94.

42. Witte, "Labor Disputes," pp. 186-87. Bing had reached a similar conclusion regarding

the government's involvement in disputes in World War I. (*War-Time Strikes*, p. 275).

43. Slichter, "Wage Stabilization," p. 53.

44. Enarson, for example, commented that disputes like the steel strike of 1952 "are intimately bound to the larger political environment. The steel dispute was shaped at every turn by considerations relating to the Taft-Hartley Act, the Defense Production Act, and the upcoming 1952 elections. As the struggle deepened, political antagonisms were aroused" ("The Politics of an Emergency Dispute," p. 73).

Chapter 11

1. See, for example, Herbert Stein and John T. Dunlop, testimony of the Cost of Living Council to the Joint Economic Committee of Congress, May 23, 1973, regarding price inflation in the revised January–May 1973.

2. Walter Heller, quoted in the *New York Times*, January 13, 1973, p. 10.

3. See John T. Dunlop, "Remarks to Nationwide Business and Financial Writers," May 29, 1973, transcript, p. 1.

4. John T. Dunlop and Derek Bok have suggested such a policy, which they have labeled "an active industrial relations policy." (Bok and Dunlop, *Labor and the American Community*, pp. 247–50). See also Robert O. Ader's (chairman of the board of directors, Kroger Corporation) call for reform of collective bargaining structure and practices in the retail food industry (speech to the Supermarket Institute, Dallas, May 8, 1973).

5. Ross, "The Lessons of Price and Wage Controls," p. 8.

Index